Adaptive Use

Development Economics, Process, and Profiles

ULI - the Urban Land Institute
1090 Vermont Ave., N.W.
Washington, D.C. 20005

About ULI-the Urban Land Institute

ULI-the Urban Land Institute is an independent, nonprofit research and educational organization incorporated in 1936 to improve the quality and standards of land use and development.

The Institute is committed to conducting practical research in the various fields of real estate knowledge; identifying and interpreting land use trends in relation to the changing economic, social, and civic needs of the people; and disseminating pertinent information leading to the orderly and more efficient use and development of land.

ULI receives its financial support from membership dues, sale of publications, and contributions for research and panel services.

Ronald R. Rumbaugh
Executive Vice President

ULI Staff

Director of Publications   Frank H. Spink, Jr.
Project Editor   W. Paul O'Mara
Manuscript Editor   Nancy H. Stewart
Production Manager   Robert L. Helms
Production Assistant   Patricia E. Thach
Art Director   Carolyn de Haas

Funding for the initial preparation of the Trolley Square, Stanford Court, Long Wharf, and Guernsey Hall case studies came from the National Trust for Historic Preservation, Washington, D.C.

Metric Conversions
meters = feet × 0.305
kilometers = miles × 1.609
square meters = sq. ft. × 0.093
hectares = acres × 0.405
(1 hectare = 10,000 square meters)

Recommended bibliographic listing:
Urban Land Institute. *Adaptive Use: Development Economics, Process, and Profiles.*
Washington: Urban Land Institute, 1978.
ULI Catalog Number A-08

International Standard Book Number 0-87420-582-4
Library of Congress Card Catalog Number 78-56054

Printed in the United States of America

Authors

Part One

Thomas J. Martin
Melvin A. Gamzon

Part Two

Nathaniel M. Griffin
W. Paul O'Mara
Frank H. Spink, Jr.
Joseph D. Steller, Jr.
Margaret A. Thomas

Part Three

Margaret A. Thomas

About the Authors

Melvin A. Gamzon is a senior associate and real estate economist in the Boston office of Economics Research Associates. His principal consulting assignments for both private and public clients include market and financial feasibility studies and implementation strategies for adaptive use projects. Many of Gamzon's projects involve recycling economically obsolete older structures as an integral component of overall redevelopment strategies for urban areas including downtown business districts. Prior to his association with ERA, Gamzon was a senior officer of a New York real estate development and consulting firm. He has a B.A. degree in economics from the University of Cincinnati and has completed graduate work at the Real Estate Institute of New York University.

Nathaniel M. Griffin is director of planning for the city of Little Rock, Arkansas. Before moving to Little Rock, Griffin was a publications associate with the Urban Land Institute. He was editor of the Project Reference File, a case study series on innovative development projects. He is a co-author of the *Shopping Center Development Handbook* and contributing author to the *Industrial Development Handbook,* both published by ULI. He holds a master's degree in planning from Ohio State University.

Thomas J. Martin is a vice president and manager of the Boston office of Economics Research Associates. He has lectured at a number of universities, including Harvard, M.I.T., and Roosevelt University, on topics related to market and feasibility analysis as well as economic impact evaluation techniques. He is a co-author of *The No-Build Alternative* (1975), an analysis of the development impacts associated with transportation projects, and of *Impact Assessment Guidelines* (1977). Before his association with Economics Research Associates, Martin was associated with major architectural and planning firms in Chicago and Kansas City. He has a master's degree in urban planning from the University of Washington.

W. Paul O'Mara, senior associate in ULI's publications division, participates in the division's task of producing publications on state-of-the-art development practices. He is editor of the monthly *Urban Land* magazine and author of the *Residential Development Handbook,* published by ULI. Recently O'Mara spoke at the annual conference of the National Trust for Historic Preservation on the economics of adaptive use. Before joining ULI, he was managing editor of *Planning* magazine with the Chicago-based American Society of Planning Officials. He received bachelor's and master's degrees from the University of Notre Dame.

Frank H. Spink, Jr., as director of publications for the Urban Land Institute, is responsible for the planning and content of all ULI publications. He received a bachelor's degree in architecture from the University of Illinois and a master's degree in urban planning from the University of Washington. Before joining ULI in 1967, Spink held a variety of planning positions on the West Coast, including director of planning for the city of Pleasanton, California.

Joseph D. Steller, Jr. is a publications associate with the Urban Land Institute and is editor of ULI's Project Reference File. He has worked as an architect, urban designer, and planner for various consulting firms in Ohio and Massachusetts, where he is a registered architect. Steller received a Master of City Planning in Urban Design degree from Harvard University and a Bachelor of Architecture degree from Kent State University.

Margaret A. Thomas is an architectural historian with the Heritage Conservation and Recreation Service of the U.S. Department of the Interior. She received a master's degree in preservation planning from Cornell University. Before attending graduate school, Thomas was assistant director of the Preservation Alliance of Louisville and Jefferson County, Inc. During the summer of 1976, she was an intern with the Urban Land Institute.

Contents

Part 1: Economics and Process

Part 2: Case Studies

Part 3: Profiles

Illustrations

Foreword

Adaptive use—converting a building originally designed for one purpose to a different and contemporary use—is becoming a widespread form of development. The trend toward adaptive use started with a general change in public attitudes during the 1960s. No longer was all *new* good and all *old* bad. The heritage and charm of things old, but not necessarily historic, began to be valued by the many rather than only by an appreciative few.

Reuse of buildings first began with housing when charming and sometimes not so charming old neighborhoods in major cities underwent interior modernization while preserving the original architectural form of the exterior. As an example of nonresidential adaptive use, Ghirardelli Square in San Francisco has probably received more attention and acclaim than any other adaptive use project. It is the pioneering example, eminently successful, and embodies all of the elements that typify adaptive use.

Although preservationists have long been committed to protecting the most historically or architecturally significant structures, it has been only recently that an interest has begun to develop in the preservation of less significant older buildings as well and, in effect, in preserving the city itself.

Like the subject it examines, this book evolved out of a series of events that made it an exciting prospect. ULI's role has always been to seek out and report on new ways to improve the quality of development. We have published studies and books on urban redevelopment and on isolated examples of adaptive use, but the full scope of the concept was brought to our attention by the National Trust for Historic Preservation in 1975. Aware of ULI's Project Reference File—a subscription service providing profiles on innovative developments—the Trust contracted with ULI to prepare five case studies of adaptive use. Then in its fifth year of publication, the Project Reference File had already reported on several adaptive use projects. The focus had not been on traditional historic preservation but on the economics of adaptive use as a type of development. The Trust felt that the case studies prepared for them from this perspective would be useful tools for their field service offices in encouraging further adaptive use. The first five case studies were published by the Preservation Press in pamphlet form in 1976.

The National Trust for Historic Preservation was so enthusiastic about the potential of private investment in the reuse of older buildings that it held a conference in Seattle, Washington, (July 31-August 2, 1975) on the "Economic Benefits of Preserving Older Buildings." I had the good fortune to attend this meeting in conjunction with our case study work. It was at this meeting that Dana Crawford, the developer of Larimer Square in Denver (whose involvement with ULI dates back to a ULI meeting in Denver in September of 1968), and I talked about the need to inform the private development community of the opportunities in adaptive use. The idea for a book to be published by ULI was formed and pursued over the next 2½ years.

To build on the case studies we already had in hand, we added projects to the Project Reference File. Then, in the summer of 1976, through an intern program funded by a grant from the J. C. Nichols foundation and administered by the Urban Land Research Foundation, Margaret Thomas, a second year student in preservation planning at Cornell University, did the field work on several other case studies and, more importantly, researched and collected most of the profiles on 180 adaptive use projects that make up Part 3 of the book. We almost had a book in hand. Missing only was an overview of the economics of adaptive use.

Through happy circumstances Melvin Gamzon and Thomas Martin of the Boston office of Economics Research Associates became aware of our work. They had been involved in feasibility studies for several adaptive use projects and agreed to prepare an overview piece that would tie the two other parts of the book together. All the case studies were updated by ULI staff, and additions were continually made to the profiles. In order to test our findings, we asked Dana Crawford and Robert T. Nahas, a past president of ULI and a sensitive and disciplined entrepreneur, for a final review of the manuscript.

We hope this book will be supportive of and a guide to future adaptive use projects. The evidence makes it clear that adaptive use can be a means to revitalization of our cities—revitalization without rebuilding. It is a wise and conserving use of existing resources.

It is rare that one form of development offers so many apparent advantages. Any possible disadvantages seem to be largely those created by institutional rules or procedures which can be rectified if the economic opportunities are truly understood. We believe that through ULI's publication of this book the elements of economically sound adaptive use will reach those who can best increase adaptive use activity—developers, design professionals, financial institutions, and agencies of government. It is these audiences who must measure the worthiness of a project. It is they who will develop projects which are sound business and community investments. And by doing so, it is they who will help preserve our historical and architectural heritage.

Frank H. Spink, Jr.
Director of Publications

Part 1
Economics and Process

Introduction

During the past three decades, the historic preservation movement has grown from a small group of history-minded preservationists to a large popular movement with a wide and varied constituency. During this same period, the real estate industry witnessed a great boom of new construction and development. This activity capitalized on the post-war economic expansion, population shifts, and the suburbanization of the 1950s, 1960s, and early 1970s. Over the last few years changing economic conditions—rising costs, decreasing availability of developable properties, and fewer attractive large-scale development ventures—have forced real estate professionals to seek alternatives which will maximize investment objectives.

Growing interest in history and in preservation of the built environment has led to increased awareness of the value of old buildings and historic areas. In areas such as New Orleans' Vieux Carré and Boston's Back Bay historic district legislation has long influenced development. A greater, more general interest in historic preservation has recently developed in many communities across the country. Numerous communities have created historic districts and attractions. City administrators have commissioned evaluations of historical and architecturally significant buildings in attempts to preserve these buildings and their environments. Many buildings have been entered in the National Register of Historic Places or in similar state or local registers.

The need to conserve and often convert the current stock of historically and architecturally significant buildings to economic and market-rate uses has risen sharply as the supply of public and quasi-public uses, such as museums and private foundations, has dwindled. As many preservationists and others have discovered all too late, there are only so many "museums" or related uses which can be supported in a given community. Often more conventional, "economic" functions must be found if the buildings are to be saved.

The real estate development community, for its part, is also finding that it must respond more vigorously to concerns from a variety of public and quasi-public interest groups. More than ever before, real estate developers are required to consider the social, economic, and environmental consequences of proposed new construction in areas surrounding the development project. These factors can add further "costs" to the development process, creating a special interest in the adaptive use of existing buildings. Strong reuse potential has been recognized in buildings which have distinctive physical and locational characteristics, and which appear to be economically viable projects. With creative development goals and financial support from the community, reuse of such properties can be an attractive option not only to developers but also to property owners, preservationists, and public and quasi-public groups.

Adaptive use has become of mutual interest to those groups concerned with the preservation of our cultural, historic, and architectural heritage, and to the real estate investment community striving to widen development opportunities. Knowledgeable investors and developers in the last few years have increasingly turned their attention to this arena, and as a result, a new type of real estate development has appeared in the form of adaptive use.

Opposite page: 1-1 Early 20th century view of Faneuil Hall's South Market, Boston, now converted to specialty shopping.

Defining Adaptive Use

While historic preservation is not a new phenomenon, until recently most efforts were undertaken by private citizens, by nonprofit historic preservation groups, or by the local, state, or federal governments. Beginning in the 1950s, however, there was a growing interest on the part of the private sector in reuse preservation as a business investment.

One of the earliest examples of this type of preservation was the Gaslight Square area of St. Louis. This area, which consisted of a gaslit street several blocks long, came into prominence around 1960. Most of the old buildings were simply repainted or refurbished and converted into antique shops and boutiques. Other buildings were extensively remodeled. One of St. Louis's top quality restaurants was thus established in handsome quarters at considerable expense. The project received a good deal of public attention and generated some very favorable publicity. This spawned a number of imitators, including the Old Town district along North Wells Street in Chicago. Despite enthusiastic public reaction, both Gaslight Square and Old Town in Chicago deteriorated rapidly, generally because neither area had any common ownership or quality control. Burglarized shops, assaults on patrons, and vandalism of automobiles parked on nearby streets also dampened the popularity of both projects. But in spite of the problems which beset Gaslight Square and Old Town, adaptive use was beginning to receive serious consideration from private business.

Shortly after Gaslight Square attracted attention in St. Louis, a project was launched in San Francisco which capitalized on the same general idea. But instead of the conversion of old shops lining an existing street which took place in Gaslight Square, Ghirardelli Square was developed in a self-contained area in which a special environment could be created.

Located approximately two blocks from San Francisco's famed Fisherman's Wharf, Ghirardelli Square, a speciality shopping center, has become identified worldwide as the prototype of adaptive use. The site, which originally housed a chocolate factory built in 1893, occupies an entire waterfront block of 2.5 acres which offers an unexcelled view of San Francisco Bay, the Golden Gate Bridge, and Marin County. Conceived for adaptive use as a high-quality complex for dining, entertainment, and specialty merchandise, Ghirardelli Square brings to life the renowned North Waterfront area of old San Francisco.

Purchased by William M. Roth and Mrs. William P. Roth for $2.5 million, the former chocolate factory was converted into a 175,000-square-foot specialty shopping center at a cost exceeding $10 million. The square officially opened in November 1964, with 55,000 square feet of rentable space, and was completed in 1968. It has since been an extremely popular and profitable center.

1-2 Ghirardelli Square, which was completed in 1968, is the best known of all large-scale adaptive use projects.

1-3 Larimer Square in Denver is also a well-known project with retail space at street level and offices above.

As the interest of the business community has grown, public and quasi-public groups have become increasingly active in historic preservation, initiating legislation and funding aimed at supporting the preservation of the built environment. Substantial amounts of time and money are now being devoted at all levels to neighborhood rehabilitation and restoration, and to renovation and the adaptive use of structures across the country.

The distinctions between restoration, renovation, and adaptive use of structures are relatively clear. The purpose of restoration is to refurbish a building's original architectural details as closely as possible. Such is the case at Old Sturbridge Village in Massachusetts, which represents a carefully detailed restoration of structures in a New England rural village during the half century following the American Revolution. The renovation of a structure refers to the physical upgrading of materials and support systems while retaining a building's original use.

Adaptive use, on the other hand, is the process by which structurally sound older buildings are developed for economically viable new uses. Such buildings may be historically important, architecturally distinctive, or simply underutilized structures which exhibit signs of life under a facade of age and neglect.

Old mills, railroad stations, municipal buildings, warehouses, theaters, department stores, and a multitude of other unique buildings have been successfully recycled to new uses. Many of these structures, which were once sitting ducks for the bulldozer, are now returning healthy financial rewards to their developers as a result of imaginative planning and support by sponsors and financial backers.

The following sections of this chapter discuss the adaptive use development process, illustrate some of the projects accomplished to date, and amplify key considerations in the implementation and development of adaptive use projects.

Project Initiation

Project Feasibili

Private Sector Participation
▶

- R.E. Developer
- Financial Institutions
- Private Sources/Owners
- Chamber of Commerce

Development Process
▶

Public/Quasi-Public Sector Participation
▶

- Funding of Studies
- Staff Support
- Background Studies

- Funding of Studies
- Staff Support
- Fund Raising
- Liaison
  with Public Groups

The Adaptive Use Development Process

The adaptive use development process has much in common with the process of real estate development in general. Information shown in Figure 1-4 illustrates the adaptive use process schematically in four basic steps: project initiation, project feasibility, project planning and financing, and project implementation. Each step has specific issues and considerations that need to be addressed in the overall process. Not all of the steps will be represented in every project, for each project is unique. The diagram, however, illustrates the key considerations which may be involved in a successful adaptive use project.

Figure 1-4 indicates the roles that private, public, and quasi-public groups may play in the adaptive use process. Projects initiated by the public sector, for instance, often draw participation from the private sector while projects initiated privately may attract resources and financing from the public. Many

adaptive use projects unite the private and public sectors because of the mutual goal of maintaining and protecting architecturally and historically important buildings and their environments. The unique opportunities presented by many of these buildings, which as well as being viable economic projects are desirable from the standpoint of tax revenues and social benefits, tend to bring into harmony the objectives of both the public and private sectors.

While many of the same basic factors involved in any successful real estate development project apply to adaptive use investments, there are variations that can be highly important in successfully adapting an old structure to a new use. Differences relate to the development process itself and the need for substantial front-end technical evaluation of the projects. Most companies involved in new development have considerable experience in site evaluation and negotiations related to new development, but few

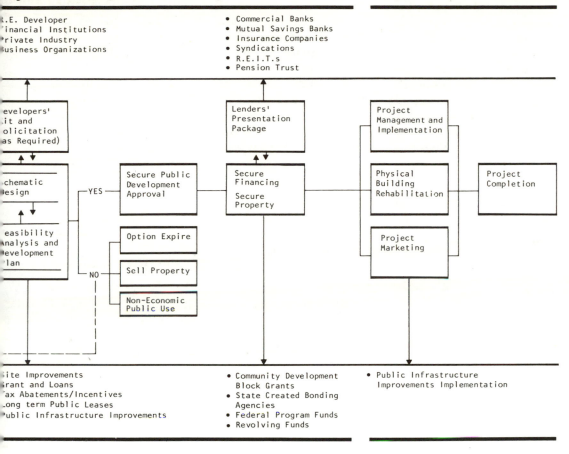

R.E. Developer
Financial Institutions
Private Industry
Business Organizations

- Commercial Banks
- Mutual Savings Banks
- Insurance Companies
- Syndications
- R.E.I.T.s
- Pension Trust

Developers'
Kit and
Solicitation
(as Required)

Lenders'
Presentation
Package

Project
Management and
Implementation

Schematic
Design

— YES —

Secure Public
Development
Approval

Secure
Financing

Secure
Property

Physical
Building
Rehabilitation

Project
Completion

Feasibility
Analysis and
Development
Plan

Option Expire

— NO —

Sell Property

Project
Marketing

Non-Economic
Public Use

Site Improvements
Grant and Loans
Tax Abatements/Incentives
Long term Public Leases
Public Infrastructure Improvements

- Community Development
  Block Grants
- State Created Bonding
  Agencies
- Federal Program Funds
- Revolving Funds

- Public Infrastructure
  Improvements Implementation

have the experience or expertise to evaluate opportunities related to existing buildings and their reuse. Because of this, architects and engineers with the requisite knowledge are becoming more directly involved in real estate development. Those development companies lacking experience in adaptive use often find it necessary to use outside consultants when they undertake such projects.

Another consideration which affects the development process relates to the goals and objectives as perceived by those taking part in the process. Typical participants might be a building owner primarily interested in protecting or liquidating his investment, a real estate developer looking for a good investment opportunity, a preservation group concerned with saving the integrity of the built environment as well as of an individual building, and a municipal government needing to increase the city's tax base. The successful adaptive use project will hopefully satisfy the differing objectives of all the various interest groups.

Because reuse of significant architectural or historic buildings is thought to further public aims, it is often possible for such projects to obtain various kinds of financial and planning support from the public sector. These supports take many forms, but most are related either to the type of use (for example, when the provision of subsidized housing is involved), or to the overall development of an area. This latter public concern is typically expressed in terms of tax incentives or abatements and public infrastructure improvements related to various redevelopment efforts. The factors of public support can be critically important to the financial success or failure of a project.

Project Initiation

As indicated in Figure 1-5, the adaptive use of a structure can be initiated by any number of participants. A real estate development group, for instance, that is looking for prospective adaptable buildings can initiate the reuse process. Both large-scale and small-scale developers are "in the field" more and more attempting to identify buildings with reuse potential. A number of these developers are relatively new groups who have made a specialty out of adaptive use projects. They can initiate the process and carry it through to completion, often with little assistance from the public sector or other groups.

1-5
Project Initiation

Private Sector Participation
▶

Development Process
▶

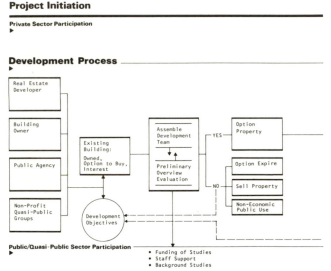

Public/Quasi-Public Sector Participation
▶
 • Funding of Studies
 • Staff Support
 • Background Studies

The development of Quaker Square in Akron, Ohio, illustrates the private initiative that has gone into adaptive use projects. In 1974, a group of private investors acquired the old Quaker Oats Company buildings in downtown Akron with the intention of reusing the buildings. The purchasers recognized that a large, untapped market potential for specialty retail and restaurant activity existed in the Akron metropolitan area. The old Quaker Oats buildings were near the University of Akron whose enrollment of 20,000 students provided a sizeable market potential.

The investment group purchased five of the old buildings and 2.8 acres for $325,000. After the initial purchase, 7 additional acres and four more structures were acquired and rehabilitation work began. Since the project opened in November 1975, some 85,000 square feet of gross leasable space have been successfully leased to a diversified blend of specialty shops, restaurants, and offices. Restaurants have been a major factor in Quaker Square's apparent success. The renovated building which houses the REA Restaurant on the first floor and a large model train display on the second floor was the local receiving and shipping headquarters for the Railway Express Agency from the turn of the century to the 1960s.

Other projects which illustrate private initiative include the Larimer Square development in Denver and the Grand Central project in the Pioneer Square area of Seattle, both of which have been implemented and developed by private groups.

In other instances a private developer will utilize a series of techniques and approaches to stimulate the public and quasi-public sectors to assist in planning and ultimately in financing the project. As a result, several state housing finance agencies have become involved in financing adaptive use projects. The Massachusetts Housing Finance Agency has been a leader in this regard, having provided both construction and permanent mortgages for a wide range of such projects in Massachusetts.

The Crowninshield Corporation was helped in this way while developing the Tannery project. When purchased by the Crowninshield Corporation, the 8.7-acre Tannery property located in Peabody, Massachusetts, was an eyesore to the community and appeared to have little or no prospect for future use. Its only apparent asset was its close location to downtown.

Involved were three buildings: the Crowninshield mansion—a three-story building constructed in 1814—and two buildings constructed in the 1890s as part of a leather tannery. The mansion was converted to a community center, management office, and security checkpoint. Leading from this building are glass-enclosed, elevated walkways to the two tannery buildings which were recycled into 284 apartments.

The project was financed by the Massachusetts Housing Finance Agency, with the requirement that 25 percent of the units be allocated to low-income and 50 percent to moderate-income persons. Construction financing was at 6.5 percent and permanent financing was at 7 percent for a 40-year term.

1-6   The REA Restaurant at Quaker Square in Akron was formerly the headquarters for the Railway Express Agency.

For the Ice House project in Burlington, Vermont, a grant from the Federal Economic Development Administration (EDA) was used to provide partial funding for the redevelopment of a mattress company building. The rehabilitation of the Cairo Hotel in Washington, D.C., is being partly financed under the Federal Housing Administration's 221d(4) program. These examples illustrate only a few of the approaches to financing from public agencies in adaptive use projects.

The owner of a building with unique reuse potential may also initiate the reuse process by offering his building for sale, or by acting as the developer of the project, or as a partner in the redevelopment. For example, in Wilmington, Delaware, the owners of the Brandywine Mills and others interested in redevelopment played active roles in the reuse plans for the building.

In other instances, the development process is initiated by a public agency that owns or has direct con-

trol over certain buildings. When the building owner is a public agency, nonprofit or quasi-public group, the reuse project will typically be developed with close attention to the public goals and objectives to be served. Surplus and underutilized structures (for example, schools and courthouses) owned by public agencies at the federal, state, and local levels, often have intrinsic value to a community. The particular government agency may encourage reuse by giving preference in sales or leases to developers who will adaptively use the buildings. The public agency may also assist the project financially and take an active role in the development process.

The development of the Old Boston City Hall is such a case. When the old city hall was vacated in the late 1960s, the city advertised unsuccessfully for developers to rehabilitate the building. Subsequently, a report was presented to Boston's Mayor Collins indicating that preservation of the building would be extremely costly. Although local historic preservation groups supported efforts to save the building, the property was destined for demolition unless a reuse could be found. At that point, the Old City Hall Landmark Corporation, a local group, came forward with a plan to save the building and turn it into commercial and office space. The Boston Redevelopment Authority, by a narrow vote, approved the plan. The building was leased to the corporation for $1 per annum plus a percentage of the gross annual rents collected. Financing was obtained from five local savings banks. Renovation was begun in 1970, the first tenants occupied space in 1971, and by 1973 the building was fully leased.

In other cases public agencies may act more directly in initiating the adaptive use process through zoning, providing for the transfer of development rights, planning for urban redevelopment, or through the selective uses of Community Development Block Grant funding.

Numerous cities have initiated adaptive use efforts in this manner. In Lockport, New York, for example, the old city hall was converted to commercial space by a private developer who leased the building from the city. Because of its unique character, the building was entered on the National Register of Historic Places in 1973. After the building was vacated by the city, a resolution was adopted which authorized the advertising of the property for lease to the bidder with the best proposal. A proposal was accepted from a private developer for a 25-year lease on the building with a fixed payment for rent to the city. As part of the agreement, the city committed Community Development funds to bring the building within compliance of building codes and ordinances.

Another outstanding example of this approach is the Faneuil Hall Marketplace project in Boston. Strategically located between the downtown and waterfront in Boston, Faneuil Hall Marketplace is being developed as a major retail and office complex by the Rouse Company of Columbia, Maryland. Faneuil Hall itself was built in 1722 as the first public market in Boston. In 1826, Quincy Market was built as an annex to the original building. Shortly afterwards, the North and South Market Buildings began a process of change in appearance and use that has continued since.

These three buildings are now under the control of the Boston Redevelopment Authority (BRA), which has spent in excess of $10 million for property acquisition, exterior building rehabilitation, and public infrastructure improvements in the project area.

As part of the overall urban redevelopment plan for Boston and following a competitive bidding process, the BRA signed a 99-year net lease agreement with the Rouse Company, which has the responsibility to continue restoration, find tenants, arrange financing, and manage the project on an ongoing basis. As part of its commitment, the Rouse Company will spend an estimated $30 million to rehabilitate the three buildings into 225,000 square feet of specialty retail/restaurant space and 150,000 square feet of upper floor office space.

Because of the creative initiatives taken jointly by preservation groups, public agencies, and the private developer, the Faneuil Hall project has become a successful venture for all concerned.

In Sacramento, California, the city and state have joined efforts to encourage redevelopment opportunities in the Old Sacramento section of Sacramento. The state has provided funds for a railroad museum on the site of the first terminus of the transcontinental railroad, and the city has used tax increment bonds to make substantial improvements in the 28-acre site which is one of the largest historic preservation areas in the West.

Adaptive use development may also be started by nonprofit and quasi-public groups that either own buildings of historic or architectural merit, or are concerned with the preservation of such buildings in their communities. These groups can range from preservationists interested in saving the environment, to chamber of commerce or business development groups interested in the economic vitality of a city.

Initiatives to rehabilitate and reuse The Arcade in Providence, Rhode Island, illustrate this approach to adaptive use. The Arcade, located in downtown Providence, was built in 1828 as the first enclosed shopping mall in the United States. It has been widely imitated in this country and remains one of the chief surviving examples of American business arcades. Public concern that the building might be demolished to make way for new construction led, in 1944, to its acquisition by the Rhode Island Association for the Blind. This assured its preservation as a historic monument and also provided a source of revenue to support the programs of the nonprofit association.

In 1976 a feasibility study of The Arcade which was sponsored by the Providence Foundation was undertaken for the Rhode Island Association for the Blind. The Providence Foundation is a nonprofit corporation founded by the Greater Providence Chamber of Commerce in 1974 specifically to represent, in cooperation with local government agen-

1-7 Aerial photo shows the strategic location of Faneuil Hall Marketplace between downtown Boston (bottom of photo) and the waterfront (top of photo).

cies, the private sector's interests in the redevelopment of Providence. The Foundation's interest in The Arcade was to encourage a rejuvenation of the building that would have a catalytic effect on other development in downtown Providence.

As a result of the initiative taken by the Providence Foundation and the Association for the Blind, a redevelopment plan was formulated. Based on the feasibility study prepared for the property owners and the Providence Foundation, the city of Providence has made a commitment of Community Development funds for capital improvements on this project.

Often nonprofit and quasi-public groups find themselves more heavily involved in the actual development process as projects move from conceptualization to detailed planning and implementation.

The Central Grammar School project in Gloucester, Massachusetts, illustrates the role that such groups may find themselves playing in the adaptive use process. The Central Grammar School was built in 1889 and enlarged in 1924. It is bordered on one side by the Civic Center District and on the other sides by residential neighborhoods. Until the time that the building was abandoned in 1971, no attempts were made to find an alternative use for the structure. When the school committee declared the building surplus property and turned it over to the city council, a number of ideas for the building's reuse began to surface. Proposals for demolition of the building were rejected, and the mayor assigned a committee to study its potential reuse for government needs. When no municipal users were found for the building, the local housing authority was asked to investigate the possibility of converting the building to housing. Its response was that such a conversion would be prohibitively expensive. During initial discussions on the reuse of the building, a local nonprofit community action program, Action, Inc., suggested a number of potential uses for the school, including housing for the elderly. The following is a description made in 1976 of the development process from the Gloucester Development Team, Inc.:

In June of 1972, Action made a formal request of the city to allow the agency to act as a development catalyst for conversion of the school into apartments for the elderly. The technical consulting services of Greater Boston Community Development, Inc., and a $9,000 seed money loan from New England Non-Profit Housing Development Corp. lent some credibility to Action's proposal. After considerable debate and public advertising the city entered into a purchase and sales agreement with Action in December of 1972. The agreement cost $1.00 and the purchase price was to be $1,400 per apartment, with a minimum of 60 apartments.

Action's Housing Development Program was staffed by two people, one with an architectural background and the other with a business administration education. This staff, after many interviews, chose four architects for a community representative group to interview. From these interviews the architectural firm of Anderson-Notter was chosen. An interview/bid process was also used to choose a general contractor. In February of 1974 Action set up a new non-profit development corporation, Gloucester Development Team, Inc. (GDT), to handle the ownership and conversion supervision of the school. In March the planning Board approved special tax treatment of the property and in May the City Council approved a Special Permit which allowed construction to begin. Model apartments were ready in September of 1975 and within 12 working days all 80 apartments had been rented. On October 15th the first tenants moved into the once abandoned school.

The Development Team

When a building has been identified and a project initiated, it is important to assemble a knowledgeable development team to prepare a preliminary evaluation of the building's potential. Since existing structures and fixed locations may offer unusual opportunities as well as constraints, the early assistance of an architect, engineer, real estate economist, contractor, attorney, and possibly even an architectural historian is often essential, not only in estimating the cost of rehabilitation but also in getting a general evaluation of the project.

For the building owner, this evaluation should give some indication of the building's market potential from the standpoint of rehabilitation costs and markets for space. For the prospective owner it is necessary to evaluate the building in terms of an owner's goals and objectives, and particularly in terms of the future economic value of the investment. Based on

this evaluation, the prospective owner will decide whether to option the building or pass up the project.

The owner will need to decide whether to proceed with a market rate project, sell the property, use the property for a non-market public use, or redefine the development objectives in light of new information from the preliminary evaluation.

In the case of public and quasi-public agencies owning properties, it is also important to get an early indication of whether the property under consideration is suitable for reuse, both physically and economically. When estimating the costs of rehabilitation it is unwise to go by rules which generally apply to new construction, as no two reuse projects are exactly alike.

In 1976 the Advisory Council on Historic Preservation undertook a survey of construction costs for completed adaptive use projects. The results of that survey indicated that demolition and structural costs tended to be minimal, while architectural and mechanical work could be substantial. The survey did not show a uniform advantage in cost savings of reuse projects over new construction, but did indicate that in many cases adaptive use was less costly.

As stated before, the sponsor's most effective method of cost estimating is to work with a development team experienced in the recycling process. By obtaining quick, accurate project cost and planning parameters, the sponsor can determine whether to proceed with a more detailed analysis.

Other members of the development team will be expected to contribute expertise regarding potential markets, legal aspects, construction management, and financial feasibility. Because of these inputs front-end planning costs associated with such projects are generally higher than for new construction. Such costs should be factored into the overall development as a necessary expense, for it is only with a competent planning team that a building space which was previously a liability can be successfully transformed into an asset. A carefully selected development team can win the confidence of the investor and the tenant or user—an additional benefit to be considered.

Preliminary Overview Analysis

The initial task of the development team is to conduct a preliminary property analysis to determine the factors which will most strongly affect project feasibility and thus provide guidelines for later, more detailed planning. The building should be inspected by the architect, engineer, and, if possible, the proposed contractor. When property purchase options have not been obtained, thereby preventing complete access to the structure being considered, the skills of these professionals will be instrumental in determining, if only superficially, any apparent physical deficiencies which could prove costly in a rehabilitation. With this preliminary understanding of the building's conditions, and a working knowledge of zoning and building/fire code regulations and requirements, recycling options can begin to be evaluated. In addition, a brief survey of the surrounding area is necessary to identify transportation services and accessibility; uses of adjoining properties; current and proposed public improvements in the area; and potential market opportunities that will need more thorough study in subsequent phases of the development process.

Once the property is purchased, the building's tenants require attention. The type of users and their lease terms should be investigated, if possible, before obtaining a property option, since laws protecting tenants may affect the timing of the recycling effort.

This preliminary evaluation should establish an understanding of the existing building, site, and neighborhood conditions which may affect recycling alternatives. If the structure is underutilized in its current capacity, that is, below market potential, the property may be undervalued and therefore purchased at a reasonably low cost. While this has been often true in the past, it is becoming less so as owners of such properties realize they may possess a "priceless heirloom."

An example in Dover, New Hampshire, illustrates how the preliminary evaluation was applied in efforts to preserve and recycle buildings slated for demolition in an urban renewal area. Dover is the oldest city in New Hampshire and has a dominant 19th century mill heritage. Initiated by local community groups who were concerned with Dover's place in history and the fate of certain buildings in the downtown, the services of the New England Field Service Office of the National Trust for Historic Preservation and the Society for the Preservation of New England Antiquities were used to prepare a preliminary historical and architectural evaluation of seven older structures in the city's downtown area. The city housing authority then retained consultants in economics and architecture to determine the feasibility of saving the buildings from demolition as proposed in the original urban renewal plan. The subsequent study was based on the properties' architectural, historical, visual, and commercial

reuse qualities. An economic overview of the downtown area revealed that market support existed for various new commercial uses within these structures. In addition, from the perspective of land use and visual design, the buildings were important to the overall character of the area. Preliminary costs of rehabilitation were worked out. Public subsidies needed for building improvements in order to attract private developers were determined.

If a preliminary evaluation indicates that a project is not suitable for his original plan, the sponsor will either have to give up the project or, if he already owns the property, alter his development objectives. Other options for an owner would be to sell the property or plan to reuse it for a non-economic public purpose.

Assuming that a decision to go ahead is made after the preliminary evaluation, the next step, if the property is not already controlled by the sponsor, is to secure a property option which will allow sufficient time to complete a comprehensive project feasibility study and to explore potential financing sources for the proposed adaptive use.

A property option is an exclusive right or privilege to buy or sell a specific property at a given price within a specified time. In a typical real estate transaction, the option agreement is initially unilateral—that is, binding upon the seller—and becomes bilateral when accepted by the purchaser. In the case of a building owned or controlled by a public or quasi-public group (such as a preservation organization), however, a private or nonprofit developer may be tentatively selected to recycle a property. In such instances, an option may be offered by the public or quasi-public group to a designated developer who may be asked during a specified period to obtain certain commitments (such as financing) to effectuate the recycling program. If he fails to get these commitments within this period, the option may lapse.

When a property option includes financial "consideration," it generally becomes a valid and irrevocable contract for a fixed period of time. If there is no such consideration, the option may typically be withdrawn at any time. At the execution of the option, monies paid for the consideration are usually applied to the purchase price of the property. If no action is taken on the part of the purchaser, and the option lapses, the consideration is often forfeited to the seller for holding the property off the market during the option period. This provides incentive for purchase of full property rights.

Project Feasibility

Following this initial overview of a project's potential, a detailed feasibility evaluation is often required. This more detailed evaluation should encompass four key areas: market support and economic evaluation; site and locational characteristics; structural considerations; and architectural and historical aspects.

At this point in the process the developer or the building owner may find financial support from various public or quasi-public groups for studies of background material concerning architectural, historical, site, and locational considerations. For buildings that are owned by public or quasi-public groups, resources often have already been applied to evaluation of some of these key factors. Market and economic studies, as well as structural and architectural evaluations have often already been undertaken jointly by public and private groups interested in historic preservation.

The approach used by the Historic Pullman Foundation, Inc., in determining the reuse of buildings in Pullman, Illinois, illustrates the evaluation process. In 1880 George Pullman began constructing a new town, which would be headquarters for his Pullman Palace Car Company. Pullman was built south of Chicago and included factory buildings, a hotel, commercial buildings, and various types of residential units. The town was eventually absorbed by the city of Chicago and ownership of the buildings passed into various private hands. As part of efforts to preserve and restore the community, the Historic Pullman Foundation, Inc., acquired four of the more historically significant structures in Pullman and is considering the acquisition of other buildings in the same neighborhood.

Recognizing that the preservation of the historic structures in Pullman was contingent on economic considerations, the Historic Pullman Foundation applied for and received a Technical Assistance Grant from the Economic Development Administration. The purpose of the grant was to prepare an economic development program based on the reuse of the historic buildings in Pullman, identify potential reuses for the several structures under study, and determine financially feasible alternatives for effective implementation of the development plan. The feasibility study was completed in 1977, and included a number of recommendations concerning reuse opportunities for the properties under consideration.

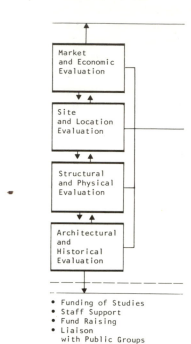

Project Feasibility

- R.E. Developer
- Financial Institutions
- Private Sources/Owners
- Chamber of Commerce

- Market and Economic Evaluation
- Site and Location Evaluation
- Structural and Physical Evaluation
- Architectural and Historical Evaluation

- Funding of Studies
- Staff Support
- Fund Raising
- Liaison with Public Groups

Market and Economic Evaluation

While developments such as Ghirardelli Square in San Francisco and Faneuil Hall Marketplace in Boston have received favorable market acceptance, in smaller communities the market for adaptive use space, particularly for specialty shopping or other unique uses, would not be as strong, and potential tenants might not be able to support the rent levels required after rehabilitation investments. In converting an older industrial building to a residential space, for example, it is essential to assess the market for residential use at projected price levels in the context of neighborhood quality and services.

In a recycling project it is important to identify unusual market opportunities, such as specialty shopping development, commercial recreation development, or artists' housing. Before the reuse of the Chickering piano factory in Boston's South End neighborhood, for instance, the developers undertook a market survey to test the idea of special housing for artists. The results of the survey confirmed the general feeling of the developers that there was a market for large, moderate-rent apartments that combined living and working space. Based on the idea of housing for artists, the Chickering piano factory was converted into 174 apartments and a 30,000-square-foot gallery area for display of art works. Since the market survey also indicated that over half of the artists also had low incomes, the project was financed by the Massachusetts Housing Finance Agency under a formula similar to the HUD 236 Program: one-fourth of the units are at market rate, one-half are at a subsidized rate for moderate-income families, and one-fourth are rented to low-income persons at 25 percent of their income.

A thorough market feasibility survey and analysis will help to test potential acceptance of the proposed project and is essential to proper evaluation of a recycling project. The following paragraphs illustrate the basic approach used by the real estate economist to quantify probable market support for any proposed recycling effort.

Initially, the economist will conduct interviews with persons experienced in community market dynamics, including, among others, public administrators and local real estate professionals. Through these interviews he will quickly identify local characteristics which will affect the marketability of the proposed adaptive use. Public agencies, especially a planning or redevelopment office, can usually provide the researcher with valuable information and impressions that will be useful in future analytical steps. In the majority of cases, the public sector is actively encouraging recycling and can be counted on to cooperate by providing information that may be essential to the sponsor's market study.

Next, local socioeconomic and demographic characteristics should be reviewed, and projections made of key indicators such as trends in population, employment, household income levels, and retail sales levels. This information is basic to realistic evaluation of the market affecting the proposed recycling.

In addition, recent development trends in the general area should be reviewed. Information regarding the type, quantity, pricing, and market acceptance of such developments must be obtained. If it is found that absorption of new or rehabilitated space is progressing slowly, and that a sizeable inventory is already available, the probability of market acceptance may be greatly diminished. A unique idea for reuse may then be required if the proposed

project is to succeed. It is also at this point that the salesmanship ability of the development team can be a key factor in the success of a project, or in just keeping it alive.

A major task next is to prepare a detailed analysis describing specific markets for each of the reuse alternatives. Using growth factors developed from the analysis of socioeconomic and demographic characteristics, the existing and future total market potential for each proposed use can then be identified.

An evaluation of the competition, both successful and unsuccessful, will be useful in defining operating characteristics of comparable facilities in the trade area; the extent to which other similar uses are satisfying market demand; the opportunities for pricing available to the proposed adaptive use; and the preferences in physical design of potential users. Because similar reuse projects are rare in a local market area, it may be necessary to evaluate projects outside of that area, even in another part of the country, in order to gather information on operating and physical characteristics similar to those of the proposed development. Like the architect and engineer of the development team, the economist should have a wide knowledge of both local and national developments in recycling in order to understand the unique market potentials of the proposed project.

The next important step is to examine locational factors which will affect the project's marketability. Obviously, a superior location will command higher rents, but the income potential of a project requires evaluation over the long term as well. The reuse project may itself stimulate other development which in turn will increase the value of the location.

The final task is to pull all findings together in a preferred development program with economic sizing guidelines based on the market analysis. Detailed information should be given concerning the development concepts to be considered; the amount of space which can be marketed all at once or in stages; the appropriate sizing and pricing units; and special design features and amenities which will give the project a competitive edge over other similar uses in the market area. If the recycling effort is to be a major endeavor which would require an extended construction and marketing program, a space absorption schedule should also be prepared.

Site and Location Evaluation

The location and site characteristics of a property are always important factors in the evaluation of development potentials. This is especially true for recycling projects in that an existing structure is tied to a fixed location. Accordingly, a thorough analysis of both public and private activities (within the neighborhood of the property) should be initiated as soon as the feasibility phase begins. Key characteristics of the surrounding area include parking availability, transportation access, plans in progress which will alter site accessibility, and the overall level of public services and safety. In conducting a site analysis, the principal factors to be considered are the existing and planned uses of adjoining properties and their compatibility with the proposed reuse, recreational and entertainment offerings in the area, the social and environmental quality of the area, and the competitive structure of real estate sales and rentals.

In short, the current location of many buildings is not always considered an asset and should be thoroughly investigated before making a commitment to recycle. Often, however, older buildings are in locations which offer proximity to transportation, jobs, markets, and "hidden" assets (such as waterfronts). These structures have frequently been overlooked during the suburban expansion of the past two decades when real estate investments were typically concentrated outside central cities.

The Boston Waterfront is an excellent example of rejuvenation in one of that city's forgotten areas. Following more than 300 years of history and economic change, the waterfront's mile of wharfs and about 65 acres of land extending to the new city hall area is now being transformed into a vital center for commercial, residential, and cultural activities.

The waterfront area was overlooked as a prime location for many years. Not until the 1960s did public agencies, private developers, community groups, and preservationists join forces to begin the process of recycling vacant or underused wharf buildings and other commercial structures in the area. Factors such as nearness to the employment centers in Boston's downtown area and accessible transportation facilities have been important to the waterfront's rebirth. With public improvements in the general waterfront area totaling approximately $50 million, several major recycling efforts have been completed or are in varying stages of development.

Considerations of site and location are especially important with regard to public buildings. Such buildings (for example, city halls, schools, railroad depots) may still be symbols of the community, even though their original functions have been taken over by newer structures. Many of these buildings are now being effectively recycled into a variety of new, economically responsive uses. A number of recent reports have outlined the costs and benefits of recycling various types of public and quasi-public buildings, from railroad stations to county courthouses.

Structural and Physical Analysis

Physical and structural characteristics must be thoroughly inspected to determine a structure's suitability for the proposed new use. For example, utility systems which were adequate for original users may not be sufficient to service the proposed new uses.

Buildings with severe structural problems may not be suitable for recycling. While the quality of original materials and craftsmanship in older buildings may be superior to that found in new construction, years of neglect can leave bricks and interior and exterior wood details, as well as structural and support systems, in need of extensive work.

Furthermore, the local building department may create difficulties for this type of development even though the municipal planning or redevelopment agency encourages recycling. Since each adaptive use project is unique and may be setting a precedent in the community, a careful evaluation of the building's potential to be upgraded to safety and structural codes is required.

Most building codes are based on characteristics that relate to new construction. Factors such as floor area ratios, building setbacks, interior and exterior common area potentials, height restrictions, floor loading capacities, foundation and structural requirements, stairway configurations, height characteristics and limitations, parking requirements, access for the physically disabled, and ventilation and sanitary facilities represent major considerations that need to be examined in light of the building and fire codes' disposition toward new buildings. Generally, a reused structure will need to be brought up to the modern standards of the building codes, with code compliance certified. If code compliance cannot be obtained, insurance for the project may be jeopardized. Many insurance companies hesitate to provide fire, building risk, and extended coverage insurance for a structure which does not fully meet code requirements. In certain cases, when only partial insurance is available, the developer must be self-insured for the balance.

The cost of upgrading building materials and structural and support systems for code compliance must be carefully examined. Such costs may be a major factor in determining the economic viability of the recycling effort.

Recycling of the Prince Spaghetti Factory Building into luxury residential and commercial uses is an example of the use of imaginative design to solve a difficult building configuration. Constructed in 1917 on Boston's waterfront, the Prince Building, which was slated for demolition in the late 1960s, found new life because of the initiative and creative talents of a local architect.

As is typical with many turn-of-the-century industrial structures, the Prince Building was overdesigned structurally for its original purpose. Its capacity for excess floor loads was a disadvantage as well as an advantage. The structure's 12-inch thick concrete

1-9, 1-10 The Prince Building was converted from a spaghetti factory (top photo) to residential condominiums. Extra stories were possible because in its use as a factory the building had been designed for heavy floor loads. (Bottom photo: Fisher Photography.)

slab floors made it difficult to install mechanical equipment and piping for the residential units. The problem was solved, however, by placing the ducts and pipes horizontally on top of the floor slabs and building up the floors over the equipment. Flexible and interesting floor plans resulted, as well as savings in rehabilitation costs. (The only punctures required through concrete slab were for the toilets.) What is more, because of the concrete construction, the developers were able to add three floors to the original structure for duplex and penthouse apartments.

Architectural and Historical Evaluation

The architectural potential of a structure is a primary consideration in successful recycling. The architect's ability to recognize and develop this potential can be the difference between financial success or failure of a project. Space utilization, interior circulation, architectural graphics and lighting, as well as imaginative use of materials and colors, can all be combined to give the structure unique character with economically efficient use of space.

Especially when an older structure is believed to have architectural or historical significance and even when it does not, the sponsor should consider enlisting the skills of an architectural historian (or the project architect) to prepare an evaluation of it as a historic structure. Questions which should be addressed include: Who built the structure? What style is it? When was it constructed? What were the original and subsequent uses of the building?

The architectural historian or architect would study the original type of construction and any modifications or additions to the building. He could then analyze the original materials used—their age and exposure, their composition and condition, and finally the types of decay, if any, and the causes of deterioration.

Until recently, it has been difficult to inspect the structural components of and alterations to a building's fabric without removing the woodwork or wall materials. The inspection of historic buildings has often been impeded by the fear of damaging valuable architectural details. Organizations such as the Society for the Preservation of New England Antiquities (SPNEA), through its Consulting Services Group, are actively involved in studying significant older structures. Non-destructive evaluation techniques, such as X-ray analysis, are used by

SPNEA on those parts of a structure not visible without removing surface elements. Other techniques used by the architectural historian to study a building's physical elements include spectroscopic paint analysis, microscopic paint analysis, and chemical analysis of mortars and stone work.

The architectural historian will determine: options for correcting the causes of deterioration; repairs necessary to stabilize the structure; elements which should be preserved in the adaptation to contemporary use; and finally the compatibility of adaptive use plans with the original use intended for the structure.

The historical evaluation of a building will sometimes result in its being placed on the National Register of Historic Places or on an equivalent state or local register of historic properties. Such recognition for a structure may benefit the owner or developer of the adaptive use project in terms of tax abatements, increase in the image and marketability of the property, access to public funding for certain improvements, or other related benefits. Such designation, however, may also lead to additional costs and requirements in implementing a reuse project. The costs may be related to delays caused by the need for permits or design review. For structures located within districts or neighborhoods zoned as historic areas, these requirements for permits and design review may already exist and will need to be checked as part of the overall architectural and historic evaluation.

Project Planning and Financing

Once a project's feasibility has been established, planning and financing can proceed towards final implementation. During this phase of the process, schematic designs and a detailed feasibility analysis are undertaken to determine whether development objectives are suitable or will need to be redefined or reevaluated. The property itself is secured, and public development approvals and financing are obtained. If necessary, developers' kits and lenders' presentation packages are prepared.

In the case of public or quasi-public owners, a developer's kit may need to be assembled and interested real estate developers solicited for their participation in a project. This is a typical approach with urban renewal properties, when the renewal agency requests plans from developers for given parcels. It is also being used when a recycling plan or alternative plans have been developed for buildings being disposed of by public agencies.

Project Planning and Financing

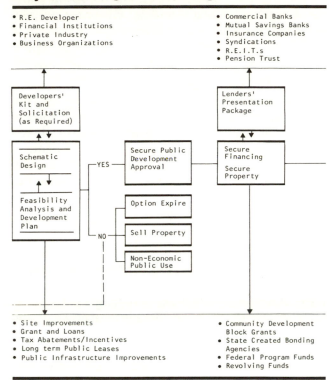

- R.E. Developer
- Financial Institutions
- Private Industry
- Business Organizations

- Commercial Banks
- Mutual Savings Banks
- Insurance Companies
- Syndications
- R.E.I.T.s
- Pension Trust

Developers' Kit and Solicitation (as Required)

Lenders' Presentation Package

Schematic Design

Secure Public Development Approval

Secure Financing Secure Property

YES

Feasibility Analysis and Development Plan

Option Expire

NO

Sell Property

Non-Economic Public Use

- Site Improvements
- Grant and Loans
- Tax Abatements/Incentives
- Long term Public Leases
- Public Infrastructure Improvements

- Community Development Block Grants
- State Created Bonding Agencies
- Federal Program Funds
- Revolving Funds

1-11

The city of Salem, Massachusetts, for instance, recently prepared a "prospectus for development" for a waterfront site and associated buildings in that city. The purpose of the prospectus, which was supported by detailed architectural, engineering, and market analysis, was to suggest a range of possibilities which might be undertaken by developers for reuse of properties so that they would contribute to the commercial viability of downtown Salem while enhancing the historic waterfront areas of the city. The range of reuse schemes that were prepared were also subjected to "policy analysis" from the city and surrounding community groups. While providing basic project feasibility information, the prospectus also recognized that private interests might suggest other development options for the property, based on assumptions about construction costs, marketability, and project financing.

For the private developer, key considerations which will help to secure financing are to make certain that the proposed plan is economically feasible and can obtain all required approvals. Approvals for development, as well as construction and long-term financing, can pose problems, particularly when private lending sources tend to be negative about "old" buildings.

Most developers of adaptive use projects find that they will spend considerable time with local building inspectors, fire department officials, and other agencies, coordinating plans and working out solutions to various code problems. Trepidation at the building inspector's office over potential code problems has undoubtedly terminated many projects. When the reuse of a building requires a zoning variance or change—such as when an industrial building in an area zoned for industry is reused for housing—the sponsor may have the additional job of securing the change. Depending on the individual city, such changes in land use or zoning can be difficult to make.

The experience of the developer of Trolley Square in Salt Lake City illustrates the type of problem that can arise in trying to implement adaptive use projects. While the Trolley Square project itself is located in a zoning district permitting commercial use, the off-street parking provision of the city zoning ordinance created unexpected problems. The zoning ordinance requires one parking space per 3,000 square feet for a commercial building, one space per 10 seats for a theater, and one space per 200 square feet for a restaurant. The zoning order does not take into account the fact that peak parking demand spreads over a long period in a combined shopping-entertainment center featuring extensive

1-12 The water tower at Trolley Square in Salt Lake City is an important visual element in the redesign of the trolley barns into a specialty shopping center.

17

evening activities. Expansion of restaurant and theater space was blocked until the developer constructed a three-level parking structure on-site to meet the requirements of the ordinance.

All such issues must be dealt with in this phase of the process or the entire project can be jeopardized.

Financing is the other main issue which developers must address at this time. It is the most difficult step to be made in the adaptive use process. If possible, good general advice for a developer would be to involve a banker from the beginning.

Construction and long-term financing have been key stumbling blocks to the implementation of adaptive use projects. Often the first adaptive use project in a community is not financed locally, or, if so, it obtains local financing only with substantial difficulty. Financing difficulties are typically related to the unique nature of most adaptive use projects, speculation as to the marketability of the reuse, and other factors.

Many developers of adaptive use projects have had difficulties similar to those reported in the *Denver Post* (October 26, 1975) by William Saslow in his efforts to recycle a Denver warehouse into housing:

> Our trouble has been that we can't convince bankers that people want to live down here and that the old buildings of solid brick often well over a foot thick can be renovated into offices and apartments of charm, dignity, and more durable construction than new buildings. We have a waiting list. People have more taste than the lenders give them credit for.

Saslow said the developer partnership had finally reached substantial agreement on financing after receiving rejections to loan applications from 38 other financial institutions.

In anticipation of such difficulties, a great deal of effort may be spent tailoring a presentation package to the specific financial institution. Included in such packages may be lease agreements already executed for substantial floor areas of the building. The planning for tenant "mix" can also be key here in bolstering the financial feasibility of the project.

The public sector can also provide assistance through various kinds of financial leverage or actual financial commitments to the project. State housing finance agencies have become particularly active in a number of states such as Massachusetts where financing has been provided to reuse old commercial buildings for housing. Other examples include financing from local or state foundations and trust funds, and from Economic Development Adminis-

tration and Small Business Administration loans and revolving funds established for historic preservation projects.

The St. Johnsbury House development in St. Johnsbury, Vermont, illustrates the diversity of funding that often goes into an adaptive use project. A 75-room hotel, originally built in 1850, was converted by the Northeastern Vermont Development Association, Inc., into 42 units of housing for the elderly, with additional space for offices. Financing for the building, which is listed on the National Register of Historic Places, came from local subscriptions, a local mortgage, Community Development Block Grant funds, a National Park Service Historic Sites Grant, and an Economic Development Administration Title X Grant. The total redevelopment and acquisition costs of $550,000 were thus drawn from five different sources.

Possibilities for adaptive use financing must be carefully examined within the specific local context, and the appropriate steps taken to assure that the project will go forward in the most cost-effective manner for the sponsor, as well as in keeping with community objectives.

Schematic Design

In recycling a building, schematic design involves synthesizing all of the physical, locational, market, architectural, and historical considerations into design alternatives. These alternatives should clearly reflect the sponsor's development objectives as well as provide a range of conceptual options.

The financial characteristics of the project should be clearly understood by the development team. Economic criteria—such as overall cost and projected levels of return on investment—should be made clear to the development team. During the schematic design phase, the architect may present designs which will provide the most rewarding "bottom line" to the sponsor while preserving the integrity of the structure and maximizing the efficiency of both the structure and its outside common area.

An important consideration in developing schematic designs is to work with the fabric of the building rather than to fight it. By understanding a structure's physical constraints and eccentricities, the creative architect can take advantage of features such as large windows or cast-iron columns which give the building its own identity.

The unusual forms and patterns which older buildings typically provide can be a marketing asset, while minimizing construction and operating costs for the sponsor. One unusual aspect of many older buildings is the extra space provided by high ceilings which can be converted, for example, into sleeping lofts or extra storage space. These features are highly desirable when compared to the box-like environment seen in many new structures.

One use of the interior space is the creation of open-air center courts in the interiors of large older buildings. These provide circulation, common space, and aesthetic effect. The Mercantile Wharf project in Boston, the Century Theater in Chicago, and the Galleria in Portland, Oregon, have all used this concept to create varied and interesting internal effects. In the case of the Galleria in Portland, an original 75-foot-high light court, closed in 1949 during a remodeling of the five-story building, was reopened to become the main feature of the multi-story complex.

Because the net to gross square-footage ratio is a key determinant in the revenue capability of a building, imaginative design must be used to maximize the useable space within a structure. High ceilings, when not used for their spacious effect, can contain mechanical equipment which would reduce rentable square footage if installed elsewhere. In many instances, with older structures, exterior load-bearing walls allow interior space to be specifically tailored to a tenant's requirements. With adaptive use projects, the many possibilities for creative solutions to the use of space can be a great advantage. In this regard, the architect's imaginative use of space, when consistent with market realities, will increase the probability of success.

During this planning phase, the architect, structural engineer, and contractor will formulate a statement of projected rehabilitation and construction costs based on alternative site and floor plans. The experience of these members of the development team in preparing reliable cost estimates is an important aspect of the project's financial feasibility study.

George Notter, a Boston architect with an extensive adaptive use practice, has summarized the real economic aspects of adaptive use:

> . . . more often than not, the total dollar expenditure for preservation, including the acquisition of the property involved, is about the same as new construction. Thus the plus factor is achieved by developing the potential assets into a final project of

greater amenity—one having the right location, more space in either height or volume, more area or more character, materials of special quality, or a potential for time savings in construction.[1]

Feasibility Analysis and Development Plan

An in-depth feasibility analysis is often required to test the schematic designs in terms of the financial criteria of the sponsor. Whether a recycling plan is initiated as a profit or nonprofit project, a clear understanding of the financial analysis is essential.

Basically, a structure must be at least self-sustaining as far as generating sufficient revenues to cover, at a minimum, operating and fixed expenses. In the case of a for-profit sponsor, private lending sources will require adequate income to meet operating and fixed expenses. They will also want to be assured that funds are available to reduce the project's mortgage commitment and still provide a reasonable return on investment for the sponsor and equity investors.

Because of the relative newness of adaptive use, many private institutions are still wary of providing financing. Innately conservative, most commercial lenders will insist that the financial feasibility of the project be well established and relatively free of risk.

Some basic questions which must be answered in the financial evaluation are:

- How much money can the sponsor borrow from a commercial lender based on the economic value of the project?
- What is the amount of equity required to complete the financing package?
- Are project development costs comparable to the maximum private financing justifiable?
- How can both public and quasi-public actions and incentives affect the financial viability of the recycling project?

The following hypothetical example describes the primary approach to a financial feasibility analysis. For this case, we have assumed that an underused warehouse in a prime downtown location has been selected for possible recycling into a first-class office building. The overall size of the structure is

---

[1] Advisory Council on Historic Preservation, Special Issue Report, *Adaptive Use: A Survey of Construction Costs* (Washington, D.C.: author, June 1976), p. 22.

Hypothetical Development Costs for Recycling a Warehouse to Office Uses*

Acquisition Costs

Property Purchase	$ 350,000
Closing Costs and Fees	7,000
	$ 357,000

Renovation/Construction Costs

Building (60,000 Sq. Ft. x $20/Sq. Ft.)	$1,200,000
Site Improvements	100,000
	$1,300,000

Indirect Costs

Architectural and Engineering Fees	$ 117,000
Legal, Engineering, Market Consultation	26,000
Interim Financing for Acquisition and Construction	125,000
	$ 268,000
Contingency (4% of Project Costs)	**77,000**

Total Development Costs **$2,000,000**

*Numbers have been rounded off.

60,000 square feet. Schematic designs have shown that 85 percent of the building, or 51,000 square feet, is adaptable to the proposed new use. It is assumed that the sponsor will initially try to obtain conventional private financing for the redevelopment.

Figure 1-13 shows the hypothetical development costs established for this case. Total costs are estimated at $2 million, or $33 per square foot. It must be emphasized that all costs are presented for illustrative purposes only and should not be related to one's specific project.

Figure 1-14 shows that by applying a figure of $11 per square foot for rent and assuming a 3 percent vacancy factor, gross annual revenues from the property will be $544,000. Next, the gross annual income is reduced by operating and fixed expenses with the residual being net income before debt service. By debt service, we mean the sponsor's periodic repayment of the principal and interest on the unpaid balance of the mortgage.

The prospective lender will then be concerned with establishing a realistic economic value for the project. In most cases, a prospective mortgage loan is based on at least one and possibly two or more appraisals which will determine the economic value of the project. Many financial institutions have their own staffs conduct such an appraisal. Before giving a mortgage commitment, however, a lender will generally require an independent appraisal of the project as well.

To arrive at the economic value, a capitalization rate is selected. The capitalization rate is an integral part of appraising the "mortgageability" of the adaptive use project. Simply stated, the capitalization rate indicates the relationship between a project's net income, usually on an annual basis, and the property's economic value. It can be expressed as follows:

$$\frac{net\ income}{capitalization} = economic\ value$$

The selection of an appropriate capitalization rate can be extremely important in determining the overall economic value of the project and usually requires the expert judgment of a knowledgeable developer, mortgage lender, real estate economist, or appraiser. Small variations in this rate can result in sizeable differences in the total economic value of the project.

Referring to the previous hypothetical case, by dividing the net income ($231,000) by the selected capitalization rate (.10), we find that the economic value of the project is $2,310,000. But had we used a rate of .11, the economic value of the project would of course be considerably less.

Hypothetical Financial Analysis*

Gross Annual Revenues

Gross Building Area .... 60,000 sq. ft.

Net Leasable Area .... 60,000 sq. ft. x
85% = 51,000 sq. ft.

Annual Rent/Sq. Ft. .... $ 11.00

Annual Income at 100% Occupancy .... $ 561,000

Vacancy Factor (3%) .... −17,000

Gross Annual Revenues .... $ 544,000

Net Income Before Debt Service

Gross Annual Revenues .... $ 544,000

Operating Expenses $198,000

Fixed Expenses

    Taxes 112,000

    Insurance 3,000

Total Building Expenses .... − 313,000

Net Income Before Debt Service .... $ 231,000

Economic Value

Capitalization Rate 10%

Net Income .... $ 231,000

Economic Value .... $ 231,000 ÷ 0.10 =
$2,310,000

Mortgage Loan Obtainable

Loan to Value Ratio 75%

Economic Value $2,310,000

Maximum Mortgage $1,732,500

Annual Debt Service

Assume Mortgage

    Interest Rate and Term of Loan 8½% for 30 yrs.

Mortgage Constant

    (Computed from Amortization Schedule) 0.093

Maximum Mortgage $1,732,500

Annual Debt Service .... 0.093 x $1,732,500 =
$ 161,000

Cash Flow Before Adjustment for Income Taxes

Net Income .... $ 231,000

Debt Service .... −161,000

Cash Flow Before Taxes .... $ 70,000

**Maximum Equity at 15% Annual
Return on Investment** .... $ 466,000

Maximum Project Cost

Maximum Mortgage $1,732,500

Equity 466,000

Total $2,198,500

*Numbers have been rounded off.

In deciding whether to grant a mortgage for the recycling project, a lender wants to be assured that net operating income will be sufficient to cover the debt service payments. Essentially, the lender is looking for a margin of safety if in fact income projections fall short of expectations. In many cases this "debt coverage factor" is in the range of 1.20 to 1.40. This means that net income should be at least 20 to 40 percent higher than debt service payments. With riskier situations, which adaptive use projects may be considered, a higher debt coverage factor is typically required—in the range of 1.40. The commercial lender, however, usually will not grant a mortgage for the full economic value of the project. While the "loan-to-value" ratio varies with each lending source, a commonly used figure is 75 percent of economic value. Applying this factor to our case results in a maximum mortgage of $1,732,500.

The annual amount of funds necessary to meet debt services or "pay down" the interest and amortization of the mortgage is then calculated by using a mortgage constant figure. (Refer to annual constant in the Mortgage Amortization Schedules.) By applying this figure, which relates to the interest rate and term of the mortgage, the annual debt service is defined. In our case the mortgage constant (0.093) is multiplied by the maximum mortgage ($1,732,500) with a resulting annual debt service of $161,000. Cash flow before adjustment for income taxes is then calculated by subtracting the debt service from net income.

If the interest rate or term of the mortgage is changed in our example, the annual debt service would be substantially affected. For instance, if the lending source only gave a 20-year mortgage, which is more often the case with adaptive use projects, the resulting annual debt service would then be on the order of $183,000.

In addition to the 75 percent mortgage commitment, other funds will be required to complete the financing package. These funds, which are referred to as equity capital, will need to be provided by the sponsor or outside investors. No matter who puts up the equity funds, it must always be recognized that this capital represents an investment. Accordingly, a reasonable financial return must be assured, as prospective investment partners or the sponsor will carefully weigh the merits and security of this investment against other more conventional investment alternatives. (In the case of a nonprofit sponsor, outside interests may provide equity funds through contributions and fund-raising efforts without requiring a cash return. These investors include preservation groups, foundations, private firms who are seeking public recognition, and government agencies.)

With a for-profit project, if we subtract the annual debt service payments from net income, the resulting figure is referred to as cash flow before taxes. Equity partners customarily would require a return on their investment (R.O.I.) of 15 percent or more. As shown by Figure 1-14, a 15 percent R.O.I. on cash flow before taxes of $70,000 yields a maximum equity of $466,000.

If we assume that our hypothetical sponsor can secure the equity funds, the maximum project cost justifiable is $2,198,500, calculated by adding the mortgage amount ($1,732,500) and the equity funds ($466,000). With development costs estimated at $2 million, it is clear that our sponsor requires only $266,000 in equity. Accordingly, a 26 percent return on investment can be appropriated to equity funds, thus making this project more financially attractive to both the sponsor and potential investors.

While the numbers in our hypothetical case work in favor of the sponsor, it should be noted that we are dealing with an ideal rental situation. Such a situation is usually rare. Market constraints in terms of a prevailing rent structure in a defined area, competition from both new construction and other recycling efforts, and location of the property may affect the property's rental capabilities.

The data in Figure 1-15 show the effect of reducing rental rates to $9 and $10 per square foot while keeping development costs at $2 million. The loss in net income before debt service results in a lower economic value for the project and thus a smaller mortgage commitment. Equity requirements in Case 1, assuming a 15 percent required R.O.I., do not match the necessary capital needed to initiate the project. By reducing the R.O.I. in Case 1 for equity capital to 10 percent the project is marginally feasible. As shown in Case 2, the financial situation becomes worse and the maximum project financing falls far below the required funds.

In all cases the final development plan must try to maximize economic advantages and minimize the negative aspects of the project which might affect financing. The creative project sponsor will explore ways of controlling expenditures by attention to acquisition costs, rehabilitation costs, marketing and other "soft" costs, operating costs, and financing costs.

Hypothetical Financial Analysis: Cases 1 and 2*

	Case 1	Case 2
Gross Annual Revenues		
Gross Building Area	60,000 sq. ft.	
Net Leasable Area	60,000 sq. ft. x	
	85% = 51,000 sq. ft.	51,000 sq. ft.
Annual Rent/Sq. Ft.	$ 10.00	$ 9.00
Annual Income at 100% Occupancy	$ 510,000	$ 459,000
Vacancy Factor (3%)	−15,000	−14,000
Gross Annual Revenues	$ 495,000	$ 445,000
Net Income Before Debt Service		
Gross Annual Revenues	$ 495,000	$ 445,000
Operating Expenses	$ 198,000	$ 198,000
Fixed Expenses		
Taxes	102,000	92,000
Insurance	3,000	3,000
	− 303,000	− 293,000
Net Income Before Debt Service	$ 192,000	$ 152,000
Economic Value		
Capitalization Rate	10%	10%
Net Income	$ 192,000	$ 152,000
Economic Value	$ 192,000 ÷ 0.10 =	$ 152,000 ÷ 0.10 =
	$1,920,000	$1,152,000
Mortgage Loan Obtainable		
Loan to Value Ratio	75%	75%
Economic Value	$1,920,000	$1,520,000
Maximum Mortgage	$1,440,000	$1,140,000
Annual Debt Service		
Assume Mortgage Interest		
Rate and Term of Loan	8½% for 30 yrs.	8½% for 30 yrs.
Mortgage Constant		
(Computed from Amortization Schedule)	0.093	0.093
Maximum Mortgage	$1,440,000	$1,140,000
Annual Debt Service	0.093 x	0.093 x
	$1,440,000 = $134,000	$1,140,000 = $106,000
Cash Flow Before Adjustment for Income Taxes		
Net Income	$ 192,000	$ 152,000
Debt Service	134,000	106,000
Cash Flow Before Taxes	$ 58,000	$ 46,000
Maximum Equity at 15% Annual Return on Investment	$ 387,000	$ 307,000
Maximum Project Cost		
Maximum Mortgage	$1,440,000	$1,140,000
Equity	387,000	307,000
Total	$1,827,000	$1,447,000

*Numbers have been rounded off.

The financial analysis which has been described is essentially the same for all types of real estate development. With regard to adaptive use projects, however, opportunities do occur to reduce acquisition and financing costs.

The following discussion will identify ways in which acquisition, financing, and operating costs may be controlled in adaptive use while later sections will discuss rehabilitation and marketing costs. In all of these areas, the track record of the developer will be a major factor in financing the project.

The high cost of property acquisition can seriously impede the economic viability of the project. Older structures may be situated in dense, urban areas where land values have accelerated due to the limited supply of useable sites. Often the commercial value of the property is greater than the revenue capabilities of the building being considered for recycling. In terms of economic realities, the existing structure may not represent the highest and best use for the property and thus, pressure is exerted to demolish the building.

The problem of providing the front-end capital needed to acquire a property can be eliminated, for example, when dealing with structures in the public sector's domain. Buildings which are controlled by public agencies may be available to the sponsor on a "net lease" basis. In simplest terms, a net lease refers to an agreement whereby the lessee (sponsor) is responsible for all maintenance and operational expenses of a property and pays to the lessor (in this case a public agency) a fee for the use of property.

This approach has been used in a number of cities including Boston where the Boston Redevelopment Authority (BRA) has acquired buildings using federal urban renewal funds and has initiated long-term net leases with private developers. Such an agreement was made between the BRA and the Rouse Company concerning the Faneuil Hall Marketplace development near Boston's waterfront. The long-term lease of the Faneuil Hall Marketplace includes a fixed sum of $1 per year plus an annual payment (in lieu of taxes) of 20 to 25 percent of gross revenues. The BRA also acquired the District 16 Police Station in Boston, which was built in 1886, and has leased it to the Institute of Contemporary Art for use as a museum, theater, and restaurant.

Other techniques which may be used to reduce acquisition costs include facade easements, transfer of development rights, and revolving fund loan programs. Depending on whether the owner of the building is a private individual, real estate developer, or a public group, different techniques may come into play. In Salem, Massachusetts, the facade easement approach has been used. The Salem Redevelopment Authority purchased properties for $1 each, rehabilitated the exteriors of the buildings, and then resold the buildings to the original owners who were required to rehabilitate the interiors. A restrictive covenant on the properties required that the owners maintain the condition of the properties until the year 2012.

In still other cases, a governmental agency may be able to create a revenue agency which can sell revenue bonds for projects considered within the public interest. These bonds, which generally have longer terms and lower interest rates than conventional mortgages, can be used to acquire properties for preservation or adaptive use purposes. The buildings may then be sold to a person or group interested in recycling, with the land being retained by the public agency and leased to the recycling sponsor on a long-term, rent-lease basis. This will reduce the total development costs of the project, thereby making marginal recycling projects more attractive to both mortgage lenders and equity investors.

Financing costs are critically important to the economic success of an adaptive use project. These costs are related to the overall interest rates and mortgage terms that are available to the prospective developer. The form of the development entity can also affect the costs. Public agencies that act as adaptive use developers can often utilize public revenue sources of various kinds—including general obligation and revenue bonds—much as they would for any development project. Nonprofit developers can use various financing sources such as federal and state housing finance agencies or economic development corporations established by federal, state, and local laws. Private for-profit developers and owners are generally restricted, on the other hand, to the more conventional sources of financing associated with real estate developments.

A variation in interest rates can significantly affect the maximum project cost. When a 6.5 percent interest rate is compared to the 8.5 percent originally assumed in the hypothetical Case 1, the effect on the maximum cost is illustrated in the data in Figure 1-16. At 8.5 percent the maximum supportable project cost is $1,827,000, while at 6.5 percent the maximum supportable cost is $1,980,000.

Operating costs represent a major area of economic concern. These costs may or may not be within the control of the sponsor. For example, utility and maintenance costs have, in many cases, increased faster than project revenues. However, through the efficient design and long-term maintenance of utility systems, mechanical equipment, and common area spaces, operating costs can be held within an acceptable range of project feasibility. In addition, a sponsor may try to pass the costs of operation to users by employing net leases and cost-of-living clauses. As previously discussed, the net lease tenant is responsible for utilities, maintenance, and taxes on a prorated basis. The cost-of-living clause allows a property owner to increase rents in relation to increases in the cost-of-living index as reported by the Bureau of Labor Statistics.

Most often the largest single building expense is property taxes. High taxes are a major deterrent to the reuse of existing structures; excessive taxes will reduce the cash flow of a project, lessening the amount of mortgage and equity financing obtainable.

Recognizing the importance of adaptive use and preservation projects and their potential for secondary economic effects on surrounding propery values, the public has, in recent years, begun to respond to the economic pressures placed on older structures by offering tax abatements and incentives.

Figure 1-17 demonstrates the effect of a tax abatement or incentive on Cases 1 and 2 which were previously presented in Figure 1-15. As indicated, a 25 percent reduction in the tax burden of Case 1 translates into a maximum project cost of $2,068,000, making this case feasible based on total development costs of $2 million. For Case 2, a 60 percent tax abatement or incentive is required to increase the maximum allowable project costs of $1,973,000, making this case marginally feasible.

Tax incentives have been used by the public to attract private lending sources to recycling projects. Many forms of incentives are used across the country.

1-16

Impact of Interest Rate Change on Maximum Project Cost: Case 1*

Gross Annual Revenues	$ 495,000	$ 495,000
Net Income Before Debt Service	192,000	192,000
Economic Value	$1,920,000	$1,920,000
Mortgage Loan Obtainable	$1,440,000	$1,440,000
Annual Debt Service		
Assume Mortgage Interest Rate and Term of Loan	8½% for 30 yrs.	6½% for 30 yrs.
Mortgage Constant	0.093	0.077
Maximum Mortgage	$1,440,000	$1,440,000
Annual Debt Service	0.093 x $1,440,000 = $ 134,000	0.077 x $1,440,000 = $ 111,000
Cash Flow Before Adjustment for Income Taxes	$ 58,000	$ 81,000
Maximum Equity at 15% Annual Return on Investment	$ 387,000	$ 540,000
Maximum Project Cost		
Maximum Mortgage	$1,440,000	$1,440,000
Equity	387,000	540,000
Total	**$1,827,000**	**$1,980,000**

*See Table 3, Case 1

Impact of Tax Abatement/Incentive: Cases 1 and 2

	Case 1	Case 2
Gross Annual Revenues	$ 495,000	$ 445,000
Net Income Before Debt Service		
Gross Annual Revenues	$ 495,000	$ 445,000
Total Building Expenses (incl. tax abatement/incentive*)	278,000	238,000
Net Income Before Debt Service	$ 217,000	$ 207,000
Economic Value	$2,170,000	$2,070,000
Maximum Mortgage	$1,628,000	$1,553,000
Debt Service	$ 151,000	$ 144,000
Cash Flow Before Adjustment for Income Taxes	66,000	63,000
Maximum Equity at 15%	$ 440,000	$ 420,000
Maximum Project Cost		
Maximum Mortgage	$1,628,000	$1,553,000
Equity	440,000	420,000
Total	**$2,068,000**	**$1,973,000**

*Assumes a tax abatement/incentive of 25 percent for Case 1 and 60 percent for Case 2.

In Massachusetts, Chapter 121A of the Massachusetts General Laws, which applies to reuse projects as well as to new construction, provides for the formation of a nonprofit or limited dividend corporation to redevelop a "blighted" area or other specific property. The developer of such a property must pay a predetermined percentage of gross revenues in lieu of taxes for a period of 15 to 20 years. Chapter 121A has been applied in the recycling of the Mercantile Wharf Building on Boston's waterfront into 121 mixed-income apartments and 17,000 square feet of ground floor for commercial uses. After tax stability through Chapter 121A was shown, the developer was able to demonstrate a financially viable project and thus was able to get financing for the $5.1 million project through the Massachusetts Housing Finance Agency.

Various forms of tax abatements are also offered in other states. Several of these tax laws, such as Connecticut Law C-127A, while on the books, have never been used. According to the Connecticut law, any municipality by ordinance can "provide for the abatement in whole or in part of real property taxes on structures of historical or architectural merit." The property can be made eligible by either the municipality or a local private preservation organization. The abatement is available to the owners of designated properties when they can show that the "current level of taxation is a material factor which threatens the continued existence of the structure, necessitating either its demolition or remodeling in a manner which destroys the historical or architectural value."

In New York City a tax abatement law (Section J51-2.5 of the Administrative Code of the city of New York) is being used to help recycle commercial buildings to residential use. Section J51 allows the developer a 12-year exemption from any increase in assessed valuation due to the "reasonable cost" of renovation. In addition, the law provides for an abatement of the rest of the property taxes, for 9 to 20 years, up to 90 percent of the reasonable cost of the rehabilitation work.

Of nationwide significance, the Federal Tax Reform Act of 1976 was signed into law on October 4, 1976 and included a section which deals with the preservation and reuse of certain historic structures. Section 2124, "Tax Incentives to Encourage the Preservation of Historic Structures," provides several new tax changes which are intended to stimulate the preservation and rehabilitation of certified historic structures and to discourage destructive actions to such properties. The 1976 tax law attempts to adjust the rates at which the costs of certified historic structures can be written off as amortization or depreciation deductions so that a financial incentive for preservation is established.[2]

The major provisions of Section 2124 and related comments are interpreted in the following paragraphs from an October 26, 1976 report prepared by the National Register of Historic Places, Office of Archaeology and Historic Preservation, National Park Service. It should be emphasized that Section 2124 of the Tax Reform Act of 1976 incorporates many generalizations regarding the effect of the tax law on preservation and adaptive use. Accordingly, the reader is advised to consult legal counsel for specific reference to provisions included within Section 2124.

Amortization of Rehabilitation Expenditures, Section 2124 (a)

A new part, Section 191, "Amortization of Certain Rehabilitation Expenditures for Certified Historic Structures," was added to Part VI of Subchapter B of Chapter 1 of the tax code, relating to itemized deductions. It provides that a taxpayer may amortize over a 60-month period any capital expenditure incurred in a certified rehabilitation of a certified historic structure, in lieu of depreciation deductions otherwise allowable.

The law defines certified historic structure as a building or structure which can be depreciated as provided in Section 167 of the tax code (i.e., the property must have some commercial characteristics; residential property may qualify if it is rented), and which

(A) is listed in the National Register,
(B) is located in a Registered Historic District and is certified by the Secretary of the Interior as being of historic significance to the district, or
(C) is located in a historic district designated under a statute of the appropriate state or local government if the statute is certified by the Secretary of the Interior as containing criteria that will substantially achieve the purpose of preserving and rehabilitating buildings of historic significance to the district.

The law defines certified rehabilitation as any rehabilitation of a certified historic structure that the Secretary of the Interior has certified as being consistent with the historic character of the property or the district in which the property is located.

To take advantage of this provision, rehabilitation expenditures must occur after June 14, 1976 and before June 15, 1981.

The effect of this new section is that owners will be encouraged to rehabilitate their historic commercial properties because of the availability of substantial tax savings in a short period of time. Before the passage of the Tax Reform Act, an owner was required to spread this tax deduction over the life of the property; now the deductions can be taken in 5 years.

Demolition, Section 2124 (b)

A new part, Section 280B, "Demolition of Certain Historic Structures," has been added to Part IX of Subchapter B of Chapter 1 of the tax code, relating to items not deductible. It provides that an owner or lessee of a certified historic structure cannot deduct any amounts expended for its demolition or for any loss sustained on account of its demolition. Furthermore, the law provides that any building or other structure located in a Registered Historic District will be treated as a certified historic structure unless the Secretary of the Interior has certified, prior to the demolition of the structure, that [it] is not of historic significance to the district.

This provision applies to demolitions beginning after June 30, 1976 and before January 1, 1981.

For tax purposes, demolition costs or losses sustained as a result of demolition must be added to the capital account as part of the cost of the land, rather than being deductible as part of the cost of the replacement structure. The effect of this provision is to discourage the demolition of certified historic structures because taxpayers will not be able to deduct these costs in later years through depreciation.

Depreciation of Improvements, Section 2124 (c)

A new part has been added to Section 167 of the tax code, relating to depreciation. This portion of the Tax Reform Act prohibits the accelerated method of depreciation for any property in whole or in part constructed, reconstructed, erected, or used (after December 31, 1975 and before January 1, 1981) on a site which was, on or after June 30, 1976, occupied by a certified historic structure which is demolished or substantially altered, other than by a certified rehabilitation.

---

[2] See Sarah G. Oldham and H. Ward Jandl, "Rehabilitation and the Tax Reform Act," *Urban Land* (Washington, D.C.: the Urban Land Institute, December 1977).

The effect of this provision is to discourage the demolition of certified historic structures by limiting taxpayers to the straightline method of depreciation, which provides less of a tax deduction in the early years of a project than does the accelerated method.

Substantially Rehabilitated Property, Section 2124(d)

Another new subsection has been added to Section 167 of the tax code, relating to depreciation. Taxpayers will be allowed to depreciate substantially rehabilitated historic property as though they were the original users of the property.

The law defines substantially rehabilitated historic property as any certified historic structure with respect to which capital expenditures for any certified rehabilitation during the 24-month period ending on the last day of any taxable year, reduced by depreciation or amortization deductions, exceed the greater of the adjusted basis of the property or $5,000.

To take advantage of this provision, rehabilitation expenditures must occur after June 30, 1976 and before July 1, 1981.

The effect of this provision is to encourage owners of certified historic structures to substantially rehabilitate their properties because they are allowed a more advantageous method of depreciation.

Transfers of Partial Interests in Property for Conservation Purposes, Section 2124(e)

Section 170(f) (3) of the tax code, relating to income tax deductions for charitable contributions, was amended by the Tax Reform Act. The Act provides that a deduction is allowed for the contribution to a charitable organization or a governmental entity exclusively for conservation purposes of (1) a lease on, option to purchase, or easement with respect to real property of not less than 30 years' duration or (2) a remainder interest in real property.

The law defines conservation purposes as the preservation of land areas for outdoor public recreation or education or scenic enjoyment, the preservation of historically important land areas or structures, or the protection of natural environmental systems.

Public Development Approvals

Before implementation of the project can begin, the sponsor must secure all required public development approvals in order to prevent unnecessary delays. Bringing the building up to code requirements will also be important in obtaining insurance.

With most buildings, securing public development approvals will mean zoning and building code approvals. In some instances, when buildings have landmark status or are located in historic districts, additional development approvals may be required, relating to the facade treatments and building renovation. Under the New York City Landmarks Preservation Law of 1965, for instance, the Landmarks Commission has the power to designate historic districts and to require a permit from the commission for any exterior alteration, demolition, reconstruction, or new construction. Public hearings are required for each permit application.

Buildings that are on the federal, state, or local historic registers may also require various forms of review or clearance before construction can begin. The reuse of the Butler Brothers Warehouse in Minneapolis illustrates the type of approvals often required.

In 1971, the Butler Brothers building was added to the National Register of Historic Places. Such properties are protected against demolition or impairment by federally funded, licensed, or approved programs that are provided by the National Historic Preservation Act of 1966.

Of far greater significance to the reuse potential of the Butler Brothers Warehouse was its designation for historic preservation by the Minneapolis City Council in 1973. This designation meant that the exterior of the building could not be altered or destroyed without the approval of the Minneapolis Heritage Preservation Commission, established in 1972 to serve as an advisory body to the council in recommending buildings and areas to be designated for heritage preservation. In its advisory capacity, the commission must review and then request that the council approve or disapprove all city permits to remodel, change, or destroy designated buildings. A renovation scheme respecting the exterior of the building, therefore, needed to be developed for Butler Square.

Financing

Various types of financing may be required for the project, ranging from funds for acquisition to permanent financing. Depending upon the type of development entity and the nature of the project, an array of financing possibilities might be available. As previously discussed, many public agencies on the federal, state, and local level are sympathetic toward and actively involved in the preservation and adaptive use process.

Many communities have been using Community Development Block Grant monies to partially finance adaptive use projects while some have used urban renewal funds. The change from categorical to discretionary community development funding has been a positive factor in increasing the use of community block grant monies. This type of funding has been particularly effective for projects developed by the public sector. The Louisiana Arts and Science Center, developed in the Illinois Central Railroad Passenger Station, was financed by an urban renewal grant.

Other examples of the use of renewal funds have occurred in Salem and Newburyport, Massachusetts. Newburyport, for instance, has employed federal funds to rehabilitate a major portion of the downtown urban renewal area. The local redevelopment authority was able to write down to zero the cost of buildings in the project area by using federal funds and was able to charge approximately $3,000 to $4,000 per building for the land value. Public monies were used to provide public improvements (underground utilities, sidewalk and street repairs, multilevel access, and plantings). These public improvements were made up to the facades of the buildings. With exterior public area treatments being handled by the town, a reduction in the sale price of individual buildings in the project area, and guidance by the town of repair and rehabilitation of structures, the process has benefited property owners by creating a better environment. The town also benefited by being able to collect additional taxes.

Other approaches to financing relate to the creation of various types of local development corporations and nonprofit corporations. The Massachusetts 121A Corporation, mentioned previously, is one such vehicle. Others include small business investment corporations created under Section 301 of the Small Business Investment Act, and local development corporations set up under Section 502 of the same act.

The development of the Franklin Square House in Boston represents another approach to financing which has been used often with conversion to housing. In this instance, the conversion was carried out using a 121A tax agreement with the city and financing from both the Massachusetts Housing Finance Agency and the federal Department of Housing and Urban Development through Section 8. Section 8 replaced Section 236 in the federal housing subsidy programs and pays the difference between unit operating and financing costs and the assisted tenants' rents, fixed at 25 percent of income.

Most states currently have state housing finance agencies and it was recently estimated that these agencies had given financing commitments throughout 1976 to approximately 200,000 units of housing. In some states such as Massachusetts, a considerable number of the projects that have been financed are for adaptive use.

Revolving funds present an increasingly popular financing approach for adaptive use projects. At the national level, the National Historic Preservation Fund, established in 1971, operates such a revolving fund. More and more, communities have been establishing such funds, usually administered through preservation groups at the local level. The purpose of the fund is to provide loans and grants for buying and rehabilitating historic structures. As loans are made and income generated, more loans can be made.

Notable examples of the use of revolving funds to finance historic preservation include those of the Historic Charleston (South Carolina) Foundation, Historic Savannah Foundation, and the Pittsburgh History and Landmarks Foundation. The Pittsburgh Restoration Fund, established in 1966 with a $100,000 grant from the Sarah Mellon Scaife Foundation, has grown to over $700,000. The fund has been used to pay for acquisition and rehabilitation of property, holding of unrestored property, public education, and marketing.

In many cases, public funding sources can take a prospective reuse sponsor just so far without the need to tap private funding sources. In such instances, public funds have been used essentially as seed money to spark a private commitment for funds.

With regard to private financing sources, it is generally true that commercial lenders are very conservative when it comes to projects thought to be speculative. Because of the limited proven track record of adaptive use projects, it can be difficult for a developer to justify a loan request. There is no private funding source specifically available for adaptive use projects. There are funds, however, for shopping centers, office buildings, residential developments, or any development venture which makes sound economic sense.

But because adaptive use projects have been increasingly accepted by the public, lenders have generally been evaluating such projects more favorably. The idea that new is better than old has been slowly changing, and private financing sources are beginning to evaluate carefully a recycling project's economic potential.

Understandably, the likelihood of obtaining private financing for an adaptive use project is greater in larger cities than in communities where there have been a minimum number of such projects initiated or where there is a large supply of land available for development.

Financial institutions, which generally have a strong commitment to cities, are beginning to appreciate the benefits of adaptive use. Many of these institutions have within their loan portfolios a significant number of aging structures located in our cities. For such buildings recycling is often an alternative. This possibility can be particularly important when considering how existing loans can be fully amortized rather than foreclosed.

In obtaining conventional financing for an adaptive use project, it is important to appreciate the lender's motivations and needs. In brief, lenders want to maximize their investment potential while minimizing their risks. As previously stated, the real estate investor will only become associated with projects which can produce the needed revenues to cover operating expenses and debt service while providing a good return on investment. Therefore, marginal adaptive use ventures, in terms of market and financial parameters, are extremely difficult to finance without government funding programs.

As a case in which recycling was a new phenomenon to the local market, the Quaker Square project in Akron, Ohio, illustrates the creative efforts used by its developers to obtain private financing. In 1973, the initial acquisition of property for Quaker Square was funded by a local commercial bank on a 1-year loan at 2 percent over the prime rate per year. This financing was guaranteed personally by the developers. Once the property had been secured, the development group attempted to raise rehabilitation funds through a limited partnership underwriting for $3,000,000. This public offering ultimately failed in 1974, and the developers were forced to seek alternative methods of obtaining financing. Since lenders, both locally and around the country, were unwilling to finance a recycling project in this untested market, the developers instituted a unique method of obtaining rehabilitation capital for the project. They sold the machinery parts which were left by the Quaker Oats Company to grain and cereal related industries as replacement parts. Through the sale of replacement parts, used equipment, and scrap metal, approximately $200,000 was raised to start the recycling effort. By leveraging the payments to contractors, approximately $500,000 of improvements were made to the buildings. Only after these efforts were completed and cash flow from the project was realized would a local savings and loan association provide the permanent financing.

There is no magic in obtaining private financing for an adaptive use project. Lenders analyze the attractiveness of these investments on the basis of the safety of the principal, the liquidity factor, and the yield. It is important for the sponsor to identify and learn to work with the principal sources of private financing. A mortgage banker can act as the intermediary between the sponsor and the financial institution. The sponsor can save both time in processing the mortgage application and financing costs with the assistance of a knowledgeable mortgage banker who can help in selecting a lender with the best financial arrangement for the project. It should be understood that a combination of financing sources may be required to complete the financing package for a project.

Commercial banks represent the principal source of short-term construction or interim financing. This is due in part to their sources of funds which are obtained from demand deposits of corporations or individuals and checking accounts which require short-term liquidity. These banks typically are not a source of funding for long-term mortgages.

In the case of the Faneuil Hall Marketplace project in Boston, construction financing was provided by a commitment of 50 percent of the necessary funds by the Chase Manhattan Bank with the remainder coming from a consortium of Boston banks. The construction loan is secured as a general obligation of the project developer.

Life insurance companies are a source of long-term or permanent financing for major projects. This is because of their constant inflow of insurance payments which are not subject to the same fluctuations which affect commercial banks or other lending sources. By obtaining a permanent loan commitment, the sponsor may more easily obtain interim financing needed during the construction period.

Connecticut General Life Insurance Company, for instance, provided financing for Ghirardelli Square in addition to the Stanford Court development in San Francisco, based on a formula related to project performance. New York Life Insurance has provided long-term financing on conventional terms for Larimer Square. In many cases long-term financing is secured after projects are well on their way to completion.

Savings banks, although they are located predominately in the northeastern portion of the country, represent a major source of financing throughout the country. Many of the smaller savings banks provide conventional financing primarily for one- and two-family dwellings, while they are heavy lenders of government-insured loans. The larger banks provide mortgage financing for commercial, industrial, and multifamily residential projects.

As previously discussed, financing for the recycling of Boston's Old City Hall into first class office and commercial space was provided by five Boston savings banks. These financial institutions provided both construction and permanent financing for this development.

Real estate investment trusts (REIT) are another potential source of financing. The real estate investment trust obtains its funds from the sale of stock and from short-term borrowing. The largest category of loans made by an REIT is for construction financing. Other types of financing provided by these organizations include long-term mortgages with maturities of 20 to 30 years, development loans necessary to prepare a site for construction, and intermediate-term loans used by developers to provide time to generate sufficient operating revenues to justify a permanent mortgage. In recent years because of serious financial difficulties many REITs have become more cautious in selecting their loan investments.

Financing for the Century Theater reuse project in Chicago, for instance, was difficult to obtain because of the recycling nature of the project and the fact that no major "triple A" long-term tenants had been signed up for the project. Accordingly, with the assistance of a mortgage banker, the developers obtained a 5-year standby permanent mortgage commitment from an REIT. This commitment assured the construction lender that funds would be available to pay the construction loan.

Savings and loan associations are a principal source of residential mortgages for single and multifamily dwellings as well as of construction financing for commercial projects. The following is an example of how savings and loan associations can be used.

In 1968, the River Square development in San Antonio, Texas, was recycled. Financing for the acquisition of this property and seed money were provided by a syndicate of 11 local businessmen who collectively invested $150,000 in cash and debentures. Construction financing was then provided by a local savings and loan association. The developers were able to obtain this interim loan as a result of their personal financial strength.

Pension funds represent a potentially major source of mortgage investments in future years. The tremendous increase in their assets has caused many pension funds to seek real estate mortgage investments which will maximize their investment criteria. The income from pension funds is second only to insurance companies. Pension funds are primarily involved in long-term permanent mortgage commitments. Permanent financing for the Faneuil Hall Marketplace is provided by the Teachers Insurance and Annuity Association. This long-term mortgage commitment is secured by a first mortgage on the leasehold interest of the project.

Individual investors are an important source of mortgage financing. They are willing to assume greater financial risks than an institutional lender and understandably require higher interest rates. They are especially useful in short-term mortgage commitments which represent potentially hard-to-finance ventures such as recycling efforts.

The recycling of Chattanooga, Tennessee's Terminal Station into the Chattanooga Choo-Choo complex was initiated by an investment group comprised of 24 local individuals. This group invested a total of $2.4 million in the development venture.

Syndications provide a vehicle by which the general public can be actively involved in the real estate development business. Such real estate entities range from joint venture syndicates to complex limited partnerships. In the latter case, the syndicate will purchase income-producing property by selling investment shares to individuals. These persons in turn can then receive investment yields as tax-free cash income and a pro rata share of the project's depreciation allowance for tax purposes.

In recycling the Chickering piano factory in Boston, the sponsors of the project established a limited partnership syndication so that they could recapture their own equity in the development.

Lender's Presentation Package

In many instances, the potential lender or investor for a recycling project has had limited experience with adaptive use financing. Such potential financing sources must be educated to appreciate the advantages of recycling and the unique character of the individual project to be financed. The sponsor should prepare a carefully detailed, straightforward presentation of the project. In many respects, the basic package of information described below is essentially the same for all types of real estate development. The prospective lender reviewing a reuse project, however, is certain to examine both the information presented and the experience of the development team more closely than he would a financing proposal for new construction.

The basic information which a prospective private lender will require includes:

- Project documentation such as the purchase agreement and terms of the sale if the property is to be bought; confirmation of zoning and code compliance for the use proposed; proof that the building is structurally sound and is suitable for the new use; and assurance that other legal issues or present building users will not encumber recycling the structure.
- The qualifications of all members of the development team—developer, architect, engineer, contractor, real estate economist and appraiser, and property manager. Information regarding the developer's financial capabilities and credit rating will also be highly important; lenders want to be assured that the developer has sufficient financial stability to cover debt service if the project's cash flow becomes inadequate. Lenders also allow for the unknown factors in an adaptive use project which could increase costs. They therefore want to be assured that experienced people will be directing the recycling effort.

- A market analysis to ascertain the development opportunities and constraints from a market perspective. When a firm commitment has been obtained from new building users, the market evaluation becomes less important.
- Schematic designs sensitive to the original architectural detail of the building and to market considerations.
- A cost analysis of physical improvements provided by the project engineer, architect, and contractor to be used as a basis for the project's financial analysis.
- A detailed financial analysis to convince both the potential lender and the developer that the recycling effort is an economically viable venture which justifies the expenditure of both time and financial resources.
- Signed commitments or letters of intent from potential space users. Such assurances will signify that cash flow is forthcoming and that the project is being accepted in the marketplace.

The process that the Massachusetts Housing Finance Agency goes through, for instance, in terms of making loan commitments, illustrates the general nature of materials required to obtain financing. The following is taken from the Eighth Annual Report (September 1976, pages 16, 18, 21) of the MHFA.

> The qualifications of the members of the proposed development team are reviewed to determine whether they have the financial strength and skills needed to undertake a housing development of the size being proposed. The staff also evaluates the performance of team members who have done business with the Agency on previous occasions. If the team is acceptable and the site meets the Agency's standards, the developer is invited to submit a formal application and begin negotiations for a mortgage loan. The mortgage application is analyzed by the staff to see whether the combination of proposed rents and subsidies will be sufficient to repay the loan. The market area is studied to determine the level of rents that people are able and willing to pay. The analysis includes the establishment of the value of the land and, in the case of rehabilitation, of the building, a review of construction and other development costs, and an estimation of the costs of debt service, real estate taxes, and operating expenses. In this analysis, comparisons of the projected construction and operating costs are made with data accumulated by the staff and based on MHFA's experience with other housing developments of similar type and construction. The density of the housing, the number and size of the apartments, and the amenities to be included

are directly related to the economic feasibility of a proposal. The quality of the design and the economic feasibility of the plan are regarded as equally important by the Agency and its staff. After the design and economic feasibility of a development plan have been approved by the staff, the proposal is submitted to the MHFA Security Committee, which decides whether such a loan would be a sound investment for the Agency. With the Committee's approval, the proposal is then recommended to the MHFA members for a vote of a legal commitment to funds from the Agency's authorization to sell notes and bonds. A loan commitment is subject to the satisfactory completion of a number of requirements. The developer must produce evidence of title to the property, legality of the zoning, appropriate insurance policies, performance and payment bonds for the contractor, and other legal documents necessary for the protection of the Agency. The MHFA construction engineer must be satisfied that the mechanical, electrical, heating, and ventilating systems meet the Agency's standards and that the plan is consistent with the minimum property standards of the federal subsidy programs. Working drawings and specifications of construction materials must be approved by the design review officer. Tax agreements and other financial arrangements must be satisfactory to the mortgage department. The projected operating expense budget must be sufficient in the opinion of the management department, and a reservation of subsidies to reduce rents for low- and moderate-income people must be in hand before the loan is closed. The legal documentation, the basis for the loan closing, contains all the controls that the Agency will need to enforce its policies and meet its goals. The contracts include a mortgage, mortgage note, construction loan agreement, regulatory agreement, and additional documents reflecting the specific conditions of the loan that have been negotiated by MHFA and the development team. After the legal closing the documents are reviewed by the Agency's bond counsel, short-term notes to fund the construction loan are sold, and construction begins. The proceeds of the note sale are deposited in a special account for the loan, and investments are purchased which will mature periodically in accordance with the projected construction schedule. A title clearance is obtained before each release of funds, and a portion of each amount is retained until the housing has been completed and the construction costs have been certified. A construction loan is converted to a permanent mortgage loan after a housing development has been completed, the apartments have been rented, and operating experience indicates the housing is economically stable. The long-term loan is funded through the sale of bonds. Amortization of the loan begins after permanent financing.

Project Implementation

After the detailed planning and financing phase, the last step in the process is implementation. This critical stage includes the physical rehabilitation of the property, project management, and marketing. Without close construction management and effective on-the-spot decision making, the chance for project cost overruns increases substantially. Cost overruns and time lost in rehabilitation, as with any type of construction activity, directly affect the economic viability of the project, not only in direct cost increases, but also in lost rents due to delays in completion.

Project marketing can also be an important part of implementation. The fact that a building is already in place allows for significant marketing lead time. This factor can be an important plus when project financing is sought. Early marketing also generates early cash flow, which may mean savings in financing costs for the project.

When the project is completed, management of the facilities often will be critical to the overall success of the reuse. This is particularly true in regard to commercial buildings, when turnover of merchants and related management problems can lead to failure of a project which has otherwise been successfully recycled.

1-18

Project Implementation

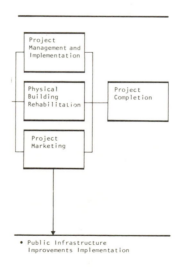

Rehabilitation

During the physical rehabilitation of the structure close attention should be given to construction management. Given the nonstandardized nature of adaptive use projects, the assistance of an experienced architect and contractor can be invaluable in controlling rehabilitation costs. Underestimating the costs can be a financial catastrophe for the sponsor who has structured a financing package based on the project's development costs and cash flow projections. Costs can be saved by determining at the beginning whether the building is suitable for the use or uses proposed and then preparing and sticking to realistic development parameters.

Secondly, it is important to try to abide by construction budgets once they have been established. This is not always possible because of the many unknown factors which can be encountered in older buildings. Through tenacious construction management, however, the potential rehabilitation cost overruns can be minimized.

Recycling of existing building materials can also be a cost savings and should be investigated prior to the actual rehabilitation work. When combined with close attention to design details, such recycled material can be handsomely used. An example of the cost savings that are possible during rehabilitation by attention to details is illustrated in the recycling of the Chickering piano factory. Its developers employed such construction shortcuts as:

- Sanding down and, where necessary, patching the flooring at a cost of $60,000 instead of replacing it at a cost of $375,000.
- Rebuilding three existing elevators for $60,000 instead of installing new ones for $150,000.
- Installing one drain-waste-vent stack to serve two units each per floor instead of the conventional one-stack-one-unit configuration. Savings: $400 a unit.
- Repainting the exterior brick for $15,000 instead of exposing the brick, which would have cost $85,000 for sandblasting, pointing, and sealing.
- Applying electric lines—in conduits—directly to brick walls. Savings: a 15 percent reduction on conventional wiring costs.
- Leaving piping—sprinkler, steam, water, etc.—exposed wherever practical. Savings: approximately $200,000.

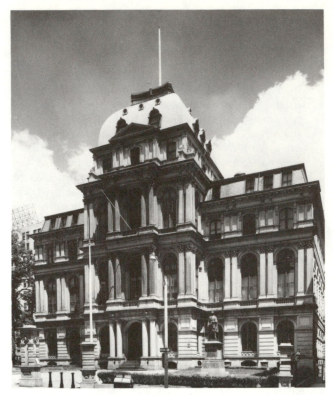

1-19 Boston's Old City Hall was converted to commercial and office space in 1971 for $2.7 million. (Photo: Carol Rankin.)

The developers deliberately did not expose the ceiling beams. "Even though exposed beams have great tenant appeal, they would have created an acoustical problem. To stop noise transmission, concrete flooring or carpeting would have had to be installed. And the beams would have had to be sandblasted clean. So the total cost for exposed beams would have been $2.25 a square foot."[3]

As noted before, experience has shown that by preparing and implementing well conceived architectural plans, rehabilitation costs associated with adaptive use projects can be comparable to costs of new construction and in some cases they have been 25 to 30 percent less than new construction costs. Recycling projects are primarily labor intensive with less materials required than new construction. Therefore, for basically the same dollars, through adaptive use efforts one can offer a highly competitive product.

[3] *House and Home* (New York: McGraw-Hill, Inc., February 1975), pp. 69-70.

Management

Overall project management from initial development through completion and into the future represents one of the most significant areas of responsibility for a real estate venture. This is particularly true for the adaptive use development where a greater number of variables may occur in terms of the physical characteristics of the structure.

The selection of a competent project manager can aid in the smooth flow of implementation functions. If project budgeting permits, the manager should be located on site. When the sponsor cannot give complete attention to the development, the close supervision of the manager combined with rigorous project standards can translate into greater control of time and costs.

Management functions such as ensuring continued liaison among the sponsor, building occupants, and others involved in the daily functions of the recycling venture are important. In a commercial reuse project, ongoing promotional efforts for the development should be coordinated by a project manager.

In the case of Trolley Square, the developer assumes overall responsibility for management of the project. Close coordination is maintained between the developer and tenants through a merchants' organization which promotes the interests of all tenants of Trolley Square. Tenants are required to belong to the merchants' association and voting rights and dues are based on a sliding scale according to square footage leased. The developer further controls the operations of this specialty retail center by writing stringent performance clauses in the tenant's lease. If these performance standards are not met, the developer may terminate the lease.

Long-term property management and maintenance are also critically important to the viability of the development and, as such, the importance of these functions should be reflected in the project's operating budget. Since we are working with older structures, continued preventive maintenance should be practiced to further extend the economic life of the building.

Marketing

Since existing structures are in most instances protected from the outside elements, with visible potential floor layouts, early marketing is possible in adaptive use efforts. In new buildings, on the other hand, marketing is more constrained by construction phasing. Thus, with recycling projects, space requirements can be discussed with potential users earlier in the development process. The sponsor can save time and money by initially designing and providing space to meet the needs of specific users. If, for example, a prospective office tenant requires a full floor and the sponsor has not already subdivided the area, the prospective tenant may be satisfied with the available block of space. In addition, the sponsor may be capable of "passing through" to contracted full-floor users the operating costs on common areas, including, for example, corridors, lavatories, and lobbies. Small space users might not be required to contribute to these common area charges.

Creation of a completed sales or leasing area will be important in demonstrating what the final building product will look like. Moreover, in many cases, it is not essential to rehabilitate completely all common area spaces before putting into effect the marketing program.

Since most individuals are not familiar with the advantages of older structures, careful architectural and design treatment in the marketing areas may prove very useful in the leasing or sales effort. Accordingly, the areas set aside for marketing, including model units, should reflect the quality and image of the project which makes it unique and noteworthy compared to conventional new construction. Graphics and marketing brochures which describe the historic significance and distinctive physical features of the building will contribute to a successful marketing venture.

An important component of the marketing program is the selection of building uses. The proper combination of uses can be essential to the success of the recycling venture. For example, specialty shopping centers, such as Ghirardelli Square and Larimer Square, are typically "anchored" by restaurants which may occupy more than 20 percent of the gross

Development Loan Graph

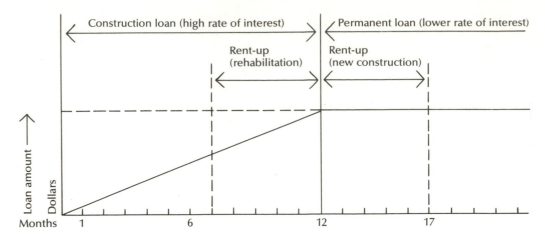

1-20   In adaptive use parts of a building often can be marketed during construction. With early rent up the developer receives rent while construction continues. Since the construction loan does not run the same length of time as the actual construction, the rent offsets the expense of the construction loan, and the developer can often obtain permanent financing sooner because the marketability of a building has been proven.

leasable area. In return, specialty retail stores, which offer quality and unique merchandise that cannot generally be found in conventional retail establishments, should complement the restaurant and entertainment offerings of the center. In leasing space in a specialty retail center, a balance should also be achieved between chain operations and local merchants. The former are important because they are proven generators of sales, the latter because they contribute the local flavor that is important to a specialty center.

With regard to project feasibility, early marketing and thus potentially earlier occupancy can mean the difference between paying higher interest rates on a construction loan and reduced financing costs on a permanent mortgage commitment. This point is described in Figure 1-20.

A case for accelerated marketing was seen in the recycling of the former 102,000-square-foot *Record American* Building in Boston's downtown area. This structure, now referred to as One Winthrop Square, was recycled successfully into Class A office space. The time required from interior demolition to tenant occupancy was only 18 months. This compares favorably with new construction in which tenant occupancy of a building of this size could require at least 6 additional months.[4]

---

[4] See Charles Tseckares, "One Winthrop Square," *Urban Land* (Washington, D.C.: the Urban Land Institute, July/August 1976).

Summary

This section has attempted to explain many of the reasons for the growing interest in reusing older buildings and the planning and development process and techniques used to implement successfully such projects. Realistic planning parameters must be formulated early in the development process. The benefits of retaining older structures should be evaluated from the perspectives of market, financial, and physical planning, as well as from the standpoint of preserving our built environment.

While adaptive use is still in the embryonic stage in many areas of the country, it is quickly gaining the attention of the real estate and financial communities, public sector agencies, preservation groups, architects and planners, and existing property owners who are beginning to recognize the intrinsic values of older structures. Factors such as quality and inherent character of the original structure; potential cost savings during the construction period; availability of underutilized properties with strategic locations; positive effects associated with property values and taxes on surrounding land uses; and increased awareness, understanding, and cooperation of varied interest groups which jointly develop such properties are but some of the influences which have generated this recent surge of adaptive use developments and proposals.

If comprehensive planning and implementation are carried out, the "bottom line" should be rewarding in terms of financial returns to the sponsor. Equally rewarding is the fact that a product has been created which can have a long-term positive effect on the community.

Part 2
Case Studies

Factor's Row

Empty warehouses and deserted wharves—in cities across the United States—mark the decline of old waterfront districts, once busy centers of commercial activity. As shipping and transportation patterns changed, these cities turned their backs physically on the rivers which once ruled their economies. The old riverfront buildings remained—often within sight of the new central business districts—but their uses shifted to dead storage or light industry. Today, however, attention is once again focusing on many of these waterfront districts, as private developers and public agencies begin to reassess the economic potential of such areas.

In Savannah, this cycle has come full circle. The old waterfront, at its height when "cotton was king" in the South, survived a long period of decline and neglect during the first half of this century to become, in recent years, the city's most distinctive tourist and commercial district. The key to the revitalization is the adaptive use of Factor's Row, a complex of 19th century warehouses interconnected by a special system of ramps and bridges. Within the last 5 years, more than 60 shops, restaurants, and offices have opened within the four-block row of warehouses. The conversion and renovation of these buildings represents a total private investment of more than $4 million.

It is not to private investment alone, however, that the Savannah waterfront owes its rebirth. The district has also been the scene of joint public-private efforts aimed at urban conservation, public improvements, and new construction. For over 20 years, waterfront rehabilitation has been one thrust of a broad-based community movement concerned with preserving the city's historic resources, and since 1973, the riverfront warehouses have been protected by a local historic district zoning ordinance. A $7 million waterfront urban renewal project was initiated in 1975, and a multimillion dollar hotel is planned for a block-long gap in the warehouse buildings. Despite a number of conflicts involving specific activities, the various participants recognize in common that the waterfront's revitalization means tangible, economic benefits for Savannah.

Opposite page: 2-1   Purchased in 1971 for $20,000, 206 West Bay Street was one of the first structures on the Savannah waterfront to undergo extensive rehabilitation. Boutiques with entries from the river side of the building occupy the lower floors of the former warehouse.

History

The waterfront was the most vital and vibrant part of the city for many decades in the 18th and 19th centuries. Savannah, founded in 1783 by an Englishman, James Oglethorpe, was laid out on a bluff overlooking the Savannah River. Although the earliest warehouses were along the water's edge, river merchants gradually began to move inland, building their structures into the side of the bluff. The invention of the cotton gin in 1793 caused a tremendous boom in Savannah's shipping industry and brought great prosperity to the city's merchants. In the 1840s, ballast stones from incoming ships were used to pave the riverfront streets and reinforce the bluff. A network of iron bridges spread itself among the warehouses and bluff, allowing buildings five stories tall on the river side to be entered at the second, third, or fourth floors on the town side.

Known as Factor's Walk because of the cotton factors (or agents) who worked along the river, this complex of bridges and warehouses is still the most distinctive feature of the waterfront. Many of the warehouses date from the 1850s, although the extravagant Victorian Cotton Exchange was not built until 1886. The centerpiece of the waterfront district, the bronze-domed City Hall, was built in 1906.

Although the city's economy eventually shifted away from the cotton industry, the central business district never moved very far from the river. South of the waterfront, Oglethorpe's unique city design—a grid system broken every few blocks by green squares—has endured into the 20th century. Bull Street, the major north-south thoroughfare, originates at the steps of City Hall, and Broughton Street, Savannah's main shopping avenue, runs parallel to the river, only a few blocks to the south.

Decline and Renewal

Eventually, the bustling waterfront became quiet. Offices were scattered through the upper stories of the warehouses, but from the riverside the buildings looked derelict. The walks were often empty, and the lower floors of the warehouses served as inexpensive storage space. Fortunately, however, tentative plans by private developers to clear some land by the river were dropped, and in the 1950s the district received a boost when two buildings on East Bay Street were renovated. When the Cotton Exchange closed in 1952, the Savannah Chamber of Commerce bought and restored the building, for $76,000, to use as a visitors' center. Four years later the adjacent Thomas Gamble Building was remodeled by the city for $40,000 for use as municipal offices and a branch library.

These projects paralleled a general awakening of interest in the city's historic buildings, sparked by activities of a new citizens' group, the Historic Savannah Foundation. Formed in 1955, Historic Savannah initiated an aggressive campaign to prevent demolition of the city's historic resources and to increase awareness of the social and economic values of urban conservation. A survey of buildings in a 2.2-square-mile downtown district was undertaken in 1962, and structures were rated by historic and architectural significance. In the waterfront district, 18 structures received a rating of "exceptional," one "excellent," and eight "notable."

In 1965, Historic Savannah and the Chamber of Commerce invited a consultant from Williamsburg, Viginia, to present suggestions on improving Savannah's tourist business. This report, citing the potential for tremendous economic gain by the city, urged Savannah to capitalize on its "unmatched" assets—the "fine buildings surrounding green squares in a downtown area bounded by [the] unique Bay and Factor's Walk complex." In response, the Chamber has steadily increased its annual travel promotion budget, and the results in tourist spending have been staggering. According to Chamber estimates, the income from tourism has climbed from $14 million in 1965 to $48 million in 1974.

Most of the waterfront buildings are now held by individual owners; and since the Gamble Building renovation, all adaptive use projects have been privately initiated. Much of the property has not changed hands during recent years, a characteristic which has kept real estate speculation to a

2-2 Two levels of bridges on the street side of 206 West Bay Street give access to the upper floors, which are used as a private home with studio space fo the artist/owner. The stone and brick structure, built in 1816, is one of the oldest cotton warehouses on the eastern seaboard.

minimum. The largest structure in the district, for example, has been in the family of Sylvan Byck, the present owner, since 1937. Redeveloped over a period of several years, the 51,000-square-foot building at 302–410 East Bay now has 15 office, shop, and restaurant tenants. Another major property owner, Anthony Ryan, bought 120–130 West Bay in 1958 and converted it in 1972; the building now has 33 tenants.

Byck and Ryan are presidents of the Waterfront Owners Association and the Waterfront Shop Association, respectively, two organizations which represent the interests of those involved in district revitalization. Neither of the Waterfront organizations is attempting to document the total investment by owners in the area because, as Byck points out, many landlords are renting unimproved or only partially remodelled spaces to tenants willing to do their own interior finishing. Retail tenants are predominantly small, locally owned specialty shops; restaurants include both local and franchised operations; and offices are occupied by architects and lawyers.

Although most of the adaptive use developments have been profit-oriented ventures, a few important participants have had other objectives. In 1971, artist Ann Werner Osteen and doctor Lamont Osteen purchased one of the oldest cotton warehouses on the river, 206 West Bay Street, to reuse as their home. The upper two floors provide dramatic living space, with a skylight cut through the steeply pitched roof; the third floor serves as an artist's studio; and the lower two floors, opening toward the river, are rented as boutiques.

City Involvement

With revitalization of the waterfront identified as a long-range goal in the 1950s, the Savannah–Chatham County Metropolitan Planning Commission did some groundwork which has proved to be an aid in recent private efforts. Factor's Row has long been zoned for bayfront business, a classification which permits offices, residences, retail and craft shops, restaurants, and night clubs but excludes heavy industry, adult bookstores, massage parlors, and other "undesirable" uses. A sign ordinance controls exterior advertising and prohibits the use of neon signs in the district.

The city's most constant involvement in the district, however, has been through Mires Rosenthal, Director of Inspections. Rosenthal has the sometimes delicate responsibility of seeing that conversions of warehouses to new uses conform with the city's building codes. Most of the waterfront buildings are structurally sound despite more than a century of use, and code problems generally have to do with fire safety and means of egress. Working closely with owners and architects, Rosenthal's office strives to make code requirements clear before adaptive use projects get underway, "so there will be no surprises." This pragmatic approach to code enforcement earned Rosenthal an award in 1974 from the Waterfront associations, which cited Rosenthal's assistance in the redevelopment process.

2-3   A pioneering adaptive use project on Factor's Row, undertaken by the city of Savannah in the 1950s, involved remodeling the Thomas Gamble Building as municipal offices and a branch library.

2-4 Built into a bluff, the old warehouses along Factor's Row have two or three stories on the front or street side and four or five stories on the rear or river side.

Rosenthal also serves on the city's Board of Review, which oversees exterior changes in all properties within the historic district. The board has the power to delay what it considers to be undersirable alterations or demolitions for a period of 4, 6, or 12 months, depending on the rating of the building involved. During its 3 years of jurisdiction, the board has not been involved in any serious disputes with waterfront owners.

The major impetus for investment in adaptive use came in 1968–1969 when plans were announced for a multimillion dollar urban renewal project for the narrow stretch of land between the river and the warehouses. The project, construction for which was begun in August 1975, involves the installation of bulkheads to stabilize the shoreline, improvement of automobile and pedestrian circulation by the construction of new paving and new parking facilities, and general beautification of the waterfront area. Urban renewal director Donald Nasmith sees the project as the "salvation" of the waterfront district, because, he says, "there was no other way that the community could have afforded to make these improvements." The warehouse shops on the riverside are attracting a considerable number of customers, despite the presence of heavy equipment and constant construction a few feet away.

The Market Outlook

In the opinion of Sylvan Byck, urban renewal's project could change the tone of the waterfront district within 5 years. Byck predicts that an influx of "big" money after the renewal project is completed will eventually bring about the displacement of the local mom-and-pop type of tenants who currently occupy many of the retail spaces. Byck is leaving several rental units vacant in his building until the construction is finished, although owners say there already are tenants waiting for available riverside spaces. Rental rates in the district cover a wide spectrum—from $0.50 to $7.00 per square foot—because of the range in the units' physical condition. Annual rent for one of the largest converted warehouses is more than $100,000; and this is for a building which represents a total investment of only $250,000.

Market values of the buildings themselves have significantly increased over the past 6 years, as evidenced by the only example of major real estate speculation in the district: In 1969, a developer purchased the buildings on both sides of the Osteen's warehouse for $66,000; after urban renewal plans were unveiled, the developer sold the buildings for $100,000. Within a year and a half, the buildings were again successfully marketed, this time for $150,000.

2-5 Revitalization of the Savannah riverfront is one part of a broad-based community effort to preserve the historic resources of the city.

2-6 A unique system of ramps and bridges along Factor's Row runs along the street side of the warehouses. Cotton agents originally walked along the bridges to inspect and bid on cotton displayed below.

Along with this increase in market value has come a rise in property tax assessments for the renovated warehouses. This rise, not surprisingly, is a sore point with many people who have bought and restored property in Savannah's historic district, since the tax increases are viewed by some property owners as an unfair penalty for a private investment which helps both the city and the tourist industry. Others accept the taxes philosophically, pointing out that an increased tax base has long been an argument to encourage rehabilitation. The tax problem was addressed by the Downtown Neighborhood Association, a local membership organization which successfully lobbied with the state government for passage of enabling legislation for facade easements. Although the law has not yet been used in Savannah, its backers predict that donors of perpetual facade easements will receive double benefits through a gift deduction on personal income taxes and a reduction in the taxable value of the property.

Revitalization has not always proceeded smoothly on the waterfront; various interest groups have clashed over the years. A conflict erupted in 1969 when two local developers announced plans to build a 15-story hotel and apartment complex in the block-long gap between City Hall and the West Bay warehouses. Citing a threat to the architectural integrity of the waterfront, a group of citizens formed the Save-the-Bay-Committee, Inc., to fight the development. The committee and the developers finally faced each other in court, and the time and cost of the legal proceedings shelved the hotel despite a final resolution that construction could not be restrained. After a breathing spell of several years, the same developers, businessman Merritt Dixon III and attorney Mitchell Dunn, are ready to try again. They feel that the new design, a seven-story, mansard-roofed hotel, will be compatible with the waterfront district. The proposal will be evaluated by the Board of Review, which will apply a set of guidelines for new construction within the historic district, focusing on materials, texture, scale, and other urban design details. Dixon is confident that another battle will be avoided and maintains that the hotel will be a considerable economic asset for the waterfront.

Trolley Square

Trolley Square is a novel entertainment and specialty shopping center located in a 13-acre complex composed of a trolley car barn and maintenance shops—once the home of Salt Lake City's trolley car system. The development was inspired by Ghirardelli Square in San Francisco, and its four freestanding masonry buildings incorporate an intricate network of internalized pedestrian shopping streets, courtyards, and common open areas interconnected by landscaped walkways. The project features a turn-of-the-century theme, and architectural artifacts and antiques have been used throughout for both functional and decorative purposes. These elements give Trolley Square an ambience that strongly differentiates it from the suburban shopping centers which are its primary market competition. The project has been designed to make shopping a recreational experience. With its varied and stimulating physical environment Trolley Square is in the forefront of innovative commercial design. In less than 4 years, it has become one of the city's major attractions. The developer believes the carefully devised nostalgic atmosphere, in large measure, explains the success of the project.

Trolley Square is situated in an aging low-density residential section of Salt Lake City approximately nine blocks southeast of downtown. The development contains a total of 125 tenants in 253,594 square feet of gross leasable area (GLA). Included are restaurants, apparel shops, movie theaters, a farmer's market, and a variety of other tenants with an emphasis on arts and crafts, gifts, and boutique items.

The site was acquired in two parts—the first parcel from National City Lines in 1969 and the second parcel from Utah Light and Power Company in 1973. Renovation began in 1970, following 12 months of project planning and design. The first establishments in the complex opened in June 1972. Development is being phased with expansion continuing as additional sections of the vacant industrial buildings are converted to commercial use. Of a total of 253,594 square feet of gross leasable area, 93 percent was committed to use by the end of 1977. It is anticipated that the remaining 18,000 square feet in the north building will soon be leased.

Opposite page: 2-7 Trolley Square features a turn-of-the-century theme with architectural artifacts and antiques used for both functional and decorative purposes.

Historic Overview

The trolley car complex was built in 1908 by the Utah Light and Railway Company which had been acquired 4 years previously by E. H. Harriman, the railroad magnate. Harriman was determined to make the system a model of its kind in the United States, and at a cost of more than $3,000,000, he erected the complex of mission-style buildings designed to house and serve a fleet of 144 trolley cars operating over more than 100 miles of track.

The site was a square city block, approximately 660 feet on a side and comprising 9.8 acres. Designated as the Tenth Ward Square in the original plat of the city, it had served as the Territorial Fairgrounds since 1889. In 1892 it was the site of the Utah Exposition. Centrally located and free of development, the fairgrounds were considered the logical location for the car barns and maintenance facilities.

As built by the Utah Light and Railway Company, the complex consisted of four main structures: a barn to house the trolley cars and carry out general maintenance; a machine shop for mechanical overhalls; a sand house to store grit for winter operations; and a carpenter/paint shop for car construction and body work. Total building coverage amounted to 270,000 square feet or 62.9 percent of the block. In addition, there was a 97-foot-high water tank with a capacity of 50,000 gallons.

Brick bearing walls and steel truss construction were used. The roofs were built of 8- to 10-inch slabs of concrete and contained a total of 208 skylights, each 16 feet long and 8 feet wide. The modified mission-style architecture featured an attractive curved cornice topped by contrasting concrete wainscoting. Most distinctive of this design was a series of reinforced concrete arches located at either end of the trolley car barn, supported by brick piers enclosed in concrete and encased in cast-iron boxes.

2-8   Interior of the car shop, September 1918.

The barn was the largest building, having 126,000 square feet under roof. It was built in a series of four bays, each 420 feet long, 58 feet wide, and 34 feet high at the peak. They were separated from one another by interior masonry and concrete walls. Each bay contained four streetcar tracks with grease pits located in the concrete floor and rolling steel doors placed at the entrance. A fifth bay was later added.

Following abandonment of the trolley car system in 1945, the buildings housed the city bus line until 1969, at which time a phaseout began which was completed in 1970. Because of the site's association with the early history of Salt Lake City and the Territory of Utah, as well as its involvement in pioneering streetcar development in the United States, the property was declared a State Register Site in 1973.

Development Strategy

Trolley Square is being developed by a group of 10 Salt Lake City investors and one Seattle investor headed by Wallace A. Wright, Jr., a local realtor. Wright was familiar with the success of adaptive use projects in other parts of the country, and when the facility was put up for sale in 1969, he recognized that the extensive complex of ornate masonry buildings would lend itself to similar treatment. He also brought to the project an awareness of the national trend toward restoration and preservation as well as a personal interest in architecture, design, and antiques. This personal touch is visible throughout Trolley Square and emphasizes the flexible and imaginative development strategy required for projects of this kind.

The partnership acquired the major portion of the block in 1969, and the balance in 1973 after the previous owner had vacated. Subsequent purchases in adjacent blocks have brought the total land holding to 13 acres, with acquisition continuing.

The following factors were crucial in the decision to proceed with rehabilitation:

Location. The complex had a strategic location in an older section of Salt Lake City approximately midway between downtown and the University of Utah campus. Adjacent uses consisted of a variety of low-density residential and commercial structures which were beginning to be displaced by higher intensity uses. These new uses included a concentration of multistory offices and an expanding governmental center several blocks to the west. The block itself was bordered on the east by Seventh Street East (State Route 71), a major arterial providing primary access to the city's growing residential section to the south and east. These factors, together with prevailing low land prices in the area, suggested an opportunity for a major upgrading of this part of Salt Lake City and its conversion into an important subcenter of the central business district.

Structural Type and Condition. As is the case with many adaptive use projects, the developers were attracted to the complex because it offered an extensive area under roof at relatively modest cost. Furthermore, additional useable space could be created by installing more floors under the high ceilings. Industrial structures of this type and vintage are particularly well suited for conversion to new uses. Because they are rarely compartmentalized inside, they can more easily be converted to residential, retail, and office functions. The streetcar buildings had been solidly built, and an evaluation revealed that no serious structural improvements were needed. The only major problem identified was leakage around the skylights. A strong plus factor in the case of Trolley Square was the attractive exterior appearance of the buildings.

Market Assumption. Perhaps the most noteworthy aspect of the Trolley Square project was the decision that a project of this type could succeed in a community the size of Salt Lake City (1970 SMSA population was 557,735). Although this assumption has proven to be correct, it represented a major gamble at the time the project was initiated, since this kind of development had previously been attempted only in the largest and most sophisticated metropolitan areas. Based on the experience of Salt Lake City, it would now seem probable that virtually every major American city could sustain a specialty shopping and entertainment center of this kind.

Public Involvement and Approvals. The site of Trolley Square was located in the C-3 Commercial District which permitted a commercial adaptive use

2-9   Restaurant located in the theater building.

project without a variance. This ordinance is cumulative in that it permits "higher" uses in all districts previously enumerated. In the C-3 Commercial District, residential and business uses are authorized by reference to previous sections of the ordinance.

However, unexpected problems arose related to off-street parking. The ordinance requires one space per 3,000 square feet of commercial buildings, one space per 10 seats in a theater, and one space per 200 square feet of restaurant floor space without taking into account the spread in peak demand created by a combined shopping/ entertainment center featuring extensive evening activities. The Board of Adjustment is authorized to modify these requirements but so far has not done so. The problem was solved by the construction of a 360-car, 3-level parking structure that was built to the slope of the land on the west side of all the buildings.

Historical Designations. Designation as a State Register Site by the Utah Heritage Foundation took place after Trolley Square had opened. The state register consists of noteworthy "districts, sites, buildings, and objects significant in Utah history," but has few regulations for the owners of such properties. Trolley Square has received a bronze plaque and has been placed on state highway signs. The register controls placement of billboards close to listed sites, but its primary benefit to Trolley Square has been to encourage municipal officials to maintain a flexible attitude in considering various aspects of a renovation project.

Project Planning

From the outset, Trolley Square was planned as a pedestrian-oriented shopping and entertainment complex modeled after similar successful developments on the West Coast. The turn-of-the-century theme was an integral part of the design concept. Also, the developer planned to emphasize entertainment functions more than is typical in shopping center developments. Only limited provision was made for office space.

The open and expansive interior spaces gave the designers optimum flexibility. Internal layouts of the bays were generalized and then refined in response to the commercial success of tenants and market demand. Flexibility has been the key in this development strategy. Areas originally designated for one type of tenant have sometimes been changed for alternative tenants. For example, the north building (carpenter/paint shop) was originally reserved for a large specialty department store. When such a tenant could not be obtained, occupancy was shifted to a number of smaller commercial uses.

Because there were a quarter million square feet of GLA to be rented, development has been phased. The theaters and several restaurants opened first because it was felt that the entertainment components were self-sufficient. For other commercial uses to be successful, however, they would need a scale of operation sufficiently large to generate pedestrian traffic. Commercial uses in the trolley barn have been added incrementally from a central corridor crossing the first three bays at right angles. Development expanded into the fourth bay in 1974 and the fifth bay in 1975. Planned for the future is the major addition of a 15-story hotel tower with 242 rooms above the western portion of the fifth bay.

2-10   Murals replace windows in the former machine shop.

Redevelopment Process

Several important considerations guided the redevelopment process. These included the following: capitalizing upon the spacious interior of the car barn by creating additional rental space; using discarded building materials, structural elements, and furnishings to give the completed project a distinct character as well as reduce construction costs; and minimizing structural changes within the buildings while emphasizing the visual and structural integrity of the complex through careful design modifications. This approach resulted in the twin benefits of minimizing cost outlays while creating an unusual and nostalgic shopping environment which would give Trolley Square a truly distinctive identity.

Exterior Reconstruction. After decades of hard use, the buildings were coated with grime, and the site itself was a barren, gravel-covered square of earth surrounded by a chain link fence. A thick coat of yellow paint was removed by sandblasting to reveal the original rose-colored brick with contrasting concrete wainscoting. Roof leaks around the skylights were sealed with a layer of polyurethane insulation and a new main entrance was created by widening and redesigning the doorway on the south side of the trolley barn. The few original windows in the complex were replaced, more windows and entrances added, and garage doors replaced with glass walls and rescaled doorways. The strong sense of visual unity throughout Trolley Square was enhanced by the use of uniform exterior materials including ornate steel frames painted black for the new windows and doors.

As part of its conversion into a branch office of the First Security Bank, one wall of the sand house was replaced by a Plexiglas dome containing a new stairway leading to the second floor. In the machine shop, which was converted into the theater building, murals of old movie stars were installed where garage doors had been, and a curved glass enclosure was extended from one side of the building to create a novel setting for a restaurant. The water tower was painted gold and converted into an observation tower by adding a circular wrought-iron staircase and decorative elements. The major effort, however, was required for the trolley car barn. Bay windows were located along the narrow space separating it from the theater building. Arcades were created on both ends of the structure by replacing the rolling steel doors with recessed glass and steel frame walls.

2-11 Trolley Square is located in a low-density residential neighborhood nine blocks from downtown.

That portion of the site not occupied by buildings was completely redesigned for pedestrian and vehicular use. Parking spaces for 443 vehicles were provided within the central block, and the four main buildings were landscaped and interconnected with brick-paved pathways. New plantings included flowers, and a combination of evergreen and deciduous species which included Russian olive, goldenrain, linden, pin oak, arborvitae, and pyracantha.

A steel marquee which once spanned a downtown street and had been used to advertise a movie theater was moved to Trolley Square where it forms an arched entryway to the parking area. Forty vintage street lamps were affixed to buildings along the four sides of the block. Six trolley cars were moved to the site, with one serving as a gas station and another as a savings and loan office. The other four have been converted to shops. A cupola from a demolished mansion has been turned into a gazebo.

2-12 The cupola of a demolished mansion was converted to a gazebo.

2-13 Wrought-iron railings on the second level are new but based on a turn-of-the-century design.

Proposed exterior modifications for the future include connecting the buildings with canopies and shifting additional parking to adjacent blocks in order to convert most of the site into a landscaped garden.

Interior Reconstruction. The major renovation cost was in converting the vacant building interiors to commercial use. This involved devising an overall concept for internal circulation and implementing it in stages. In the trolley barn, the pedestrian system takes the form of a modified "H" with a main central corridor crossing the five bays diagonally. It has a central opening at the second bay which provides a primary internal focus. The bays themselves consist of narrow pedestrian shopping streets 7 to 12 feet wide with shops fronting them on either side. The corridor system is interconnected by openings knocked through the masonry walls separating the individual bays. Main entrances to the trolley barn open onto the central corridor on the north and south sides of the building, with secondary entrances provided off individual bays on the east and west sides. Tenants in the machine shop and paint/carpenter shop face central corridors which are lined up diagonally and only a few steps from a secondary entrance to the trolley barn.

Useable space in the trolley barn was increased approximately 50 percent by adding second and third levels overlooking the main floor. This brings an exciting visual dimension to the project made up of shops, balconies, stairways, and elevation changes which highlight the theme of a shopping bazaar. The second and third floors are built of pre-stressed concrete core decks resting on steel beams.

Systems for heating, electricity, and lavatories had to be added. The central heating plant, consisting of a four-pipe system with fan coil units for heating, gas absorption, and cooling was located in the trolley barn. This system makes roof units unnecessary and is more efficient than having individual units in each building. It is interconnected with the separate buildings by means of an underground pipe system located in the former grease pits. The system operates on natural gas but can, if necessary, be converted to coal, oil, or electricity by changing or converting the boilers.

Use of vintage architectural elements was the most innovative aspect of the interior reuse effort. These features are found throughout the project and were provided at a cost no greater than that of furnishing conventional shopping center interiors. Included are streetcars, antique elevators, discarded street furniture, wood beams, and similar items. Facades from demolished mansions have been used to create interior streetscapes and serve as fronts for individual stores. Many of the shops incorporate stained glass windows, gables, doors, chandeliers, wood paneling, and other relics. One of the most striking features of all is a stained glass dome from a demolished California church. All store interiors, although paid for by the tenant, must first be approved by the developer.

Walls have been sandblasted and the steel roof trusses painted black. Wrought-iron railings, window screens, and similar details of modern construction but reminiscent of turn-of-the-century designs, have been used to integrate the overall interior. With the addition of natural plantings, the setting has a festive, holiday atmosphere which is further emphasized by the fact that the buildings and water tower are lighted at night.

Because Salt Lake City lies within an area prone to earthquakes, it was necessary to upgrade the buildings to modern building code standards. This was done by designing all new floors with seismic bracing. Steel seismic bracing was also added to support the old brick bearing walls which had not been reinforced.

Description of Completed Project

Trolley Square consists of 253,594 square feet of GLA of which 236,505 square feet have been committed to tenants. Through redevelopment, 80.6 percent of the original building area was converted into leasable space, a percentage equivalent to that of new buildings constructed specifically for commercial use. Occupied retail and office space amounts to 226,644 square feet. Most of the remaining space has been designated for retail functions.

Building coverage remains unchanged except for the addition of the two streetcars serving as commercial buildings. However, 50,000 square feet of landscaping have been introduced and the remainder of the block has been connected to the trolley barn by a second level pedestrian bridge crossing 6th Street South. This will make the outlying parking areas more useable. Two old brick houses adjacent to Trolley Square have been refurnished by the developer and converted to office use. Because of the success of Trolley Square several other projects on adjacent properties are also underway.

Market

Trolley Square was planned as an alternative to the conventional shopping center from which it differs in several important respects. Heavy emphasis is on entertainment activities, including theaters and restaurants, which account for one-third of the GLA. This orientation with its design scheme creates a festive atmosphere and extends patronage of the complex into the evening hours.

Most tenants are local merchants rather than national franchise outlets and bring to Trolley Square an understanding of local interests and tastes—an invaluable marketing asset.

A full range of retail outlets is provided, but the tenants also include a number of stores selected because they would help generate additional vitality and interest. Among these are a farmers' market, a flower shop, and craftsmen workshops which are home to a leatherworker, silversmith, and diamond cutter. The other major tenants, in terms of square footage, have to do with clothing and shoes (14 percent of GLA).

Visitors number between 50,000 and 70,000 per week, of whom an estimated 60 percent are from the Salt Lake City area, 25 percent from other areas of Utah, and 15 percent from elsewhere. One objective of the tenant mix was to stimulate return traffic on a daily or weekly basis, thereby establishing Trolley Square as a major shopping center. The developer believed that the only way Trolley Square could succeed would be for it to become an integral part of the community, meeting the recurring shopping needs of residents rather than becoming a novel tourist attraction to be visited once or twice a year. To a considerable degree, this objective has been achieved.

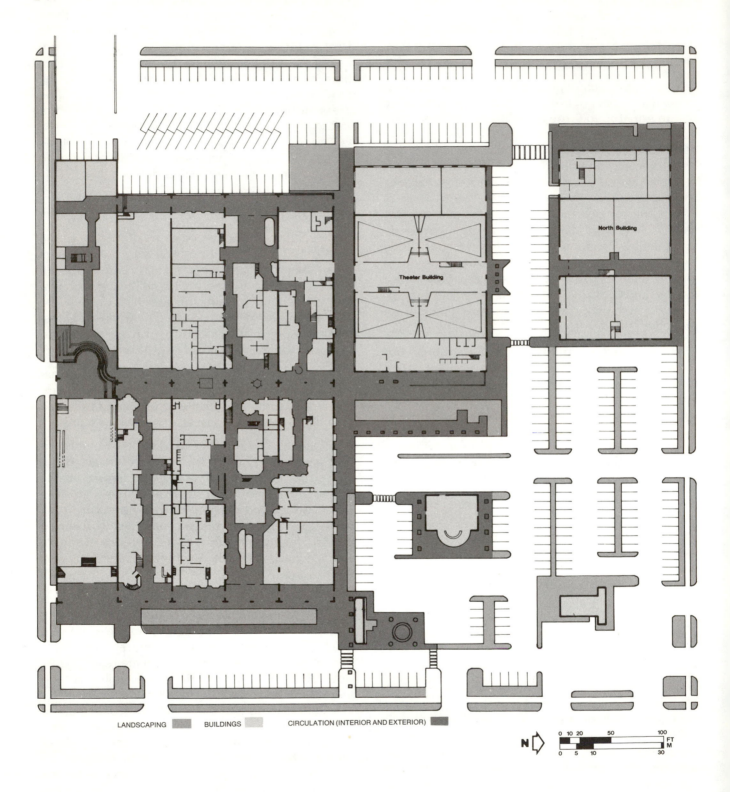

LANDSCAPING ▨ BUILDINGS ▨ CIRCULATION (INTERIOR AND EXTERIOR) ▨

Financing

The land and buildings were acquired for a total of $1.5 million in two major purchases. Some additional property was also acquired in adjacent blocks for parking. Construction financing was increased several times at a revolving rate of from 8¾ to 10½ percent. A permanent loan of $8 million at 9⅞ percent over a 25-year period was placed with a savings and loan association.

The rehabilitation cost amounted to $25 per square foot. Good quality new commercial construction has an estimated cost of $25 to $30 per square foot. In no way, however, could the physical character of the Trolley Square buildings be reproduced for that figure. A comparable new structure could cost $40 to $50 per square foot.

Operation and Management

Trolley Square is operated like a conventional shopping center with the developer leasing space to individual tenants and assuming responsibility for overall project management and control. There is a merchants' association to which all tenants must belong. Its purpose is to promote the interests of all occupants of the center by conducting promotions, special events, and a publicity program. Voting rights and fees are based on a sliding scale which varies from $.12 to $.50 per square foot according to the space used by individual tenants. Annual operating and maintenance costs for common areas and facilities are shared by tenants on a prorated basis.

Minimum retail leases generally range between $6 and $8 per square foot. Office space is priced at $5 per square foot. Most leases run from 3 to 5 years. The lease specifies rules and regulations established by the developer. Among these are a percentage clause which gives the developer an average of 6 percent of the gross of certain tenants above their guaranteed minimum rental, and a performance clause which authorizes the developer to terminate a lease if predetermined sales levels are not reached in a specified time. The renewal option, if given, adjusts the rent according to shifts in the Consumer Price Index.

The project is being managed by Trolley Square Associates. The partnership employs a manager; an operations manager; and a secretarial, security, and janitorial staff numbering approximately 10 full-time and 15 part-time personnel. Much of the actual reconstruction work was carried out by the building arm of the firm called Trolley Square Construction Company. It has employed as many as 150 persons and retains a skilled cadre of 25 craftsmen to complete the remaining rehabilitation work.

Experience Gained

- Opening the entertainment component as the initial feature of Trolley Square was essential for success. It was important for the public to know at the outset that Trolley Square would contain many activities having more than a tourist orientation. Without strong and continuing support from local residents, the project could not have succeeded.

- The original cost was projected at $5 million. Market response, however, has been sufficient to justify enlarging the scope of the project.

- In order to create a self-contained shopping center of this type, a minimum of 150,000 to 200,000 square feet of space is needed. Where less space is available, adjacent commercial uses must be relied upon in part to reach the market scale needed.

- Important savings were made by using recycled building materials. The value of these items when imaginatively used is frequently unrecognized. A wide variety of structural materials and architectural details were available from wrecking companies and junk yards at prices which did not reflect their reuse value. Money was saved by buying old buildings slated for demolition for their material contents rather than buying salvaged items after structures had already been demolished.

- The unique design of the buildings and the materials used give Trolley Square an intangible quality that is unobtainable in new construction. While new construction for the activities contained in Trolley Square might be provided at a competitive cost, the character of the new construction would be entirely different, and most likely not as appealing.

- Establishment and maintenance of a merchants' association is a major responsibility of the commercial developer. This should be done when the development is first opened in order to involve the merchants from the beginning.

- Security is essential and must be strongly implemented from opening day. Uniformed off-duty sheriffs' deputies are employed to give a professional and highly visible dimension to security at Trolley Square. Visitors know that competent but non-intimidating security forces are "watching the store."

PROJECT DATA

Land Use Information:

Total Site Area:	566,280 sq. ft. (13.0 acres)
Central Block:	429,000 sq. ft. (9.8 acres)
Floor Area Ratio	
(FAR):[1]	.7
Parking:	
Spaces:	1,084 surface spaces, plus 200 street spaces
Ratio:	4.9 spaces per 1,000 sq. ft. GLA[2]

Land Use Plan:[3]

	Acres	Percent of Total
Buildings	6.2	47.7
Parking and Paving	5.6	43.1
Landscaping	1.2	9.2
Total	13.0	100.0

Buildings:

Gross Building Area (GBA):[4]	314,619 sq. ft.
Gross Leasable Area (GLA):[5]	253,594 sq. ft.
Percent Rentable:	80.6

Name	GBA	GLA	Rented[6]	Vacant[6]	Percent Rented	No. of Tenants
North Building (Carpenter/ Paint Shop)	38,713	38,713	21,624	17,089	55.9	3
First Security Bank (Sand House)	4,151	4,151	4,151	0	100.0	1
Theater Building (Machine Shop)	39,926	39,926	39,926	0	100.0	8
Trolley Barn (Car House)	224,129	163,104	153,243	9,861	94.0	109
Other (S&L, Gas Station)	7,700	7,700	7,700	0	100.0	4
Total	**314,619**	**253,594**	**226,644**	**26,950**	**89.4**	**125**

Tenant Information:[7]

Classification[8]	No. of Stores	Percent of Total Tenants	Sq. Ft. of GLA	Percent of GLA	Dollars & Cents of Shopping Centers: 1978 Regional Shopping Centers' Composition by Tenant Classification Group (Table 8G-4)
General Merchandise	—	—	—	—	19.3
Food	6	4.8	6,243	2.5	7.3
Food Service	21	16.8	56,370	22.2	5.8
Clothing	21	16.8	28,656	11.3	23.0
Shoes	4	3.2	6,010	2.4	6.2
Home Furnishings	2	1.6	2,757	1.1	2.4
Home Appliances/ Music	—	—	—	—	3.2
Building Materials/ Garden	1	.8	3,082	1.2	.8
Automotive Supplies/ Service Station	1	.8	4,000	1.6	1.2
Hobby/Special Interest	7	5.6	15,353	6.1	3.1
Gifts/Specialty	11	8.8	13,861	5.5	4.0
Jewelry and Cosmetics	7	5.6	4,040	1.6	2.1
Liquor	1	.8	725	.3	.3
Drugs	1	.8	7,077	2.8	3.6
Other Retail	16	12.8	13,748	5.4	3.6
Personal Services	8	6.4	9,746	3.8	2.1
Recreation/ Community	7	5.6	35,740	14.1	4.1
Financial	4	3.2	9,458	3.7	2.6
Offices (other than financial)	7	5.6	9,778	3.8	1.6
Other	—	—	26,950	10.6	3.7
Total	**125**	**100.0**	**253,594**	**100.0**	**100.0**

Sq. Ft. of GLA	Number of Tenants	Percent
0–999	60	48.0
1,000–1,999	36	28.8
2,000–4,999	22	17.6
5,000+	7	5.6
	125	100.0

Lease Information:

Commercial Rent: $6.00–$10.00 sq. ft.
Average $5.00 sq. ft.
Office Rent: $5.00 sq. ft.
Length: 2–15 years Average 5 years
Clauses:
- Performance clause with option to terminate if predetermined sales levels are not reached within a specified time.
- Renewal option provides for adjustment of rent based upon fluctuations in the Consumer Price Index.
- "Percentage rent" giving developer between 4 and 20 percent of most tenants' gross. Averages 6 percent.

Economic Information:

Acquisition Cost:[9] $1,500,000
Land Cost Per Sq. Ft.: $2.64
Building Cost: Nominal, included in land cost
Rehabilitation Cost:[10]

Buildings	**$6,847,924**
Trolley Barn	5,336,245
First Security Building	68,629
Theater Building	923,059
North Building	519,991
Improvements	**$1,868,188**
General Construction on Square	194,570
Tower	94,467
New Boiler Room	111,754
Lighting	83,657
Grounds	598,938
Heating and Air Conditioning Plant	377,991
Tunnel	106,438
Power Vaults	4,790
Trolley Cars	7,940
Kiosks	13,510
Parking Lot Improvements	71,011
Capital Theater Sign	8,511
Unallocated Construction Costs	1,693
Machinery-Equipment-Tools	120,191
Automotive Equipment	6,541
Patio Furniture	2,369
Furnishings	22,015
Office Furniture and Equipment	10,649
Double Decker Bus and Motorized Trolley Car	31,153
Total	**$8,716,112**

Financing:

Mortgage	Rate	Amount	Time Period
Construction Loan	8¾-10½%	$7.5 million	1972-1975
Permanent Loan	9⅞%	$8.0 million	25 years

Operations (projected 1977):

Income

Rent Minimum	$1,000,000
Rent Overage	290,000
Total	1,290,000

Operating Expenses

Office Salaries	52,685
Promotion Salaries	12,000
Payroll Taxes	8,409
Advertising	2,500
Custodian and Supplies	2,060
Insurance	29,908
Accounting Fees	8,000
Office Expenses	12,000
Public Relations	3,000
Taxes and Licenses	650
Telephone	1,920
Travel	1,350
Utilities	8,400
Common Area	54,000
Miscellaneous	2,400
Office Rent	12,780
Legal Fees	6,000
Trolley Bus	3,500
Total	**$ 221,562**

Other Expenses:

Interest	$ 800,000
Property Taxes[11]	100,000
Roof and Building Expenses	6,000
Loan Amortization	84,653
Total	**$1,212,215**
Net Cash Flow	$ 77,785

Notes:

[1] FAR—gross building area divided by net land area.
[2] Based on rented square footage as of December 31, 1977.
[3] For entire property.
[4] GBA—all square footage within the structure.
[5] GLA—revenue producing portion of the structure.
[6] As of June 30, 1977.
[7] As of June 30, 1977.
[8] Based on *Dollars & Center of Shopping Centers: 1978*.
[9] Including land and buildings.
[10] Trolley Square Association Balance Sheet, June 30, 1977.
[11] Approximate.

Development:

Trolley Square Associates, Inc.
Wallace A. Wright, Jr., General Partner
199 Trolley Square
Salt Lake City, Utah 84102
(801) 521-9877

Architecture:

Architect/Planners Alliance
Albert L. Christensen, Project Architect
139 Trolley Square
Salt Lake City, Utah 84102
(801) 359-7777

Management:

Trolley Square Associates, Inc.
Richard G. Robins, CSM
199 Trolley Square
Salt Lake City, Utah 84102
(801) 521-9877

Old Court House and Jail

In numerous towns across the country and particularly in the Midwest, the dome, tower, or cupola of a county courthouse dominates the townscape, rising above other buildings to serve as a visual landmark for the community. These courthouses, which often date from the second half of the 19th century, reflect the aims of the town's early citizens to construct a dignified and contemporary building in which to house the offices of the local government. As a public symbol, the courthouse is frequently still the focal point of the town square or central business district, just as it was at the time of its construction.

Many of these grand old structures represent a local architect's interpretation of the newest American architectural style for public buildings. But few 19th century architects could anticipate the growth and changing needs of local government over a century. County offices have outgrown courthouse space; interiors have been remodeled again and again. Too often the county's new physical demands have been answered by destroying the old courthouse and replacing it with a larger, modern facility.

Demolition could easily have been the fate of the county courthouse and jail in Woodstock, Illinois, a town of 12,000 located 60 miles from Chicago. Having outgrown its courthouse and jail, the government of McHenry County decided in 1972 to consolidate its scattered offices by constructing a new complex of offices and courts on the outskirts of town. When the old courthouse and jail were put up for auction, the county received two bids. The low bid, from a group of Woodstock businessmen, called for demolition and replacement with an at-grade parking lot. The higher offer, from Woodstock resident Clifford Ganschow, proposed conversion of the buildings into a commercial complex. Sold for $50,500 to Ganschow, who owns a publishing firm in Milwaukee, the courthouse and jail were redeveloped to accommodate eight retail shops, a broadcasting studio, an ice cream parlor, and a restaurant.

Opposite page: 2-16   Adaptive use of the courthouse and jail contributed to the revitalization of Woodstock's central business district. The county sold the property to the developer for $50,500.

Historic Overview

Dominating the town square and situated on its west side, the courthouse and jail face a 2-acre landscaped park. A Richardsonian-Romanesque opera house, built in 1890, dominates the south side of the park, and low-rise commercial buildings, dating primarily from the late 19th century, occupy the remainder of the square.

The red brick courthouse and the buff brick jail, joined together by a narrow passageway, were constructed in 1857 and 1887, respectively. The courthouse, capped with a white wooden dome, was designed by John Mills Van Osdel, one of Chicago's earliest architects. Van Osdel practiced architecture in the area during the middle of the last century, when Chicago was changing from a small trading town into the transportation and commercial center of the Midwest. Although he concentrated primarily on building residences and commercial structures in the city, his design of the Cook County Courthouse in Chicago in 1853 probably led to the commission in nearby Woodstock.

The courthouse was originally built in the shape of a Greek cross, but extra bays were later added to either side. Two stories tall on a raised basement, the building has an at-grade basement entry and a central flight of stone steps leading to the main floor. Limestone was used for the foundation and for window and door details; original exterior and interior walls are of solid brick construction. The roof trusses are hand-hewn beams, 10 inches square with spans of 23 feet.

Inside the courthouse, office suites opened off a central hallway, with spaces designated for the sheriff, the county clerk, and other officials. Originally a pair of curving wooden staircases led to the second floor; however, one staircase was removed early in the 20th century to allow for construction of a vault. The second floor accommodated the courtroom, judge's chambers, jury rooms, and county supervisor's office.

2-17   The domed courthouse dominates Woodstock's 2-acre town square. Rehabilitation of the courthouse and jail required a private investment of $450,000.

By the 1880s, the original prison facilities, located in the basement of the courthouse, had become inadequate, and a structure was built to the immediate north of the building to house the jail and to serve as the sheriff's office and residence. The two-story jail, like the courthouse, has a raised basement, central entrance pavilion, and limestone detailing. The front half of the building, with four rooms on each floor, provided quarters for the sheriff, and the rear half contained a prefabricated two-story cell block.

The jail gained a place in national history when it held Eugene V. Debs, labor leader and founder of the socialist party, who was imprisoned in 1895 for disregarding a federal injunction during a railroad union workers' strike. Debs later wrote that his conversion to socialism came during his 6-month term in the Woodstock jail.

The interior of the courthouse was remodeled several times during its ownership by the county, but no major renovations had been undertaken within recent years. As the size and functions of the McHenry County government had expanded over the years, additional office space had been rented in other buildings around the square. In the 1950s, the county purchased the old Woodstock junior high school, one-half block off the square, and adapted the structure to serve as a courthouse annex. Following the decision to consolidate offices and construct a new $3.5 million government complex, the county had the courthouse and jail evaluated by three private real estate appraisers. All three estimates placed the value of the property between $50,000 and $60,000.

Redevelopment Strategy

Ganschow's decision to undertake this adaptive use project was based on his evaluation of the economic potential of the structures as a retail and restaurant complex and his belief that the continued use of the buildings was important to the health of Woodstock's downtown. Although no formal marketing studies were undertaken, the developer examined market statistics, population projections, and other demographics from such sources as Commonwealth Edison and the Northeastern Illinois Planning Commission, a regional public planning agency, to determine the feasibility of the project before he purchased the property.

The developer felt that commercial reuse of the courthouse and jail, familiar landmark buildings on the square, could attract substantial local business. The town square has been the central focus of Woodstock—physically and commercially—since the town was established in 1832. Woodstock also serves as the county seat of McHenry County (population 125,000), a strong agricultural as well as developing suburban county.

Woodstock's access to several urban centers, in addition to Chicago's continued growth toward the Northwest, were further factors which were expected to contribute to the success of the project. Linked by commuter train to Chicago, Woodstock is 12 miles north of a northwest interstate route. Rockford, the second largest city in Illinois, is 40 miles to the west of Woodstock, and Milwaukee is 70 miles northeast.

Although the property was sold in late 1972, the county continued to occupy the courthouse complex until the spring of 1973. A small architectural firm in Oak Park, a suburb in western Chicago, was chosen for the project because the developer wanted as much flexibility and opportunity for personal input into the project as possible. A construction management firm, rather than a general contractor, was employed in order to eliminate some of the lag time between design and reconstruction, and to better deal with the unknowns that exist with adaptive use.

As sole owner of the courthouse, Ganschow took an active role in lining up tenants for the project. Four lease agreements had been signed by January 1974, in order to help secure financing for the project as well as show activity in the building. These included one short-term tenant which occupied several unrenovated second floor rooms while redevelop-

2-18   A decorative iron fence, wooden doors, and stone trim are among the architectural details which contribute to the character of the courthouse and jail.

ment work focused on other parts of the building. To encourage businesses which he felt would contribute to the long-term success and stability of the project, the developer entered into joint-venture agreements with two tenants and, with a partner, formed a separate corporation to establish a restaurant in the courthouse complex. He also established a retail operation of his own.

As county property, the courthouse and jail had no zoning classification; after the sale, the city council zoned them for commercial and restaurant use. A special use permit was later granted to allow craft demonstrations, and a liquor license was obtained for the restaurant. With the assistance of an architectural historian in Chicago, the buildings were placed on the National Register of Historic Places in November 1974.

2-19 Decorative signage shows the tenant mix at the project.

Design Scheme

The guiding philosophy behind the adaptive use process was to preserve the original character of the buildings, both inside and outside, while adjusting interior spaces to modern retail use. The design called for retaining the original courthouse entrance lobby as public space, with entrances to individual businesses off either side of the halls on the first two floors. The restaurant was planned for the basement, with direct access from the square through the at-grade basement entrance. Existing entries to the main floor and basement would provide access to shops in the jail. Further access would be created by reopening old prisoner walks which had once connected the jail with the courthouse.

The primary design problem for the interior of the courthouse was to provide a circulation system which would meet the approval of the state fire marshall, but be compatible with the character of the building. To achieve this without enclosing the curving front staircase, a secondary fire stairway was placed in a well to the center rear of the building. This stairway, a prefabricated steel unit, runs from the basement to the third floor.

Retained and restored were original features such as the pressed metal ceiling moldings, hand-painted iron vault doors, the judge's bench and jury box, and a pair of decorative plaster ceiling medallions in the courtroom. In the former county clerk's office, now part of a clothing store, a blackboard was saved because it carried the official county tabulations of the 1972 presidential elections, the last votes to be recorded in the courthouse.

Reconstruction Sequence

Initial work concentrated on exterior restoration, renovation of the mechanical and electrical systems, and compliance with the fire code requirements. Work on the retail areas followed, first on the main floors of the courthouse, then on the basement for the restaurant, and finally on the jail.

The electrical systems in both buildings were replaced, at a cost of approximately $70,000. The old boiler was retained, but the distribution system was revamped to provide baseboard heating (rather than radiator steam heat). Because central air conditioning could not be tied into the boiler system, separate air conditioning units with electric coolers were installed in each tenant area. The dropped acoustical ceilings which the county had placed in most offices were removed, and some heating pipes were left exposed, but painted.

The original walls were retained, for the most part, and steel beams were added where new entries were cut. New openings were made the same height as the original doorways, and the original wood trim was duplicated for the new doors. Large interior windows were cut through the walls on either side of the main floor hallway in the courthouse, to provide display space for the retail shops. Masonry walls were constructed toward the rear of the second floor hall, to provide a fire-resistant separation between the shops and lobby space.

Only the courthouse basement required extensive reconstruction to accommodate dining rooms, a bar, and kitchens for the restaurant. The existing concrete and gravel floors were covered and several brick walls were pierced to provide additional access through the spaces. The brick walls in the kitchen were tiled or whitewashed.

In the jail, existing room arrangements were retained to keep reconstruction work to a minimum.

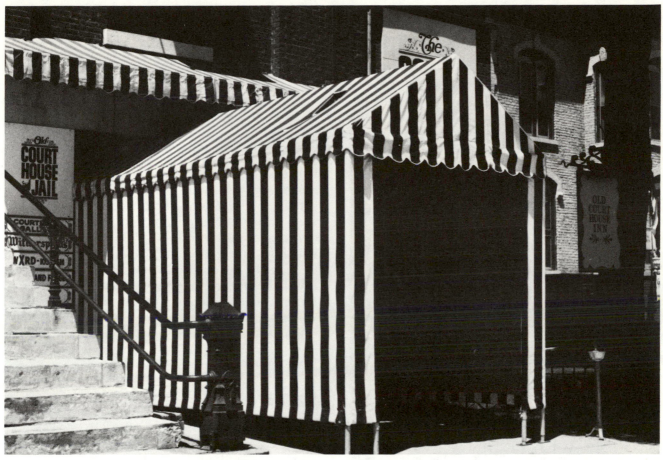

2-20   An eye-catching awning provides direct access from the street into a restaurant in the basement of the courthouse.

Description of the Completed Project

The two buildings face the town square on a site containing somewhat over 20,000 square feet. The complex does not provide any parking facilities, but free parking is allowed on all sides of the town square.

The complex has a gross building area of approximately 30,000 square feet, with 18,000 square feet of leasable space in the courthouse and 7,000 square feet in the jail. A gourmet kitchenware shop, a plant shop, and a clothing store each occupy several rooms on the first floor of the courthouse; second floor tenants include a radio broadcasting studio and an art gallery. The courtroom is used in conjunction with the restaurant as a banquet facility, accommodating parties of up to 200. It is also used for craft demonstrations and houses a permanent historical display. The restaurant occupies the entire basement. The three floors of the jail contain a specialty gift shop, an ice cream parlor and tea room, an antique store, and a woman's clothing store.

Financing

The courthouse project was undertaken during a period of particularly tight mortgage money (1973-1974), and met resistance from many of the financial institutions which were approached for loans. Construction financing for $450,000 was arranged primarily through a local commercial bank and its correspondent institution in Chicago. The State Bank of Woodstock extended its maximum loan of $150,000, and the Harris Trust and Savings Bank in Chicago contributed $200,000. An additional $100,000 in construction funds were secured by the developer from his own private sources.

Neither of the banks providing construction money was willing to assume the long-term mortgage on the property. The developer approached institutions in Chicago, Rockford, Elgin (Illinois), and Milwaukee without success; rejection of the loan was generally based on bankers' skepticism that the project could be fully leased and thus able to carry the debt load on the basis of its rental income.

The developer was not able to secure a mortgage loan until he had lease commitments from several tenants, covering about 50 percent of the total leasable area. On the basis of these commitments, a team of three banks agreed to provide a permanent mortgage of $450,000. All of the participating banks are small institutions, a characteristic which the developer felt gave them a better understanding of the nature of small retail development. A savings and loan in Marengo, Illinois, formally holds the full mortgage but provides only $300,000 for the package; the State Bank of Woodstock supplies $75,000, as does a commercial bank in Princeton, Illinois. The mortgage amortizes over a 25-year term; interest rates vary from 9 to 9½ percent among the banks. The loans are personally guaranteed by the developer.

Market

Four years after restoration began, the two buildings were fully occupied. The developer is owner of one business, a joint-venturer with two tenants, and the major partner in the corporation which owns the restaurant. He anticipates an eventual consolidation of the joint-venture projects into a single retail corporation.

Lease arrangements vary from 3 to 5 years, except for the restaurant, which holds a 10-year lease with an option for an additional 10 years. The leases, which carry inflationary clauses, require a base rent at an average of $5.00 per square foot plus a percentage of sales. A merchants' association for courthouse and jail tenants was established to make decisions concerning public space and advertising for the complex. The developer is now beginning a limited marketing campaign in the Chicago area to advertise the complex.

Rents for the courthouse and jail are higher than the average rates for the square. In 1973, when the courthouse project was initiated, commercial rents on the square ranged from $2.00 to $2.50 per square foot; the current average is estimated at $3.00 to $4.00. This significant rise in rents over a 4-year period can be attributed in part to a general sense of revitalization on the square, boosted by several municipally supported activities.

While the courthouse project was underway, a nonprofit community organization began a successful fund-raising campaign for renovation of the city-owned opera house, the other landmark building on the square. The opera house rehabilitation was completed in late 1977. City government offices, which had been housed in the opera house since 1890, were moved to the old junior high school (vacated by the county government upon construction of the new office and courts complex).

Low-cost architectural consultant services were arranged by the city to owners of buildings on the square, for a week-long period during the winter of 1975. For $10 per front foot of building, property owners could purchase renderings of their buildings, illustrating improvements which could be made to the facades. Approximately 12 owners used the services, and several have since carried through the architectural firm's recommendations. Woodstock's city manager and planning consultant estimate that $2.25 million in public and private funds were invested in the square between 1972 and 1977. Other projects are now underway.

Experience Gained

- With the exception of one, all of the retail tenants in the complex were small ventures just beginning, rather than established businesses. A lease agreement with an established "anchor" tenant might have helped significantly in the search for mortgage money, since the banks were predominately interested in the rental income which the building could produce.

This viewpoint is supported by the developer's experience with a separate adaptive use project which he undertook following rehabilitation of the courthouse. He approached the owner of a well-established independent department store in Elgin, Illinois, about opening a second outlet in an F. W. Woolworth building on the Woodstock square. On the basis of a lease commitment from this store, the developer was able to negotiate both purchase financing and a long-term mortgage for the property.

- Mortgage applications for the project also suffered from the banking community's lack of guidelines for adaptive use work. The same criteria used to make loan decisions concerning new construction were applied to adaptive use although many different factors affected the latter. Several bankers did ask for "comparables," but data on related adaptive use projects were not easily available. Therefore, the developer had to "sell the potential" of the building, a task which proved particularly difficult during a long period of tight money.

- The use of a construction management firm, rather than a general contractor, allowed construction work to begin before the final design stage for the project had been reached. In addition to saving time for the overall rehabilitation work, the developer also realized more effective cost controls on the construction work.

- Since the project was initiated, the developer has been contacted by several individuals and organizations concerned with the future use of other courthouses as well as other old buildings. This interest in the Woodstock experience suggests that other communities are recognizing the historical and physical value of their courthouses and are taking steps to prevent their loss. Also apparent, however, is the fact that courthouse obsolescence is a dilemma which unfortunately faces increasing numbers of county governments.

- The courthouse project did not have as much immediate effect on the surrounding square in terms of encouraging prompt rehabilitation of other buildings as the developer had anticipated. However, the leadership provided by Ganschow and the city government through other major rehabilitation projects has had a long-term effect on the vitality of the square. This impact is now beginning to be measured in such concrete terms as the amount of money invested in the square, the number of buildings undergoing rehabilitation, property value escalations, and sales tax increases. Many property values in the downtown area have more than doubled in the 5 years since the courthouse and jail restoration began. Building vacancies have been almost eliminated, and retail sales in Woodstock doubled during this period.

2-21

PROJECT DATA

Land Use Information:
  Site Area: 20,000 sq. ft.
  Parking: None[1]
Buildings:
  Number of Buildings: 2
  Gross Building Area: 30,000 sq. ft.
  Gross Leasable Area: 25,000 sq. ft.[2]
  Percent Rentable: 83.3
Economic Information:
  Acquisition Cost: $50,500
  Construction Cost: $450,000
Lease Information:
  Rate: $5 per sq. ft.
  Length: 3 to 5 years[3]
  Clauses: based on minimum rent plus
    percentage of sales with inflationary clauses.

Notes:
[1] Free parking on all sides of the town square.
[2] 18,000-sq.-ft. courthouse; 7,000-sq.-ft. jail.
[3] Restaurant has a 10-year lease with option to renew for additional 10 years.

Development:
Clifford Ganschow
424 Oakwood Avenue
Woodstock, Illinois 60098
(815) 338-2053

Architecture:
Sturr Young Associates, Limited
115 North Marion
Oak Park, Illinois 60301
(312) 383-0890

Construction Financing:
State Bank of Woodstock
101 South Benton
Woodstock, Illinois 60098
(815) 338-3131

Harris Trust and Savings Bank
111 West Monroe Street
Chicago, Illinois 60690
(312) 461-2121

Permanent Financing:
Marengo Federal Savings and Loan Association
200 East Grant
Marengo, Illinois 60152
(815) 568-7258

State Bank of Woodstock
  (see above)

Citizens First National Bank of Princeton
606 South Main
Princeton, Illinois 61356
(815) 875-4444

Court House Square

Much existing commercial development in central city locations takes the form of one- and two-story buildings strung out along major arterials. Approriate to the streetcar era, this form of development is now functionally obsolete. Nevertheless, opportunities to redesign these areas and restore their commercial vitality do exist, as evidenced by the Court House Square. Demolition, rehabilitation, and new construction were combined to convert a deteriorated two-square-block area into a modern office complex.

This project occupies a 1.3-acre site just south of downtown Columbus, Ohio, and has 160 feet of frontage on High Street, a major north-south thoroughfare. The immediate environs are characterized by a mixture of commercial, residential, and industrial uses. Just west of the property is a vacant complex of buildings formerly used as a brewery and now used primarily for warehousing. Because of its association with early German settlement in Columbus and its unique architectural character, this area of the city is experiencing spontaneous renewal. The city has assisted this process by establishing the German Village Commission and creating a historic district designed to protect the character of the neighborhood. Although Court House Square is just outside the boundaries of the historic district, it was originally developed simultaneously with the rest of German Village and contains several buildings which date back to the pre-Civil War era. The project has been developed in keeping with the intent of the municipal legislation.

As completed in mid-1974, Court House Square consists of five buildings, one new and four restored, with 49,428 square feet of gross building area (GBA). Overall site coverage amounts to 25 percent, and there is sufficient surface parking to accommodate 100 cars. The site was assembled during 1972, and the redevelopment work took 1 year beginning in 1973.

Before redevelopment, the Court House Square site consisted of eight separate parcels and 10 commercial and residential buildings. A local street which provided access from the brewery to South

High Street divided the property into two contiguous blocks. Between 50 and 60 persons lived in the multifamily residences and in apartments located on the upper floors of the multistory commercial buildings fronting on South High Street.

The initial developer, a law firm, planned to build on the southernmost parcel within the site. When the design firm hired to evaluate the site discovered that the parcel would be insufficient to provide parking in addition to a building of required size, they suggested that greater benefits could be obtained by assembling the entire two-block area and redeveloping it in a comprehensive fashion. A joint venture partnership was formed to undertake the project.

The site had important locational advantages despite its generally rundown condition. These included ready access to both the inner belt expressway and German Village. The key consideration in the decision to convert the property to office use, however, was the construction of a new county courts complex one block to the north across the inner belt on South High Street. Development strategy presumed that the new office space would be attractive to legal firms and other professionals desiring locations close to the new complex.

2-23 The South High Street frontage as it looked after redevelopment.

Opposite page: 2-22 A former street has become a pedestrian way.

2-24   South High Street before redevelopment.

Planning and Engineering

Most of the original buildings were structurally sound, even though they had suffered from neglect and inadequate maintenance over many years and exhibited varying degrees of deterioration. The decision as to which of the structures to retain and which to remove was based primarily on the amount of building necessary to satisfy the parking requirement and on each building's reuse potential within the framework of the redevelopment plan.

Brewer Street was converted from a vehicular thoroughfare into a landscaped area for pedestrians, paved with concrete accented by contrasing insets built with brick retrieved from the old street. Building and street frontages have been softened with shrubbery and trees which will grow in a few years into a lush, park-like environment. The pedestrian area is bound by three of the original buildings; two residences which were combined into a single structure and a 10-unit apartment building which was converted into a restaurant. At-grade parking, landscaped and partially screened by brick walls, was placed at the edge and rear of the site. Along

South High Street, three substandard buildings were replaced by a single new structure four stories high and set back 20 feet from the property line along the thoroughfare. A fifth building to be retained was subsequently demolished in order to gain enough space to provide sufficient at-grade parking spaces. The gross rentable area lost in this manner was regained by adding a fourth floor to the new structure.

Although the structures were old, those to be retained were structurally sound and required no major reconstruction. Renovation consisted primarily of modernizing interior spaces by adding stairways, elevators, toilet rooms, and completed mechanical and electrical systems. A uniform exterior appearance was achieved by cutting in new window and door openings, sandblasting, and tuck-pointing and repainting brick. The new structures were proportioned and detailed to blend in with the older buildings.

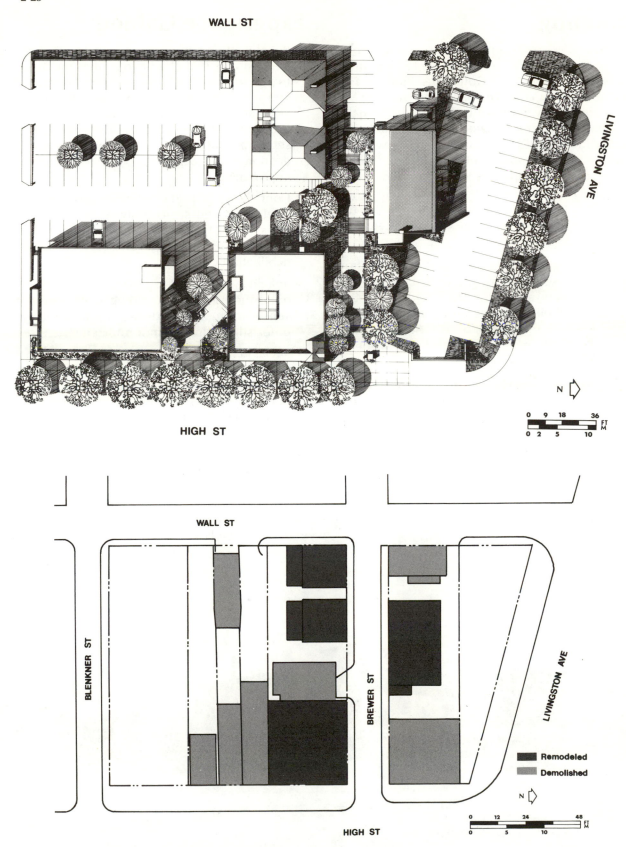

WALL ST

LIVINGSTON AVE

HIGH ST

N

0 9 18 36 FT
0 2 5 10 M

WALL ST

BLENKNER ST

BREWER ST

LIVINGSTON AVE

Remodeled

Demolished

N

0 12 24 48 FT
0 5 10 M

HIGH ST

2-26   Land use pattern before redevelopment.

Marketing

Court House Square was planned as an office complex with rents generally comparable to new office construction in downtown Columbus. Parking is included at no extra cost. The economic value of the existing buildings was built into the project from the start. The developer calculated which would be removed, which would be retained, and how much new space would be built before initiating the development. Most properties were acquired at current market value, and the city of Columbus, feeling that a project of this kind would be a real asset to the community, cooperated by agreeing to vacate Brewer Street.

Flexibility was a key developmental consideration since the precise nature of the tenants occupying space could not be ascertained beforehand. For this reason, the building designated for restaurant use was designed so that it could be rented as office space if a suitable restaurant tenant could not be found.

All space within Court House Square, 42,609 square feet of net rentable area, had been leased before work was completed, and the project is fully occupied. The rehabilitated buildings are each occupied by a single tenant, while the new structure has six tenants.

Experience Gained

- Rehabilitation and reuse of existing buildings can be accomplished at a savings of as much as one-fourth to one-third less than new construction. The actual amount will vary depending upon previous and proposed use, structural condition, location, and other factors. Careful analysis is essential because each case will be unique, and the economic viability of the restored structure is all important.

- Contrary to popular belief, older buildings are rarely impaired structurally. Where such conditions do exist, they can usually be identified before the work has begun and corrected in the rehabilitation process.

- Imagination is required to visualize an economic opportunity in an old building. Conversions make sense when they permit capitalizing on the preexisting value of underutilized structures.

- Site assembly did present problems. Most parcels were purchased at fair market value, a price most owners were willing to settle for, but the "hold out" seller must be anticipated. Land leases can be combined with outright purchases to make land parcel assembly possible.

- The developer had to educate both appraisers and bankers as to what he was trying to accomplish. More often than not, this is the case when a project is unique or unusual in some way. Good presentation graphics and precise economic models are essential.

2-27   The 7,000-square-foot Vineyard restaurant (to the right of the photo) was formerly a 10-unit apartment building.

- Downtown "fringe" locations which cannot justify high-rise redevelopment can be redeveloped as low rise, either with new construction, renovation, or a combination of both. High-rise rents can often be charged because of easily accessible parking and the unique environment created by a carefully articulated rehabilitation project.

- Relocation of the persons living within the project area presented no serious problems. Most were elderly and had the financial means to relocate themselves. The city of Columbus, impressed that private developers showed concern for the people being relocated, made their services available.

2-28

PROJECT DATA

Land Use Information:

Site Area: 1.32 acres

Floor Area Ratio (FAR):[1] 1.14

Parking:
Spaces: 100 surface spaces
Ratio:[2] 2.3 spaces per 1,000 sq. ft. of NRA

Economic Information:

Land Cost: $6.49 sq. ft. (average of eight parcels)

Rehabilitation Cost: $18 per sq. ft.
(average for three buildings)[5]

Cost of Comparable New Construction: $22 per sq. ft.
(new four-story building)[5]

Buildings:

Number of Buildings: 4

Gross Building Area (GBA):[3] 49,428 sq. ft.

Net Rentable Area (NRA):[4] 42,609 sq. ft.

Percent Rentable: 86.2

Land Use Plan:	Gross Acres	Percent of Site
Building Coverage	.33	25.0
Parking	.64	48.5
Landscaping	.35	26.5
Total	1.32	100.0

Characteristics:

Name	Year Built	Treatment	Tenant	GBA	NRA	Percent Rentable	Former Use
499 South High	Early 1900s	Conversion	The Vineyard Restaurant	7,036 sq. ft.	6,129 sq. ft.	87.1	10-unit apartment
501 South High	1925	Conversion	Law firm	12,756 sq. ft.	10,180 sq. ft.	79.8	Two-story commercial bldg.
503 South High	Pre-Civil War	Conversion	Engineering firm	9,727 sq. ft.	8,670 sq. ft.	89.1	Two residential buildings
505 South High	1974	New construction	Six office tenants	19,909 sq. ft.	17,630 sq. ft.	88.6	NA

Lease Information:

Rate: $7.50 to $8 per sq. ft. (New York Method)

Length: Five 3-year leases, two 5-year leases, two 10-year leases

Clause: No signs permitted unless approved by developers.

Notes:
[1] FAR—gross building area divided by net land area (NLA = 43,152 sq. ft.).
[2] Parking Ratio—number of spaces divided by 1,000 sq. ft. NRA.
[3] GBA—all square footage within the structure.
[4] NRA—revenue producing portion of the structure.
[5] 1973-1974 cost.

Development:
South High Development, Ltd.
(a limited partnership of)

NGB Corporation
505 South High Street
Columbus, Ohio 43215
(614) 224-7145

Twyford and Donahay,
Dziamba Alexander,
Attorneys
501 South High Street
Columbus, Ohio 43215
(614) 224-8166

Architecture/Planning:
Charles A. Nitschke
Nitschke Associates
31 East Gay Street
Columbus, Ohio 43215

James W. Godwin
Frederick Bohm
Godwin-Bohm-NBBJ
505 South High Street
Columbus, Ohio 43215

Construction Financing:
Huntington National
Bank & Trust Company
17 South High Street
Columbus, Ohio 43215

Permanent Financing:
Nationwide Properties,
Inc.
236 North High Street
Columbus, Ohio 43215

Stanford Court

Between the turn of the century and the late 1920s urban living attracted upper-middle and upper-income groups, and many handsome apartment buildings of architectural quality and spacious design were constructed. Often these buildings were located in prestigious "uptown" neighborhoods, close to downtown. Later, as life-styles changed and such locations became less attractive to these income groups, these apartment structures experienced decline and loss of economic viability. Many buildings were torn down or, as more frequently occurred, were subdivided into smaller units and gradually became shadows of their former elegance.

The Stanford Court Hotel is an outstanding example of a return to the elegance of an earlier era. The Stanford Court apartment building was erected in 1912 on the site of the Leland Stanford mansion near the top of San Francisco's Nob Hill. For the first 25 years of its existence, this was a good location but gradually decline set in and by 1963 the building was slated for demolition as stipulated in the will of Lewis Marsten, then the owner. Fortunately, that did not happen. After various adaptive use strategies were considered, it was finally decided that the best economic solution for the Stanford Court Apartments was to convert the building into a luxury hotel. In February 1972, the Stanford Court began its new life. The building exterior has been retained almost unchanged while the new interiors equal or exceed the former quality of the building.

Historic Overview

The site of the Stanford Court Apartments was selected in the 1870s by Leland Stanford, railroad mogul, governor of California, U.S. Senator, and founder of Stanford University, as the location for his San Francisco mansion. The mansion, located on the corner of Powell and California Streets, was completed in 1876, at a cost of some $2 million and was said by many to be one of the most elegant in the country. During that period, Nob Hill was the site of numerous mansions including those of Mark Hopkins next door and Charles Crocker across the street. The Baldwin, Huntington, and Nabob (legend has it the name Nob Hill came from "where the Nabobs live") mansions were all nearby.

In 1906, the great earthquake struck San Francisco and the devastating fire which followed destroyed the Stanford mansion along with much of San Francisco. Leland Stanford had died in 1894, his wife in 1905, and his son Leland, Jr., after whom Stanford University is named, had preceded them both in 1884. The property was purchased in 1907 by Lucian H. Sly whose modest fortune was made initially in Alaska and increased by real estate investments in San Francisco. All that was left on the site was the outer basalt and granite wall, which reached 30 feet in height on the downhill side of the property and was topped by a wrought-iron fence. In 1911, construction began on the Stanford Court Apartments; they were completed in the fall of 1912.

As documented in the December 1911 issue of *The Architect and Engineer of California,* Stanford Court Apartments, at the time, was the largest fireproof reinforced concrete apartment building west of Chicago. Eight stories high with two basement levels, the building was 168 feet by 214 feet with a center court 91 feet by 137 feet. A tri-arched entrance to the court from California Street consisted of a center arch for vehicles, with a walkway on each side. An eliptical drive and walkway around a garden with a central fountain provided direct pedestrian and vehicular approaches from the court to the six entrances to the building located in each corner and at the midpoints of the court. Each of the entrances gave access to an elevator lobby with two apartments on each floor. In addition, there were four service elevators, each serving four apartments. The building contained a total of 95 apartment units of 5 to 10 rooms each. The majority of the apartments had operating fireplaces and the larger units included maids' rooms. The building had a four-pipe water system with both hot and cold fresh water and hot and cold salt water. Below the eight main levels, the first basement included a garage, tradesmen's entrance, office, extra bedrooms with lavatory for servants, kitchen, servants' dining room, and laundry. The sub-basement included more servants' quarters, storerooms for tenants, and space for machinery.

Opposite page: 2-29 Stanford Court Hotel as completed.

2-30 Excavation of the Pine Street side for ballroom addition and sub-basement.

Stanford Court had several owners over the years until 1953 when it was purchased by Lewis Marsten, president of Mohawk Petroleum. In 1961, it was leased to Trans Hill Corporation, which was also at the time the lessee of the adjacent Mark Hopkins Hotel. A. Cal Rossi, Jr., then food and beverage manager at the Mark Hopkins, acquired the 99-year lease in 1963 for an initial investment of $40,000. By that time, the apartments were run-down, and there were $89,000 in debts against the leasehold. Losses totaled $130,000 annually. The picture was further darkened by a provision in Marsten's will calling for razing of Stanford Court by 1968.

Over the next few years, Rossi pursued various schemes for the site. Initially he planned to renovate the building and convert it to condominiums. This of course was inconsistent with the demolition provision of the will. Later, he considered building a 50-story apartment-hotel with 25 stories of hotel space and 25 stories of apartments. This scheme was followed by adaptive use plans for a 338-room hotel, then a 600-room new hotel, and finally by a grand scheme for a 1,000 to 1,300-foot-high aluminum observation tower designed by Raphael Soriano. Ultimately, however, it was decided to convert the apartments into the Stanford Court Hotel.

The Adaptive Use Strategy

The adaptive use history of the Stanford Court Apartments really began in 1968 with the preparation of a schematic concept by the San Francisco architectural firm of Botsai and Overstreet for A. Cal Rossi. Alternatives ranged from a hotel with 462 rooms to one with 391 rooms. Finally a plan for a 423-room hotel was evaluated by real estate counselor, Hubert D. Eller. A firm commitment for financing was obtained. Rossi realized, however, that he needed a new financial partner and with the assistance of Eller, ultimately entered into a partnership arrangement with three general partners—A. Cal Rossi and Associates, the Royal Street Development Corporation (a group of investors headed by Edgar Stern of New Orleans who had been responsible for the Royal Orleans Hotel and was at the time completing the Royal Sonesta Hotel, both located in the New Orleans French Quarter), and Stancourt Corporation, a wholly owned subsidiary of UAL, Inc. The partners decided that to be successful Stanford Court should be an independent hotel under independent management, rather than a national chain affiliate. Therefore, the Stanford Court

Hotel Management Company was created with James Nassikas as president. Nassikas' broad background in luxury hotels at the Royal Orleans and Royal Sonesta in the New Orleans French Quarter and at the Plaza in New York were drawn upon throughout the redevelopment process. The architectural firm of Curtis and Davis was also commissioned to prepare a new set of plans under the new ownership entity.

The concept for the Stanford Court Hotel was clearly established with the new partnership. Stanford Court would be a luxury hotel offering a special personality and superior service. As such, the building's elegant and genteel appearance would be an asset.

Demolition began December 1, 1969. The construction contract was awarded to Dinwiddie Construction on April 6, 1970. The first occupants moved in on February 25, 1972, and the grand opening was held on April 4, 1972.

Site Description and Building Condition Before Reuse

Location was a key factor in the various feasibility studies for conversion of the Stanford Court Apartments to a luxury hotel. The famous San Francisco cable cars cross at the corner of Powell and California Streets. Nob Hill is a particularly desirable location for San Francisco's elegant and famous hotels.

While the building was not unique in architectural design or exterior beauty, it was well proportioned with strong and well-arranged fenestration. It had an attractive if not overly dramatic entrance. The only exterior defacements were the fire escapes and minor remodeling which had been done for an office entrance on California Street off Powell. In addition, because of a lack of maintenance, the building had the general appearance of decline.

For adaptive use as a hotel, the site and building had three unique characteristics in its favor—the shape of the building, the availability of sublevels suitable for conversion into public spaces, and the presence of vacant land on the Pine Street front and in the courtyard for additional spaces. The building is rectangular with a gracefully proportioned central court. The bays were wide enough to accommodate a hotel room layout with some innovative adjustments made to the orientation of the room and to the width of the hotel corridor.

2-31   Completed ballroom addition to the Pine Street frontage.

The courtyard provided an area for expansion. Expansion below the courtyard allowed suitable areas for the hotel's kitchen facilities, restaurant, and some meeting space. By depressing the grade level of the court a handsome, covered auto court and entrance lobby were created. What had been the first basement level could then be converted to administrative offices, shops, and other public spaces including a registration area, lobby lounge, coffee shop, and other shops. The vacant land on the Pine Street side allowed the additon of an unobtrusive ballroom of modest size to satisfy the need for meeting space and below it provide space for mechanical equipment.

Government Approvals

Stanford Court is located in the city's R-5 residential district, primarily an apartment zone, but with hotels permitted as conditional uses. The site is also in the Nob Hill Special Use District which specifies the Nob Hill area as appropriate for hotel and institutional uses. Under City Planning Commission Resolution No. 6241, of July 11, 1968, a special use permit was granted to the Stanford Court Apartments and the Rolls Garage for conversion to a hotel

2-32   View of a portion of the Powell Street facade where proposed "greenhouse" addition to Fournou's Ovens restaurant will provide a window to the San Francisco streetscape.

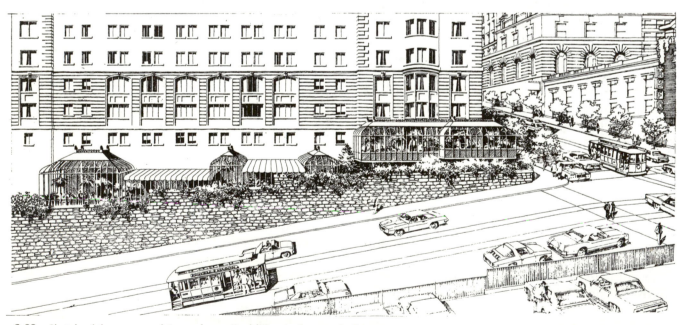

2-33   Sketch of the proposed "greenhouse" addition to Fournou's Ovens.

with the following provisions: that the exterior walls of the apartment building and the boundary wall be preserved; that there be a limit of 424 rooms; that there be no increase in building height; that there be 100 off-street parking spaces, including 10 at the hotel entrance; and that there be a limitation on commercial uses and on dining and conference space. The user permit approval and the conditions applied clearly recognized the importance of the reuse concept.

Structural Condition

The building is of reinforced concrete and was structurally sound. Subsurface investigation established the existence of good foundation conditions and the feasibility of additional excavation at reasonable cost. Because San Francisco is in a major earthquake zone, design requirements for resistance to seismic loadings are stringent. While Stanford Court was well constructed and an excellent example of post-1906 earthquake construction, the engineers state it would have been impossible to bring the structure into full compliance with current codes. In earthquake zones this can be a key problem in the adaptive use of a structure of any significant age.

Adaptive use required a creative response to the objectives of the code to assure both safety and an improved level of conformance to its provisions. It was decided that the conversion from apartment to hotel did not involve a change of occupancy under the San Francisco Building Code. Therefore, upgrading of the existing structure was not required. However, lateral strengthening with shear walls in new elevator and stair shafts and elsewhere in the building has, in the opinion of the engineer, resulted in a building which is safe and which meets the spirit of the code while achieving approximately two-thirds compliance with it. All new construction in the ballroom addition and in sublevel expansion was designed to full code specifications. The subsurface excavation to find new space required substantial modifications of the foundations and called for some innovative construction techniques.

After demolition all that remained of the Stanford Court Apartments was the exterior shell and the interior structural frame. Total reconstruction of the interior space was required by the design concept. The boundary wall and entrance gate posts, the only remnants of the Leland Stanford mansion, were preserved and restored.

2-34 New main entrance arch.

Rehabilitation Process

The first eight floors which were the original apartment floors were redesigned for hotel rooms. The width of the building bay was approximately 37 feet. With some modification of traditional hotel room design, this dimension allowed for a central corridor with rooms on either the court side or street side. To produce a satisfactory design, four departures from the traditional design of hotel rooms were necessary. First, the corridor width was reduced to 5 feet (the usual width is 6 feet or more). To avoid the appearance of long narrow halls, the corridor was widened to 6 feet at the room entrances and special lighting and ceiling treatment provided. Second, the traditional approach to room design with the narrow dimension of the room parallel to the corridor and the long dimension perpendicular to the corridor (in order to maximize the number of rooms) was reversed. This meant that almost every room has two and in many cases three windows, an attractive feature not found in most hotel rooms. Third, the bath and dressing room areas were placed between rooms on the court side rather than in the traditional position between corridor and room. Fourth, a wide variety of room sizes and layouts was necessary to accommodate the existing structural elements and window locations. Therefore, while the floor plans are identical vertically (with some differences on the first and second floors because of building variations and on the eighth floor because of several large suites), practically every room on each floor is in some way unique. The unusual room arrangement resulting from these design elements required a complete re-thinking of basic room design and furnishing. For example, a special armoire was designed which incorporated blanket storage, a television set, a writing desk, and drawer space in a single vertical unit which when closed is a handsome piece of furniture and removes from view much of the clutter typical of hotel rooms.

Circulation between floors was completely changed. The original six entrances and the elevators did not lend themselves to hotel operations. Hotel entrances should be arranged for guests and for service to provide security control and efficient elevator service. As noted earlier, these vertical improvements provided opportunities to introduce structural reinforcement. The general location of the elevators was determined by the points where full vertical circulation could be given to new lower levels as well as to upper floors, thus saving the cost of a second system to serve the lower level meeting rooms.

Main Floor Design

The main, or lobby floor of the hotel occupies what was formerly the first basement level. Located at this level are the auto entrance court, main lobby, registration area, lobby lounge, shops, coffee shop, and the restaurant's cocktail lounge. To achieve this arrangement the entry courtyard was depressed to the level of the first basement. The original three-arched entrance was redesigned as a wider single arch to provide a driveway access of modern dimensions flanked by walkways that give access to the enclosed arcade walkway which surrounds the auto court. This was the only exterior modification, and it can be persuasively argued that the new arch is better proportioned to the building than was the original. The auto court has been paved and landscaped and covered by a Tiffany-style glass dome over a central fountain. This creates both a pedestrian plaza and a forecourt to the hotel entrance, as well as a parking lot with more than the 10-space capacity required by the use permit. The fountain is reminiscent of the original fountain that was in the center of Stanford Court, and the glass dome is similar to the amber glass dome which once graced the vestibule of the Stanford mansion. The remainder of the original courtyard area is occupied by the entrance lobby which also has a glass dome, flanked by two 19th century crystal chandeliers acquired from the Grand Hotel in Paris when it was modernized.

The courtyard level provides another example of a unique solution to a problem presented by the adaptive use of a structure. Where the new lobby connects to the old building, the floors are even because the courtyard was depressed. While a higher ceiling could be provided in the main lobby, the ceiling heights of the remainder of the floor had to conform to the original building. The development of a small lobby lounge together with an open staircase to the lower meeting room areas was the solution. The result is effective; a lobby of modest proportions, but one which compares favorably with the extravagant lobbies of most new open court hotels. It creates the feeling of spaciousness that belies the smallness of the actual area.

Lower Level and Ballroom Addition

A hotel has many space needs not required by the typical apartment building. Excavation of a second level under the courtyard provided the "found" space for one suite of meeting rooms, the kitchens, and a unique multilevel restaurant which includes two well-appointed private dining rooms and a wine cellar. The ballroom addition and its sub-basement space for mechanical equipment take up the rest of the added space.

The site did not permit the location of garage facilities on the premises. The parking requirement established by the use permit required provision of 100 parking spaces, including 10 on site. To meet this condition initially, a long-term lease was acquired on an existing garage, one-half block away, which was later purchased. All parking is done through valet service, which is consistent with the character of the hotel and works well for an off-site garage.

Description of Completed Project

Completed, the Stanford Court has 402 guest rooms, including 34 suites. Commercial shops include a newsstand, book shop, beauty shop, men's clothing shop, two specialty shops, and car rental and travel counter. Restaurants include the Cafe Potpourri on the main floor (which serves breakfast and lunch) and Fournou's Ovens Restaurant (which serves dinner). Fournou's Bar (adjacent to but a level above Fournou's Ovens) and the Promenade Lounge in the lobby are available for cocktail service.

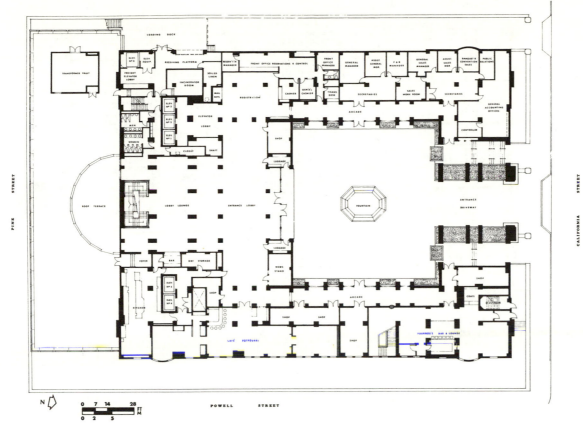

2-35   Main floor plan.

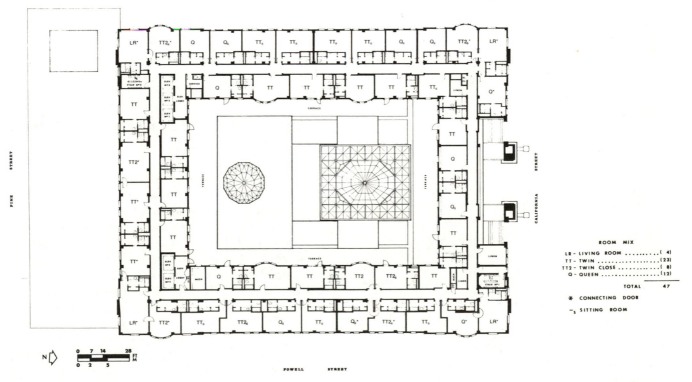

ROOM MIX

LR - LIVING ROOM ....(4)
TT - TWIN ....(23)
TT2 - TWIN CLOSE ....(8)
Q - QUEEN ....(12)

                 TOTAL   47

✻ CONNECTING DOOR

‒ₛ SITTING ROOM

2-36   First floor plan.

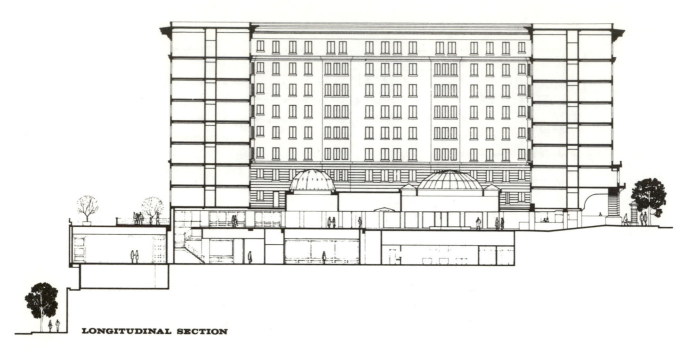

LONGITUDINAL SECTION

2-37 Longitudinal section.

Meeting spaces include the 5,062-square-foot Stanford Ballroom with a meeting capacity of 800 and a dining capacity of 500, and the 1,944-square-foot India Suite with a meeting capacity of 275 and a dining capacity of 160. Each of the two rooms can be divided. While modest in size, these meeting spaces are consistent with the overall scale of the hotel.

Art works have been installed, with an appraised value of almost $130,000—well over the normal expenditures for hotel furnishings. These include antique furniture, paintings, and chandeliers.

Market

The plan for the hotel was to provide a first-class luxury hotel featuring understated elegance, a residential decor, and outstanding service. The Stanford Court is not a convention hotel although a modest amount of meeting space was provided as a necessary adjunct. Its primary competition was the Clift Huntington, Mark Hopkins, and Fairmont Hotels. During the planning of Stanford Court it was forecast that the supply of new first-class hotel rooms in San Francisco would increase 50 to 65 percent over the next several years. By the time it was completed, however, the number of such hotels had actually increased by 100 percent with the opening of the San Francisco Hilton, two new Hyatt Hotels, the Westbury, a major addition to the St. Francis Hotel, five Holiday Inn Hotels, and several smaller hotels at Fisherman's Wharf.

Despite the new competition, Stanford Court has done extremely well. The initial analysis in 1968 projected an average room rate of approximately $30 with an annual occupancy of 75 percent. Because of severe competition, the initial 10-month period of 1972 achieved only a 48.4 percent occupancy level; however, the average room rate was $40.71. In the first half of 1977, occupancy exceeded 83 percent and the average daily room rate exceeded $61.00. House profit for the first half of 1977 was 35.5 percent (25 percent is considered good), and the hotel has generated a positive cash flow.

Development Organization and Financing

As noted earlier, the original development entity for Stanford Court was composed of three general partners and a separate hotel management company for operational control. Subsequent to the completion of the project the ownership structure changed. The initial investment to acquire leasehold rights in the site was $40,000. The leasehold is for $200,000 per year on a 99-year lease with escalation after 10 years based on the Consumer Price Index. The garage was purchased for $487,000 in 1969. Financing was provided by Connecticut General Life Insurance Company through an initial commitment in 1968 of $9 million for 27 years and 2 months at 8 percent interest and a percentage of gross annual sales. This was revised in 1970 to increase the loan by $2.3 million to $11.3 million at 9 percent interest. Total project costs upon completion were $17,215,519.41.

Experience Gained

- The development entity for Stanford Court went through several evolutions during the project's development and following its completion. Since adaptive use projects are by nature more complex and require continual rethinking as the projects proceed, having the decision-making role in a single entity is an obvious advantage that should be achieved if possible.

- Using an already existing structure made it easier from the beginning to create a first-class hotel with a unique character of its own. The personality of the structure helps to set the tone of the design concept, and details that conflict with the inherent nature of the building are more easily identified as planning and design are completed.

- Of major importance in any adaptive use project is the ability of the structure and site to accommodate the additional facilities required by the proposed reuse. At Stanford Court the additional space needed was found by excavating the courtyard to produce the lower levels and by making use of vacant land to build the meeting room.

- Unlike a new hotel facility in which the number of rooms is decided and then a building designed to house that number, the adaptive use of an existing structure requires a compromise between the number of rooms necessary for economic success and the ability of the existing structure to accommodate that number. In the case of Stanford Court, various schemes considered called for between 391 and 462 rooms. Ultimately a 402-room plan was selected, but experience has shown that somewhat fewer rooms at a higher average daily rate might have been a better solution. The rate structure should be a major focus of the economic analysis for a project of this type.

- Within the development entity there was a difference of opinion as to the necessity for or the amount of meeting space needed in a luxury hotel not catering to conventions. The conclusion of the hotel management company was that even in this type of facility some meeting space is necessary for economic success. Operating experience has show that there is a need for more small function rooms and in anticipation of this, the reuse

2-38   Street entrance to Fournou's Ovens.

design included a provision for access to the roof of the present ballroom area where four rooms for 30 to 40 people can be provided.

- The physical constraints of the building required an innovative approach to room planning and design that proved to be an asset in establishing the special character of the hotel. These constraints required an imaginative approach to the use of furniture and interior design with the result that a guest at Stanford Court experiences a room environment significantly different from that of a typical hotel.

- The cocktail lounge of Fournou's Restaurant has not been successful. The lobby lounge is far more attractive. Modification of the cocktail lounge is planned to improve its competitive position and the relationship between the hotel and its outside environment.

2-39 Room interior illustrating its residential character. The specially designed armoire is a combination desk, T.V. console, dresser, and storage space.

- The reuse design failed to utilize the Powell Street corner of the Stanford Court Apartments effectively. To maintain the integrity of the original structure as completely as possible, only a modest entrance to Fournou's Ovens Restaurant and Bar, at the site of an existing office entrance, was provided at this corner. In general, the plan of Stanford Court at the street level focuses inward with only the redesigned archway entrance to draw people to the hotel from the street. It has been proposed that a greenhouse be added to Fournou's Ovens Restaurant and Bar. This would provide a "window" to the excitement and activity on the corner of Powell Street. The proposed addition would not detract from the basic mass of the structure and for those acquainted with the details of the Leland Stanford mansion, it would be reminiscent of the elegant conservatory which was a prominent feature of the mansion.

- While the parking provided meets the requirements of the use permit, the demand for parking was underestimated. Original estimates indicated that 20 percent of the guests would come by automobile which would mean that 100 parking spaces would be adequate. Actual experience has been that 28 percent of the guests arrive by automobile, which occasionally creates parking problems.

- The only clearly identifiable cost penalty in fitting hotel facilities to an existing building was the requirement to install two kitchens, one major kitchen for the banquet areas and Fournou's Restaurant and a second kitchen to serve the Cafe Potpourri. This added cost, which might have been avoided with a new structure, was $90,000, or less than 1 percent of construction, furniture, and finishings costs.

- Of major concern in any reuse project are unforeseen circumstances which result in increased costs. An analysis of the $819,000 spent in changing orders because of such circumstances indicated that only $80,646 of additional costs could be specifically tied to unforeseen circumstances. This is less than 1 percent of construction costs. Careful exploratory studies plus the fact that interior demolition was completed before seeking bids for reconstruction were factors which probably helped avoid miscalculations.

- Because adaptive use requires many compromises during the design phase, it is important from the beginning that management participate with the architect in these decisions. Failure to do this may result in design compromises that will adversely affect efficient economic hotel operations and management.

Development: (a limited partnership joint venture with three general partners)

Royal Street Development Company, Inc.
Edgar B. Stern, Jr.
521 Royal Street
New Orleans, Louisiana 70112

Stanford Court Investment Company
c/o A. Cal Rossi, President
A. Cal Rossi Company, Ltd.
1130 Sacramento Street
San Francisco, California 94108

Stancourt (a wholly owned subsidiary of UAL, Inc.)

Management:

Stanford Court Hotel Management Company
James A. Nassikas, President
905 California Street
San Francisco, California 94108
(415) 989-3500

Architecutre:

Curtis and Davis Associated Architect and Planners, Inc.
Morton Bernstein, Senior Vice President and Project Architect
111 Iberville Street
New Orleans, Louisiana 70130
(504) 581-2600

Real Estate Counselor:

Hubert D. Eller
111 Sutter Street
San Francisco, California 94104
(415) 989-5247

PROJECT DATA

Land Use Information:

Site Area:

Hotel .... 56,250 sq. ft.
Garage .... 9,507 sq. ft.

Building Area for Hotel:

"Found" Gross Building Area Originally ...... 224,613 sq. ft.
Added New Space .... 47,509 sq. ft.
Gross Building Area after Reuse .... 272,122 sq. ft.
FAR (final) 4.8
New Space as Percent of Existing Building 21%

Parking:

Spaces: 100 in garage and auto court. With valet parking, more are available.
Ratio: 1 space per 4 guest rooms.

Economic Information:

Project Costs:

Building and Construction[1] $8,982,405
Landscaping 58,969
Architect, Technical Consultants, and
Interior Design[2] 824,900
Furniture, Furnishings, and Equipment 1,642,695
Pre-opening Expenses[3] 715,400
Operating Equipment 424,372
Partnership Operations[4] 4,486,644
Licenses, Permits, and Fees[5] 80,134
Total Project Costs **$17,215,519**

Comparable Costs Per Room for Construction:

Stanford Court	$22,344	(1972)
Royal Sonesta (New Orleans)	21,400	(1968)
Marriott Hotel (New Orleans)	21,900	(1969)
Westbury (San Francisco)	25,240	(1972)

Land Lease Information:

Hotel Site: $200,000 per year, 99-year lease (1961 to 2060) fixed for first 10 years (to 1971). Then adjusted up and down yearly based on variation in Consumer Price Index. Lessee has right of encumbrance, pays all taxes, assessment, and utilities.

Garage: Purchased in 1969 for $487,000.

Financing: Permanent loan of $11,300,000 @ 9 percent plus 15 percent of gross room sales above $3.4 million but below $4.1 million and 5 percent of gross room sales above $4.1 million. However, in no case may total payments exceed 10 percent under the usury laws of the state of California.
Partner Equity $1,500,000

Occupancy Pattern:

Pre-Opening Expectations: Average room rate of $30.00 with 75 percent occupancy.

Actual Performance:

Year	Room Rate	Percent Occupancy
1972 (10 months)	$40.71	48.4
1973	42.23	55
1974	45.93	65
1975[6]	50.05	71
1976	56.88	76.4
1977 (first half)	61.84	83.3

House Profit:

35.5 percent for the first half of 1977.[7]

Building Information:

Total Guest Rooms: 402, including 34 suites

Typical Guest Room Floor: 23,487 sq. ft. (51 rooms including 4 living rooms for suites)

Public and Commercial Spaces:

Meeting Space	Sq. Ft.
Ballroom	5,040
India Suite	1,944
Foyer	2,650
Restaurant & Lounge	
Fournou's Restaurant	2,628
Fournou's Bar	1,646
Lobby Lounge	2,496
Cafe Potpourri	2,134
Lobby Areas	
General Lobbies	5,030
Arcades	1,800
Shops	
Barber Shop	284
Smoke Shop/Newsstand	398
Beauty Shop	149
Specialty Shops (3)	563
Travel Desk	64

Notes:

[1] Building and construction includes all permanently installed construction including all change orders.

[2] Consultants include basic architectural fees and all technical consultant services.

[3] These expenses include all salaries, special events, public relations, and other one-time costs related to the period before opening when no income is occurring.

[4] Partnership operation expenses include insurance, property taxes, rents, mortgage payments interest, cost of money, loan fees, and improvements to garage.

[5] Includes utilities connection charge, building permit, etc.

[6] The year would have been better except for a weak first quarter. The period from April to December exceeded 80 percent occupancy at $50.00. For comparative purposes, national room occupancy for center city locations averaged 62.2 percent in 1974 and the average room rate was $21.72.

[7] In general, specific income/operating expense information is not available on an individual basis in this highly competitive industry. Comparative statistics are available via industry-wide publications on regular basis. Basic measurement of success is *house profit*. This is defined as the percentage relation of the difference between total sales (including all income centers, rooms, restaurants, shops) over the total cost of merchandise (payroll and other expenses, both direct and indirect, such as administrative and general, advertising, heat, light, power, and repairs, but not including taxes, fire insurance, interest, depreciation, amortization of leasehold and bound discount and other capital expenses).

Grand Central

Downtown commercial buildings offer a great potential for adaptive use. They have often been demolished as new technology and a shift in the location of a city's commercial and industrial district made them obsolete. Many, however, have been recycled with skill and imagination into a variety of new and interesting uses. Because such buildings are frequently clustered in one section of a city, renovating one of them often leads to the revitalization of the entire area with a subsequent increase in property values. The Grand Central Hotel in the Pioneer Square Historic District of Seattle is one example.

The Grand Central Hotel has been converted to an office complex with a shopping arcade on the main floor and in the basement. The central arcade with high arched brick walls opens from the street entrance and leads to Occidental Park on the other side of the building. The offices are completely modern but offer tenants amenities such as high ceilings and exposed brick walls not found in newer construction.

The development was conceived in June 1971, and the site was acquired in July. Rehabilitation began immediately and was completed in 1973.

Location and Site Description

The Grand Central Hotel is located in Seattle's Pioneer Square Historic District, one block from the waterfront, four blocks from the general office and banking districts, nine blocks from the commercial "uptown," and two miles from the Seattle Center. The building is in a neighborhood characterized by handsome, low-rise commercial buildings dating back to the turn of the century or earlier.

The site on which the hotel is situated came into prominence in the 1870s when arms magnate Philo Remington purchased several blocks of property in the area on speculation. Later, his son-in-law and manager of his arms factory in Ilion, New York, Watson C. Squire, purchased Remington's property for

$55,000 and built on it a three-story opera house, Seattle's first real theater. Theatrical performances in the opera house included local talent, traveling minstrels, and acting troupes.

Squire remodeled the opera house in 1882, converting the second and third floors into the Brunswick Hotel. On June 6, 1889 a fire razed the entire business district of Seattle causing damages estimated at $9 million. Although Squire suffered one of the largest losses, he was among the first businessmen to decide to rebuild his burned out properties.

With financier N. H. Latimer, Squire erected the four-story Squire-Latimer building which was used for offices until 1897 when gold was discovered in Alaska. With gold fever turning Seattle into a boom town, the Squire-Latimer building was converted into a hotel to serve the influx of hopeful miners. The Grand Central Hotel, as it was then called, prospered for several years, but as the gold strikes dwindled, so did the prosperity of the hotel. The entire Pioneer Square area gradually became a haven for the transient and penniless.

Today Pioneer Square has undergone a resurgence to become a highly attractive section of the city with specialty shops and offices. The city of Seattle has actively contributed to this revitalization by upgrading public facilities; it has installed pedestrian malls, planted trees along the streets, renovated existing parks, and added new parks. Alan Black, one of the developers of Grand Central, views the revitalization of Pioneer Square in three phases:

> In Phase 1, from 1962 to 1970, modest but important renovation work was done on an informal and somewhat amateur basis with limited outside financing. Phase 2, beginning with passage of the Pioneer Square Historic District Ordinance in 1970, saw the complete restoration of three major buildings and important municipal recognition and support for the area. Phase 2 also established the financial feasibility of restoring major buildings. Proven rent structures were established for these buildings and financing became available. Phase 3 is beginning now, in the summer of 1975. The Pioneer Square area is an established and recognized vital part of the city, where many buildings remain to be restored. There is a market for attractive, first-class space, and financing is available for the right development team . . . .

Opposite page: 2-41   The brick exterior of the Grand Central was restored as closely as possible to its original appearance.

2-42 Arcade is to the left of the main entrance to the Squire-Latimer building. (Photo: Richard Bush.)

The investment and restoration that took place in Pioneer Square from 1962 to 1970 during the Phase 1 period certainly was the most profitable. Indeed, it should have been, because it demanded the imagination and courage that started the area going.

Phase 2 was a period of high risk and long wait for a return on investment—in short, a testing period for Pioneer Square. Expensive restoration work was done before rental rates had adjusted to reflect the true cost of the work or the fine quality of the product.

Phase 3 can be approached less emotionally and with more logic. Rents are established for top quality space in well-restored buildings. Financing is easier to obtain for projects that show economic feasibility based on a record of work recently done in the area. The period of highest risk is over. . . .[1]

---

[1] Alan Black, "Making Historic Preservation Profitable—If You're Willing to Wait," *Economic Benefits of Preserving Old Buildings* (Washington, D.C.: National Trust for Historic Preservation, 1976), p. 27.

Architectural Character

The 80,000-square-foot brick building, constructed in the 1890s, is Victorian Romanesque in style and occupies completely its 16,650-square-foot site. Major cornices were removed from the building 10 years ago because of damage from earthquakes. The brick exterior of the building was restored as closely as possible to its original appearance, and the storefronts were given the general scale and character of the early architecture. The developers have control over all architectural and color changes made by tenants on both the exterior and interior of the building. They also control all commercial signage on the building exterior and in the arcade.

Approximately 48,000 square feet is set aside for office space and 32,000 square feet for retail use. No provision has been made for parking, but parking is available near the Grand Central Hotel, including daytime parking adjacent to the new municipal stadium.

2-43   Interior of arcade.

2-44   Occidental Park was constructed by the city of Seattle from a parking lot east of the Grand Central.

Redevelopment Sequence

When the developers purchased the building they had no concrete plan for redevelopment. In the fall of 1971, the city of Seattle bought the parking lot east of the Grand Central for use as a park. From this purchase, the concept of an arcade developed; the passageway would be from the First Avenue entrance through the building to the park, with shops opening onto the arcade. Three floors of office space were planned for the area above the arcade.

The exterior reconstruction took 8 months to complete and required the replacement of several courses of rotten brick. In addition, the parapet was lowered, and the upper section rebuilt, incorporating a bond beam that would tie the parapet together. The cleaning and repairing of the exterior was completed in early 1972. A silicone sealer was then applied. The Seattle building code posed an interesting structural requirement. The building department was concerned about the seismic risk of unreinforced brick buildings, the primary type of construction used in Pioneer Square during the immediate post-fire era. In a seismic disturbance the walls might pull away from the floors. According to developer Black:

The building code required that whenever more than 50 percent of the assessed value of a building was spent on improvements in any one year the building would have to meet current building code seismographic requirements . . . .

The architects and structural engineers for the building, together with the Building Department staff, developed a compromise solution for this type of unreinforced masonry building. The walls on each floor of the building had to be tied to the floors by the installation of a properly sized steel angle around the inside perimeter of the floor, with 4-foot-on-center steel strips welded to the channel and running back along the surface of the floor. These strips were then nailed and bolted to a new plywood overlaid floor, which tied the floor together so it would act as a single diaphragm. The perimeter steel angle member was then tied to the outside of the walls by bolts drilled through the walls and fastened on the outside with escutcheon-like plates that could be decorative in design.[2]

Interior reconstruction involved cutting through the 18-inch thick brick bearing walls to create the arcade and partitioning the upper floors for office space. The basement area was not part of the original plan. On first inspection it appeared unuseable. As work on the main arcade progressed, however, it became apparent that the basement space could be used if tied to the main arcade by a stairway.

---

[2] Black, "Making Historic Preservation Profitable," p. 24.

2-45　Exterior before redevelopment.

2-46　Arcade interior. (Photo: Richard Bush.)

Ownership and Management

The developers own the building and the site. Leases are for a fixed minimum rent with tenants paying an extra pro rata share for maintenance, night security, and refuse collection. The building is managed by a real estate management company. Office space is leased for between $5.00 and $6.50 per square foot. Many of the original retail tenants on the main arcade rented space for approximately $2.00 per square foot on 3- to 5-year leases.

The developers believed that the building, with its colorful history, would attract shoppers visiting the Pioneer Square Historic District. The area is alive with art galleries, restaurants, and shops, most of them new additions. The retail tenants are small specialty shops with food, arts and crafts, jewelry, clothing, and other goods.

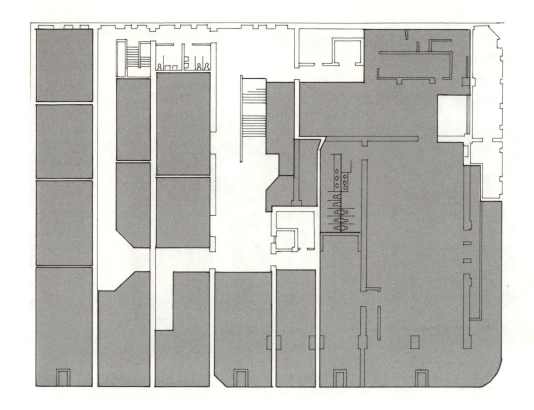

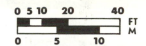

2-47 Lower arcade plan.

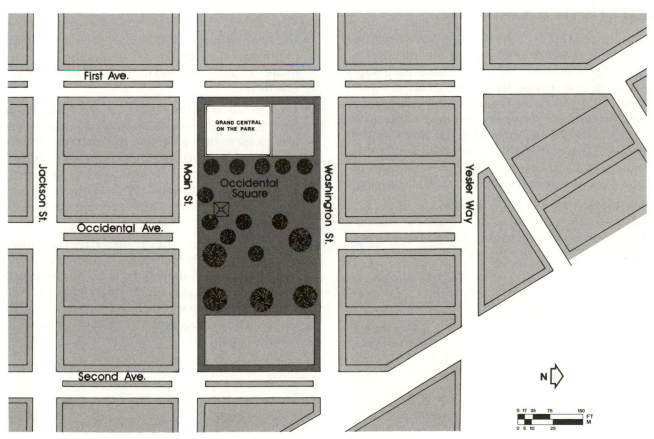

First Ave.

GRAND CENTRAL
ON THE PARK

Jackson St.

Main St.

Occidental
Square

Washington St.

Yester Way

Occidental Ave.

Second Ave.

N

2-48

2-49   Entrance detail. (Photo: Richard Bush.)

Experience Gained

- The developers feel they should have exercised stronger control over leases and advertising at the start; for example, the lease should have stipulated that all stores would maintain the same hours. Initially stores regulated their own hours, which confused shoppers and made advertising difficult. The developers also felt that the lease should have stated that a percentage of profits must go toward advertising. With no central control it is difficult to coordinate joint advertising.

- More effort should have been made to attract a better balance of shops. The developers found a tremendous demand for small retail shops of high quality.

- The financial stability of tenants should have been better investigated at the beginning. Insecure financing of tenants led to the early failure of several businesses.

- The operation of the Grand Central Hotel would have gone much more smoothly had there been a business manager from the outset. Having diversified interests and backgrounds, the three business partners were not able to manage the enterprise satisfactorily. With a business manager, the operation is now running much more smoothly.

- The developers feel they should have put a provision in the lease which would require tenants to pay a percentage of gross sales to the landlord to cover such items as taxes and maintenance. However, if a percentage had been required at the outset, the project would not have attracted as many tenants.

PROJECT DATA

Land Use Information:
　Site Area: 16,650 sq. ft.
　Gross Building Area (Before Renovation): 66,600 sq. ft.[1]
　Gross Leasable Area: 80,000 sq. ft.
　　Retail Space: 32,000 sq. ft.
　　Office Space: 48,000 sq. ft.

Economic Information:
　Acquisition Cost: $230,000[2]
　Construction Cost: $18 per sq. ft.
　Amenities Cost: $0.50 per sq. ft.[3]

Rental Information:
　Total Minimum Rent (1st Year): $274,722
　　　　　　　　　　(2nd Year): $276,522
　Common Area Charges: $30,472
　　Maintenance and Night Security: $29,672
　　Refuse Collection: $800

Tenant Information:

Classification	No. of Stores	Sq. Ft. of Space	Percent of Total
Food	3	8,177	13.5
Clothing/Boutique	1	723	1.2
Art/Crafts	9	5,003	8.2
Specialty	13	8,633	14.2
Offices	21	34,802	57.4
Services	2	636	1.1
Other[4]	—	2,695	4.4
Total	**49**	**60,669**[5]	**100.0**

Notes:
[1] Not including basement which was thought to be unuseable.
[2] 1971.
[3] Including cost of landscaping, fireplace, etc.
[4] Nonrentable space.
[5] Rented as of October 1973. The building is now completely rented.

Development:
Ralph D. Anderson
119 South Main Street
Seattle, Washington 98104
(206) 623-6832

Alan Black
4834 Southeast 32nd
Mercer Island, Washington
(206) 232-3702

Richard White
311 Occidental Avenue
Seattle, Washington 98104
(206) 682-7333

Architecture:
Ralph D. Anderson and
　Partners
119 South Main Street
Seattle, Washington 98104
(206) 623-6832

Management:
Leonard Gerber Real Estate
216 First Avenue South
Seattle, Washington 98104
(206) 622-3718

The Garage

The Garage is a 72,000-square-foot mini-mall with an urban setting in Harvard Square, Cambridge, Massachusetts. The project is of particular interest because it combines adaptive use with a specialty retail orientation, two innovative and often economically tenuous forms of development.

The Garage occupies a multilevel masonry and concrete structure which has gone through numerous transformations in its 116-year history. The most recent change occurred in 1972, when the building was converted from a parking garage to a shopping center at a cost of $2 million. At that time, the interior of the structure was completely rebuilt, the exterior upgraded, and a fourth floor added to obtain maximum allowable floor-to-area ratio. Subsequently, however, the developer failed to meet mortgage payments and the lender, Connecticut General Life Insurance Company, foreclosed.

Today, The Garage stands on the threshold of yet another transformation. The lender has elected to retain ownership of the property and carry out an improvement program designed to accomplish the original objective identified for the project, that of creating a specialty shopping complex appropriate to the unique environment of Harvard Square. Connecticut General believes that this strategy will enable it to recoup its investment in the property and obtain a return of 8 to 10 percent.

The Building and Its Setting

Built as a stable for horse-drawn trolleys in 1860, The Garage is one of the oldest three or four survivors of early mass transit-related structures. In 1916, the building was renovated into a two-level parking garage. Entry ramps were constructed, the gable replaced by a flat roof, and a concrete structure inserted inside the brick exterior. Subsequently, the parking operation was expanded and a third level was added to the top of the old building. New concrete auto ramps were built into the structure and the old ramps removed. The building operated as a parking garage and service station with few alterations for the next 50 years. Increasingly, however, it became more inefficient as parking design improved, automobiles became larger, and the area became more congested.

Opposite page: 2-51 Entrance to The Garage.

Location was the crucial factor in determining a new use for the block-long masonry building. Harvard Square is a unique pedestrian environment, functioning not only as the retail business area for Harvard University, but also as the central business district for a substantial portion of the Cambridge community. Vehicular movement on the irregular network of streets is difficult. The Garage is one block south of Harvard Yard on a 17,000-square-foot parcel bordered on three sides by public streets. The obvious development opportunity was to capitalize on the market potential.

2-52 The Garage before conversion to a 72,000-square-foot mini-mall. (Photo: George Zimberg.)

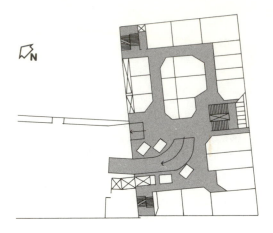

2-53   Mezzanine level: 1972 redevelopment.

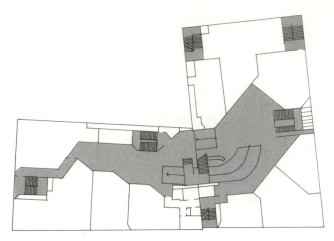

2-54   Mezzanine level: 1977 redevelopment.

1972 Renovation

The conversion created a mini-mall with four levels of retail space, including the basement, first floor, a bazaar, and third floor. Gross leasable area (GLA) totals 53,000 square feet. To maximize useable space the basement was converted to retail use, a mezzanine was sandwiched between the street-level arcade and the bazaar floor, and a floor was added to the top of the structure.

An entirely new utility system including electricity, lighting, heating, and air conditioning was installed. Major structural alterations, including post tensioning of some floor slabs, were required. New elevators and stairs were inserted into the building shell. Two of the existing automobile ramps were removed; the third was reused as a main circulation route. The entire interior was sandblasted. Exterior brick was washed and repainted. Bricked-up windows and entrances were reopened and glazed to emphasize openness of the structure, and major entrances were added to attract and direct pedestrian flow. An interior arcade on the ground floor level provides access to the mezzanine and upper levels of the center. Total cost of this renovation was $2 million above the $1 million required to purchase the property.

Failure of the project as a commercial venture can be attributed to the following factors: poor management, inadequate upkeep, inability to lease the third level for office space as anticipated, specific design deficiencies, and inadequate signs.

1977 Renovation

An evaluation of the visual, architectural, and operational deficiencies of The Garage prepared by the architect provided the basis for the decision to renovate the structure. A property management firm was retained simultaneously to carry out a reevaluation of the merchandising mix.

The scope of the program was limited. Major elements included redesign of the three main entrances, implementation of a new signage program intended to unify the exterior facade and enhance the project's visibility, and reorganization of the interior circulation system and retail areas. A new management program to upgrade maintenance, service, and security was established.

2-55   Interior of The Garage before conversion.

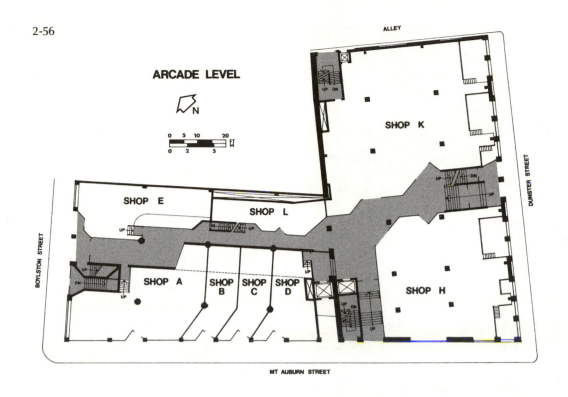

2-56

ARCADE LEVEL

N

0 5 10   20
0 2   5

SHOP E

SHOP L

SHOP K

SHOP A

SHOP
B

SHOP
C

SHOP
D

SHOP H

BOYLSTON STREET

DUNSTER STREET

ALLEY

MT AUBURN STREET

2-57   Building reveals numerous additions over its more than 100-year history.

93

2-58 One auto ramp was reused as a main circulation route.

Interior Modifications

The Bazaar, an open shopping area located on the middle level and encompassing 24 small shops, was one of the unique features of the first renovation of The Garage. After being supplied with utilities, the tenants simply moved in and opened for business. This merchandising technique proved difficult to manage, however, and in the 1977 renovation the number of Bazaar tenants has been reduced, the original pedestrian loop system replaced with a smaller common area, and individual tenant space more precisely defined.

The first level is being converted into a concentrated food service area with 3,500 square feet of GLA. The third floor is occupied by entertainment services, including three mini-theaters and a nightclub. Basement tenants and those with exterior access remain unchanged.

The quality of interior materials and accessories was upgraded to the standards of an urban shopping center. For example, quarry tile floors were installed and handrails, curbing, and lighting refurbished or replaced as required.

Experience Gained

- Difficulties experienced by The Garage point up the need for careful management and operation of specialty shopping centers in an urban location. Initial failure derived only partially from the concept itself, which was overly trendy in nature. Of greater importance was the way in which the concept was implemented. Connecticut General Life Insurance Company believes that with a minimum of investment and improved management practices the development can be placed on a sound footing.

- Flexibility in adapting to changing economic and market conditions is essential in real estate development generally. At The Garage, this fundamental requirement to some extent has been met, given the nature and structure of the use. The 1977 renovation represents a strategy to minimize some of the uncertainties by shifting to a more conventional marketing approach.

- Adaptive use has become an established development technique in New England because of the high cost of new construction, growing public pressure to retain existing buildings, and market preference, which places a premium on space in well restored older buildings.

- All participants must be closely involved with projects of this type. The Garage could not have been completed had its principals not been in close touch to supervise carefully all phases of redevelopment and operation.

- The original renovation was particularly difficult because the building's new uses had to accommodate a solid concrete frame. The construction process was also unusually demanding because the renovation was done by "negotiation." The owner was the contractor as well, and the architect served as an advisor. Sometimes the architect's advice was taken and sometimes it was not.

- Specialty tenants frequently do not have staying power and can contribute to instability. The Bazaar's orientation has been shifted from arts and crafts to popular priced retail shops while still retaining the novel character of a Harvard Square location. The marketing challenge, therefore, is to appeal to the specialized interests of the Harvard Square shopper within the framework of a sound business operation.

PROJECT DATA

Land Use Information:
   Site Area: 17,000 sq. ft.
   Floor Area Ratio:[1] 4.6:1
   Parking: No parking spaces are provided on site.

Building Information:
   Number of Buildings: 1
   Gross Building Area (GBA):[2] 78,000 sq. ft.
   Gross Leasable Area (GLA):[3] 52,770 sq. ft.

Economic Information:
   Rent Range Per Sq. Ft. of GLA: $12 to $25
   Common Area Expenses: $1.25 per sq. ft.
   Percentage Rents: 3% to 10%
   HVAC: $1.10 per sq. ft.
   1972 Renovation:
      Acquisition Cost: $1,000,000
      Redevelopment Cost: $2,000,000
      Renovation Per Sq. Ft.: $25.60
      Mortgage Loan: $3,000,000
   1977 Renovation:
      Redevelopment Cost: $500,000
      Renovation Per Sq. Ft.: $6.41

Tenant Information:[4]

Tenant Group	No. of Stores	Sq. Ft. of GLA	Percent of Total GLA	Dollars & Cents of Shopping Centers: 1978—Neighborhood Shopping Centers' Composition by Tenant Classification Group (Table 8 G-4)
General Merchandise	—	—	—	11.2
Food	2	1,078	2.0	30.2
Food Service	6	22,410	42.5	6.4
Clothing	7	8,521	16.2	3.7
Shoes	—	—	—	1.0
Home Furnishings	3	4,038	7.7	2.4
Home Appliances/Music	3	4,291	8.1	1.7
Building Materials/Garden	—	—	—	3.2
Automotive Supplies/Service Station	—	—	—	2.4
Hobby/Special Interest	1	1,690	3.2	2.4
Gifts/Specialty	1	1,000	1.9	1.5
Jewelry and Cosmetics	—	—	—	.5
Liquor	1	1,110	2.1	1.3
Drugs	—	—	—	9.9
Other Retail	1	632	1.2	2.4
Personal Services	—	—	—	5.0
Recreation/Community	1	6,500	12.3	4.0
Financial	—	—	—	3.3
Offices (other than financial)	—	—	—	2.1
Other[5]	1	1,500	2.8	5.4
Total	**27**	**52,770**	**100.0**	**100.0**

Notes:
[1] FAR—the square-foot amount of total floor area (all stories) for each square foot of land area of a property.
[2] GBA—all square footage within a structure.
[3] GLA—total floor area designated for tenant occupancy and exclusive use. The median GLA of the nine centers included as specialty centers in

Dollars & Cents of Shopping Centers: 1978 was approximately 68,000 square feet.
[4] *Dollars & Cents of Shopping Centers: 1978* tenant classifications which reflect the mix after completion of renovation in spring 1977.
[5] Vacant.

Ownership/Development:
Connecticut General Life
   Insurance Company
Hartford, Connecticut 06115
(203) 243-8811

Architecture:
ADD Inc.
1158 Massachusetts Avenue
Cambridge, Massachusetts
   02138
(617) 661-0165

Management:
Wilder Manley Associates
66 Long Wharf
Boston, Massachusetts
   02138
(617) 726-1500

The Dewitt Building

As educational needs and standards have changed over the years, many school systems have chosen to build new facilities rather than invest large amounts of money in the modernization of old schools. An obsolete school building often occupies a large site in a central location, and, as a public building, pays no taxes to the city. These factors have proved fatal to a great number of early 20th century schools, and, without the intervention of a local architect-developer, they probably would have led to the demolition of the old city high school in Ithaca, New York. Instead, the Dewitt School, built in 1915 and declared surplus public property in 1970, provides an excellent example of the popular and economic success that can accompany the adaptive use of an old structure. The building, which contains 115,000 square feet, was converted to multiple use, including apartments (adapted from the original classrooms), offices, and shops opening onto an interior mall.

The Dewitt occupies a half-block site and is one of the largest buildings in downtown Ithaca, a city of 26,000. Despite a general atmosphere of pessimism in the early 1970s concerning the future of the downtown, the developer felt that the location and character of the building would have an appeal for residents, commercial tenants, and shoppers. The immediate success of the project, which opened in 1972, helped to reestablish confidence in the downtown area and most likely helped spur a major community renewal program which featured construction of a pedestrian mall on part of the city's main commercial street, one block from the old school.

Opposite page: 2-60 The exterior of the Dewitt Building was largely unchanged during conversion of the former high school into apartments, offices, and shops.

Historic Overview

Dewitt High School was the last important commission of William Henry Miller, a prominent Ithaca architect. Miller, whose architectural practice spanned half a century, was the first student of architecture at Cornell University in Ithaca; he later designed several campus buildings and numerous local residences. The red brick school follows the Gothic style which was fashionable for educational buildings during the early 20th century. A tower with a narrow octagonal turret dominates the main facade, and limestone archways with carved stone details emphasize the front and side entrances. Named for Simeon Dewitt—Revolutionary War soldier, surveyor-general of New York, and founder of Ithaca—the high school was originally built with three floors above a partially below-grade ground floor. In 1935, a fourth floor with four classrooms was added and a one-story cafeteria wing was constructed on the rear of the building. Corridors and classrooms in the school were arranged around a central core which included a gymnasium on the ground floor and a 1,000-seat auditorium with a balcony on the first and second floors.

In 1960, crowded conditions in the building prompted the construction of a new high school on the southern edge of the city. Dewitt functioned as a junior high school from 1960 until 1970, when state officials determined that the building did not meet stringent fire code and smoke detection standards necessary for public educational facilities. To comply with these standards would have been costly. Because of this and the fact that state funds were available for new construction, the Board of Education decided to build a new junior high and place the Dewitt school on the market.

2-61 Apartments on the north side of the building look out onto a small city park. The top portions of some of the three-tiered windows were inconspicuously blocked off to improve insulation.

Redevelopment Strategy

Following the closing of the school, several public and nonprofit agencies, attracted by its central location and its prominence as a city landmark, considered possible adaptations for the building. Located in the central business district within two blocks of most city and county government offices, the building is part of the Dewitt Park Historic District, named to the National Register of Historic Places, and designated by Ithaca's Landmarks Preservation Commission in 1970. None of the adaptations studied—including one in a report prepared for the city and the New York State Urban Development Corporation to convert the building to a community services center—resulted in a feasible reuse proposal.

After the Dewitt building had been on the market for a year without attracting purchasers, the Board of Education put it up for auction through closed bids. A local architect, William S. Downing, submitted an offer of $20,000. This low bid prompted a counter offer of $122,000 by the Savings Bank of Tompkins County for purchase of the property "free of existing structures." With demolition of the Dewitt building estimated at $55,000, the Board of Education could have netted $67,000. The bank planned to use the site as an at-grade parking lot which would yield about $6,000 annually to the city in property taxes. Downing's redevelopment scheme, on the other hand, involved a major investment of private money in the downtown area with an annual real estate tax return in excess of $30,000. The Board used this long-term economic rationale to justify its rejection of the bank's offer and acceptance of Downing's bid.

A subsequent legal suit by an "irate taxpayer" against the Board of Education, charging "unlawful and unconstitutional gift of property" for underselling the structure, was dismissed from court because of lack of standing by the suing party.

Downing's careful evaluation of market conditions and the design potential of the Dewitt building helped lead to the sale. The Board recognized that redevelopment of the building according to Downing's plan would be an economic asset to the city. Downing had used the original architectural plans for the school to draw up a scheme of reuse as apartments, shops, and offices. Estimates were made for heating, plumbing, electrical, and mechanical renovations, and for general construction work. According to the terms of the sale, Downing agreed to invest $500,000 in the conversion of the school to a mixed-use complex. Because of the size of the investment needed for the conversion, he offered a minimal purchase price to make the project financially feasible.

As the owner of a 42-unit apartment house elsewhere in Ithaca, Downing had several years of experience as a landlord and felt confident that a demand existed, especially among the elderly, for well-constructed, fire-resistant apartments in the downtown area. His architectural office was adjacent to the school property in a Federal-style townhouse which he also owned. Downing had also organized and opened a commercial art gallery and boutique, giving him additional background in retail business ventures.

At the time of the sale, the property was zoned for residences and offices (B-1); Downing received a variance allowing shops. When a request for a second variance, to allow a restaurant, was denied by the zoning board, Downing appealed to the city council and the entire block was rezoned for residences, offices, shops, and restaurants (B-2). Requirements for off-street parking were waived because of a city-owned parking garage nearby.

Design Scheme

Downing served as architect and interior designer for the project, which got underway immediately after his purchase of the building in August 1971. His design concept called for conversion of the school classrooms to apartments, redevelopment of the ground floor for retail shops opening onto an interior mall, and reconstruction of the auditorium space into office suites with a two-story atrium lobby. In order to keep interior demolition to a minimum, the plan retained the existing corridors, stairs, and exterior exits, and generally did not require alteration of the original classroom walls. Access to the building is unrestricted during business and shopping hours but limited at other times when exterior entries are kept locked for security.

2-62 A restaurant on the ground floor hangs its shingle in a new plate glass window which opens onto a terrace.

Individual apartments on the first, second, and third floors are contained within single classrooms through the addition of dry-wall partitions and kitchen and bathroom units. Special design features include a luxury three-bedroom apartment in the old school library and a "penthouse" apartment with a sleeping loft and spiral staircase in the fourth floor tower. A ground floor hallway running the length of the building was opened up to serve as the interior mall with at-grade entrances at each end of the building. The central entrance under the tower leads to the first floor and gives the offices access to the atrium lobby through an oak-paneled wall which once marked the school's administrative offices.

Reconstruction Sequence

Initial work on the project concentrated on renovation and replacement of the mechanical systems and on conversion to residential use. The second phase focused on preparing the ground floor for retail occupancy, and the final work involved reconstruction for the office complex. The first apartment units were available 12 months after the purchase of the building, and the first shops had opened by October 1972.

The building, which has steel framing and concrete slab floors, had no structural deficiencies. Four staircases were enclosed to meet fire code requirements, but the existing smoke detection and fire alarm systems passed inspection. The electrical and forced air heating systems were in good condition, and renovation was limited to the addition of more distribution lines. Water pipes were replaced, but the additional plumbing facilities for the apartments were connected to existing waste lines. Windows were replaced throughout the building, and plate glass was used in the ground floor to give the shops exposure and display space. The top portions of the tall, three-tiered windows in the upper floors were blocked off to improve insulation, an alteration which is unnoticeable from the outside of the building.

Each apartment is equipped with an 8-foot-square kitchen unit with range, refrigerator, dishwasher, and garbage disposal. An intercom and door release system for the building's main entrance are installed in each residential unit. The first, second, and third floors are provided with laundry, trash disposal, and storage facilities.

A new floor was laid on part of the ground floor and the rows of shops there were broken by an open space midway along the mall corridor. Interior finishes for the retail areas were left to individual tenants. To construct the office complex, the sloping floor of the old auditorium was covered by a new, level floor, and offices were arranged around a two-story atrium lobby with an open stair. Both the stage and balcony areas were adapted as office suites, with plate glass windows opening onto the lobby.

No exterior changes were made to the structure, and landscape design focused on the construction of a terrace on the south side of the building. Parking on the rear of the lot was retained, with spaces assigned to residents of the building.

Description of the Completed Project

With a gross building area of 115,000 square feet, the Dewitt Building provides 69,480 square feet of rentable space. The structure occupies a site of 61,446 square feet, which has at-grade parking facilities for 51 cars.

Dewitt contains 48 rental apartments, with 18 one-bedroom units (each averaging 575 square feet), 28 two-bedroom units (875 square feet), and two three-bedroom units. Space is available for approx-

2-63

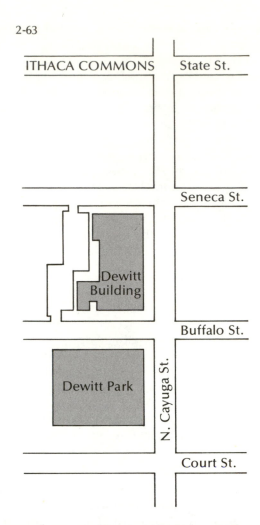

2-64 Shoppers head for the arched entrance to the interior shopping mall on the ground floor of the old school.

100

2-65 Tents on the lawn outside the building attract shoppers to a sporting goods store in the ground floor shopping arcade. A penthouse apartment occupies the central tower.

imately 17 retail and restaurant tenants, which include a camping and sporting goods store, a guitar workshop, hobby and woodworking shops, a health food restaurant, a delicatessen, a bakery, a women's boutique, a soap shop, and antique and used book stores. The central open space in the mall is used as a sidewalk café and as a public meeting area for poetry readings, music, and other events.

Offices are available for approximately 14 tenants, which include a U.S. House of Representative's home office, two attorneys, a doctor, two life insurance companies, and a realtor. The developer's architectural firm occupies the top floor of the building.

Financing

Permanent mortgage financing was obtained outside of Ithaca, from a financial institution which had previous experience with a similar adaptive use project. During 1968 to 1969 the Savings Bank of Utica (New York) had provided construction and permanent financing to a local developer for the conversion of St. Luke's Hospital and Nursing Home in Utica into an apartment and office complex. The same bank holds a $650,000 mortgage on the Dewitt Building, at 8¾ percent over 20 years. The project can be refinanced after 15 years. Construction financing was obtained from various commercial banks in Ithaca and out of town; loans are open notes, at 10 percent.

Market

Dewitt is one of the few fire resistant buildings containing apartments in the immediate downtown area, and monthly rents for units are slightly higher than average for rental housing stock in Ithaca. One- and two-bedroom apartments in Dewitt average $210 and $250 per month, respectively. The rent structure has resulted in a high proportion (about 70 percent) of elderly residents, as the developer anticipated. The remainder of tenants represents a cross section of ages, including some students. Turnover is low, and the building generally operates at full residential capacity.

Commercial rents are competitive with other downtown space, although somewhat lower than average rates in buildings on the major commercial street (now partially a pedestrian mall) one block to the south. Retail tenants, predominately small, locally owned specialty shops, pay between $4 and $5 per square foot (no percentages); office tenants pay between $3 and $5. Leases vary from 1 to 5 years, with inflationary clauses included. Downing owns two of the mall businesses, the women's boutique, and the sidewalk café. Retail space is 100 percent occupied; office space is about 70 percent rented.

Experience Gained

- The location of the school building in the downtown area, with immediate access to both shopping and residential neighborhoods, was one key to the project's success. Having mixed uses undoubtedly contributes to the project's vitality by tapping several markets at one time (residential, commercial, and professional).

- The architect-developer's ability to assume many roles "in-house"—acting as engineer, landscaper, interior designer, general contractor, building manager—resulted in significant savings in the cost of professional services. In addition to Downing's architectural training, his background as a landlord and an entrepreneur was important in his evaluation of the potential market for the redeveloped building.

- The low acquisition cost of the building was a vital factor in the financial viability of the project. The price paid for the property was well below the value of the building and a fraction of the value of the downtown site. Because of the guarantee of a substantial private investment in a downtown property and the prospect of high property tax returns to the city on the rehabilitated building, the Board of Education chose to accept a low bid rather than a high bid which required demolition.

- The developer emphasized the necessity for buildings such as the Dewitt to be taxed according to their earning ability rather than their replacement value. Without this pragmatic approach to assessment, annual property taxes could prove to be an impossible financial burden for many adaptive use projects.

PROJECT DATA

Land Use Information:
 Site Area: 61,446 sq. ft. (1.41 acres)
 Total Dwelling Units: 48
 Gross Density: 34.04 du per acre
 Parking Spaces: 51[1]

Building Information:
 Gross Building Area: 115,000 sq. ft.
 Net Rentable Area: 69,480 sq. ft.
 Percent Rentable: 60.4

Unit Information:

Type	Number	Sq. Ft.	Rents
One bedroom	18	575	$210
Two bedroom	28	875	$250
Three bedroom	2	Variable	$350

Lease Information:
 Retail—Rent: $4 to $5 per sq. ft.
 Length: 1 to 5 years with escalator clauses
 Office—Rent: $3 to $5 per sq. ft.
 Length: 1 to 5 years with escalator clauses

Economic Information:
 Acquisition: $20,000[2]
 Building Cost: $0.17 per sq. ft. of GBA
 Rehabilitation Cost: Not available[3]
 Financing:
  Construction: Open notes at 10 percent
  Permanent: $650,000 at 8¾ percent for 20 years

Notes:
 [1] City-owned parking garage nearby.
 [2] The low acquisition cost was vital to the financial viability of the project. The price paid was well below the value of the building and a fraction of the value of the downtown site. Because of the guarantee of a substantial private investment in a downtown property and the prospect of high property tax returns to the city on the rehabilitated building, the Board of Education chose to accept a low bid rather than a higher bid which required demolition of the school but would have yielded lower property taxes.
 [3] According to the terms of sale the developer agreed to invest $500,000 in the conversion.

Development/Architecture:
William S. Downing
William Downing Asso-
 ciates, Architects
The Dewitt Building
Ithaca, New York 14850
(607) 273-6427

Permanent Financing:
Savings Bank of Utica
233 Genesee
Utica, New York 13501
(315) 792-4800

Long Wharf

Older buildings, especially those which have been used for warehousing or manufacturing, typically have hidden assets which, when tapped, make reuse of the buildings attractive to developers. These assets can have to do with a structure's height, space, or volume or with such intangibles as its character and personality, all of which can add to the value of the property. For example, if a developer buys a building with a special configuration and square footage and can "find" additional, useable space within it, then he has tapped the hidden assets of the structure.

Two projects which reflect the resilience of older buildings are the Custom House Block and the Gardner Building, both located on Long Wharf on Boston's historic waterfront. The Custom House Block has been redesigned to house 29 luxury rental apartments, 15,110 net square feet of retail space, and 18,450 net square feet of office space, including the corporate headquarters for the developer. The Gardner Building has been renovated to accommodate a West Coast restaurant chain, Chart House, with 7,140 net square feet of space.

The Custom House Block consists of nine bays or buildings, each four stories high with full attic and separated by masonry party bearing walls. Floors are of heavy timber, mill construction. The Gardner Building is an older structure and consists of three separate buildings or bays which are similar in construction to the Custom House Block but are smaller in size. Each has three stories with an attic. Bearing walls are 16 inches thick at the base and 8 inches thick at the roof.

Opposite page: 2-67   The Chart House restaurant occupies the Gardner Building, which was built between 1784 and 1805, and is the last remaining building of its type on the Boston waterfront.

Historic Overview

Long Wharf dates back to the early 18th century, having been completed in 1715. It stretched some 1,700 feet into Boston Harbor in 1829. The Gardner Building was built between 1784 and 1805 and is the last remaining building of its type on the Boston waterfront. It is also the oldest. Warehouse structures before the Revolutionary War were built of wood, and during the 1770s most of Long Wharf burned down. Subsequently, the Boston selectmen passed a law requiring all new warehouse construction to be of masonry. The Gardner Building was part of a long string of buildings which reached from the tip of Long Wharf back to Faneuil Hall over the entire length of the original Long Wharf.

Built between 1845 and 1847 during the heyday of Boston shipping, the Custom House Block replaced buildings similar to the Gardner Building. The south face, which is the front, is granite. The remaining facades are brick. Originally somewhat longer on the sea end, the building was shortened in 1865 to provide space for tin sheds. The Custom House Block represented a break in style from the rooflines of the earlier Gardner-type warehouses. In fact, it was the only granite structure on Long Wharf.

The primary use for the building up until 1900 was for warehousing. Ships unloaded their wares into the back of the building, and goods were sold from the front. This accounts for the elaborate granite facade on the front of the Custom House and for the lack of windows on the back. Usually the back side consisted of large loading doors through which merchandise could be hoisted for storage.

The three bays in the Gardner Building are all the same size—25 feet by 36 feet. Each of the first four bays in the Custom House is 25 feet by 60 feet, the next two, 20 feet by 60 feet, and the last three, 25 feet by 68 feet. This accounts for the angular bend on the back portion of the Custom House.

2-68　The Boston Redevelopment Authority owns all of Long Wharf, except for the actual area on which the buildings stand.

In 1869 the Wharf was shortened considerably by the construction of Atlantic Avenue, cutting the wharf nearly in half. In the early 20th century, the inner harbor of Boston became less important because of its shallow depth, and the waterfront buildings fell into disrepair. Large portions of both the Gardner Building and the Custom House remained unoccupied or were used for dead storage and some light industry such as soap manufacturing, pipe cutting, and metal fabrication. After World War II, portions of the buildings were converted to residential use, consisting of small, one-bedroom apartments. Fire balconies and fire escapes were installed, and the old mud cofferdams, which had kept basements dry for 120 years, were pierced to accommodate new utilities.

Redevelopment Strategy

The Long Wharf properties were absorbed from Dreyfuss Realty in 1970 by the Berenson Corporation, a real estate management firm, which had arisen when Dreyfuss Realty went out of business. The property was put in a trust which in turn contracts with the Berenson Corporation (now called Wilder Manley Associates) for management services. The trust was established to maintain continuity with the

Berenson Corporation's other investments and operations. The owners chose to redevelop the buildings rather than tear them down to make way for new construction. The Long Wharf area had come under the purview of the Boston Redevelopment Authority (BRA) since it was in the BRA's waterfront renewal area. As part of its redevelopment plan, the BRA had taken all of Long Wharf for redevelopment, leaving only the actual area on which both buildings stood for private ownership.

As such, the BRA had substantial authority to direct the work on the buildings to make certain that their final appearance was historically appropriate and that their uses were compatible with the waterfront redevelopment plan. In order to maintain private ownership of the parcels the developer had to negotiate an agreement with the BRA guaranteeing a full renovation. This agreement gave the BRA the right to acquire the property by eminent domain if the agreement was broken. The Redevelopment Authority was primarily interested in the preservation of the exteriors of the buildings and was amenable to many design solutions for the interiors. In fact, substantial design coordination was carried out with the BRA's design staff. They provided many suggestions about the design of the buildings and coordinated their plans for the upgrading of the immediate area to be consistent with the uses which the developer proposed to house.

The Custom House Block is listed on the National Register of Historic Places, a listing which serves notice that these buildings are historically significant and protected from demolition or adverse effects which might be caused by federally aided programs.

Structural Condition Before Reuse

The Custom House Block is composed of nine separate buildings or bays; the Gardner Building, three. Load-bearing walls are constructed as party walls. These masonry walls are corbelled over three to six courses to make a shelf about 4 inches in depth. The wood structural beams, which are of southern hard pine, generally 14 inches by 8 inches, rest on the shelf. Floor construction over the beams is two layers of 1-inch, rough-cut boards, some 2 feet wide.

The brick for both buildings was probably hand cast. The granite facing is of large, rough-faced slabs and is only 4 inches thick, backed by 4 to 8 inches of brick. All lintels for original openings are also granite.

Foundations for both buildings are constructed over what was originally water. The Gardner Building is built on a rubble foundation which spreads from the bottom of the outside bearing walls at approximately a 45-degree angle. The Custom House, built some 50 years later, is supported by friction piles inside a cofferdam which was constructed first. This cofferdam is composed of two vertical sheets of plank approximately 5 feet apart driven into the harbor bottom and backfilled with harbor clay. The top 5 to 10 feet of piles inside the cofferdam were then backfilled with clay to provide a waterproof barrier. On top of the piles are pile caps, large slabs of granite spanning the piles, from which rise the brick bearing walls. The elevation of the pile caps was established by tides in order to keep all of the wooden piles under water to prevent rot.

The structural condition before reuse was substantially sound except for some superficial problems. Underneath the Custom House are deep cellars which are normally dry. However, with the piercing of the cofferdam after World War II to install utilities and its general decay over time, the soundness of the foundation was in question.

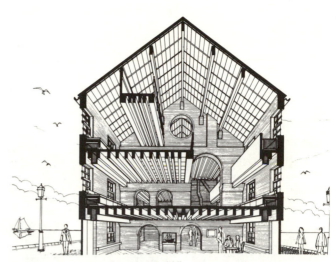

2-69 Section drawing of the Chart House restaurant.

Redevelopment Process

Custom House Block. A large portion of the Custom House was unoccupied when the developer considered rehabilitation. The rest of the building consisted of 26 apartment tenants and a few commercial uses. Initial plans called for a two-stage conversion of the building to all residential occupancy except for the ground floor, which was to be developed into small shops catering to tourist trade as Long Wharf was upgraded by the BRA. The first stage was to develop all of the vacant space in the building. The second phase was to rehabilitate the existing residential space which had been constructed in the 1940s.

While the vacant portions of the building were being rehabilitated, the existing residential space came under new rent control laws in Boston. These apartments had been rented after World War II at minimal rents to artists and others and finally in the 1960s to young professionals. The developer proposed to upgrade substantially the part of the building already occupied by apartments. Code compliance would have cost approximately $4,000 per unit, but the developer proposed only moderate rent increases to the Housing Board, which was authorized by the city to enforce the rent control law. The Housing Board passed favorably on the matter.

2-70 Fifth floor mezzanine apartment with deck in the Custom House Block.

An organization of tenants in the Custom House took the developer to court and won, the court ruling in favor of rent control over code compliance. This action proved fatal to the second phase which was the upgrading of the existing apartments. Therefore, the developer reprogrammed this space to accommodate substantial office use. Eventually, the developer negotiated a relocation plan with the tenants. Some moved into the new apartment units constructed in Phase One; some into Harbor Towers, the developer's project next door; and others elsewhere. All received 3-year leases and rents negotiated on the basis of their previous rents. There was no option to renew at the same rental.

Gardner Building. The developer had a somewhat easier time in securing a tenant for the Gardner Building. It was tentatively planned for residential use until it became possible to develop the building as a restaurant. The trust in 1970 had negotiated with a restaurant tenant to occupy part of the attic space in the Custom House, but code requirements called for mandatory state review of the project, and, in addition, the existing tenants were displeased with the action. The proposal died, and the prospective tenant then considered and turned down the Gardner Building. Another prospective restaurant tenant also turned down the Gardner space. Finally, the Chart House, a West Coast restaurant chain, settled on the site. The Chart House chain has created an image for itself partly by locating its restaurants in older buildings. For example, its first restaurant on the East Coast (Boston has the fourth) was housed in a brush factory.

The first phase of construction was performed by the developer-owner (or the trust) acting also as general contractor with the architect to provide construction management services on a cost-plus basis. Although the Gardner Building was still owned by the trust, the Chart House restaurant was allowed to perform all leasehold improvements to its own specifications.

Public Approvals

The Boston Zoning Commission had zoned the Long Wharf property M-2, light industrial use, so it was necessary to go to the zoning board of appeals to seek a change. This is the procedure for most major projects in Boston, and it is not considered a problem, provided the BRA agrees to the change.

The property was rezoned B-8-U, a general business district that would allow for the variety of uses planned by the developer. The "U" designation provides for design review by BRA of rehabilitation projects as well as new construction.

The zoning approval was granted without any specific parking requirements. There could be no requirement since the BRA owned the wharf. At present the restaurant pays a nominal rent to the BRA for the use of parking space.

Two building codes have been in force during the project. In 1970 Boston adopted a new building code, which had taken 3 years to draft and implement. In January 1975, this code was superseded by a state code for all buildings. Most of the work done on Long Wharf has been carried out under the 1970 Boston city code. The architects estimate that it would have been far more difficult to complete the rehabilitation had the 1975 code been in force.

Exterior Reconstruction

Custom House. The historic district designation dictated that the exterior of the building be preserved intact. The Redevelopment Authority was interested in the building's facade. Hence, exterior reconstruction involved merely the removal of a few fire escapes, a careful cleaning of the granite and brick, and the replacement of windows.

Gardner Building. As with the Custom House, very little was done to the exterior of the restaurant. The building was cleaned and the mortar repointed; the windows were replaced; authentic shutters were added; and minor repairs were made on the slate roof.

The Chart House restaurant has constructed brick and cobblestone terraces at the front and rear of the building under an agreement with the Redevelopment Authority which owns the land. The purpose of the terracing is to serve customers from the rear patio. At all times there remains, as part of the agreement, a 30-day notice requirement for the Redevelopment Authority to come in and take over the outdoor space.

Interior Reconstruction

Custom House. The transverse masonry walls separating the Custom House into nine separate buildings or bays were pierced with new arched openings to create corridors. Modern egress stairs and a new elevator were installed, connecting to a new central lobby on the first floor. An old freight elevator at one end of the building has been upgraded to comply with code requirements for safety.

The vacant attic space was converted into 29 luxury apartment units through the construction of a mezzanine level over the attic floors. This allows for duplex apartment units, each with a large private balcony. Because of the building's internal design each apartment is spatially unique. The design approach has been to expose the structural elements of the building, the brick bearing walls, and the timber beams. All new partitions and floors were finished through the use of oak trim—custom-built oak stairs, hardwood floors, and kitchen cabinets. A new central heating system, new wiring, a complete new sprinkler system, central TV antenna, and television monitoring system tied to a lobby intercom have also been installed.

Code requirements dictated that fire separation be established between floors in the Custom House. Floors had consisted of one to three layers of 1-inch, rough-cut boards over structural beams. The developer put 3 inches of concrete over the planks and topped this with hardwood flooring. Three inches was the minimum amount of concrete necessary to prevent the concrete from cracking.

Utilities were distributed along a new horizontal corridor formed by raising the level of the central hallways on each floor, making it necessary to step down into individual apartment units. At present there are two heating systems in the building—a hot water system serving the new residential and office components, and a steam unit serving the rest of the building. Originally the attic in the Custom House was not insulated. The harsh Boston winter and conversion of the attic to residential use necessitated some insulation, but it was not possible to do this on the inside without losing the eclectic potential of exposed ceiling beams. The solution was to add another roof to the existing slate roof. A polyurethane sheet was laid over the roof followed in succession by 2 x 4s, insulation between the 2 x 4s, three-quarter-inch sheets of plywood decking, new roofing paper, and finally shingles.

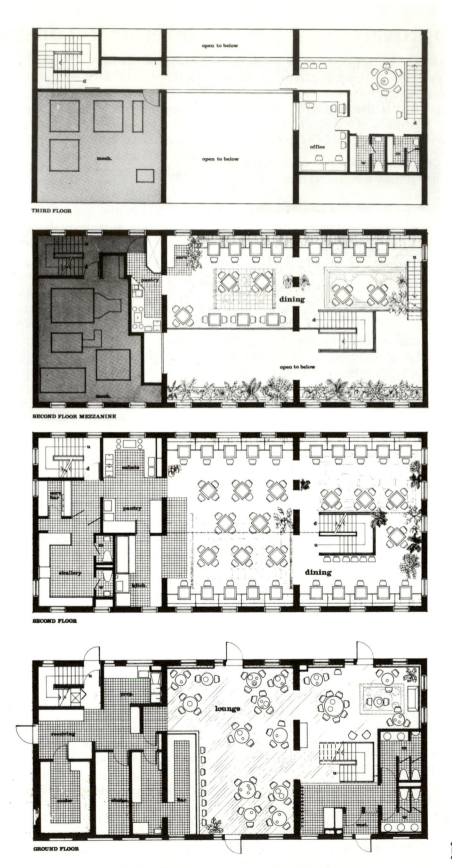

THIRD FLOOR

SECOND FLOOR MEZZANINE

SECOND FLOOR

GROUND FLOOR

2-71 Chart House restaurant floor plans.

2-72　Interior of a fifth floor duplex apartment. Exposed ceilings made it necessary for insulation to be installed from the outside.

Gardner Building. Using the same technique employed in the Custom House, the architects cut through the two masonry party walls, building arches from the bricks removed to make the openings. The architects matched the original mortar in color, the brick was then sandblasted, and the original beams and timbers were cleaned. The building still employs tie rods connected to starplates for support. A new floor was constructed out of existing beams and planks. Because the building is given over to public occupancy, the building code requires that restaurant service be limited to two floors. The solution was to remove two-thirds of the third level to create a mezzanine, which by law can only be one-third of the area of the second floor. The ground floor is a cocktail lounge; the second and mezzanine levels serve as dining space; the manager's office and mechanical equipment comprise the old attic.

The placement and routing of new mechanical equipment always presents a problem in older buildings, especially in those used primarily for warehousing. Vertical distribution is achieved by constructing flues similar in appearance to the old ones. The central air distribution system is routed in soffits and banquettes on the perimeter of the space, and the condenser units are concealed in the old roof structure in order to maintain the building's historic profile.

Natural gas was not available on the site in sufficient quantity to be used for heating and cooking. The restaurant chose gas for cooking and electricity for heating. Subsequently, and before the restaurant opened, the gas company upgraded its capacity to serve both cooking and heating, but the restaurant kept the two systems. The building is heated by a heat pump system assisted by a heat recovery wheel which transfers (and cleans) the heated air from the broiler exhaust to the ventilation air. It was necessary to cut through the roof on both sides to install louvres in order to transfer air from the outside through the heat pump system to the restaurant and to maintain the original character of the slate roof as much as possible. It is estimated that although this system is more expensive to install, it is 30 percent more efficient than other systems.

2-73 Rear of Custom House Block facing west. Note the angular bend caused by bays of different sizes.

Like the Custom House, adequate insulation was a problem. The BRA's wish that nothing be done to change the slate roof required that the architect seek an interior solution. Two inches of urethane insulation were placed in the spaces between the roof joists and covered with the planking from the original third floor which had been removed to create the mezzanine.

Detailing of the interior was made as consistent as possible with the character of the old building. A new sprinkler system had to be installed. The requirement that exit signs be lettered in white on a red background was fulfilled by lettering on the red brick background.

Description of Completed Project

The Chart House restaurant, occupying the Gardner Building, took 6 months to rehabilitate and was operating by September 1973. It is one of the chain's most successful restaurants, earning a profit in its first year of operation.

Phase I of the Custom House Block renovation which consisted of 29 rental apartment units in the attic space, and the rehabilitation of some commercial and office space on the other four floors, was completed in 1973. Phase II which involved the rehabilitation of more commercial space, the cleaning of the exterior, and the construction of corporate offices for the developer has also been completed. This latter operation involved taking two of the duplex apartment units on the fifth floor for office use and combining them with much of the fourth floor space. Left to be done is completion of Phase III which is the conversion to office space of the 1940-vintage residential units on the third floor and of one apartment on the second floor.

2-74   Much of the Boston waterfront has already been recycled. Commercial Wharf can be seen in the background.

Financing

The terms of acquisition financing were set with a commercial bank. The structure was acquired by the trust from the Berenson Corporation in 1970 for $525,000 with a standard cash and purchase money mortgage of $220,000 at approximately 6 percent. Construction also received standard financing and amounted at the end of Phase I to $2.1 million. The terms were set with the Harvard Trust Company and represented the first time local money had been invested in a Boston waterfront rehabilitation. Terms floated one point over prime and eventually converted to 8.75 percent.

The permanent financing is with State Mutual Life, a standard conversion of construction financing. It was difficult at first to interest banks in permanent financing since the agreement which the trust had negotiated with the Boston Redevelopment Authority for redevelopment constituted, in the investors' eyes, a lien on the building. The wording of the agreement was renegotiated to remove the stigma of a lien.

Though several subsidies were applied for through state agencies, based on the buildings' historic status, these applications were rejected. Total ownership remains with the trustees, and there are no outside investors or tax shelter benefits.

Of the $2.1 million construction loan, the trust picked up the cost of installing two water services—sprinkler and domestic—for the Chart House restaurant at a cost of $3,000. The rest went into the Custom House. Chart House acted as its own developer spending $587,000 for leasehold improvements, furnishings, and kitchen equipment.

Market

The residential portion of the Long Wharf project appeals to upper-income tenants who are able to afford high monthly rentals and enjoy the unique experience of living in an old warehouse. This part of the project is completely occupied with a waiting list as well. In constrast, the developers have trouble keeping the 40-story Harbor Towers project fully occupied.

Commercial tenants in the Custom House Block include two antique stores, a furniture store, and a preparation kitchen for the Chart House restaurant. Office tenants are concentrated in the design and legal fields and include an architect, two lawyers, an advertising firm, and an engineering firm, in addition to headquarters for Wilder Manley Associates and the India Wharf Rats, a private club which had been located on the waterfront's India Wharf. By the end of 1975, all commercial/office space was occupied.

Operations and Management

Apartment rents in the Custom House Block are comparable to other projects in the Boston area; the aim of the developer is to keep the entire residential portion occupied. Efficiencies rent for approximately $375 per month; one bedrooms, $475 to $500, depending on size; and two-bedroom apartments rent for $675 and up.

Commercial space in the Custom House Block rents for $10 per square foot for the shell only, including heat, air conditioning, and lighting. This is comparable to other Boston projects of this type except for ground-floor commercial elsewhere which is higher. Three of the present commercial tenants were already occupying space when the developer purchased the property. The developer has no rent projections, and hence the operation is rather loose. Demand for both ground-floor and upper-floor commercial space is about the same. However, demand for the ground-floor space should escalate once the Redevelopment Authority finishes all its improvements on the wharf. Rents for commercial space are based on 3-year leases with standard increases based on local cost of living statistics.

The Chart House restaurant was attracted to Long Wharf because of its location. The trust and the restaurant negotiated a lower rental—$5.32 per square foot—in return for leasehold improvements. The lease runs 35 years, and the trust receives a percentage of gross sales.

The trust has entered into an agreement with Wilder Manley Associates for long-term management of the Custom House operation. Wilder Manley, however, does not manage the Chart House restaurant.

Yearly income for the Long Wharf property runs at 15 percent of the total project cost. By comparison, Harbor Towers (624 apartment units) managed by the same firm reports a yearly income of 12 percent of the total project cost ($33 million).

Experience Gained

- Designation of Long Wharf as a redevelopment area had the effect of locking the developer into a reuse scheme if he wished to retain the property in private ownership. Local officials at the redevelopment authority supported the project since it was consistent with their urban renewal plan to create mixed-use projects on the waterfront.

- The architects emphasize that reuse projects would be generally unsuccessful if strict compliance with the building code was mandated. Regulations must be flexible enough to cover solutions which meet the intent, if not the exact specification, of the ordinance.

- Warehouses and factories are generally attractive buildings for reuse. Structurally, they are overdesigned which, in the case of the Long Wharf buildings, often allows the developer a great deal of flexibility in accommodating all the proposed uses.

- It remains to be seen just what the parking implications will be for the Long Wharf project once the Redevelopment Authority upgrades the wharf according to its plan. The zoning classification has no parking requirement, and, at present, the Chart House restaurant leases land from the BRA for its parking requirements at a nominal rent. Moreover, construction of any more parking garages has been terminated by the Environmental Protection Agency. There is one public garage nearby which was constructed earlier in conjunction with Harbor Towers.

- Construction costs for Harbor Towers were $30 per square foot in 1970. The architects indicate that the residential portion of the Custom House was rehabilitated for approximately $25 per gross square foot and the commercial/office space for $22, but that $35 per square foot is a more accurate figure when costs to accommodate the rent control delays are figured in. The Chart House restaurant was rehabilitated at a cost of $42.02 per net square foot exclusive of kitchen facilities, furnishings, and terrace.

- It was felt initially that adaptive use projects would be marketable and profitable during periods when money was tight because of the monetary deterrents to new construction. However, adaptive use projects have continued to be profitable even as money has become easier to obtain.

PROJECT DATA

Land Use Information:

Site Area:[1]
Custom House .... 13,500 sq. ft.
Chart House .... 2,700 sq. ft.

Gross Building Area (GBA):
Custom House: .... 74,800 sq. ft.[2]
Chart House: .... 9,740 sq. ft.[3]

Parking: NA

Custom House Block:
Gross Building Area
(After Reconstruction) .... 79,325 sq. ft.
Net Rentable Area
(After Reconstruction) .... 73,495 sq. ft.
Non-Rentable Space
Mechanical .... 740 sq. ft.
Lobbies and Corridors .... 5,090 sq. ft.
Total .... 5,830 sq. ft.

Rental Space Allocation:

	Sq. Ft.	Percent of Total
Residential	29,145	39.6
Commercial/Office[4]	33,560	45.7
Phase III Office[5]	10,790	14.7
Total	73,495	100.0

Unit Information:

Type	No.	Sq. Ft.	Bathrooms	Rental Range
Efficiency	8	478-750	1	$375
One Bedroom	8	528-900	1	$475-500
Two Bedroom	13[6]	782-1,300	1–1½	$675+
Total	29			

Tenant Information for Custom House—Commercial/Office:

Tenant Classification	Sq. Ft. of Net Rentable Area	Percent of Total
Harbor Design (Furniture) ...	4,300	12.8
Chart House (Preparation Kitchen)[7]	1,420	4.2
Traders Block (Antiques)	800	2.4
Green Dolphin (Antiques) ...	800	2.4
Attorneys (Two)	3,900	11.6
Architect	1,500	4.5
Advertising Firm	1,130	3.4
Engineering Firm	5,015	14.9
Boston Pilots	1,800	5.4
India Wharf Rats	1,900	5.6
Berenson Corporation	6,300	18.8
Vacant (three)[8]	4,695	14.0
Total	33,560	100.0

Lease Information:

Custom House—Commercial/Office:
Rent: $10.00 per sq. ft., shell only, including heating, air conditioning, and lighting.
Length: 3 years
Clauses: Rent increases based on local cost-of-living statistics. No percentages.

Chart House:
Rate: $5.32 per sq. ft.
Length: 35 years, with two 5-year options to renew
Clauses: 6 percent of gross sales between $833,000 and $1 million; 5 percent of gross sales over $1 million.

Economic Information:
Acquisition Cost:
Total Purchase Price (both buildings): $525,000
Building Cost (both buildings): $6.21 per sq. ft. of GBA

Rehabilitation Cost:
Custom House: $2,097,000[9] or $28.53 per net sq. ft. (26.44 per gross sq. ft.)
Chart House: $42.02 per net sq. ft. exclusive of kitchen equipment, furnishings, and terrace

Utility Services	$10,000
Sprinkler	$18,000
Mechanical	$80,000
Electrical	$30,000
Plumbing	$35,000
General Construction	$35,000
General Contractor's Fee	$ 7,000
Roof Insulation	$ 5,000
Exterior Cleaning	$ 6,000
Minor Subcontractors	$74,000
(millwork, carpet, tile, drywall, shutters, etc.)	
Total Building Improvements	$300,000
Front and Rear Terrace	$50,000
Kitchen Equipment and Furnishings	$237,000
Total Improvements	$587,000

Notes:
[1] The Boston Redevelopment Authority owns Long Wharf. The developer owns only the buildings and their foundations.
[2] Not including basements but including attic.
[3] Includes attic.
[4] Includes two residential units taken over by the Berenson Corporation for office space.
[5] Includes conversion of old residential on floors 2 and 3 to office.
[6] Present two-bedroom residential space consists of 11 units since Wilder Manley Associates took two units for office space.
[7] Preparation kitchen and office.
[8] Tenants secured but spaces unoccupied at the time of this writing.
[9] Original construction loan was for $2.1 million of which $3,000 is included in Chart House figures for utility services.

Development/Ownership:
Trustees of the Custom House Block Trust
131 State Street
Boston, Massachusetts 02109

Architecture:
Anderson Notter Associates Inc.
77 Washington Street North
Boston, Massachusetts 02114

Structural Engineering:
Arthur Choo Associates, Inc.
230 Boylston Street
Boston, Massachusetts 02116

David M. Berg Inc.
570 Hillside Avenue
Needham, Massachusetts 02194

Financing:
Harvard Trust Company
Harvard Square
Cambridge, Massachusetts 02138

Chart House Restaurant Only:

Electrical Engineering:
Joseph V. Herosy
Mark 128 Office Park
140 Wood Street
Braintree, Massachusetts 02184

Mechanical Engineering:
W. N. Peterson Associates, Inc.
16 School Street
Manchester-by-the-Sea, Massachusetts 01944

Acoustical Engineering:
William Cavanaugh
3 Merrifield Lane
Natick, Massachusetts 01760

Old Mill Plaza

Although the most widely known adaptive use projects are in large urban centers, developers throughout the country are proving that adaptive use can be an economically viable investment in small cities and towns as well. In any location, the economics of an adaptive use project depend to a great extent on an accurate evaluation of the costs and market potential of the building involved. But other factors may also be at work in determining the ultimate success of an adaptive use development in a small town. An older building can have particular visual and historical significance, and a community may take special interest in the preservation of these physical resources. By recycling a building, a developer may also have an opportunity to develop a space which cannot be duplicated elsewhere and will attract attention because of its unique character.

Consider the case of Old Mill Plaza in Newton, Kansas, a city of 16,000 located 30 miles north of Wichita. As the only remaining 19th century mill complex in Newton, the building symbolizes the town's part in the birth and growth of the wheat industry in the Midwest. When demolition seemed imminent despite community protest, Newton resident Lloyd Smith stepped in to purchase the mill and inaugurate a second term of useful existence for the complex.

As owner of a company specializing in the manufacture of hand tools, Smith viewed the large and sturdy mill as suitable expansion space for his growing business. In addition to satisfying the needs of his own company, Smith's redevelopment of the mill provided 11,100 square feet of marketable professional office space. A rewarding business investment, Old Mill Plaza has also earned Smith a special award from the community in appreciation of the adaptive use project.

Opposite page: 2-76   An investment of $850,000 converted this small town mill complex into office and light manufacturing space.

Historic Overview

Bernhard Warkentin purchased the Monarch Steam Mill in Newton in 1886, 7 years after its construction by a builder now unknown. A Mennonite immigrant from the Ukraine who settled in Kansas in 1873, Warkentin is credited with introducing a new and especially hardy kind of winter wheat to the Midwest. This "turkey red" wheat quickly replaced other grains and became the single most important factor in the rapid growth of the midwestern wheat industry. Soon after his purchase of the Newton mill, Warkentin converted its machinery from stone rollers to metal rollers, a significant step toward improvement of the milling process for winter wheat. These innovations in the wheat industry made Warkentin one of the region's leading citizens, and he served in his later days as a banker, insurance broker, and philanthropist. He died in 1908 during a visit to Russia, when he was accidentally murdered on the Orient Express.

During three-quarters of a century of use, Warkentin's mill grew by accretion into a complex of interconnected structures. The original mill was a 40- by 50-foot brick building with a full basement and four above-grade floors capped by a mansard roof. Built to hold massive machinery and to withstand continual vibrations, the mill has brick bearing walls and an interior frame of heavy timber with 12-inch square posts and beams. When the mill building was enlarged, rough-cut fieldstone was used on the lower two floors, with brick above. Other pre-1900 brick additions included a long one-story office extension to the east, or front, of the mill and a one-story facility to the west to house the boiler room and mechanical systems. A two-story warehouse to the north is connected to the mill by a roofed passageway and loading dock. A 100-foot chimney stack adjoins the boiler room and a cluster of four concrete grain silos stand on the southern edge of the property.

The complex was purchased in 1948 by the International Mill Company, but milling operations were terminated in the 1960s. For a time the buildings were used as warehouses for a mobile home company, but in the early 1970s the mill was bought by partners from Newton and Wichita, who considered converting the buildings to commercial space. When an architect's estimate of the investment necessary for rehabilitation exceeded their expectations, the owners began demolition of the badly deteriorated buildings.

A group of Newton citizens, opposed to the destruction of the landmark, initiated a movement to save the mill. Although the owners were willing to sell the property to the citizens' group, not enough money could be raised in the community to make the necessary $2,000 down payment. This plight, however, led to Smith's purchase of the partly demolished mill in the fall of 1973.

Redevelopment Strategy

Although the immediate impetus for the purchase was the desire to prevent further destruction of the building, Smith's long-range goal was to return the landmark to an economically useful life. Located on Main Street at the southern end of Newton's commercial and business district, the mill seemed suitably situated for retail or office use. Conversion to a shopping mall was considered but rejected on the premise that Newton did not have an adequate market for such a facility. The developer saw a greater market potential for professional office space within the city. In addition, the S/V Tool Company had grown so in the 5 years since Smith assumed ownership that it was in need of expanded facilities. Smith decided to adapt the mill for rental offices and for his own corporate headquarters and light manufacturing operations.

To assist in the project, Smith engaged Charles Hall, head of an architectural firm in Manhattan, Kansas, and Earl Adams, a contractor-engineer from Newton. Both Hall and Adams had previous experience in rehabilitation work. The three worked as a team through each stage of planning, exterior and interior design, construction, and landscaping.

Zoning changes were not required since the property was already zoned for commercial and industrial use. Newton's city council agreed to vacate a small portion of city-owned land east of the office extension to allow construction of a walkway and curb along the edge of the building. The city retains an easement on the land fragment. The council also voted to allow rerouting and replacement of a section of public sewer lines, at the developer's expense. The mill complex has been listed on the National Register of Historic Places since 1970, but the city of Newton does not exercise any local controls over historic property.

Design Scheme

Design and construction work on the mill complex was phased over a 2-year period while decisions were made concerning the best redevelopment of each space. The key to the initial design for the project was to maintain flexibility, permitting rehabilitation work to proceed before final uses had been determined. Several spaces served temporary functions but were changed to permanent uses as the project progressed.

Adaptive use work has focused on the original mill building and the two additions to the front and rear. The warehouse is still used as storage and manufacturing space for S/V. The first floor of the mill serves as a public lobby with a spiral stair dropped to the basement and an elevator added for tenants on the upper floors. Outside access to the boiler room and the front office extension was kept to provide private entries for tenants in those areas. Throughout the interior the original brick and woodwork have been retained and highlighted as much as possible. Scuffs and scars on the timber posts from mill machinery remain as evidence of the building's original use. Other mill fixtures, such as the mechanisms for an old sprinkler system and a platform scale, have also been preserved. New materials, including a good deal of cedar, were used to fit in with the natural brick and wood. Offices have been custom-designed for individual tenants.

The design scheme called for restoration of the exterior, including careful reconstruction of the mansard according to the design of a fragment of the roof remaining from the demolition. The building was painted a pale yellow, a color thought to have been used extensively by Mennonite immigrants in this country. The south side of the property has been landscaped and developed for parking, and a concrete lot on the north provides access to and parking for the warehouse. Two small, freestanding structures—a drive-in film booth and a self-service gas station—were constructed in this north lot and are compatible with the mill complex in color and design. Exterior and interior signage was designed to be subtle and harmonious with the other building materials.

Future plans include an adaptive use for the cluster of silos on the southern boundary of the property as either offices or apartments. Development has been thwarted, however, by the problem of cutting openings in the concrete structures.

2-77   The former front office of the old mill now provides a private entry for one of the building's tenants.

2-78   Interior spaces, such as this office in the old boiler room, were custom designed for the tenants.

Reconstruction Sequence

The initial phase of work called for reconstruction of the demolished roof, exterior restoration and site work, structural repairs, replacement of the mechanical systems, and renovation of the first floor for use as offices for the tool company. The second phase concentrated on interior work, including preparation of the second floor and the boiler room for tenants. The third phase involved completion of the interior renovation.

At the time of purchase, the building and site were badly deteriorated from the years of neglect and from the beginning of demolition work. Remnants of several old wooden structures, underground tanks, and pieces of equipment had to be cleared from the south side of the site, which was regraded, partially paved for parking, and landscaped. The exterior of the building was scraped and repainted after attempts to sandblast or steam clean the brick were unsuccessful. Brick arches over all the window

2-79 Bare brick arches contrast with painted brick walls at the main entrance to the offices.

openings were cleaned and left unpainted, to harmonize with the pale color on the remainder of the building. All windows in the complex were replaced and the original wooden trim duplicated. Cornice brackets for the roofline were reproduced from sheet metal to resemble the originals.

Concrete underpinnings were added to the southeast corner of the mill which had settled unevenly over the years, but no other structural problems arose. All the mechanical systems were replaced and pipes for new water, gas, and electric lines were concealed. Each floor has forced air heating and air conditioning units (small enough to permit local servicing); this split system allowed individual units to be installed as each floor was renovated and occupied.

Working with the city inspector to satisfy fire and building code requirements, the architect added an enclosed fire stair to the mill building and placed a retractable fire door in the opening between the mill lobby and the office extension. A self-service elevator opens into the lobby.

The interior timber posts were cleaned by steam or sandblasting, but no finishes were applied. Plaster was removed from the interior walls, exposing brick and a portion of fieldstone which dates from the first enlargement of the mill building. Floors in the lobby and basement were covered with octagonal tiles imported from Mexico; elsewhere, carpets have been added. Rest rooms and a kitchenette were installed in the basement, which serves as a lounge for employees of S/V.

In the next phase of work, two suites were developed on the second floor—one as a dentist's office and one as a joint office for the architect and contractor of the mill project. Part of the floor was raised several inches in the dentist's office to facilitate installation of equipment, and several small spaces were created for labs, examination rooms, and a dark room. Public rest rooms were added on the second floor. The boiler room, designed to accommodate an accounting firm, follows an open-space plan with the old brick smokestack as its central feature. Original steel beams were exposed and used as support for a mezzanine with offices arranged around two sides. A triangular arch, outlined in brick, leads into a separate office, which retains the original pressed metal ceiling.

The third floor was converted into offices for a law firm during the third phase of redevelopment. The one-story front extension on the complex, formerly used as office space for S/V, is now subdivided into five rental offices, and the fourth floor serves as S/V's headquarters. A central loft was constructed, creating "found" space on the fourth floor, which has a ceiling height of 20 feet at the roof peak.

Description of the Completed Project

Upon completion of the third phase, Old Mill Plaza contained 11,100 square feet of rentable office space, out of a total of 33,000 square feet of building area. S/V occupies 3,000 square feet in office space and an additional 13,000 square feet for warehousing and light manufacturing. The mill complex site covers 3 acres and includes parking facilities for approximately 130 cars.

Financing

Smith acquired the mill property in two parcels. The mill, office additions, and south lot were purchased for $35,000 in October 1973, and the warehouse and north parking area for $40,000 in December 1973. The conversion of the mill has been financed through loans guaranteed by the Small Business Administration (SBA) rather than through conventional construction and mortgage loans. The developer did not encounter any problems in making financial arrangements but stressed that his growing company provided sound collateral for the loans.

Through the First National Bank of Newton, Smith received from the SBA a maximum loan of $350,000 at 9½ percent interest over 10 years. This loan covered the mortgage on the property and provided enough funds to complete the first phase of adaptive use work (replacement of the roof and mechanical systems, construction of the parking lot on the south side, and renovation of the first floor and basement). For the second phase of work (including preparation of the boiler room and the second floor for tenant occupancy), Smith borrowed $245,000 from the First National Bank of Wichita. This short-term loan at 10 percent was covered by personal guarantees. The work which had already been completed on the mill no doubt made the second loan easier to secure than it might have been had the project not been underway.

2-80 A contemporary gas station, installed in the parking lot, repeats the materials and colors of the old mill complex.

Since the project began in 1974, the maximum amount available in loans through the SBA was increased from $350,000 to $500,000. Smith recently negotiated a loan at the new maximum, using the funds to pay off the existing short-term loan and to refinance the mortgage. In addition, the new loan generated $100,000 in cash, used to complete redevelopment of the third and fourth floors.

Market

Old Mill Plaza offers high quality office space at a rental rate of $5.00 to $6.00 per square foot. Generally, rental offices in Newton are in turn-of-the-century buildings along Main Street, with rates as low as $1.00 per square foot and rarely over $2.00 to $2.50 per square foot. Often these buildings have been remodeled once or more over the years, but few of them have undergone extensive renovations. There is no available space which is comparable to the mill.

As the renovation got underway, the developer actively sought tenants for the complex: between November 1975 and February 1976 four major tenants moved into custom designed spaces. In addition to these office tenants (a dentist, a stock broker, an accounting firm, and a joint office for the architect and contractor of the mill project), the self-service gas station and drive-in film booth opened for business in newly constructed facilities in the north parking lot in the fall of 1975.

2-81 The warehousing and light manufacturing needs of the developer's hand tool company are served on the north side of the complex.

More recently, two law firms and two insurance agencies moved into spaces on the first and third floors when they became available in the late fall of 1976. To complete the project, Smith moved the offices of S/V to the fourth floor in January 1977, leaving space for five additional small tenants in the first floor office wing.

The complex, when fully occupied, will yield an annual rental income of $135,000, according to Smith's projections. He anticipates that operating expenses—including utilities, taxes, and maintenance—will absorb about 20 percent of this income. Because utilities are prorated, approximately 10 percent of the operating costs will be passed on to the tenants. Each tenant holds a 10-year lease.

Smith estimates he will have invested a total of $850,000 in the mill upon completion of the project. About one-half of this amount, or $400,000, has been used for basic rehabilitation of the building and grounds, including exterior restoration, replacement of the roof and windows, electric, water, and gas lines for the mechanical systems, and construction of the parking lots. The remainder has covered the finishing work for the interior, including public areas, rest room facilities, and customized spaces for the tenants. Excluding the warehouse (where rehabilitation work has been minimal), costs per square foot for the project run approximately $33 to $34. New construction for similar space, Smith estimates, would range from $40 to $45 per square foot, without the cost of the land. This places the adaptive use project at 25 to 30 percent less in expense than comparable new construction.

Experience Gained

- The character of the old mill complex is considered a substantial asset by the tenants, who are willing to pay high rents for their unique spaces. Not only do the tenants appreciate the buildings and their individual offices, but they are confident that the complex elicits a favorable reaction from clients as well. For the developer, this represents a conversion of the intangible qualities of the old building into tangible economic gain.

- Because Smith sought a Small Business Administration loan based on improving facilities for his own company, he did not encounter the typical stumbling block of many adaptive use projects: the necessity of lining up prospective tenants before rehabilitation begins in order to secure financing. The use of a loan from the SBA to finance the mill reuse points up the availability of funding sources outside of conventional lending institutions. Other federal programs which can be explored for assistance through loans or grants include Community Development Block Grants (HUD), Business Development Loans (Department of Commerce), Farmers Home Administration Business and Industrial Program (Department of Agriculture), and Historic Preservation Grants-in-Aid (Department of Interior).

2-82

PROJECT DATA

Land Use Information:
Site Area: 3 acres
Gross Building Area:

S/V Tool Company:	21,900 sq. ft.
Office Space:	11,100 sq. ft.
Total:	**33,000 sq. ft.**

Parking Spaces: 130

Tenant Information:[1]

Classification	Sq. Ft. of Net Rentable Area	Percent of Total
Stockbroker	500	4.5
Insurance	500	4.5
Dentist	1,500	13.5
Contractor/Architect of Project	1,200	10.8
Accountant	5,000	45.1
Attorneys (two)	2,400	21.6

Lease Information:
  Rent: $5 to $6 per sq. ft.
  Length: 10 years

Economic Information:
  Acquisition Cost: $75,000
  Building Cost: $2.27 per sq. ft. of GBA
  Rehabilitation Cost: $850,000

Notes:
  [1] Does not include gas station and drive-in film booth in the north parking lot.

Development:
Lloyd T. Smith, President
S/V Tool Company, Inc.
Old Mill Plaza
Newton, Kansas 67114
(316) 283-6038

Architecture:
Charles L. Hall
The Hall Associates
404 Humboldt
Manhattan, Kansas 66502
(913) 776-6010

Engineering/Contracting:
Earl Q. Adams
Smada Enterprises, Inc.
Old Mill Plaza
Newton, Kansas 67114
(316) 283-2600

Financing:
First National Bank
128 East Broadway
Newton, Kansas 67114
(316) 283-2600

First National Bank
P.O. Box ONE
Wichita, Kansas 67201
(316) 263-5711

Central Grammar Apartments

One response to decreasing school enrollments is to reduce class sizes and establish programs to address previously unmet needs and interests. The necessity of reducing expenses, however, has caused most communities to close unwanted schools and, in many cases, demolish the vacated buildings. The conversion of Central Grammar to 80 apartments for the elderly is another community alternative.

The Central Grammar building, near downtown Gloucester, Massachusetts, was opened as a high school in 1889. In 1924 the size was doubled, and in 1940, when a new high school was opened, the structure began its service as a grammar school, a capacity in which it continued until the building was closed in 1971, being considered no longer functional. Although no attempt was made to find an alternative use before abandonment, a number of proposals emerged once the Gloucester city council became responsible for the property. Suggestions ranged from a number of public uses to demolition and use as parking. All proposals which required demolition were rejected, however. Then, when the city council voted narrowly to appropriate money for a new municipal building, the way was left open for Action, Inc., a local nonprofit community action agency, to purchase an option on the property. The agency did so in June 1972 to reuse the structure as housing for the elderly. Finally, in 1974, the city sold the building to Gloucester Development Team, Inc., a nonprofit housing development corporation formed by Action, Inc., to handle the ownership and conversion of the school building.

Construction began in December 1974, and model units were opened for inspection in September 1975. Within 12 days, all units were rented. The first tenants moved in during mid-October, and no vacancies have since occurred. Central Grammar Apartments has helped meet the housing needs of the city's elderly while preserving a Gloucester landmark and enhancing the appearance and atmosphere of the surrounding neighborhood and the downtown area.

Opposite page: 2-83   Central Grammar was originally opened as a high school in 1889.

2-84   The Central Grammar building faces the historic city hall.

Gloucester is a fishing and shipping port of about 29,000 people (1970) an hour north of Boston. Central Grammar is in Gloucester's Civic Center District and is bordered on the west by a historic residential neighborhood. Nearby structures include a post office, the city hall, a library, a YMCA building, and a historical museum. To the south lies the central business district, where public transportation, restaurants, shopping, medical offices, and social services are within walking distance. Also within walking distance are Gloucester's harbor and several churches.

Redevelopment Process

Action, Inc.'s proposal for Central Grammar had considerable professional input and support, a circumstance which also gave it credibility at the beginning with the city council and later with others. New England Non-Profit Housing Development Corporation loaned the project $9,000 in seed money in 1972, and the greater Boston Community Development Corporation served as a financial and

125

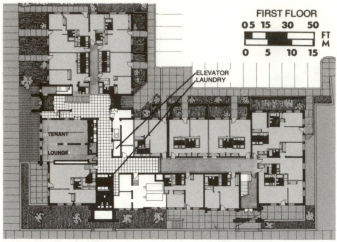

FIRST FLOOR
05 15 30 50
0 5 10 15
FT
M

ELEVATOR
LAUNDRY

TENANT
LOUNGE

TYPICAL FLOOR

FIFTH FLOOR
(Original Attic)

BALCONY

legal consultant. Senior Home Care Services, Inc., a local nonprofit community agency, also helped fund the project and was later involved in development and design. State agencies helped with financing (Massachusetts Housing Finance Agency) and staff costs (Massachusetts Department of Elder Affairs) when federal funds from the U.S. Department of Housing and Urban Development and the Office of Economic Opportunity were cut off in 1973. Community Research Applications, Inc., a private nonprofit environmental psychology consulting firm, donated its resources for social services planning as matching "funds" for the staffing grant.

The city council carefully monitored the development, requiring plan review at various stages. The council evaluated and approved the developer, the general contractor, and the tenant selection plan, which gives priority to Gloucester residents over 61 years of age. The city also retained the right to buy back the property in 50 years for $1. The city's support of the project took such form as a special tax treatment approved for the property by the city planning board, and a special permit, granted by the city council, for the construction of multifamily housing in the Civic Center District. The city also supported the formation of Gloucester Development Team as a nonprofit corporation.

Construction and mortgage loans were provided by the Massachusetts Housing Finance Agency, an independent state agency which lends money for rehabilitation and new construction of multifamily housing. MHFA, in granting loans, requires that at least 25 percent of the units it helps finance be reserved for low-income tenants. Other state subsidies were provided through the local housing authority under the state Department of Community

Affairs' 707 program, which reduced the rent of some units to a level affordable by the poorest tenant.

Central Grammar is owned by a 10-member, limited-dividend partnership, with the general contractor and Gloucester Development Team serving as general partners during construction. The contractor, who was required to guarantee completion of the project, agreed to become a limited partner once the building was 95 percent occupied. Having the general contractor tied financially into the venture obligates him to the project for almost 17 years, at the end of which time, if the project is disposed of through sale or foreclosure, the depreciation benefits allowable by the Internal Revenue Service are not subject to recapture. In addition, the local nonprofit Gloucester Development Team remains the sole general partner, and operating decisions thus remain in local hands. In the event the project requires a financial reserve, escrow accounts totaling $109,000 have also been established.

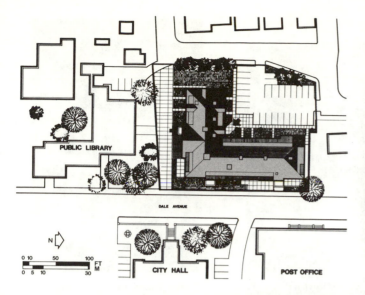

2-86

2-87 Balconies were cut into the original roof.
(Photo: Jerry Klinow.)

Design and Engineering Features

The Central Grammar building was constructed in the functional style of its time, with neoclassical details. As a school the structure contained 35 classrooms, an assembly hall on the third floor, a gymnasium on the fourth floor, a cafeteria in the basement, and an unused attic. The architect, in his design, tried to retain the beauty of the original school which was still sound at the time of conversion. To test some of his ideas, particularly for the less conventional floor plans, full-scale mock-ups were erected in the building in 1973, using wood studs, a type of corrugated board, and wrapping paper. Representatives of a number of Gloucester senior citizen groups took part in two design evaluation sessions.

The conversion makes more complete use of the building's space by including previously unfinished or unused space in the basement and attic. Throughout the structure, large hallways were retained and existing classrooms were used, where possible, for the apartments, producing units larger than those normally found in housing for the elderly. By lowering the sills of some windows to create doorways, all basement units were given direct access to private, fenced yards.

Apartments in the 1889 portion of the attic have living space on one floor and stairs leading to bedrooms on the floor above. Wooden trusses in this area were retained as architectural elements, but in the 1924 addition the roof was cut back along both sides to allow for recessed outdoor decks off the apartments. One entrance to the school building was glassed in and made into a living area in an apartment, and the basement entryway was converted into a main entrance and lobby. The coal room was rebuilt as a laundry and restrooms. In addition, former storage space was turned into a tenant lounge and small kitchen. Some of the original maple floors, oak wainscoting, and oak trim were retained, and ceilings throughout the building were lowered to 9½ feet. The structure is barrier free and has an elevator.

A Comparative Project

Another school had stood a number of blocks from Central Grammar but had been demolished a few years earlier, and a high-rise apartment building for the elderly was constructed on the site at the same time Central Grammar was being renovated. Although it is difficult to meaningfully compare any two development projects, the contrast between these two projects is informative. The average apartment in the high rise is two-thirds the size of the average at Central Grammar. In total development costs, the high-rise units averaged $25,666, whereas the Central Grammar units averaged $22,525. Rentable floor space is 61 percent of gross floor area in the new building, 79 percent in the renovation. The new building took about 18 months to construct and several months thereafter to fill with

2-89   A fifth floor unit. (Photo: Jerry Klinow.)

2-88   Central Grammar compares favorably with a new high rise for the elderly (top, center right).

tenants, whereas renovation of Central Grammar required 10 months, and all apartments were rented (and the tenants had begun moving in) within a month of completion. Finally, the high-rise units are uniform in layout and design, whereas the Central Grammar units vary in response to the school's former arrangement.

Tenants

Tenants at Central Grammar elect a committee to advise the professional resident manager on matters ranging from home improvements to health and social activities. A captain is also designated for each floor to check in with each tenant daily and to make sure that all residents are safe during emergencies. Each unit has a health alarm in the bedroom and bathroom. Nearby churches, the library, and the YMCA provide a wide range of recreational and social services. These organizations have established for Central Grammar residents an outing club, a bowling team, bingo matches, and a monthly covered plate dinner.

Most residents are retired, receive social security benefits, and have a fixed, limited income. All have had a long association with Gloucester; in addition, many attended or taught school in the building, and many still have family members in the area. Average age of the residents is over 60, although an agreement with the city provides that the age limit may be lowered to 54 if the units are not filled by Gloucester residents over 61 years of age.

2-90   Some ground floor units feature their own patios.

Experience Gained

- The use of original materials, finishes, and architectural elements can help make a project marketable. Old and new elements can be successfully mixed.

- By limiting structural change, money can be saved for amenities, quality fixtures, and special attention to details.

- Before schematics are developed, the original building should be well known to those making the architectural decisions.

- Unusual apartments—the result of retaining the original building configuration—are a selling point and help reduce the institutional feeling of a large apartment building.

- It is important to deal with professionals who have had successful experience with reuse projects.

- Previously unused areas of a building should be considered for living quarters.

- The developer of an adaptive use project should start as early as possible to work with fire department officials, the building inspector, and other public officials to assure them that the building can be made safe according to current codes and life safety standards. Codes required smoke detectors wired to the central fire station, audible alarms, hose cabinets, and standpipes, and the fire department required, in addition, a sprinkler system to cover all public areas. At one point, fire safety requirements nearly ended the Central Grammar project.

2-91

PROJECT DATA

Land Use Information:
Site Area: 43,000 sq. ft.
Total Dwelling Units: 80
Gross Density: 81 du per acre
Parking:
  Spaces: 27
  Ratio: 0.34 spaces per dwelling unit
Land Use Plan:

	Sq. Ft.	Percent of Total
Building	16,000	37.2
Landscaping	15,000	34.9
Drives and Paving	12,000	27.9
Total	43,000	100.0

Building Information:
Gross Floor Area: 72,500 sq. ft.
Net Rentable Area: 57,750 sq. ft.
Percent Rentable: 79.6

Unit Information:

Type	Sq. Ft.	Number[1]	Rent[2]	Bedrooms	Bathrooms
A	485–860	69	$185	1	1
B	846–993	7	$215	2	1
Duplex	750	4	$185	1	1½

Economic Information:
Site and Building: $96,000
Construction: $20.45 per sq. ft.
Amenities: $15,000[3]
Total Development: $1,802,000[4]

Notes:
[1] Consists of 21 low-income (Section 8 equivalent) units, 58 moderate-income units (subsidized through MHFA's bonding abilities), and 1 unit for resident manager.
[2] Includes all utilities.
[3] Includes landscaping and furnishings.
[4] Includes land acquisition and "soft" costs such as architectural, legal, filing, and survey fees, and interest.

Development:
Gloucester Development Team, Inc.
R. Kirk Noyes, Executive Director
159 Main Street
Gloucester, Massachusetts 01930
(617) 283-2135

Management:
Greater Boston Community Development, Inc.
177 State Street
Boston, Massachusetts 02109
(617) 227-7897

Architecture:
Anderson Notter Associates
77 North Washington Street
Boston, Massachusetts 02144
(617) 227-9272

The Cast-Iron Building

Conversion of existing structurally sound but functionally obsolete buildings to new and economically viable uses is becoming an increasingly important aspect of the development field. The conversion of The Cast-Iron Building from industrial to residential use is an example of how a historically significant structure can be preserved through recycling. Located on a 16,789-square-foot site in lower Manhattan, this building has been occupied by a variety of manufacturing concerns since being built in 1868. The most recent occupant was a shoe factory.

The five-story structure is of mill construction and faced with precast iron panels. This building style flourished in the decade following the Civil War and constituted the first indigenous American style of commercial architecture. It was also the first time precast components had been used in construction and as such, represented an important technological break-through. General awareness of the significance of cast-iron buildings, however, has only developed recently.

The developer originally intended to tear the structure down and construct an apartment building on the site. The property was purchased essentially for its land value. The decision to retain The Cast-Iron Building and convert it to residential use was made after it was found to be one-third cheaper to rehabilitate the structure than to replace it with new construction. This circumstance points out the primary economic opportunity to be derived from revitalizing older buildings, that of capitalizing upon their existing but underutilized structural value. In the case of The Cast-Iron Building, both the site and the structure lent themselves to new uses.

The property was acquired during 1972 and reconstruction was completed by the summer of 1974. All 144 units were rented within a 3-month period.

Opposite page: 2-92 A refurbished exterior conceals the new interior use for the cast-iron building.

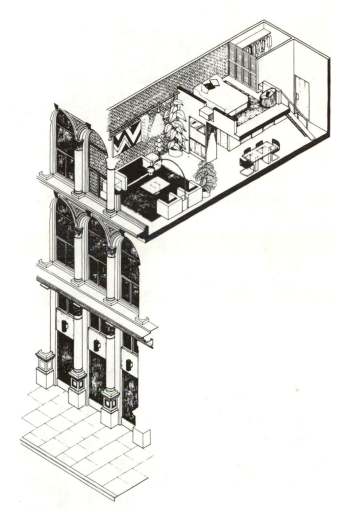

2-93 Section of a typical apartment.

The surrounding area is characterized by a mixture of multistory offices and industrial loft buildings. Most neighboring structures date back to the turn of the century and before. Built as a high-density shopping and industrial center in the pre-automobile era, this area has been functionally obsolete for many decades, and vacancy rates in the loft space are high. While the developer pioneered on this particular block, the proximity of Greenwich Village and several churches and apartment buildings constituted a stabilizing factor. As further conversions take place, the complexion of this area can be expected to change. The building occupies a corner site and covers almost the entire lot.

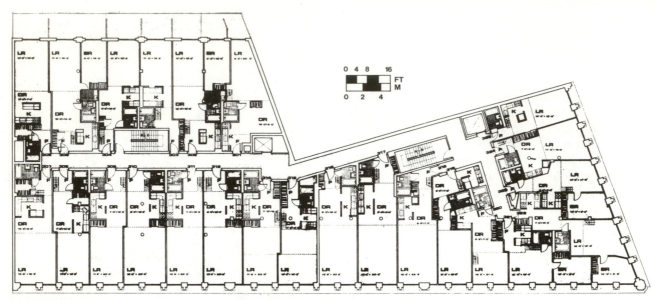

2-94 Third and fourth floor plan.

2-95 Apartment interior.

Planning and Engineering

Before reconstruction began, it was determined that the cast-iron exterior walls, interior columns, and heavy timber girders supporting the five floors were sound. No additional structural elements would be needed since the building had been originally designed to carry the heavy floor loads required for industrial use.

Reconstruction involved no major exterior modifications. Fire escapes were removed and replaced by two interior stairwells. The cast-iron panels which faced the building on its two street fronts were repainted the original buff color. The first two levels were sandblasted as well. A poorly constructed addition on the top level was removed and replaced with new construction.

In order to make the project economically feasible, two floors were added, one between the first and second levels and the other between the existing fifth floor and the top of the cornice. This modification resulted in an increase of internal space from 76,732 to 107,923 square feet of gross building area. The open bays previously used for industrial production were subdivided into apartments opening onto double-loaded corridors. Because of high ceilings, it was possible to add loft bedrooms to most units. An additional elevator was installed to supplement the existing one, and new hardwood flooring was laid throughout. The ground level, with 15,-532 square feet of commercial space, is occupied by five antique stores.

A modern style of interior decoration was adopted for the lobby and corridors since the new use in no way corresponds to the previous one. This was done by using recessed lighting, textured concrete block walls, slate flooring, and supergraphics. The cost of these changes was estimated to be one-third less than comparable new construction.

The Market

Location is a key factor in the market success of reconstruction and conversion projects. Whereas there are a great many structures which lend themselves to reuse, this approach becomes feasible only when the buildings are located where demand for new uses exists or can be created. In the case of The Cast-Iron Building, a previously unrecognized demand for unusual and sensitively designed apartment units was discovered. Because this was a large conversion and involved the reuse of a historically interesting building, the project received considerable publicity which gave it a competitive edge at a time when residential development in New York City was at a low ebb.

Single adults and working couples predominate in the mix. There are few children. Most residents have an artistic bent which caused them to seek out a unique living environment. A number of them have been sufficiently enthusiastic about their residences to make other improvements at their own expense.

Individual apartments are small, ranging from 500 square feet for efficiencies, to 900 square feet for the largest two-bedroom units. The project involves selling an environment rather than just space, and this is a trade-off many people are willing to make. The developer benefits in that a smaller unit size enhances the economic viability of a project while tenants have lower utility and other overhead costs.

Public Approvals

Existing zoning is C6-1, a high-density commercial zone which permits low residential densities. Intensification of the revenue-producing potential of the building was essential to the project's success and since the ordinance specified that structural bulk could not be changed, it was necessary to get a variance to make the conversion economically possible. The developer's original plan, with 150 units instead of the 100 units permissible in the C6-1 zone, was approved as a variance from the code by the Board of Standards and Appeals. Only 144 units were actually built.

2-96   Because of the high ceiling it was possible to add loft bedrooms to most units.

2-97   A modern style of an interior decoration was adopted for the lobby.

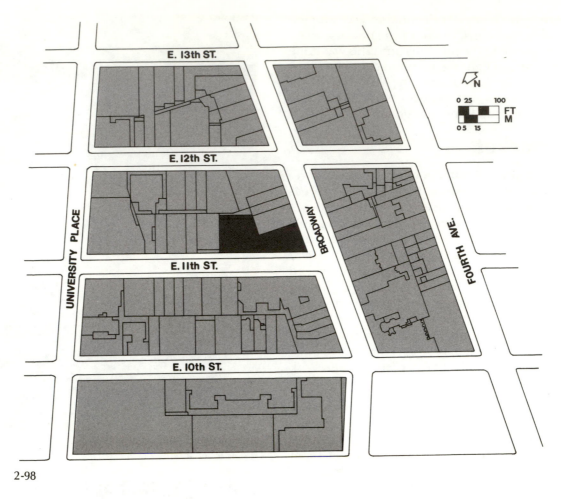

E. 13th ST.

E. 12th ST.

E. 11th ST.

E. 10th ST.

UNIVERSITY PLACE

BROADWAY

FOURTH AVE.

N

0 25 100
FT
M
0 5 15

2-98

Experience Gained

- Industrial loft buildings, with their open bays frequently occupying entire floors, are easier to convert to commercial than to residential use. Market demand, however, must ultimately determine what an older building is to be reused for.

- Although it might seem that the discovery of unexpected structural weaknesses or other physical problems would constitute the primary engineering difficulty to be faced in conversion work, these problems can usually be anticipated ahead of time.

- In many ways, conversion jobs are easier than new construction. Weather is less of a problem, and the construction time is markedly reduced. Careful supervision of the craftsmen is essential, however.

- The Greenwich Village type of tenant, although possibly unique in some respects, demonstrated a willingness, perhaps common to the public in general, to sacrifice space for a carefully articulated living environment.

- Many financial institutions are wary of conversion projects, particularly when a new or unusual approach is involved in which the developer is pioneering in a previously ignored location. This circumstance requires that the developer educate the banker in what he is trying to accomplish and seek to develop a mutual rapport.

- A traditional design approach to finishing the interior of the structure was judged to be both inappropriate and costly. Existing elements should be reused whenever possible. The developer capitalized on the unusual character of the building itself by sandblasting masonry walls and leaving the brick exposed in interior corridors. This represented a substantial savings and gave the end product additional character as well.

- Ultimately, the main difference between rehabilitation and new construction is that the developer working with an existing structure must be alert to its unexpected and unique opportunities.

PROJECT DATA

Land Use Information:

Site Area: 16,789 sq. ft.

Gross Building Area (GBA):[1]

Residential Space	92,391 sq. ft.
Commercial Space	15,532 sq. ft.
Total	107,923 sq. ft.

Total Apartment Units: 144

Floor Area Ratio (FAR):[2]   6.4

Project Density: 373.0 units per gross acre

Parking: No parking spaces are provided on site

Rental Unit Characteristics:

Unit Type	No. of Units	Rental Range	Unit Size	Bath-rooms
Efficiency	40	$300-$340	500-600 sq. ft.	1
One Bedroom	85	$450-$490	550-800 sq. ft.	1
Two Bedroom	19	$550-$650	700-900 sq. ft.	1
Total	144			

Economic Information:

Site Cost: $600,000

Reconstruction Cost: $3,200,000[3]

Notes:
[1] GBA—all square footage within the structure.
[2] FAR—gross building area divided by net land area.
[3] Includes all interior and exterior work.

Development:
Rockrose Associates, Inc.
Henry Elghanayan,
    President
31 West 16th Street
New York, New York 10011
(212) 674-3400

Architecture:
Stephen B. Jacobs
    Associates
19 East 57th Street
New York, New York 10022
(212) 421-3712

Structural Engineering:
Alvin Fischer & Robert
    D. Redlien, P.C.
167 Madison Avenue
New York, New York 10016
(212) 679-7740

Mechanical Engineering:
Harold Rosen Associates
95 Madison Avenue
New York, New York 10016
(212) 532-5498

Mercantile Wharf Building

The 120-year-old Mercantile Wharf Building on Boston's historic waterfront has been converted into 122 apartments and 13,400 square feet of commercial space. The glance of a passerby, however, would not be enough to detect the extent of renovation: the roofline and granite facade have been preserved, but the interior has been opened up with a seven-story atrium with skylights running the length of the building.

The development group was one of about 15 developer-designer teams to submit proposals in 1973 to the Boston Redevelopment Authority (BRA) to convert the vacant structure into apartments and neighborhood-oriented, ground-floor commercial space. Included in the proposal was the provision that at least 25 percent of the units be available for use as low-income housing, to be financed by the Massachusetts Housing Finance Agency (MHFA). BRA designated a development team for the project in 1974. The 15-month renovation was completed in June 1976. The project is in BRA's urban renewal plan for the Downtown–Waterfront–Faneuil Hall urban renewal area.

Multilevel duplexes and triplexes with lofts and skylights are in the roof structure on the upper two floors, and a variety of studio and one-, two-, and three-bedroom units are on the second through fifth floors. There is a total of 17 different unit plans. Forty-three units are available for low rents (tenants pay not more than 25 percent of their income), 42 units for moderate rents, and 37 units for market rents.

Opposite page: 2-100   The seven-story atrium with skylights running the length of the building.

The Site

The Fitzgerald Expressway or Central Artery, an elevated expressway built in 1952, separates Boston's central business district from its waterfront and North End neighborhoods. The Mercantile Wharf Building is situated next to the freeway on the waterfront side, overlooking a 4-acre park constructed recently by BRA. As a result, there is an unobstructed view of Boston's inner harbor from the building. A housing project for the elderly and other wharf buildings, some of which have been renovated for housing, are near the building on the other sides, and within walking distance are a number of colonial landmarks, including the Old North Church and the home of Paul Revere. Just on the other side of the freeway and also within walking distance are the newly renovated Faneuil Hall and Quincy Markets, the Boston City Hall, and historic sites in the business district. Pay parking is available for residents on lots near the project, and subway stations and bus stops are within walking distance.

2-101   Transverse section.

2-102   A virtually unchanged exterior viewed from Boston's waterfront park.

History

The 1857 building, designed by Gridley James Fox Bryant in the French Second Empire style, is in what has traditionally been called the Market District. Constructed on filled land, the building was designed primarily as a storage and distribution house for ship chandlers and sail makers. Since there was limited space on the waterfront, the commercial building went up several stories and each company occupied a small space. Items were brought in from the sea on the back side, and from the town on the front or Commercial Street side. The front was designed as offices and the back as the shipping room with a large door and a whip-hoist elevator system to haul goods to all floors, including the basement. The basement and middle floors were used for storage and by riggers who needed long, narrow spaces, while the sail makers used the loft, which was 26 feet at the highest, to bend, stretch, and sew their sails. The structure, measuring 100 feet in width, 450 feet in length, and 100 feet in height, originally consisted of 18 bays.

Land reclamation projects during the 1860s separated the building from the waterfront, and the use of railroads decreased the waterfront's importance. In the 20th century, food processors and packers occupied the building, and the widening and continuation of Cross Street through the block in the 1930s resulted in the demolition of several bays near the southern end of the building. A small part of this southern tip remained, although isolated, and was not removed until construction of the elevated expressway was begun in the early 1950s. Although structurally sound, the building's interior had fallen into disrepair by the 1970s. Only 12 bays (measuring 300 feet in length) of the original 18 remained for renovation.

Design and Engineering

The original construction employed granite-faced brick bearing walls with heavy timber floors and roof. The transverse brick bearing wall repeats approximately every 24 feet, and is 24 inches thick on the first two floors and 16 inches on the upper floors. Bearing walls in the basement are rough granite. From the Cross Street wall of the building, next to the expressway, 10 transverse bearing walls partition the building into 24-foot bays. The remainder of the building is a 40-foot section fronting on Richmond Street. The sixth and seventh stories are under a steeply pitched (30-degree), single-ridge roof, except for the Richmond Street section, which is under a hipped (but equally pitched) roof.

The renovation design, with the central atrium, was chosen because of the building's great width (100 feet), since a normal double-loaded corridor scheme would have resulted in very deep apartments with dark interiors. With the new design, each floor has a continuous balcony which is lighted from the glass roof. All units have entries directly onto these balconies, and some multilevel units have another private balcony in the atrium. The exterior has remained virtually unchanged.

To create the 24-by-100-foot core, the contractor removed the center sections of the transverse brick bearing walls, floor by floor, starting at the top. The apartments fit into the 24-foot bays and range in size from 535 to 1,540 square feet. The ground floor has 16 commercial bays, ranging from 450 to 1,325 square feet and accessible from both the street and the atrium.

Architecture

The renovation design capitalizes on the aesthetic qualities of the original building materials and emphasizes the various atrium views. Brick, stone, metal, and wood timber surfaces were left exposed and were sandblasted to restore their natural finish. Almost all remaining brickwork is in its original position, and the new columns, arches, and planters were constructed from brick torn from the core. In the roof-level units, the original trusses and skylights have been retained. Granite blocks, used as counterbalance cornices in the original structure, protrude as much as 2 feet into the apartments. New materials—including mosaic ceramic tiles, wood parquet flooring, and vinyl wall covering—complement the old. All windows and entrances have been replaced with black aluminum units.

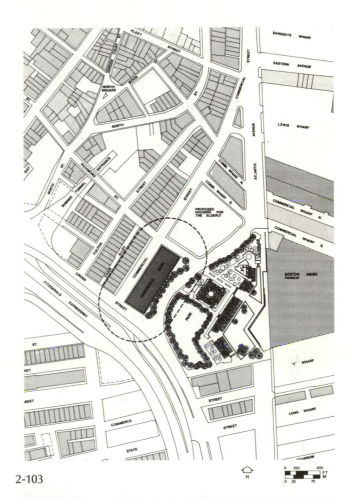

2-103

2-104   Facade facing the elevated freeway.

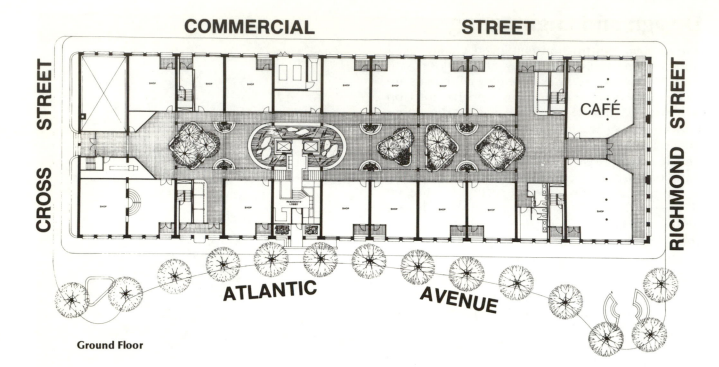

COMMERCIAL STREET

CROSS STREET

RICHMOND STREET

CAFÉ

ATLANTIC AVENUE

Ground Floor

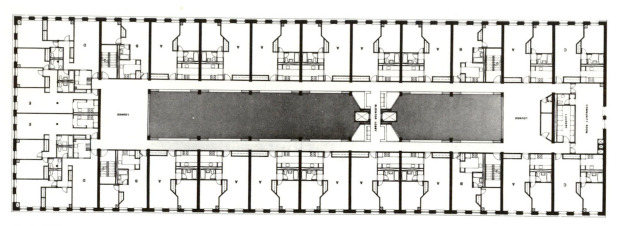

Typical Floor

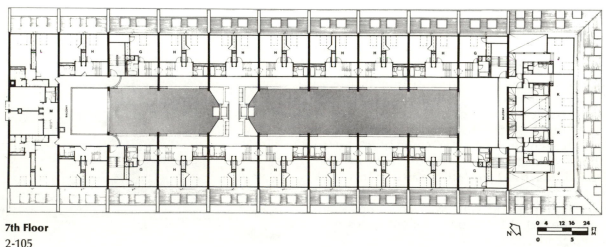

7th Floor

2-105

2-106   A café uses part of the atrium as a dining area.

Although the residents have a separate, attended entryway on the park side of the building, they travel to their floors by glass-walled elevators located in the atrium. The atrium shop level is organized around a pool, benches, and various shapes of brick planters with live trees, plants, and shrubs. A café on the Richmond Street side uses part of the atrium for its dining area. All shops look into the atrium, and some windows in the multilevel apartment units open into the core.

At the time of renovation, the construction cost of $21.70 per square foot was lower than comparable new apartment construction costs, which were $26 to $30 per square foot.

Market

In a market with a small supply of good units, the Mercantile Wharf Building—with its attractively renovated units and low- and moderate-income arrangement—had little difficulty being rented. During construction, 1,400 applications were received for the 122 units. MHFA required that 50 percent of the units be subsidized for the construction loan. The Boston Housing Authority under Section 707 subsidized 25 percent of the units to one quarter of the renter's income, and the Massachusetts Interest Reduction Program (Section 13a) reduced rents for another 25 percent of the units. All but 1,400 square feet of commercial space are occupied or committed through a contract.

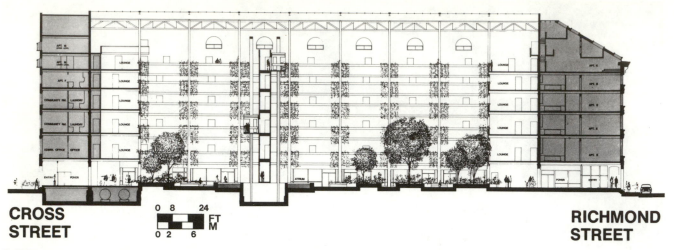

CROSS STREET

0 8 24
0 2 6 FT M

RICHMOND STREET

2-107 Longitudinal section.

Experience Gained

- An atrium is an asset in this project and is an obvious way of solving problems created by a building of great width; but the problems of maintaining and policing the atrium must also be understood. In an atrium design, one must take into account such matters as management, lighting, ventilation, and use of materials and plants.
- A close working relationship between contractor and building manager can solve many problems of detail and maintenance.
- Because of the need to preserve the building's historic exterior, views from the upper floors are limited; no vertical windows or balconies (only high, flush skylights) were permitted on the roof, to avoid spoiling the original appearance.

- A redevelopment authority in planned development should be specific in terms of neighborhood commercial use in residential projects to minimize incompatibility; being too specific, however, will make it harder for the developer to rent the space.
- In a multi-use project, entry to the apartments must be controlled and separated from the commercial space.
- In building renovation, the most difficult problems are generally related to foundation and framing.
- Success with BRA meant completing the required applications and studies on time and keeping in touch on changes and progress.
- IRS financing rules, allowing only 20 percent of the total building floor area to be nonresidential, prevented the use of mezzanine levels in the design of shops.

PROJECT DATA

Land Use Information:
Site Area: 0.88 acres[1]
Total Dwelling Units: 122
Gross Density: 138.64 du per acre
Parking: None[2]

Building Area:

	Sq. Ft.	Percent
Residential...............................	141,243	66.0
Commercial	13,444[3]	6.3
Atrium[4]	12,300	5.7
Circulation/Lounges[4]	41,400	19.3
Common Rooms[5]/Office	2,625	1.3
Mechanical	3,000	1.4
Total	214,012	100.0

Unit Information:

Type	Number	Sq. Ft.	Rents		Bedrooms	Bathrooms
			Market[6]	Subsidy[7]		
A (Studio, Standard, Duplex)	85	535–880	$490 (19 units)	$235 (66 units)	1	1
B (Standard, Duplex)	31	985–1,190	$580 (16 units)	$285 (15 units)	2	1½
C (Duplex, Triplex)	6	1,540	$650 (2 units)	$360 (4 units)	3	2
Total Units	122		(37)	(85)		

Economic Information:
Acquisition: $72,600[8]
City Site Improvement: $100,000[9]
Construction: $21.70 per sq. ft.[10]
Development: $23.83 per sq. ft.[11]

Notes:

[1] Developer project area is within the building line (0.71 acre, or 31,000 sq. ft.); the city of Boston improved the sidewalk area (0.17 acre).

[2] Sixty-one spaces at $35 per space per month are available for tenants at a nearby site, cleared by the Boston Redevelopment Authority but improved by developers of area housing projects.

[3] Includes the following retail uses: restaurant/café, furniture, dentist, hair salon, dry cleaners, jeweler, fast food and beverage, tobacco, stereo, and art supply.

[4] Atrium—2,050 sq. ft. per floor; circulation—6,900 sq. ft. per floor.

[5] Includes meeting rooms and laundries.

[6] Average monthly rents.

[7] Includes rents for 42 moderate-income units and 43 low-income units (not in excess of 25 percent of resident's income). Subsidy programs for permanent loan: HUD Section 707 (leased housing) and HUD Section 236 (interest subsidy).

[8] Purchased from Boston Redevelopment Authority.

[9] Includes granite and brick sidewalks, curbs, paving, lighting, and planting.

[10] Includes general conditions, excavation and site work, demolition, structure and finishing, plumbing, heating and air conditioning, electrical work, survey, permits, architectural fees, and general overhead.

[11] Includes interest, taxes, MHFA fee, insurance, legal, accounting, rentup, and marketing.

Development:
Mercantile Associates
3 Center Plaza
Boston, Massachusetts
  02108
(617) 724-0112

Architecture and Planning:
John Sharratt Associates
35 Fenwood Road
Boston, Massachusetts
  02115
(617) 566-3038

Management/Construction:
Peabody Properties, Inc.
Peabody Construction
  Company
536 Granite Street
Braintree, Massachusetts
  02184
(617) 848-2680

Airy View Condominiums

Is something new inherently better than something old? Will a new structure sell better on an open market than an old one? For years, the development community has answered yes to both of these questions and has shied away from rehabilitation. Recently, however, the picture has begun to change. Developers have been able to capitalize on an older building's hidden assets and they now regard reuse as a more attractive venture. It is very often the capitalization of these assets that makes a project successful.

One example of a successful reuse is the Airy View Condominiums in the Kalorama Triangle section of Washington, D.C. Built in 1911 as a luxury rental apartment building, Airy View has been converted into 20 condominium units, each selling for between $30,000 and $62,000. Typical of so many in-town garden apartments of its era, Airy View is brick, has three stories and a full basement, and is surrounded by a partially enclosed exterior courtyard which leads off a semicircular carriage drive. The building has 41,168 gross square feet, including the basement. The neighborhood generally consists of single-family attached dwellings of the same vintage and some newer brick garden apartments. In its heyday the building had 23 units, a spacious lobby, and an elevator. But by 1974, Airy View had fallen into disrepair. Fortunately, its deterioration was mostly superficial, and the structural condition of the building had remained basically sound.

The developer of Airy View is Marilyn Taylor, who had formerly worked for Inland Steel Development Corporation on its project to upgrade and reuse The Cairo Hotel, also in Washington, for rental apartments. The Airy View project was originally offered to Inland Steel but was turned down because of its size; Inland considered the project too small to justify the company's involvement. In December 1974, Marilyn Taylor, then on her own, was offered the project. She was skeptical of the project's overall feasibility, since the District of Columbia had recently placed a moratorium on the conversion of occupied rental apartment buildings to condominiums. It was discovered, however, that the building was vacant and was therefore not covered under the District's conversion law. With this obstacle removed, Marilyn Taylor decided to proceed.

The location of the project is excellent. The Kalorama Triangle section of Washington, part of the larger Adams-Morgan area, has undergone significant rehabilitation in the past 2 years. Another point in the project's favor was that there would be no protracted negotiations with District officials on zoning or building code issues; the city's building code is the same for apartments as for condominiums, and the building was already zoned R-5-B, so it was not necessary to get a variance for the condominium conversion. In addition, any rental apartment building built before 1925 was exempt from compliance with the city's current parking regulations because the District, until 1925, had no parking regulations for such buildings. Even so, if the developer had increased the residential density of the building by increasing the number of units, Airy View would have come under the city's parking requirements. But because there was actually a decrease in the number of units, from 23 to 20, the problem did not arise.

With two outside investors, James and David Carley of Madison, Wisconsin, Taylor formed a Subchapter S corporation, Carley Capital Group, Inc., to renovate the property. In April 1975, after a 3-month search for acquisition financing, the corporation purchased the property for $375,000. The corporation put $10,000 down on Airy View and financed the remaining $365,000 through a local savings and loan association at 10 percent interest with two points up front. The corporation hired Kent Abraham, an experienced local renovation architect, to plan the project. Renovation took 9 months, and the last unit was sold in April 1976.

Exterior Renovation

Exterior renovation consisted of merely repainting the existing window trim, installing a brick walkway from the carriage drive to the front entrance, and landscaping. The courtyard was sodded, and a few plants—azaleas, laurel, and pachysandra—were added. The previous owner had cleaned all the brickwork, and no repointing was necessary.

Opposite page: 2-109 Airy View was built in 1911 as a luxury rental apartment building.

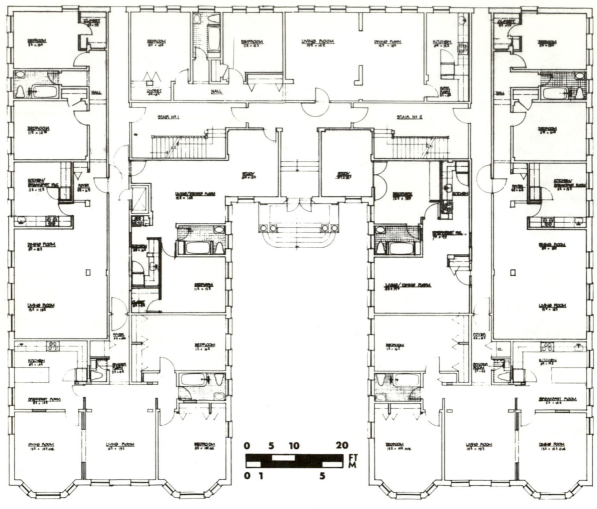

2-110   First floor plan.

Interior Renovation

The interior of Airy View required more work. The reconstruction sequence saw the developers renovate one unit immediately for use as a sales office, then begin interior demolition on one side of the building, proceeding around the building to the other side. New plumbing and wiring were installed, and each kitchen was equipped with trash compactor, dishwasher, refrigerator, and gas stove. Because the building's gas capacity could not be increased during conversion, three duplex units are serviced by electric stoves, and all units feature through-the-wall electric heating and cooling units.

The duplex units were created by cutting through ceilings and installing metal stairways with oak treads. The developer had originally considered using spiral staircases to allow more living space, but this was not permitted under the District building code. The developer worked with city officials to come up with a design which met the intent of the code without requiring too much space. In addition, part of the old lobby was closed off, yielding this space for a study in each of two apartments. In all, 15 units have been rehabilitated as two-bedroom condominiums, two as two-bedroom duplexes, two as one-bedroom condominiums with study, and one as a one-bedroom plus study duplex.

All wooden floors were retained, sanded, and covered with a polyurethane finish. The 10-foot ceilings and much of the original brass hardware have also been retained. An existing elevator was revamped.

2-111   Living room/dining room combination in a typical unit. Dining area is on a raised platform.

A laundry room has been constructed in the basement, and storage lockers have been provided for each unit. The on-site custodian's one-bedroom apartment in the basement, already in place when the building was purchased, has been upgraded. This apartment is not being used at the present, but the condominium association may later rent it out. The association has a working agreement with a custodian of a nearby building to provide maintenance services.

The basic room arrangement of most of the units remains intact. In a few units, however, kitchens have been moved and dining areas have been built on a 6-inch platform to provide some visual separation between the dining area and the living room and to hide the floor underneath, which in some cases, had served as part of the kitchen floor. In addition, the developer provided some custom renovation for the owners at a cost to them of approximately $20,000.

One surprise came up during the renovation process. Although only three stories, the building was reclassified by the city as a high rise, and city officials required the developer to install an electric generator, at a cost of $6,000, for hall and lobby illumination in time of an emergency.

2-112   Kitchen in a typical apartment.

2-113 Surrounding neighborhood in the Kalorama Triangle section of Washington, D.C.

Development:
Marilyn Taylor
Brighton Associates
2123 California Avenue,
  N.W.
Washington, D.C. 20008
(202) 232-6236

Architecture:
Kent Abraham
Office of Arthur Cotton
  Moore
1214 28th Street, N.W.
Washington, D.C. 20007
(202) 337-9083

Cost Data

The developer lists the rehabilitation cost of Airy View as $9.11 per gross square foot; comparable cost of new construction would be in the range of $25 to $30 per square foot. The local savings and loan, which made the acquisition loan, also provided approximately $375,000 in construction financing. This financial institution was impressed with the location of the project and granted the acquisition and construction loans on the contingency that they handle the permanent loan financing for the occupants. End-loan financing consisted of 90 to 95 percent, 30-year loans with 9⅛ to 9½ percent interest. The developer paid all closing costs, title work, and a one-point commitment fee on the end-loan package; purchasers were required to deposit 2 months' condominium fees in escrow. The project has made a moderate profit for the corporation.

Marketing

Very little marketing was carried out at Airy View; in fact, the project almost sold itself. Marilyn Taylor estimates that nearly $3,000 was spent on marketing for advertisement, the sales office, and its furniture. The project was not marketed to any particular age group, but the oldest of the original occupants, nevertheless, was 32. Units have been purchased by young couples and by single adults.

The project is being administered by a condominium association with a yearly operating budget of approximately $30,000. Dues average $110 per month and are based on the ownership interest in the association. Of the total budget, $17,700 is spent on utilities. The building has only one electric meter, allowing the association to get a commercial rate from the local electric company. Residents pay for the electricity for heating, cooling, lighting, elevator operation, and other normal uses for residential occupancy, as well as for the fuel oil required by the building's hot water heater.

148

Experience Gained

- It is better to use an experienced renovation contractor, even if the cost seems high. Marilyn Taylor acted as general contractor for Airy View, but it would have been better to subcontract out the renovation work. Renovation requires a great deal of close supervision and many on-the-spot decisions, since it is often impossible to predict all the changes that may be required. An experienced and trusted renovation contractor can make such decisions, thus freeing the developer from having to be on the site every day.

- It would be better to do a little more marketing to sell some units. One advantage of a rehabilitated building, however, is that prospective purchasers can see generally what the final configuration will look like, and, since the building is already up, marketing can begin sooner than with a new structure.

- The basement space at Airy View could have been used more effectively. Since there was a continuing demand for duplexes, even after the three duplex units had been sold, this basement space might have been used profitably as the lower level of more duplex apartments.

- It is sometimes better not to try saving old woodwork which has been buried under many layers of paint. Likewise, it is not always useful to save old window frames. In Airy View, although most of the frames were solid cherry, the developers now feel that all of them should have been replaced. Even so, many of the owners are refinishing the windows and moldings themselves.

- Redevelopment projects generally follow the same three criteria found with new projects: location, location, location. It is often impossible to interest lending institutions in a rehabilitation project unless the location is excellent. Even then, financing may be difficult if the institution strongly favors new construction.

2-114

PROJECT DATA

Land Use Information:
Site Area: 15,625 sq. ft.
Gross Building Area: 41,168 sq. ft.
Total Dwelling Units: 20
Parking: None

Economic Information:
Acquisition Cost: $375,000
Total Construction Costs $375,000

Electrical	65,000
Plumbing	35,000
HVAC	30,000
Sheetrock (including hallways)	70,000
Painting	30,000
Floors, refinishing	20,000
Carpentry	15,000
Kitchen cabinets, appliances	40,000
Demolition	15,000
Basement	15,000
Miscellaneous (roof, carpeting, landscaping, brick sidewalk, generator)	40,000

Building Cost:
$9.11 per gross sq. ft. of GBA

Construction Cost:
$9.11 per gross sq. ft. of GBA

Residential Unit Characteristics:

Unit Type	Unit Size	No. of Units	Price Range	Bathrooms
One bedroom + study	700 sq. ft.	2	$30,500-$31,500	1
One bedroom + study (duplex)	770 sq. ft.	1	$36,000	1
Two bedroom	1,200-1,400 sq. ft.	15	$48,000-$62,000	1-1½
Two bedroom (duplex)	1,195-1,200 sq. ft.	2	$56,000-$58,500	1½

Operating Expenses (1 Year):
Operation Costs

Utilities	$17,700
Janitorial	4,500
Trash Collection	1,200
Elevator Maintenance	1,500
Supplies and Equipment	300
Exterminating	500
	$25,700

Insurance Costs
Property, Liability, and Fidelity

Bond Insurance	$ 2,450
Legal and Accounting Services	500
	$ 2,950

Reserve Costs
Reserve for Working Capital

and Contingencies	$ 860
Reserve for Replacement of Common Elements	$ 860
	$ 1,720

Total **$30,370**

Guernsey Hall

Old mansions which have outlived their usefulness for single-family dwellings have typically met with one of two fates. Either they have been demolished to make way for new construction when no economic uses could be found for them, or they have been turned into museum pieces.

Guernsey Hall in Princeton, New Jersey, nearly met with the former fate, but today it is hardly a museum. The mid-19th century house, which was previously the home of Richard Stockton Field, New Jersey state attorney general, a founder of a short-lived Princeton University Law School, and U.S. Senator, is of stone masonry construction, designed in the Italianate villa style. Originally, the Field estate consisted of 40 acres, planted with trees from around the world. Now half of it is a public park, owned and maintained by the borough of Princeton. Guernsey Hall itself has been converted into five luxury apartments under a condominium form of ownership. Situated on an extensively landscaped 2.5-acre site, the mansion contains parking for residents and guests and a formal garden. The project has been completed and is occupied by its new owners.

Opposite page: 2-115 Guernsey Hall facing east from the formal garden which is part of the property held in common by all residents.

There was no precedent for luxury multifamily housing in Princeton. The mansion is located in an area of single-family detached houses on large lots, and there was some concern that the Guernsey Hall condominium would be the catalyst for turning other large and historic homes in Princeton into apartments—to some an indication of decline.

Historic Overview

Guernsey Hall was designed by Scottish-born, Philadelphia architect John Notman and was erected around 1852. The exact date is not known, but there is no evidence to suggest that the mansion, then called Fieldwood, was standing before 1850. The stone used for construction is a golden-yellow, local sandstone. Exterior trim is of brownstone and wood, the latter having been painted a deep buff color to blend with the stone.

There is a large, square, three-story tower, off center and pierced with arched windows. The house itself is bulky with low, hipped roofs of tin, accentuated by clusters of hexagonal chimneys. The west front terminates in two large bays. A cast-iron porch originally extended from the south front, the entrance, and around to the west side.

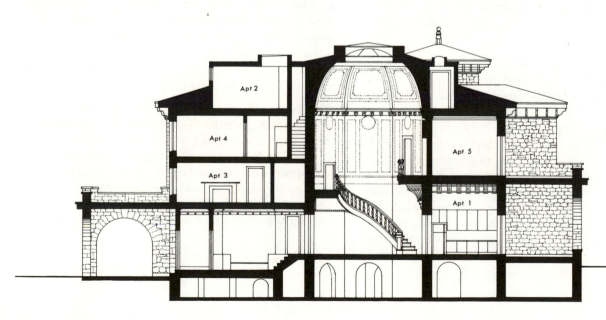

2-116   Cross section.

2-117   View of the south side which was the original entrance when the house was constructed. A cast-iron porch extended from this side around to the west (left of photo). It was replaced in 1912 with piers and arches.

All major rooms had marble fireplaces and elaborate molded plaster cornices. By far the most spectacular space in the house however, was the octagonal center stairway hall, rising 40 feet to a glazed dome. The walls here were painted trompe l'oeil to simulate stone. Around the walls rises a winding staircase, which has the effect of being supported by fluted, plaster corbels.

Field died in 1870, and one year later his heirs sold the property to Mrs. David Brown. In 1887, Mrs. Brown sold the property to Allan Marquand, who changed the name of the house to Guernsey Hall, after the English channel island of Guernsey, his ancestral birthplace. Marquand decided to modernize the house in 1912, which still depended on gas for lighting, on fireplaces for heat, and had only one bath. The house was enlarged by approximately one-third through a three-story addition with porte cochere on the north side of the house, and the carriage entrance was shifted to the same side from the south.

The cast-iron porch on the south and west fronts was removed and replaced, on the south front alone, with heavy piers and arches holding a flat roof. Many of the original marble mantels were replaced, but the elaborate plaster cornice work was left intact. The Minton tile flooring in the stairway hall was removed and replaced with hardwood. In addition, clear glass was substituted in the skylight for etched glass. Formal gardens were constructed on the west and northwest parts of the property, but only those on the west side remain.

The property was sold, in 1951, by the estate of Eleanor Marquand. When it was learned that the new owners would subdivide the property, approximately 20 acres were purchased by the Marquand daughters and donated to the borough of Princeton as a public park, called Marquand Park. Eventually the new owners sold off four house lots from the property on the south and west.

2-118   Front or north entrance was built in 1912.

Redevelopment Strategy

Guernsey Hall and the remaining 3 acres came up for sale in 1970 after the death of its last private owner. It was obvious that the house could no longer be maintained as a private residence although it had been zoned in a category (R-1) permitting only single-family residences.

The building came to public attention when a prospective purchaser wished to demolish the house and replace it with a combined house and studio for organ instruction. This was permissible under the existing zoning, which allows a home occupation if it is restricted to 40 percent of the total area of the house. For the additional space required by the organ loft the prospective buyer sought a variance from the zoning regulations. At public hearings, the opponents of the variance pointed out the historic significance of the building and its loss to Princeton if the mansion were razed. The building was in good condition as well. Opponents also objected to the proposed use and specifically to the noise that could be expected. The request for the variance was denied, but it was still unlikely that this 42-room mansion could be maintained as a single, private residence. William Short, who had testified at the earlier variance hearing, felt that a multiple dwelling would be the most feasible way to save the landmark. Others felt that conversion to office use for nonprofit institutions was possible, but no one actively pursued that route because of the objections of neighbors.

From the outset, the intent of the Guernsey Hall venture was to preserve a Princeton landmark and not necessarily to make a profit. Along with Short, eight other individuals formed a Subchapter S corporation, Guernsey Hall, Inc., with the intention of purchasing the property for conversion to a multifamily dwelling under a condominium form of ownership. Short felt that the project had to be a condominium since the interest of the corporation's investors was to save the building, not to become rental apartment owners. Moreover, rents would have had to be over $1,000 per month to justify conversion to apartments.

Guernsey Hall, Inc. entered into a nonconditional purchase agreement and took possession of the mansion in February 1972. The property was still zoned R-1 so it was necessary to petition the local zoning board for a use variance. The argument at a public hearing on the matter pointed out that the neighborhood would be worse off if the house was torn down and the acreage subdivided into five lots with an increase in roads, utilities, etc. Subsequently, the use variance was granted.

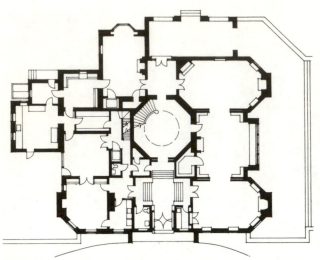
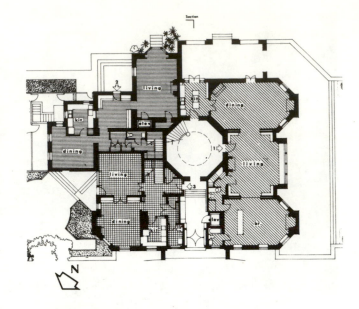

2-119   Pre-conversion and post-conversion floor plans.

Guernsey Hall, Inc. is a nonprofit Subchapter S corporation consisting of nine stockholders (there can be no more than 10). Three of the investors were Marquand daughters. Under this arrangement, the corporation can elect to have its income taxed directly to the shareholders, similar to a partnership, but it offers limited liability to the participants. Any losses in a Subchapter S corporation, however, cannot exceed the total of the capital stock and the loans by the shareholders to the corporation. Unlike partnerships, tax losses cannot be greater than the actual investment.

Financing

The nine shareholders made a capital investment of $95,000. In addition, the corporation borrowed $180,000 for construction from the Princeton Savings and Loan Association at 8 percent interest. The loan had a life span of 18 months. The corporation was allowed to borrow money as was needed and was only charged for money actually used. The mansion and grounds were purchased for $125,000, using $50,000 of the initial capital investment and $75,000 from the PSL loan. The remainder of the money was treated as working capital. In addition, a one-half-acre parcel was sold from the mansion grounds for $45,000. This brought the Guernsey Hall site down to 2.5 acres, and resulted in the irregular shape of the property, but helped make the project economics work satisfactorily.

Moreover, four out of five of the condominiums were presold and the down payments on them used as working capital. The last condominium was sold as an even trade for the new owner's existing single-family house. In all, the project incurred some $400,000 in construction costs.

Out of an initial capital investment of $95,000, shareholders have realized a return on that investment of only $89,000. However, most of the corporation's shareholders were in a position to realize some annual tax shelter benefits through operating losses during the construction period.

Redevelopment Process

Guernsey Hall, Inc. had two overriding design objectives: to save a fine, old, single-family residence by adaptation; and to keep as many of the good, original details as possible. Working from old drawings, Short, as project architect, tried to match the original stone color of the painted trim. In addition, a honeycomb concrete block was laid outside the north front and grass planted in the holes. This provided additional, inconspicuous guest parking. There were three garages standing when reconstruction began; two more were added, giving each unit one garage space plus at least one open space.

Interior reconstruction consisted of dividing the 42 rooms into six apartments, the sixth being a caretaker's apartment on the top level. The existing plaster and woodwork were retained wherever possible and the main stairway hall was repainted as it had been in 1912 to simulate stone.

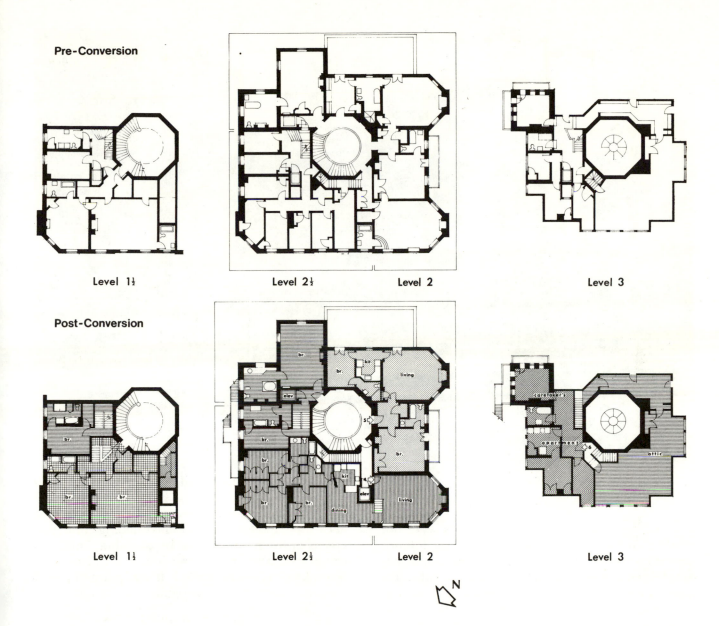

Pre-Conversion

Level 1½   Level 2½   Level 2   Level 3

Post-Conversion

Level 1½   Level 2½   Level 2   Level 3

In all, there are five different levels in the house. This was due to the fact that in many parts of the house, the ceilings are 14 feet high while in other parts they are 9 feet, a condition reflecting the original dichotomy between servants' quarters and owner's quarters. The former servants' sections also lack the elaborate plaster detailing on the ceilings and cornices of the owner's quarters.

In the redesign scheme, four out of the five apartments were each given one of the large formal rooms as a living room. One apartment received the original morning room and library, another the formal dining room, and the last two were given the large bedrooms. The fifth apartment, a duplex on the east side, consists of servant space entirely, but the owner is compensated for the coziness by a private garden.

2-120   Side view showing parking garages to one side. The fire escape was added to comply with code requirements and has been painted to match the trim.

Improvements to individual apartments were not made until the units were sold. In this way, interior amenities could be tailored to fit the individual tenant. The corporation had a base figure for individual unit improvements. If the tenant wished improvements which cost more, it was the tenant's responsibility to pay for them. Altogether, the five tenants spent over $60,000 in custom refinishing. The basement of the mansion consists of storage space for each unit, a workshop for the caretaker, and laundry facilities.

A passenger elevator existed in the mansion before reconstruction, but it was poorly located. It was incorporated as part of the largest condominium, which spans three levels, and a new hydraulic elevator was added in the vestibule of the main entrance.

Because of the New Jersey state building code, two means of fire egress had to be available. The large center stairhall provided one, and a new fire escape was added to the east front. It was painted a buff color to match the wood trim and the sandstone.

The state building code for multiple dwellings also stipulates that the main stairway under the dome in Guernsey Hall must be able to withstand a fire for 2 hours. Fortunately, there were 12 inches of brick wall under a plaster exterior which satisfied the code. In addition, doors which were considered to be primary apartment entrances off this main stairhall had to be switched from wood to steel. Moldings were applied to the flush steel doors to match the paneling of the original wood ones.

The statewide code also does not permit winders on stairs used for fire egress. An exemption from this portion of the code was secured to permit retention of the stairs when it was argued that the winders were, in fact, wider than an average stair without winders.

2-121   Interior of a duplex apartment consisting entirely of former servant space. This apartment lacks the elaborate plaster detailing on the ceilings and cornices of other apartments. Ceilings are only 9 feet high; the other apartments have 14-foot ceilings.

Description of Completed Project

The project was 80 percent complete by August 1973 with four out of five units occupied. The last tenant took occupancy in July 1974. With the exception of improved main entrance security, an elevator, and two new garages, the mansion looks very much as it did after the 1912 reconstruction. The formal garden still exists and is owned in common by all residents. A caretaker has been hired to maintain it. No trees have been removed, and, therefore, the site remains heavily wooded. Some of the specimens—cedars of Lebanon, yews, larches, horse chestnuts, white oaks, and beeches—date back to the days of Judge Field.

Market

There is no comparable project of this kind in Princeton. In fact, multiple dwellings are only now being introduced into the borough. Hence, the market for this type of project was unknown. Guernsey Hall, Inc. conducted a trial marketing study before it committed itself to rebuild. Of the 16 prospective purchasers, only two made firm offers, but it was on this basis that the decision to go ahead was made.

All of the tenants are or expect to be empty nesters for whom the cost was not the major consideration. The units sold in the range of $95,000 to $115,000. Since the project had remained in the public eye because of the variance proceedings, advertising expenses were minimal ($200-300). Four units were quickly bought either on the basis of the project's publicity or through referrals. A delay in selling the last apartment ultimately cost the corporation $4,025 in maintenance payments, while it was held for sale. A willing buyer was found for this unit initially, but because of difficulties in selling his single-family house he would not totally commit himself to the condominium. Renting the unit temporarily was decided against because that would require interior refinishing, and the corporation wanted it refinished for an owner rather than a renter. Also renting would have held up a possible sale for the period of the lease. In the end, the corporation made an even trade with the interested buyer, his single-family house for the condominium. It was reasoned that it would be less complicated to rent the house than the condominium. Subsequently, the corporation sold the house but only after the loss of $4,025 in maintenance due to the delay.

2-122 The 2.46-acre site is heavily landscaped. The fence at the left of the photo defines an outdoor patio space for the private use of the owner of the unit in Figure 2-121.

Operation and Management

Maintenance expenses in 1974 amounted to over $19,000. A major part of this—$10,000—goes to the caretaker. Because of the mansion's size a caretaker seemed mandatory although eight to 10 condominium units would have made the per-unit maintenance costs more palatable.

Expenses for ground maintenance, general fees, the caretaker's salary, liability insurance, and workmen's compensation are split evenly among the five tenants, regardless of ownership interest. Apartments are not metered separately, which saved the developer $2,000. In another project the developer would install separate metering. The initial intention was to charge for electricity on a pro rata share based on the number of outlets, regardless of occupancy time. In the end costs for electricity as well as building maintenance, fire and machinery insurance, and water were divided on a percentage basis according to ownership interest. Heating costs are allocated on a percentage basis according to the cubic footage, or volume, of each unit. Each apartment has individual hot water controls.

The administration and management of the condominium is vested in the Board of Managers of the Guernsey Hall Condominium. Each of the five unit owners designate one member. Until all of the units were sold the Board of Managers consisted of the board of directors of Guernsey Hall, Inc. Residents own their individual units from face of wall to face of wall and from floor to ceiling and are restricted from altering the central stairway hall, exterior cornices, windows, and doorways. Each unit owner has a joint access easement to use the common elements located in any other unit but serving his unit.

Units are served by a master TV antenna. Certain outside areas have been set aside for the exclusive use of individual tenants. The remainder of the outside space, including the formal garden, is common property.

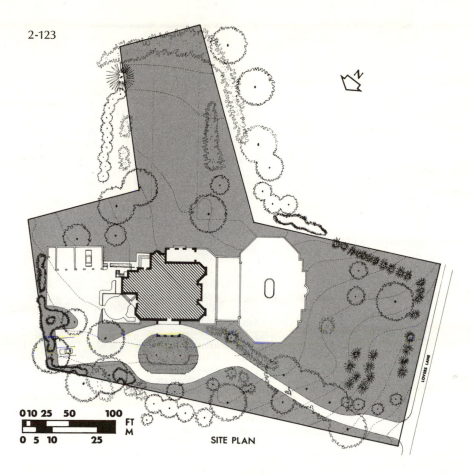

2-123

0 10 25 50 100 FT
0 5 10 25 M

SITE PLAN

Experience Gained

- Reuse, as an alternative to demolition and new construction, can be cheaper for a municipality. In the case of Guernsey Hall, which remains on the local tax rolls, the taxes collected are probably equal to or exceed the taxes that would be levied if five single-family houses were built. The reuse plan also creates less of a burden on city services—roads, sewers, schools, etc.—than would five single-family dwellings. In all, the tax assessments increased from $94,200 in 1972 to $383,600 in 1975.

- Without Notman's main center stairhall, it would have been more difficult to satisfy the building code requirements for multifamily housing. Overall, Notman's plan with thick masonry bearing walls throughout limited the flexibility in actually changing the spaces, but it made compliance with the fire code easier.

- Although it saved the developer $2,000, it would have been better to have installed five separate meters for utilities given the fact that the occupants own their individual units and that occupants now pay their percentage of heating costs regardless of whether they have used their share.

2-124   Part of the interior main stairhall.

- It probably would have been possible to charge more for the individual condominium units and thereby make up some of the loss to the investors. However, since four out of five units had been sold before rehabilitation, there was no way to make up for increased costs brought about by unforeseen circumstances. It might have been advantageous to have had some form of escalator clause built into the presale agreements, which would have accounted for the unforeseen circumstances.

159

PROJECT DATA

Land Use Information:

Site Area: 2.46 acres

Total Dwelling Units: 6

Project Density: 2.44 units per gross acre

Parking:
- Spaces: 12
- Ratio: 2 spaces per dwelling unit

Economic Information:

Acquisition Cost: $125,000

Land Cost: $1.17 per sq. ft.

Building Cost (Excluding Basement): $9.71 per sq. ft.

Construction Loan: $180,000 at 8% interest

Unit Information:

Unit	Sq. Ft.	Percent of Total	Rooms	Bedrooms	Bathrooms
Apt. 1	2,055	16.0	4	1	2
Apt. 2	2,707	21.0	6	3	3½
Apt. 3	2,085	16.2	5	2	2½
Apt. 4	1,613	12.5	6	3	2
Apt. 5	1,194	9.3	4	2	2
Apt. 6	933	7.3	4	1	1
Public Halls and Attic	2,280	17.7			
Total	12,867	100.0			

Rehabilitation Cost:

Exterior Work:

Painting and Trim	$ 4,000
Drive and Parking Area	5,781
Fire Escape	5,630
Landscaping	5,339
	$20,750

Interior Work:

General Construction*	$341,087
*Includes Besides Other Costs:	
Elevator plus Masonry Shaft and Structure	$30,000
Electrical Subcontract	46,924
Heating and Plumbing Subcontract	47,140
Kitchen Cabinets (Custom Type)	11,800
Metal Doors and Bucks—Apt. Entrances to Hall (Including Hardware)	3,600
Painting Restoration of Main Rotunda and Ceiling of Bedroom, Apt. 1	4,200
Finishing Wood Flooring	5,710
Painting	21,500
Appliances (Stoves and Dishwashers)	3,000
Furnishing and Carpeting	5,102
	$380,599

Other Costs:

Real Estate Commissions	$ 17,990
Legal Fees (Zoning Variance, Condominium Documents, 6 Sale Negotiations)	11,388
Architect's Fee	21,366
Interest on Purchase and Construction Loan	17,763
Insurance	3,566
Real Estate Taxes	9,704
Bookkeeping and Accounting	1,415
Fuel Oil (About 1 Season)	2,143
Water, Electric, Telephone	1,445
Grounds Maintenance	2,100
Building Maintenance	2,800
Maintenance Payments to Guernsey Hall Condominium for Apt. 4	4,025
Miscellaneous (Purchase Costs, Filing Fees, etc.)	1,590
	$ 97,295
Total	**$498,644**

Operating Expenses (1974):

Caretaker	$ 8,674.08
Care of Grounds	451.78
Interior/Exterior Repair	756.90
Accounting	277.00
Insurance—Workmens' Comp. and Liability	739.00
Insurance—Fire and Ext. Coverage	2,204.91
Reserve	1,000.00
Electric	2,349.17
Gas	520.15
Water	190.62
Oil (Heat)	2,318.17
Total	**$19,481.78**

Development:

Guernsey Hall, Inc.
c/o W. H. Short
10 Nassau Street
Princeton, New Jersey 08540

Architecture:

William H. Short
Short and Ford
10 Nassau Street
Princeton, New Jersey 08540

Management:

The Board of Managers of
The Guernsey Hall
Condominium
68 Lovers Lane
Princeton, New Jersey 08540

Financing:

Princeton Savings and Loan
130 Nassau Street
Princeton, New Jersey 08540

Part 3
Profiles

Catalog Directory

Introduction

Described in the following pages are 180 adaptive use projects, representing a total investment of more than $129 million. As an index of recent adaptive use activity throughout the country, this catalog illustrates a broad range of old and new uses and a diversity in size, cost, and financing techniques. Emphasis is on projects undertaken since 1966 by private developers, although a handful of public projects are also included. Conversions of buildings into private homes or into house museums have been excluded.

Project descriptions and tables are based on information supplied by developers or architects in response to a survey conducted by the Urban Land Institute. Projects are described in a brief analysis of the building type, focusing on its architectural development, construction characteristics, and general adaptability to new uses.

Catalog entries are arranged according to the original use of the building. The 10 categories covered are schools; theaters; railroad stations; public buildings (including courthouses, city halls, firehouses, and police stations); hotels, mansions, and apartments; carriage houses, garages, and stables; commercial and office buildings; mills; factories, warehouses, and industrial buildings; and miscellaneous (including churches, social halls, water towers, and gas stations). Projects within each category are listed alphabetically according to states and towns within states.

Tables have been compiled on the economics and physical redevelopment work involved in the recycling of the projects, and are given at the end of each category section. If a project does not appear on a table, the information was not made available to us.

For purposes of comparison, costs are broken down into acquisition (building and land) and redevelopment (construction, professional services, financing, and others). When costs per square foot were not supplied by the developer, an approximate figure has been computed by dividing redevelopment costs by gross building area. Estimates determined in this manner are indicated by parentheses. Because costs have not been adjusted to a single year, comparisons should not be made without considering the variables of time and inflation.

Buildings which are listed on the National Register of Historic Places (individually or within districts) or are designated as National Historic Landmarks are indicated by an abbreviation (NR or NHL) following the project name. The National Register is a federal listing of historically or architecturally significant structures, sites, and monuments throughout the United States.

Cross references, arranged according to geographical locations and new uses, are listed at the end of the catalog.

Opposite page: 3-1 One Winthrop Square was formerly the headquarters of the Boston *Record American*.

Schools

Shifting residential patterns and changing educational methods have made victims of many older school buildings left empty by declining enrollment, consolidation of schools, or construction of new facilities better suited to modern demands. As surplus property, these buildings pose a serious problem for school districts which cannot afford to maintain unused structures.

An important social institution, the school also is often a significant visual element in a neighborhood. The abandonment or deterioration of an old school—a symbol of continuity and stability from one generation to another—can have a negative effect both physically and psychologically on an entire community.

If a school building is not operating at full capacity, sharing facilities with other community programs (such as day care, vocational training, health clinics, centers for youth or for the elderly) may ameliorate the problem of underutilization. These supplemental uses not only may save a building from closing but also may increase its public service.

Rental or sale of a school building to another public agency offers an alternative if joint school-community uses are not viable. In Woodstock, Illinois, for instance, the county school board sold the high school to the city which converted the building into municipal offices.

An increasing number of school districts, however, are choosing to sell their property to private developers, often with a guarantee that the building will be rehabilitated for a predetermined new use. This option not only ensures preservation of the building but also returns the property to the tax rolls. The residential character of the neighborhoods in which many schools are located has encouraged their recycling as housing units, although redevelopment for office or commercial uses has also been successful in several areas.

Professional organizations, educators, and legislators across the nation have begun to address the problem of surplus schools. Educational Facilities Laboratories (EFL), a nonprofit corporation established to encourage constructive changes in school facilities, discusses the issue in *Surplus School Space: Options and Opportunities* (New York: EFL, 1976). This report, the most recent of several EFL publications on the subject, describes procedures for dealing with school closings and solutions for reuse. The American Association of School Administrators examines problems of energy conservation and physical obsolescence in *To Recreate a School Building* (Arlington, Virginia, 1976), a handbook which focuses on schoolhouse rehabilitation.

Two federal bills which would have a major impact on adaptive use of schools have been introduced in the Banking, Currency and Housing Committee in Congress. The Surplus School Conservation Act would make communities eligible for HUD grants of up to 80 percent of the cost of renovating schools for other productive purposes, and the Surplus School Conversion Act would allow a private developer to amortize purchase and renovation costs over a period of 15 rather than 30 years.

In the typical plan of an older school building, multiple self-contained classrooms are arranged on each side of a wide corridor. Reuse designs which retain this basic configuration of modular units opening onto a hallway are generally the most expedient and least costly. Developers of the Dewitt Building in Ithaca and the Assumption School in East Boston, for example, placed individual apartment units within the classrooms, minimizing the need for interior demolition.

School adaptive use designs can often capitalize on "found space," — underutilized or unused areas in gymnasiums, auditoriums, cafeterias, basements, or attics. In Gloucester, Massachusetts, useable square footage in the Central Grammar School increased from 60,000 to 72,500 through redevelopment of the basement and attic and through an addition of an intermediate floor within the original two-story auditorium.

In most states strict code standards must be met by buildings which are used as public schools. Because of these requirements, the heating, electrical, and fire alarm systems of a school building which has not been vacant for an extensive period of time may still be in working order. Repair of systems rather than their total replacement may be enough to meet the needs of some new uses.

Ironically, while some communities are seeking new uses for surplus schools, others are converting non-school buildings, such as factories and hotels, into educational facilities. This reverse phenomenon has saved many school boards both time and money in having to construct new buildings. Frequently, space can be leased rather than purchased, alleviating the need for bond issues or voter referendums on school construction. Industrial buildings in particular may offer flexible interior spaces which can be adapted to open classroom schools or can accommodate special vocational programs.

Several private colleges and universities have also undertaken innovative reuse projects. Described elsewhere in the catalog are the conversions into educational facilities of such diverse buildings as a railroad station and an automobile club in Baltimore and a resort hotel in St. Augustine, Florida.

1 Barton Academy (NR)
Mobile, Alabama

Origin:	Barton Academy, 1836
Conversion:	Offices for county school board, 1969
Developer:	Mobile County Board of School Commissioners, Mobile
Architect:	March-Holmes, Architects and Engineers, Mobile

Redevelopment: Constructed in 1836 by the New Orleans architectural firm of Gallier and Dakin, Barton Academy became the first public school building in Alabama. After classroom use was discontinued in the mid-1960s, the Greek Revival building was converted to school administrative offices for about $2 million. Redevelopment of the three-story brick structure concentrated on restoration of the exterior, including the rooftop cupola and dome, and renovation of the interior.

2 Griswold's Old School House
Claremont, California

Origin:	Claremont High School, circa 1911
Conversion:	Commercial use and theater, 1974
Developer:	Griswold's Restaurants, Inc., Claremont
Architect:	Willis K. Hutchason, Los Angeles

Redevelopment: As part of a large hotel and dining complex, the former school now contains restaurants, a 640-seat theater, an art gallery, and 30 retail shops. The Spanish-style buildings, constructed of reinforced concrete with tile roofs, were purchased for $600,000 and redeveloped for $3 million. Because no conventional financing was available for the conversion, the project was undertaken through the private earnings of the development company.

3 Old Town
Los Gatos, California

Origin:	Grammar school, 1923
Conversion:	Commercial use, 1965
Developer:	Max Walden, Santa Cruz
Architect:	Frank Laulainen, Los Gatos

Redevelopment: Acquisition and conversion of the stuccoed grammar school, which contains 45,000 square feet, totaled $573,000. The developer had to change lending institutions with each expansion of the project. Rental rates for retail tenants are approximately $6 per square foot.

4 Woodstock City Hall
Woodstock, Illinois

Origin:	Woodstock Central School, 1906
Conversion:	Municipal offices, 1975
Developer:	City of Woodstock
Architect:	John Vincent Anderson, Woodstock

Redevelopment: City offices, located in Woodstock's municipally owned opera house since its construction in the 1890s, were moved to the school in 1975 when restoration work on the opera house began. The conversion of the two-story brick school which had served for several years as a county courthouse annex, was financed through general revenue sharing. Original classrooms are subdivided by moveable partitions to give flexibility to the offices. City council chambers occupy the school assembly room. The former school is a block from the old McHenry County Courthouse and Jail, now reused as shops and restaurants (see case study.)

5 Center Stage
Baltimore, Maryland

Origin:	Loyola High School and College, 1856
Conversion:	Performing arts theater, 1975
Developer:	Center Stage Associates, Baltimore
Architect:	James R. Grieves Associates, Baltimore

Redevelopment: Vacant since 1941, the school complex provided an answer to the needs of Center Stage after the theater group's original facility burned in 1974. Located in downtown Baltimore, the building was sold by the Maryland Province of Jesuits to the city for $200,000; the Jesuits then donated this amount to the theater and the city sold the building to Center Stage for $5. Additional funding for the project came from a grant from the National Endowment for the Arts ($100,000); a fund drive ($150,000); and loans from a five-bank consortium ($300,000), from the city ($200,000), and from the Ford Foundation ($750,000 at 8 percent over 5 years). The first phase of redevelopment on the five-story brick structure covered 40,000 of the total gross building area of 95,000 square feet and was completed within 10 months in 1975. Work included developing a 500-seat auditorium with a balcony and "open thrust" stage, a two-level entrance lobby, a 150-seat restaurant, offices, and rehearsal space. The second and third phases will add a 300-seat theater, a restaurant, apartments for visiting actors, classrooms, and more rehearsal space.

6 Assumption House
Boston, Massachusetts

Origin:	Assumption School, 1890
Conversion:	Mixed-income apartments, 1975
Developer:	East Boston Community Development Corporation, Boston
Architect:	Childs, Bertman, Tseckares, Boston

Redevelopment: Classroom spaces in the three-story brick school were converted into 12 mixed-income housing units within a 10-month period. Apartments utilize both attic and basement spaces with a gross building area of 20,000 square feet. The Massachusetts Housing Finance Agency provided construction and permanent mortgage loans for the $228,000 project, which received a commendation from the Boston Society of Architects.

7 Central Grammar Apartments
Gloucester, Massachusetts

Origin:	Central Grammar School, 1889
Conversion:	Apartments for the elderly, 1975
Developer:	Gloucester Development Team, Inc.
Architect:	Anderson Notter Associates, Boston

Redevelopment: A local nonprofit community action group successfully campaigned for conversion, rather than demolition, of the old school despite initial city skepticism. Eighty apartments for tenants over 55 were designed for the building, which is located within Gloucester's civic center district between a residential neighborhood and the central business district. Redevelopment of the basement and attic spaces increased the gross building area to 72,500 square feet. Basement apartments have at-grade entrances with private yards, and attic apartments are either duplexes or feature outdoor terraces. Construction and mortgage loans for the $1,482,350 project were provided by the Massachusetts Housing Finance Agency. The city of Gloucester, which sold the school for $96,000, retains the right to repurchase the property in 50 years for $1.

8 Marvin Gardens
Clinton, New York

Origin:	Marvin Street School, 1892
Conversion:	Apartments, 1977
Developer:	Gaetano Realty Corporation, Utica, New York
Architect:	Ronald G. Armstrong, Clinton

Redevelopment: Classroom units in the two-story Romanesque-style school are being converted into eight one-bedroom and eight two-bedroom apartments. The 18,000-square-foot structure was purchased for $27,500. Development costs are carried by the developer on a current note account, with permanent financing solicited after substantial enough occupancy to overcome anticipated resistance by lenders to a speculative conversion.

9 German Village Center (NR)
Columbus, Ohio

Origin: St. Mary's School, 1887
Conversion: Offices, 1972
Developer: Kinetic Ventures, Inc., Columbus
Architect: Nitschke-Godwin-Bohm, Columbus

Redevelopment: Acquired for $72,000, the brick school house was converted to offices at a cost of $600,000. The renovated structure, with a gross building area of 19,929 square feet, is within a 233-acre historic neighborhood which has undergone residential and commercial revitalization since 1960.

10 SEDCO, Inc.
Dallas, Texas

Origin: Cumberland Hill School, 1888
Conversion: Offices, 1971
Developer: SEDCO, Inc., Dallas
Architect: Burson, Hendricks and Walls, Dallas

Redevelopment: Located on a prime downtown site, the two-story brick school building seemed doomed for demolition when the school board put the property up for auction in 1969. Instead, the building was purchased for $1.3 million and adapted by the president of SEDCO, Inc. as corporate headquarters for the international drilling and pipeline company. In order to recapture the character of the original design, the building's flat roof was replaced with a hipped roof, a cupola was reconstructed, and 20th century additions to the building were painted to blend in with the earliest part of the structure.

11 Southwest Craft Center at Old Ursuline (NR)
San Antonio, Texas

Origin: Ursuline Academy, 1851-1882
Conversion: Craft center, 1971
Developer: Southwest Craft Center, San Antonio
Architect: Ford, Powell and Carson, San Antonio

Redevelopment: Acquired gradually as gifts from private individuals, four buildings from the old Ursuline Academy in downtown San Antonio have been converted to new uses as a craft school. A former dormitory building houses a gallery, restaurant, and weaving rooms; the old cookhouse serves as the kiln complex; the chapel contains classroom and concert facilities; and another structure holds a printshop and studios for wood-working, pottery, and photography. Ongoing redevelopment work has included restoration of the earliest academy structure (1851) which is architecturally significant as an example of rammed-earth building construction in the United States. Construction funds have been received from the Economic Development Administration ($180,000), the Texas Historical Commission ($30,000), and the city of San Antonio ($50,000).

12 Old Female Charity School (NR)
Fredericksburg, Virginia

Origin: Female Charity School, 1835 (with 1903 addition)
Conversion: Offices, 1977
Developer: Female Charity School Partnership, Fredericksburg
Architect: Mary Ellen Wheeler, Fredericksburg

Redevelopment: The brick, Federal-style school, little-changed since its construction almost 150 years ago, has been adapted as professional office space with as few alterations as possible. An $85,000 construction loan from a local savings and loan was converted to a permanent mortgage upon completion of the redevelopment. The two-story building, which contains 3,000 square feet, was 100 percent rented before construction was finished.

3-2 St. Mary's School in Columbus, Ohio, was converted to office use at a cost of $600,000.

Project Economics
Schools

Project	Year of Conversion	Gross Building Area (sq. ft.)	Acquisition Cost	Redevelopment Cost	Approx. Cost Per Sq. Ft.	Source of Financing	Rental Rates (annual per sq. ft., unless otherwise noted)
Barton Academy	1969	60,000	Already owned	$2,000,000	$(33.33)	Public school funds	(not rented)
Griswold's Old School House	1974	75,000	$ 600,000	3,000,000	(40.00)	Retained earnings	$6.00
Old Town	1965	45,000	123,000	450,000	10.00	S&L	$6.00
Woodstock City Hall	1975	—	50,000	188,661	13.90	General revenue sharing	—
Center Stage	1975	Total 95,000 (Phase I) 40,000	5	1,800,000 (Phase I)	35.00 (Phase I)	Public and private grants and loans	(not rented)
Assumption House	1975	20,000	40,000	228,000	(11.40)	State finance agency	—
Central Grammar Apartments	1975	72,500	96,000	1,482,350	20.45	State finance agency	$185/mo./1 br, $215/mo./2 br
Marvin Gardens	1977	18,000	27,500	225,000	12.50	Development costs borne by owner-developer on current note account	$250/mo./1 br, $300/mo./2 br
German Village Center	1972	19,929	72,000	600,000	(30.11)	Local S&L	$9.00
SEDCO, Inc.	1971	40,000	1,362,667	1,000,000	25.00	—	(not rented)
Southwest Craft Center	1971	40,000	Gifts	260,000+	—	Private and public grants	(not rented)
Old Female Charity School	1977	3,000	60,000	55,000	(18.33)	Local S&L	$6.50

Dashes indicate data not available.
Figures in parentheses were not supplied directly but were derived from other data.

Redevelopment Work
Schools

Project	Exterior Restoration	New Exterior Construction	Structural	Mechanical	Interior Demolition	Interior New Construction	Site Restoration	New Facilities, Parking	Landscaping
Barton Academy	Extensive	Moderate	Moderate	Extensive	Extensive	Extensive	Moderate	Moderate	Moderate
Griswold's Old School House	Moderate	Moderate	Extensive	Extensive	Moderate	Moderate	Extensive	Extensive	Extensive
Old Town	Extensive	Extensive	Moderate	Extensive	Extensive	Extensive	Extensive	Extensive	Extensive
Woodstock City Hall	None	Minor	Moderate	Moderate	Minor	Moderate	Extensive	Extensive	Extensive
Center Stage	Minor	None	Extensive	Extensive	Extensive	Extensive	None	None	Minor
Assumption House	Moderate	Minor	Minor	Extensive	Extensive	Extensive	Moderate	Extensive	Moderate
Central Grammar Apartments	Moderate	Minor	Extensive	Extensive	Moderate	Extensive	Minor	Minor	Moderate
Marvin Gardens	Moderate	Minor	Minor	Extensive	Moderate	Extensive	Minor	Extensive	Moderate
German Village Center	Extensive	Moderate	Moderate	Extensive	Extensive	Extensive	Extensive	Extensive	Extensive
SEDCO, Inc.	Extensive	Extensive	Extensive	Extensive	Extensive	Extensive	Extensive	Extensive	Extensive
Southwest Craft Center	Moderate	None	Moderate	Extensive	None	Minor	Extensive	Moderate	Extensive
Old Female Charity School	Minor	Moderate	Minor	Extensive	Minor	Minor	—	Moderate	Minor

Dashes indicate data not available.

Public Buildings

Although architectural styles have changed dramatically, a common theme of dignity, strength, and permanence has remained in the design of public buildings throughout two centuries of American history. These buildings are physical symbols not only of government institutions but also of community pride.

Expenses were seldom spared during the construction of state capitals, courthouses, city halls, and federal office buildings, and designs generally represented the highest standards of the period. Stone or brick, because they were more durable than wood, were used on exteriors, and interiors were often lavished with rich details. Public buildings are generally the most monumental and impressive structures in large cities, and in small towns they may be both the visual focus as well as the physical gathering place for the downtown area.

Unfortunately, the future of many older public buildings is now uncertain; office space has been outgrown, and older firehouses, jails, hospitals, and other structures have become obsolete. Demolition of a familiar public building may cost a community a vital landmark in terms of historical associations, social significance, and urban design. Adaptive use of public buildings by the private sector, however, represents an alternative to continued public use or to demolition, often with the economic bonus of returning a property to the rent rolls.

Post offices, firehouses, libraries, and other small buildings often are suitable for a single new use, such as a store, office, or restaurant. Larger buildings may present more complex reuse problems which can best be solved by joint public and private cooperation.

Three recent studies, helpful to both private developers and government planners, have focused on strategies for conserving public buildings. Public responsibility for preservation is stressed in *Federal Architecture: Adaptive Use Facilities* (Washington, D.C.: Federal Architecture Project, 1975), a task force report funded by the National Endowment for the Arts as part of a review of federal architectural policy. In *A Courthouse Conservation Handbook* (National Trust for Historic Preservation, Washington, D.C.: Preservation Press, 1976), the challenges of rehabilitating older courthouses for continued use are explored. *Recycling Public Buildings*, a Planning Advisory Service Report by Judith N. Getzels (Chicago: American Society of Planning Officials, 1976), discusses public and private opportunities and incentives for reuse of surplus schools and civic buildings.

Many of the legislative and policy decisions which determine the role of public agencies in the conservation of public buildings also affect private sector involvement in adaptive use of this kind of building. On the federal level, individual agencies are required under law to inventory their real estate, nominate all eligible structures to the National Register of Historic Places, and undertake proper steps for maintenance and preservation of buildings in the Register.

The purchase, construction, alteration, or sale of federal buildings, however, comes under the jurisdiction of the General Services Administration (GSA). Surplus federal buildings which are of historic or architectural value may be transferred without charge from GSA to state or local governments, under the Surplus Properties Act of 1944. Although transfers originally were limited to buildings which were to be used as museums or historic monuments, an amendment in 1972 expanded the Act to allow transfer of buildings for compatible revenue-producing purposes.

This new provision gives local governments an opportunity to use former federal buildings for municipal purposes, such as offices, schools, cultural centers, or to initiate a public-private cooperative reuse effort by leasing all or part of a building to a private developer. The city rent return from a private tenant, over and above the cost of restoration and maintenance, must then be for public preservation, park or recreational needs.

The city of St. Paul was among the first municipalities to take advantage of the new amendment by accepting title to the Old Federal Courts Building in October 1972. The structure is being reused as a metropolitan cultural center with art galleries, theaters, restaurants, and shops.

In more recent federal legislation, the Public Buildings Cooperative Use Act authorizes GSA to acquire or lease historic structures for adaptive use as office space and encourages mixed (public-private) use of existing federal buildings.

Unlike historic federal buildings, surplus public buildings under state or local ownership often can be transferred directly to the private sector. The method of transfer, however, may depend on a complex equation of public interests rather than on a simple choice of the highest bid. For instance, a structure may be donated rather than sold to a private nonprofit organization for use as a museum or youth center if a public agency feels the reuse of the building will be of general benefit to the community.

In the sale of a public building, the highest offer may not represent the best prospect for long-term tax revenue returns to a city. Because a rehabilitated building pays a much greater annual property tax than an at-grade parking lot, a low bid which proposes adaptive use may be financially more rewarding to a city than a high bid which proposes demolition.

Transfer of a public building may also be contingent on the fulfillment of certain obligations by the buyer. These restrictions can take the form of deed covenants—such as prohibiting demolition of the structure—or they may be written into the purchase agreement. The sale of the Dewitt School in Ithaca, New York (see case studies), for example, stipulated that the developer had to invest $500,000 in conversion of the building into mixed apartment and commercial units.

Alternatively, a public agency can lease rather than sell its surplus property. A long-term lease arrangement offers certain advantages to both the public owner and the private developer. Through its choice of a lessee, the public agency retains some control over the use of the building. Reuse is achieved without cost to the community and the building produces a steady rental income. The private developer, on the other hand, escapes the high cost of acquisition of a property and may have an easier time in securing renovation financing. Old City Hall in Boston and the National Bank of the Commonwealth (formerly a courthouse) in Indiana, Pennsylvania—both award-winning adaptive use projects—represent successful applications of long-term leasing arrangements of public buildings to private developers.

**13 Mobile County Department of Pensions and Security (NR)
Mobile, Alabama**

Origin:	Mobile City Hospital, 1834
Conversion:	Public administrative offices, 1975
Developer:	City of Mobile
Architect:	Grider and Laraway, Mobile

Redevelopment: In a cooperative effort between the city and the county of Mobile, the former hospital (closed in 1966) was returned to public service as county offices. The exterior of the three-story building, a fine example of Greek Revival architecture, was restored. A private donation of $500,000 initiated the project with additional funding of $600,000 each from the city and the county.

**14 Cooper House
Santa Cruz, California**

Origin:	Santa Cruz County Courthouse, 1895
Conversion:	Commercial uses, 1971
Developer:	Max Walden, Santa Cruz
Architect:	None

Redevelopment: The rich interiors of the buff brick courthouse were largely preserved in the $600,000 conversion to a shopping complex. Two commercial banks and a savings and loan were products of the redevelopment of the building which contains 21,000 square feet. Interior features of the Richardsonian-Romanesque structure, an architectural style which is uncommon on the West Coast, include a circular stained glass dome.

**15 Customs House (NR)
Wilmington, Delaware**

Origin:	U.S. Customs House, 1855
Conversion:	Offices and bank, 1976
Developer:	Customs House Square Associates, Wilmington
Architect:	Victorine and Samuel Homsey Inc., Wilmington

Redevelopment: Designed in 1855 by Ammi B. Young, Supervising Architect of the U.S. Treasury, the Customs House needed only minor remodeling for its conversion to commercial banking and other office needs. The two-story building, an early example of fireproof construction, is part of a 14-acre downtown redevelopment project, which also includes extensive new construction by Customs House Square Associates.

16 Old Idaho State Penitentiary (NR)
Boise, Idaho

Origin:	Idaho State Penitentiary, 1870-1911
Conversion:	Historic, recreational, and commercial complex, in planning stage
Developer:	Idaho State Historical Society, Boise
Architect:	Not designated

Redevelopment: On a 510-acre site, the state-owned penitentiary is undergoing redevelopment as a recreational and commercial complex integrated within a historical site, according to a master plan completed in 1976. Turreted sandstone walls surround 12 buildings, including the original two-story, mansard-roofed prison (1870). Parts of the complex will be leased to private developers, with rents applied to operating funds and continuing restoration work. Some of the buildings may be used as laboratories for studies on the craftsmanship and conservation of building materials.

17 Allen House, Inc. (NR)
Louisville, Kentucky

Origin:	Firehouse, 1873
Conversion:	Commercial space, 1971
Developer:	Allen House, Inc., Louisville
Architect:	Donald J. Allen, Louisville

Redevelopment: Horse-drawn fire trucks once passed through the wide-arched entry of Firehouse No. 10, a narrow brick building located within the Butchertown Historic District. Acquired for $19,000, the 3,000-square-foot building was redeveloped for $60,000 as a studio for interior design.

18 Jail Arcade (NR)
Louisville, Kentucky

Origin:	Jefferson County Jail, 1905
Conversion:	Commercial and office space, in planning stage
Developer:	Jefferson County, Kentucky
Architect:	Not designated

Redevelopment: Left vacant by the construction of a new detention complex, the old jail will be recycled as one part of a multimillion dollar urban redevelopment plan which includes an office tower, parking garage, and urban park. The freestanding steel cell block within the fortress-like brick jail will be gutted to create an interior arcade with four levels of offices, shops, and restaurants. The administrative wing of the jail, also to contain office and commercial space, will open onto a four-story atrium which will replace a boiler plant. Both the atrium and the arcade will be connected to the lobby of the proposed 16-story office tower. The land which the jail occupies has been leased by the county to a developer.

19 Boston's Old City Hall (NHL)
Boston, Massachusetts

Origin:	Boston City Hall, 1865
Conversion:	Commercial and office space, 1971
Developer:	Old City Hall Landmark Corporation, Boston
Architect:	Anderson Notter Associates and F.A. Stahl Associates, Boston

Redevelopment: The city of Boston and the principals of the Old City Hall Landmark Corporation (a subsidiary of Architectural Heritage, Inc., of Boston) were the major participants in a project which has become one of the most widely known examples of adaptive use. The exterior of the French-Second-Empire-style building was restored and the interior was gutted for adaptation into modern offices. Before conversion, useable space in the building—which has six full stories and an additional three floors in the dome—comprised less than 50 percent of the gross building area; today, 75 percent of the total 90,000 square feet is useable. Rental rates in Old City Hall are competitive with neighboring skyscrapers, and the building has been fully rented since 1973. The property is leased from the city for 99 years for $1 plus 25 percent of gross rents, an arrangement which is expected to yield the city more than $25 million. Completed for approximately $2.7 million, the redevelopment received construction and permanent financing from a consortium of local savings institutions. Roger S. Webb, president of the development corporation, received an award from the Boston Society of Architects for his work on Old City Hall and other reuse projects.

20 Institute of Contemporary Art (NR)
Boston, Massachusetts

Origin:	Police Station 16, 1886
Conversion:	Art museum, 1975
Developer:	Institute of Contemporary Art, Boston
Architect:	Graham Gund Architects, Inc., Cambridge

Redevelopment: Recognizing the need to raise funds through rental income, the Institute reserved major spaces for a restaurant, a theater, and a shop in its redevelopment of the Richardsonian-Romanesque police station as an art facility. The first phase began modestly with conversion of the small, two-story horse stable into offices and a gallery. With the first phase completed in 1975, the second phase involved redevelopment of the main building, a three-story, rusticated stone and brick structure, as gallery and restaurant spaces. The last phase, now in progress, includes adaptation of the stable into a theater and shop complex and completion of renovations of the third floor of the main building. The complex, which contains a gross building area of 22,750 square feet, is leased to the Institute by the Boston Redevelopment Authority.

21 Landmark Center (NR)
St. Paul, Minnesota

Origin:	Old Federal Courts Building, 1892-1901
Conversion:	Civic center for the arts, history, and education, 1976-1977
Developer:	Ramsey County/Minnesota Landmarks, St. Paul
Architect:	Stahl Associates, Inc., Boston; and Winsor/Faricy Architects, Inc., St. Paul

Redevelopment: In a transaction which marks a turning point for public involvement in adaptive use, this building was transferred in October 1972 from federal to city ownership for the token fee of $1. Transfer of the Romanesque building was allowed under a 1972 amendment to the Surplus Properties Act of 1944 which permits the General Services Administration to convey surplus federal property with architectural or historic value to public or nonprofit agencies without charge. The structure has since been conveyed from city to county ownership. Redevelopment of the granite, two-towered building will feature restoration of the original four-story atrium into a landscaped, skylighted interior court. The gross building area of 190,207 square feet includes theater facilities, galleries and exhibition spaces, assembly rooms, shops, and restaurants. A fund drive by Minnesota Landmarks has raised money from both public and private sources, including the state legislature, the U.S. Department of Interior, local and national foundations, local corporations, and individuals. The project received awards from the General Services Administration (1975) and from the National Trust for Historic Preservation (1976).

22 Old Post Office Shops
Stillwater, Minnesota

Origin:	United States Post Office, 1903
Conversion:	Commercial space, 1975
Developer:	Melvin Doyle, Plymouth, Minnesota
Architect:	None

Redevelopment: Used for storage of heavy machinery for 8 years following its sale by the post office, this one-story building was rescued from continued deterioration by its conversion into a retail complex. Nine small shops occupy the brick structure, which has stone details on the exterior and marble and terrazzo finishings inside. The slate roof was repaired, the exterior cleaned, and mechanical systems renovated by the owner. Additional interior remodeling was undertaken by the lessees.

23 Oxford City Hall
Oxford, Mississippi

Origin:	United States Post Office and federal building, 1886 (with 1936 addition)
Conversion:	Municipal offices, 1975
Developer:	City of Oxford, Mississippi
Architect:	Robert Parker Adams, Jackson, Mississippi

Redevelopment: In a cooperative effort between federal and municipal authorities, the city of Oxford exchanged a parcel of land in return for the former post office. Revenue sharing provided $359,922 for redevelopment of the Romanesque-style brick building, which contained a gross building area of 19,500 square feet.

24 CEMREL
St. Louis, Missouri

Origin:	City buildings for the poor, chronically ill, and insane; 1900-1903
Conversion:	Educational research facility, 1973
Developer:	CEMREL, Inc., St. Louis
Architect:	Anselevicius / Rupe / Associates, St. Louis

Redevelopment: Prompted by a federal grant's stipulation that its new facility must be in an existing building, CEMREL chose a complex of old hospital buildings for conversion into an educational laboratory. Two structurally sound masonry buildings, opening onto a newly landscaped courtyard, were linked by a new brick tower containing circulation and reception space for the complex. Combined new and old construction provided a gross building area of 70,000 square feet. Purchased from the city of St. Louis for $325,000, the buildings were redeveloped for $2,200,000. The project has received several design and landscape awards.

25 Team Four, Inc.
St. Louis, Missouri

Origin:	Newstead Avenue Police Station, 1905
Conversion:	Design and planning offices, 1973
Developer:	Station Partnership, St. Louis
Architect:	Anselevicius / Rupe / Associates, St. Louis

Redevelopment: First reused in 1960 as a studio for documentary films (a film truck occupied the original stable and television operators worked in a former cell block), the two-story police station was extensively remodeled during its most recent conversion into offices. To emphasize the open-space plan desired by the owners, suspended ceilings and non-load-bearing walls were removed, providing large drafting and design studios. A mortgage loan through the Small Business Administration assisted redevelopment of the 10,000-square-foot building, which was acquired for $55,000.

26 Yellowstone Art Center
Billings, Montana

Origin:	Yellowstone County Jail, 1882
Conversion:	Art center and museum, 1964
Developer:	Yellowstone County
Architect:	Robert Fehlberg, Billings

Redevelopment: Private citizens raised $25,000 to renovate the two-story brick jail, which remains in county ownership. Cell blocks were removed and the interior was completely remodeled to provide galleries, an auditorium, meeting and classroom space, a ceramics studio, and a shop. Donated materials and volunteer labor kept project costs low.

27 Children's Museum, Arts and Science Center
Nashua, New Hampshire

Origin:	Central Fire Station, 1870
Conversion:	Children's museum, 1973
Developer:	The Arts and Science Center, Nashua
Architect:	Carter, Woodruff and Cheever, Nashua

Redevelopment: Nashua's Arts and Science Center, a union of old construction with new, juxtaposes the tower and gables of the century-old firehouse with the low horizontal lines of a contemporary addition. Purchased for $100,000, the firehouse contains a children's museum and several classrooms and offices. The old building comprises 14,000 square feet of the total gross building area of 30,000 square feet. A fund drive provided the major source of financing for the complex.

28 Jefferson Market Regional Branch Library (NR)
New York, New York

Origin:	Jefferson Market Courthouse, 1876
Conversion:	Public library, 1967
Developer:	City of New York, Department of Public Works
Architect:	Giorgio Cavaglieri, New York

Redevelopment: The polychromatic, exuberant architecture of this Victorian Gothic building has made it a distinctive Manhattan landmark since its design by Frederick C. Withers and Calvert Vaux more than a century ago. Vacated in 1958, the structure, which features a round nine-story clock tower, was the object of an ardent preservation campaign culminating in its $1,165,282 conversion to a branch library. Redevelopment work on the building, which now provides 18,642 square feet of floor space, included installation of new lighting, placement of a catwalk across the high ceiling of the main reading room, structural repairs, and extensive restoration and repairs of the interior finishings. The project won awards from the American Institute of Architects (1968) and the American Library Association (1976).

29 East Side Recreation Center
Troy, New York

Origin:	Hope 7 Firehouse, 1885
Conversion:	Recreation center and library, 1976
Developer:	City of Troy
Architect:	Garry J. Kearns, Troy

Redevelopment: Combined efforts of government and citizens led to the adaptive use of Troy's old two-story firehouse which had been closed in 1974 following construction of a new fire department facility. The large engine room now serves as a neighborhood recreational area and the second floor houses a branch library. Completed in 5 months, the redevelopment was funded through a Community Development Block Grant with an additional $1,000 from the city's general account.

30 Zino's Firehouse
Cincinnati, Ohio

Origin:	Firehouse, 1871
Conversion:	Restaurant, 1969
Developer:	Zino, Inc., Cincinnati
Architect:	Hefley/Stevens, Cincinnati

Redevelopment: Conversion of the two-story masonry firehouse into a restaurant was facilitated by 16-foot ceiling heights, which allowed development of a dining mezzanine over approximately one-third of the main dining area. A new wall was built inside the existing front wall; the area between can serve as a sidewalk cafe during good weather when specially designed doors in the original 14-foot-square firehouse entrances are opened. The project, which won a local American Institute of Architects design award in 1970, was completed for $175,000. Renovation of the firehouse caused a rekindling of interest in the Corryville area, which has since undergone substantial revitalization.

31 Jefferson Center for Vocational Rehabilitation (NR)
Toledo, Ohio

Origin:	Central post office, 1911
Conversion:	School, 1971
Developer:	Toledo Public Schools
Architect:	Hahn and Hayes, Toledo

Redevelopment: Sold by the federal government in 1966 to the Toledo Public Schools for $1, the former post office was converted for $2,119,000 with funds from the Bureau of Vocational Rehabilitation and the state of Ohio Department of Vocational Education. The interior of the limestone-faced building, originally having 35-foot ceilings, was redeveloped to accommodate three stories, increasing the gross building area to 122,000 square feet. The building contains 45 learning laboratories and 28 offices, in addition to conference rooms, lounges, and storage facilities.

32 Old City Hall (NR)
Tulsa, Oklahoma

Origin:	City hall, 1919
Conversion:	Offices, 1974
Developer:	Coleman-Ervin and Associates and Kothe and Eagleton, Inc., Tulsa
Architect:	Coleman-Ervin and Associates, Tulsa

Redevelopment: Jointly purchased by an architectural firm and a law firm, Tulsa's Beaux Arts city hall was fully leased before renovation was completed. Public lobbies on the first and second floors were restored, but the remainder of the interior was gutted and redeveloped as professional office space at a cost of $448,150. Vacant since municipal offices were moved to a new civic center in 1967, the building was sold for $150,000 by the city of Tulsa. The four-story stone structure, recipient of an AIA regional honor award in 1975, contains a gross building area of 27,140 square feet.

33 Trone and Weikert, Inc.
Hanover, Pennsylvania

Origin:	Post office, 1912
Conversion:	Retail store, 1972
Developer:	Trone and Weikert, Inc., Hanover
Architect:	Harold E. Trone, Hanover

Redevelopment: Built of granite and marble in a Renaissance Revival style, Hanover's old post office now houses "Mail and Femail," a clothing store. In order to convert the rear of the building into the main entrance with access from the former mail truck parking lot, the developers replaced the old loading dock with a ramp and landscaped terrace. Interior changes to the 10,800-square-foot structure, purchased from the post office for $47,500 and redeveloped for $91,800, were minor.

34 National Bank of the Commonwealth (NR)
Indiana, Pennsylvania

Origin:	Indiana County Courthouse, 1870
Conversion:	Bank, 1974
Developer:	National Bank of the Commonwealth, Indiana
Architect:	William Kerr Associates, Pittsburgh

Redevelopment: With a 50-year lease from the county, National Bank of the Commonwealth invested about $450,000 to restore the brick courthouse for use as its central offices. The French Second Empire building, 3½-stories tall with stone columns and exterior details, is dominated by a tall clock tower. The bank has received several awards for the restoration, including a national award for corporate contributions to the arts from Esquire Magazine and the Business Committee for the Arts (1975).

35 Old City Hall (NR)
Tacoma, Washington

Origin:	City hall, 1893
Conversion:	Commercial space, 1974
Developer:	Robert Nyquist and Associates, Inc.
Architect:	Barnet Schorr, Seattle

Redevelopment: Sold by the city of Tacoma in 1969 for $17,400 (the estimated value of the property without structures), the old city hall survived demolition threats to be converted into a shopping and restaurant complex. An initial effort at rehabilitation ended in bankruptcy, and a new development team acquired the structure in 1972 through an agreement with the project's creditors. Perhaps because of the first experience, local lenders were not interested in the project and construction financing was secured through a REIT in San Diego. High ceilings allowed the addition of several mezzanines, which increased the gross building area for the four-story Italianate structure to 77,000 square feet. The building is occupied by more than 30 businesses including a jewelry store in the clock tower, and restaurants both in the roof gardens and in the former jail cells in the basement.

36 Old Courthouse Apartments (NR)
Moorefield, West Virginia

Origin:	Hardy County Courthouse, 1792
Conversion:	Apartments, 1972
Developer:	Mrs. C. B. Allen, Moorefield
Architect:	Marjorie Pierce, Weston, Massachusetts

Redevelopment: After more than 60 years of service as the county's first courthouse, this building was variously used as a girls' school, a print shop, offices, and housing. A need for small, modern, well-designed apartments in the Moorefield area prompted redevelopment of the building into five one-bedroom units. The exterior (including a rooftop cupola) was restored and the interior was completely remodeled with new dry walls, floors, wiring, and electrical heat.

37 Ashland City Hall (NR)
Ashland, Wisconsin

Origin:	Post office and federal office building, 1894 (with 1926 addition)
Conversion:	Municipal offices, 1976
Developer:	City of Ashland
Architect:	Thomas J. Shefchik and Associates, Inc., Duluth, Minnesota

Redevelopment: The building was given to the city of Ashland by the federal government in 1937 in exchange for other property and was used for many years as a vocational school. A 100-foot tower, once used for meteorological observations, dominates the Romanesque-style brownstone structure which had stood vacant for 7 years before its conversion into municipal offices. Although interior alterations to the first floor and basement were extensive, floor plans for the second and third levels remained essentially unchanged. The original oak woodwork was retained throughout the 18,800-square-foot building. Funding for redevelopment of the structure came from the Upper Great Lakes Regional Commission ($300,000) and the Ashland City Council.

Project Economics
Public Buildings

Project	Year of Conversion	Gross Building Area (sq. ft.)	Acquisition Cost	Redevelopment Cost	Approx. Cost Per Sq. Ft.	Source of Financing	Rental Rates (annual per sq. ft., unless otherwise noted)
Mobile County Dept. of Pensions	1975	32,000	City-owned	$1,560,000	$48.75	City and county funds, private donation	(not rented)
Cooper House	1971	21,000	$ 75,000	600,000	30.00	S&L, commercial banks	$9.00
Customs House	1976	10,200	115,000	165,000	16.15	Local commercial bank	$5.85
Old Idaho State Penitentiary	Planned	(510 acres)	State-owned (to be leased to private developers)	—	—	Private capital, state funds, rental revenue	(not rented)
Allen House, Inc.	1971	3,000	19,000	60,000	10.00	Local commercial bank	(not rented)
Jail Arcade	Planned	56,000	Leased	1,960,000	35.00	Undetermined	$10.00 commercial, $6.50–8.50 office
Boston's Old City Hall	1971	90,000	Leased	2,700,000	30.00	6 local savings banks	$9.00
Institute of Contemporary Art	1975	22,750	Leased	800,000 Phases I and II	(35.16)	Local commercial bank, fund drive	(leased by developer)
Landmark Center	1976–1977	190,207	1.00	8.5–9.0 million	40.00–45.00	Fund drive, public grants	$5.50 turnkey; $2.00–6.00 + percentage, commercial
Old Post Office Shops	1975	8,000	—	5,000 (Interior)	—	Private	—
Oxford City Hall	1975	19,500	Trade	359,922	18.46	Federal revenue sharing funds	(not rented)
CEMREL, Inc.	1973	70,000	325,000	2,200,000	25.00	Federal funds	(not rented)
Team Four, Inc.	1973	10,000	55,000	(63,000)	11.45	Local bank and SBA	(not rented)
Yellowstone Art Center	1964	11,000	County-owned	25,000	(2.27)	Private donations	(not rented)
Children's Museum	1973	Old 14,000 New 30,000	100,000	1,200,000 (Old and new)	35.00	Fund drive	(not rented)
Jefferson Market Regional Branch Library	1967	18,642	City-owned	1,165,282	62.50	City funds	(not rented)
East Side Recreation Center	1976	4,900	City-owned	105,590	21.55	Community Development Block Grant	(not rented)
Zino's Firehouse	1969	8,700	66,000	175,000	20.00	Local commercial bank	$2.40
Jefferson Center for Vocational Rehabilitation	1971	122,000	1	2,119,000	16.68	State and federal funds	(not rented)
Old City Hall (Tulsa)	1974	27,140	150,000	448,150	16.50	Local bank	$6.00
Trone and Weikert, Inc.	1972	10,800	47,500	91,800	8.50	Local savings bank	—
National Bank of the Commonwealth	1974	23,000	$12,000/year Leased	450,000	(19.57)	In-house	(leased by developer)
Old City Hall (Tacoma)	1974	77,000	17,400	1,500,000	(19.48)	REIT	—

Project	Year of Conversion	Gross Building Area (sq. ft.)	Acquisition Cost	Redevelopment Cost	Approx. Cost Per Sq. Ft.	Source of Financing	Rental Rates (annual per sq. ft., unless otherwise noted)
Old Courthouse Apartments	1972	—	25,000	85,000	—	Private	—
Ashland City Hall	1976	18,800	City-owned	400,000	22.85	Public funds (city and regional)	(not rented)

Dashes indicate data not available.
Figures in parentheses were not supplied directly but were derived from other data.

Redevelopment Work
Public Buildings

Project	Exterior Restoration	New Exterior Construction	Structural	Mechanical	Interior Demolition	Interior New Construction	Site Restoration	New Facilities, Parking	Landscaping
Mobile County Dept. of Pensions	Extensive	Minor	Moderate	Extensive	Extensive	Extensive	Moderate	Extensive	Moderate
Cooper House	Minor	Moderate	Minor	Extensive	Moderate	Moderate	Moderate	Minor	Minor
Customs House	Minor	Minor	Minor	Moderate	Moderate	Moderate	Minor	Moderate	Minor
Old Idaho State Penitentiary	Moderate	Minor	Moderate	Extensive	Minor	Moderate	Minor	Moderate	Moderate
Allen House, Inc.	Moderate	Minor	Extensive	Extensive	Minor	Moderate	Moderate	Minor	Extensive
Jail Arcade	Moderate	Minor	Extensive	Extensive	Extensive	Extensive	Minor	Extensive	Minor
Boston's Old City Hall	Minor	Minor	Moderate	Extensive	Extensive	Extensive	Minor	None	Moderate
Institute of Contemporary Art	Minor	Minor	Moderate	Extensive	Extensive	Extensive	Minor	Minor	Minor
Landmark Center	Extensive	Minor	Moderate	Extensive	Moderate	Extensive	Moderate	Minor	Extensive
Old Post Office Shops	Moderate	—	—	Extensive	—	Moderate	—	—	—
Oxford City Hall	Moderate	Minor	Minor	Extensive	Moderate	Moderate	Moderate	Minor	Minor
CEMREL, Inc.	Moderate	Moderate	Minor	Extensive	Moderate	Extensive	Extensive	Extensive	Extensive
Team Four, Inc.	Minor	—	—	Moderate	Extensive	Extensive	—	Moderate	—
Yellowstone Art Center	Minor	Minor	Minor	Moderate	Extensive	Extensive	Moderate	Minor	Moderate
Children's Museum	Minor	Moderate	Moderate	Moderate	Moderate	—	Extensive	Extensive	Extensive
Jefferson Market Regional Branch Library	Moderate	Moderate	Extensive	Extensive	Extensive	Extensive	Moderate	Minor	Minor
East Side Recreation Center	Moderate	Minor	Minor	Extensive	Moderate	Extensive	Moderate	—	Moderate
Zino's Firehouse	Moderate	Minor	Minor	Extensive	Moderate	Extensive	Minor	Minor	Minor
Jefferson Center for Vocational Rehabilitation	Moderate	Moderate	Extensive	Extensive	Extensive	Extensive	Extensive	Extensive	Extensive
Old City Hall (Tulsa)	Extensive	Minor	Minor	Extensive	Extensive	Extensive	Moderate	Moderate	Extensive
Trone and Weikert, Inc.	Minor	Minor	Minor	Moderate	Minor	Moderate	Minor	Minor	Moderate
National Bank of the Commonwealth	Extensive	Minor	Minor	Extensive	Moderate	Extensive	Moderate	Minor	Extensive
Old Courthouse Apartments	Extensive	Extensive	Extensive	Extensive	Extensive	Extensive	Extensive	Extensive	Extensive
Ashland City Hall	Minor	Minor	Minor	Extensive	Moderate	Extensive	Minor	Minor	Minor

Dashes indicate data not available.

Movie Theaters

Once the "palaces" of public entertainment, the fancy movie theaters of the 1920s and 1930s are often underutilized, neglected, or threatened in today's economy. The popularity of these downtown theaters, frequently built with seating capacities for 2,000 or more, waned in the 1950s, as television began to provide comfortable home entertainment. The older theaters are no longer competitive in a movie market which currently encourages the design of small auditoriums, often in clusters of two or more.

Although a lucky combination of good location with well selected movies might rebuild a lost reputation, many theater buildings are proving to be better suited for new uses than for movies. Within the last 15 years, for example, movie houses in at least a dozen cities have been successfully rejuvenated through conversion into performing arts facilities. Other theaters, such as The Century in Chicago, contained large spaces which have been imaginatively redeveloped to accommodate commercial uses.

Ironically, the movie theater originated architecturally as an adaptive use, for the first movies—the nickelodeons of the early 20th century—usually occupied former storefronts. The movie industry experienced such rapid growth, however, that by 1915 more than 25,000 theaters had been built across the United States. In architectural design the movie theater did not vary substantially from the traditional playhouse (often providing space for vaudeville or road shows), but in decoration it marked a new era of extravagance and grandeur.

The theater building itself played an important role in the movie-going experience, providing an escapist environment of richness and fantasy which could not be found elsewhere. Theater owners claimed that "the audiences increase in proportion to the amount of ornamentation,"[1] and architects obligingly created Baroque palaces, Moorish castles, and Grecian ruins. John Eberson, designer of more than 100 "atmospheric" theaters, added artificial clouds and twinkling stars to the architect's repertoire of exotic details.

Despite the faded splendor of the movie palaces, many cultural groups are now recognizing the unique potential of the theaters for redevelopment into contemporary performing arts centers. St. Louis pioneered in this conversion movement in 1968, with the adaptation of a 1925 movie house into Powell Symphony Hall. Like many other old theaters, Powell was well-located in the central city and had an auditorium capacity which was sufficient for concert audiences.

Redevelopment of an existing theater as a performing arts center can offer substantial savings over new construction in both time and money, as a feasibility study for The Paramount in Oakland emphasized. Restoration of a theater's original decoration, such as the Pittsburgh Symphony undertook for Heinz Hall, can result in an opulence which could not be achieved in a new building.

Conversion generally requires major technical alterations to improve acoustics and lighting and some redesign of performance and support facilities. The extent of the redevelopment work can vary from the minor repair work needed to open The Fox in Atlanta to the major structural adaptations necessary for completion of the Lederer Theater in Providence. Omaha, Columbus, Youngstown, Miami, Aurora (Illinois), Manchester (New Hampshire), and Elmira (New York) are other cities with contemporary performing arts centers housed in old movie or vaudeville palaces.

Although reuses oriented toward entertainment usually have been able to capitalize on the existing plan and decoration of a theater, other successful conversions have completely departed from the original configuration of the building. The redevelopment may call for restoration of the original street facade, but frequently the new interior has little or nothing to do with the original character of the building.

Commonly built with structural systems of steel or reinforced concrete, theaters provide large open spaces which can be subdivided horizontally as well as vertically. Adaptive use of The Century, for example, resulted in seven floor levels within the old auditorium. In other projects the auditorium has been reduced in size and modified for present use with remaining spaces remodeled to meet other needs.

Although only projects involving movie or vaudeville theaters are described here, many of the same considerations can be applied to the reuse of surplus opera houses, concert halls, or playhouses. During the second half of the 19th century, the

---

[1] R. W. Sexton, *American Theaters of Today*, Vol. 2 (New York: Architectural Book Publishing Company, 1930), p. 3.

opera house was often one of the most architecturally distinguished buildings in a community. An encouraging number of these buildings have been restored and reopened for continued use for live performances. Examples range from Wilmington, Delaware, and Woodstock, Illinois, to What Cheer, Iowa, and Nevada City, California.

The Theatre Historical Society (P.O. Box 4445, Washington, D.C. 20017) publishes a quarterly journal which deals in part with the documentation, preservation, and reuse of movie houses and other theater architecture.

38   Paramount Theatre of the Arts (NR)
Oakland, California

Origin:	Movie theater, 1931
Conversion:	Performing arts center, 1973
Developer:	City of Oakland, Paramount Theatre of the Arts, Inc., Oakland
Architect:	Skidmore, Owings and Merrill, San Francisco

Redevelopment: The Paramount Theatre, purchased in 1972 by the Oakland Symphony Association, is a masterpiece of art deco design second only to New York City's Radio City Music Hall. Acquisition and conversion of the theater cost $2 million and took only 9 months, in comparison to a study report's estimated cost of $13 million and construction period of 4 years for a new performing arts center for the city. Timothy L. Pflueger, original architect for the building, served as consultant for the restoration, which included cleaning and refinishing of the original decor, installation of new seating, and replacement of the carpets, upholstery, and curtains according to the original designs. The theater is now owned by the city of Oakland and is partially subsidized by the local hotel-motel tax.

39   The Fox (NHL)
Atlanta, Georgia

Origin:	The Fox Theater, 1929
Conversion:	Performing arts center, 1975
Developer:	Atlanta Landmarks, Inc., Atlanta
Architect:	Members of the Board of Trustees, Atlanta Landmarks, Inc.

Redevelopment: Nicknamed the "Fabulous Fox," the onion-domed theater originally featured live performances in a 5,000-seat hall, silent and sound movies on a curved cinemascope screen, and the largest ballroom in Atlanta, all within an interior of lavish, neo-Mideastern and eclectic decor. The building, designed by Marye, Alger and Vinour of Atlanta, was initially planned as a shriner's mosque and included rental space for stores and offices within a 200,000-square-foot complex. Atlanta Landmarks, a nonprofit organization, purchased the building in 1975 with a $1.8 million loan from a 5-bank consortium. Renovation has largely concentrated on maintenance—putting on a new roof, improving mechanical and electrical systems, and making stage repairs. Although box office receipts are now paying operating expenses for the theater, Atlanta Landmarks is raising funds through private donations, benefit performances, and souvenir sales in order to repay the loan principal which comes due in 1978. If the organization defaults on the interest or principal payments, the building will revert to the previous owners who have a demolition permit for the structure.

40   Paramount Arts Centre
Aurora, Illinois

Origin:	Paramount Theatre, 1930
Conversion:	Performing arts center, 1977
Developer:	Aurora Redevelopment Commission and Aurora Civic Center Authority
Architect:	ELS Design Group, New York City; and Frazier, Orr, Fairbank and Quam, Geneva, Illinois

Redevelopment: The $2 million rehabilitation of the 2,000-seat vaudeville and movie palace, designed by Rapp and Rapp of Chicago, is part of a city-funded civic center development program. Terra-cotta decoration on the exterior and extravagant plaster details within the theater are being cleaned and restored to complement the remodeled stage and support facilities and the new sound and lighting systems. A landscaped pedestrian promenade separates the theater from the banks of a river.

41 The Century
Chicago, Illinois

Origin:	The Century movie theater, 1925
Conversion:	Shopping mall, 1976
Developer:	E and S Realty Corporation, Chicago
Architect:	Jerome Browne and Associates, Chicago

Redevelopment: The Century made its grand premiere as a shopping center in 1976, 50 years after its construction as a 3,000-seat vaudeville and movie palace. Capitalizing on the high-density, upper-income population of Chicago's New Town area, the developers purchased the building for $1 million and invested about $9 million in redevelopment and in new construction for an attached 550-car garage. The ornate terra-cotta theater facade was retained but the interior of the building was gutted to develop a seven-level shopping space around an 80-foot high atrium. As a mall, The Century has a gross building area of 150,000 square feet (compared to 29,000 square feet in the original theater) and accommodates almost 100 retail shops, "ministores," and restaurants.

42 Scottie's On Seventh (NR)
Minneapolis, Minnesota

Origin:	Theater, later the Forum Cafeteria, 1911
Conversion:	Nightclub, 1976
Developer:	Scott W. Smith, Burnsville, Minnesota
Architect:	Scott W. Smith

Redevelopment: The Art Deco interior of the former theater, installed in 1929 when the building was converted into a cafeteria, has been refurbished as the major attraction of the nightclub. A mezzanine provides two levels of seating in the building which was acquired for $135,000.

43 Columbia Racquetball Club
St. Louis, Missouri

Origin:	Columbia movie theater, 1925
Conversion:	Racquetball club, 1976
Developer:	Dico Finance Corporation, St. Louis
Architect:	Hunter Hunter Associates, St. Louis

Redevelopment: The former auditorium space of the Renaissance-Revival-style movie theater now accommodates eight racquetball courts and several locker rooms. The theater floor was leveled and a new ceiling was hung during the conversion of the steel frame building. It now contains a gross building area of 12,000 square feet.

44 Orpheum (NR)
Omaha, Nebraska

Origin:	Creighton Orpheum movie theater, 1927
Conversion:	Performing arts center, 1975
Developer:	Omaha Performing Arts Center Corporation
Architect:	Leo A. Daly Company, Omaha

Redevelopment: Purchased for $135,000 and donated to the city of Omaha by a nonprofit civic association, the extravagant movie palace was adapted with $1.8 million in city revenue bonds. Access to the 2,700-seat theater, designed by Rapp and Rapp of Chicago, is through an ornate lobby within an adjacent 16-story bank building; the lobby had to be separately purchased for $72,000 by the Omaha Symphony Association, which has granted the city free use of the space. Major acoustical renovations were necessary and a hydraulic stage lift which can raise and lower the enlarged orchestra pit was installed.

45 The Palace Theatre (NR)
Manchester, New Hampshire

Origin:	Vaudeville theater, 1915
Conversion:	Performing arts center, 1974
Developer:	Palace Theatre Trust, Manchester
Architect:	None

Redevelopment: The Palace Theatre, variously used in the 1960s and early 1970s as a college classroom and as manufacturing and storage space, reopened in 1974 following basic renovations by the New Hampshire Performing Arts Center. A local foundation holds a 5-year mortgage on the building, which was purchased for approximately $100,000. The first phase of redevelopment, totaling $150,000, included enlargement of the orchestra pit, rewiring and improving lighting, recarpeting, and replacement and repair of seats. An additional $100,000 will be invested in the second phase to renovate the heating system, install air-conditioning and major insulation, and reconstruct a marquee which is historically appropriate.

46 The Ohio Theatre (NR)
Columbus, Ohio

Origin:	Loew's Ohio Theatre, 1928
Conversion:	Performing arts center, 1969
Developer:	Columbus Association for the Performing Arts
Architect:	Karlsburger and Associates, Columbus

Redevelopment: Restoration of the 3,000-seat theater, designed by Thomas W. Lamb, continues as funding from foundation grants and private donations becomes available. Major work has involved replacement of seats on the lower floor and in the loges, enlargement of the orchestra pit, renovation of the mechanical systems, and remodeling of staff and ticket offices. The theater was purchased for $1.8 million and $1.5 million has been invested in its redevelopment.

47 Heinz Hall for the Performing Arts
Pittsburgh, Pennsylvania

Origin:	Loew's Penn movie theater, 1927
Conversion:	Performing arts center, 1971
Developer:	Pittsburgh Symphony Society, Pittsburgh
Architect:	Stotz, Hess, MacLachlan and Fosner, Pittsburgh

Redevelopment: Before undertaking this $12 million project, the Pittsburgh Symphony made several test performances to check the acoustics of the plush movie palace, originally built by the architectural firm of Rapp and Rapp. The lobbies and 2,847-seat hall were restored to the original marble and crystal opulence of the twenties, and an addition was made to the rear of the building to accommodate backstage facilities. Acoustical innovations by Austrian consultant Dr. Heinrich Keilholz further contributed to the success of the conversion which was largely funded through the Howard Heinz Endowment. Opened in 1971 after a 16-month period of redevelopment, Heinz Hall serves not only the symphony but also Pittsburgh opera and ballet companies and the youth orchestra.

48 Lederer Theatre (NR)
Providence, Rhode Island

Origin:	Emery's Majestic vaudeville house and movie theater, 1917
Conversion:	Performing arts center, 1973
Developer:	Foundation for Repertory Theatre of Rhode Island, Providence
Architect:	Providence Partnership, Providence

Redevelopment: One theater became two in the conversion of Emery's Majestic into a performing arts center for the Trinity Square Repertory Company. Architects for the adaptive use had a horizontal concrete slab placed across the length of the building at the level of the old Majestic's lowest balcony. The lower theater now seats 300 in an arena arrangement and the upper theater houses a flexible space for 500 to 800 theatergoers. Colored tile decorations on the building's facade have been restored—as well as interior features made of marble, brass, and leaded glass, including a stained glass dome in the lobby. Redevelopment costs totaled $1.3 million.

49 Madison Civic Center
Madison, Wisconsin

Origin:	Capitol movie theater, 1928; and adjacent department store, 1941
Conversion:	Performing arts center and restaurant, 1978
Developer:	City of Madison
Architect:	Hardy Holzman Pfeiffer Associates, New York

Redevelopment: Behind the Moorish-style facade of the former movie house, a 2,100-seat auditorium and a 299-seat small theater with a thrust stage will be developed for contemporary use. New construction joins the theaters to a former department store which now houses gallery space and administrative offices, and serves as an interior pedestrian link between two city blocks.

Project Economics
Theaters

Project	Year of Conversion	Gross Building Area (sq. ft.)	Acquisition Cost	Redevelopment Cost	Approx. Cost Per Sq. Ft.	Source of Financing	Rental Rates (annual per sq. ft., unless otherwise noted)
Paramount Theatre	1973	(2,400,000 cubic feet)	$1,000,000	$ 1,000,000	$30.00	Private donations for initial restoration; public (local)	$425–575/ performance, plus 5 percent of ticket sales
The Fox	1975	200,000	1,864,000	100,000	(0.50)	5-bank consortium, private donations, benefits, souvenir sales	—
Paramount Arts Centre	1977	23,000	435,000	2,000,000	—	City funds	—
The Century	1976	Old 150,000 New 208,000	1,000,000	9,000,000 (includes new construction for garage)	(25.14) (Old and new)	REIT construction loan, insurance company mortgage	—
Scottie's On Seventh	1976	—	350,000	—	20.00	Commercial bank	—
Columbia Racquetball Club	1976	12,000	60,000	440,000	41.67	Commercial bank	—
Orpheum	1975	—	135,000	1,800,000	—	City revenue bonds	—
The Palace Theatre	1974	—	100,000	150,000 ($100,000 more planned)	—	Mortgage held by private foundation	—
The Ohio Theatre	1969	—	1,800,000	1,500,000	—	Donations, foundation grants	$600–800/ performance
Heinz Hall	1971	124,000	1,000,000	11,000,000	(88.71)	Private donations	—
Lederer Theatre	1973	42,100	750,000	1,300,000	(30.88)	Local banks	—
Madison Civic Center	1978	—	300,000	5,000,000	50.00	Bond issue, fund raising	—

Dashes indicate data not available.
Figures in parentheses were not supplied directly but were derived from other data.

Redevelopment Work
Theaters

Project	Exterior Restoration	New Exterior Construction	Structural	Mechanical	Interior Demolition	Interior New Construction	Site Restoration	New Facilities, Parking	Landscaping
Paramount Theatre	Minor	Minor	Minor	Moderate	None	Minor	Minor	Moderate	Minor
The Fox	—	None	None	—	Minor	Minor	None	None	None
Paramount Arts Centre	Moderate	Moderate	Minor	Extensive	Moderate	Moderate	Moderate	Minor	Minor
The Century	Minor	Minor	Extensive	Extensive	Extensive	Extensive	Extensive	Extensive	Extensive
Scottie's On Seventh	Minor	—	—	Minor	Minor	Minor	—	—	—
Columbia Racketball Club	Minor	Minor	Minor	Extensive	Extensive	Extensive	None	None	None
Orpheum	Minor	Extensive	Minor	Moderate	Moderate	Minor	None	None	None
The Palace Theatre	Minor	Minor	Minor	Extensive	Moderate	Moderate	Minor	None	None
The Ohio Theatre	Moderate	None	None	Moderate	None	Minor	None	None	None
Heinz Hall	Moderate	Minor	Moderate	Extensive	Extensive	Extensive	Extensive	Minor	Minor
Lederer Theatre	Moderate	Minor	Extensive	Extensive	Extensive	Extensive	Minor	—	Minor
Madison Civic Center	Moderate	Moderate	Extensive	Extensive	Moderate	Extensive	Moderate	—	Extensive

Dashes indicate data not available.

Hotels, Mansions, and Apartments

At a time when recycled schools, barns, mills, and warehouses are providing unique and comfortable homes for thousands of people, many buildings which were originally designed as living spaces are instead serving different functions. Virtually every town in America has an example of an old house which serves a new use, perhaps as a restaurant, a library, an antique store, or a real estate office. Indeed, for many years the adaptive use movement was primarily identified with the reuse of residential buildings.

The most traditional conversion is that of an architecturally or historically significant residence into a house museum. Unfortunately, the income from admission charges seldom meets the cost of maintenance and operation of the building. Although these museums are usually valuable cultural assets in a community, economic realities make it impractical to preserve many structures in this manner.

A broad range of imaginative and profitable uses are possible not only for city houses but also for country estates, apartment buildings, hotels, and resort complexes. Often the residential character of a building can be retained despite an adaptive use: mansions are split into condominiums; hotels become apartment houses; apartments serve as nursing homes or dormitories. Other conversions introduce unrelated new uses, primarily as office, commercial, or educational space.

Social changes, economic pressures, and technological innovations have all influenced the style of the buildings in which we live. The single-family house—urban mansion, suburban bungalow, rural farmhouse—spans every period of American history, providing a physical record of changing tastes in life-styles, architectural design, building materials, and interior decoration. The apartment house was developed in the second half of the 19th century, when an increase in population and a rise in land values precipitated a crisis in urban housing. Like the more stylish apartment houses, the city hotel was designed to offer modern conveniences in a luxurious atmosphere. The proliferation of great resort hotels began with the rise of the railroads; vacationers crowded the rambling wooden spas of upstate New York, the Mediterranean-flavored holiday hotels of Florida and, later, the mission-style inns of southern California.

Changes in our living and recreation patterns have now made many of these older buildings obsolete and in need of alternative uses. Without large staffs of servants, for example, it has become impractical to maintain most of the urban mansions and rural estates of the 19th century. Since early in the 20th century, subdivision of large city houses into apartments has seemed to offer the most economically feasible solution to this dilemma. The resulting shift in the character of a neighborhood from single-family, owner-occupied houses to high-density, absentee-landlord apartment units has too frequently been accompanied by a decline in the condition of the buildings. Many of these neighborhoods are experiencing a revitalization today, as a renewed interest in urban living by some sectors of society has led to rehabilitation of areas such as Beacon Hill, Society Hill, and Georgetown.

A new approach in this neighborhood revitalization movement involves conversion of large houses into condominiums. In the redevelopment of Guernsey Hall in Princeton, New Jersey (see case studies), the architect was able to incorporate elegant and indigenous features of the mansion into each condominium unit. Although new entry and circulation patterns had to be developed, much of the original design and detail could be retained.

In some situations, continued residential use of an older house or apartment building may not be practical or desirable. A single mansion or a row of once-fashionable homes or apartments may have become physically isolated as surrounding houses have been demolished and replaced by commercial buildings. Economic pressure to redevelop the property for more intensive use may sometimes be met through conversion into commercial or professional office space. Reuse as offices in buildings such as the Speed House in Louisville provides a reasonable rental return for the owners and also prevents the encroachment of new construction for commercial uses in a National Register district which is residentially oriented. A luxury apartment house in Washington, D.C., was purchased in early 1977 by the National Trust for Historic Preservation for use as the organization's national headquarters.

The inner-city location of many older hotels may have cost them their business to the modern suburban motel, but it also has encouraged their recycling into downtown offices or into high-rise urban apartment buildings such as the Belvedere in Baltimore, The Cairo in Washington, D.C., and The Dewitt Clinton in Albany. The extent of redevelopment work varies: in The Dewitt Clinton, each apartment unit was created by combining two former hotel rooms and replacing the second bath with a kitchen; in The Cairo, the interior was gutted and reconstructed.

In an urban environment, zoning can sometimes be a delicate factor in an adaptive use problem involving older residences. Mansions which no longer seem feasible for residential use may be located in neighborhoods zoned exclusively for single-family homes. A 1973 proposal by the planning office of Washington, D.C. to allow nonprofit organizations to use mansions in some of the city's residentially zoned districts as office headquarters was criticized by citizen groups as offering a foothold for further development pressures on urban neighborhoods. In another situation, if zoning allows conversion of large houses into multifamily dwellings, it may simultaneously encourage their replacement with new, higher-density apartment buildings.

A major decision involved in the adaptive use design for former residential buildings concerns the treatment of the interior space. Meticulous restoration represents one solution, while complete gutting of the interior offers the other extreme. Among the catalog projects are examples of both approaches. In Chicago there is the Glessner House in which several rooms were restored according to the original design by H. H. Richardson. In the old Van Rensselaer Mansion in Philadelphia, on the other hand, the interior was extensively altered to accommodate the retail needs of Design Research. Although no definitive guidelines for interior treatment can be established, the design solution should generally be determined by the architectural significance and condition of the building's interior fabric and by the requirements of the new use.

50 French Flats
Fort Payne, Alabama

Origin:	Boarding house, 1889
Conversion:	Dental office and apartments,1973
Developer:	Dr. Stephen Brewer, Fort Payne
Architect:	None

Redevelopment: A two-story, wood-frame building containing 6,000 square feet, French Flats originally served as a boarding house for wealthy bachelors. Purchased for $6,500 and redeveloped for $40,000, the building now mixes professional offices with residential uses.

51 Murphy House (NR)
Montgomery, Alabama

Origin:	Private residence, 1851
Conversion:	Offices, 1970
Developer:	Water Works and Sanitary Sewer Board, Montgomery
Architect:	Jim Seay, Montgomery

Redevelopment: When space problems squeezed the Water Works and Sanitary Sewer Board out of its city hall offices, representatives of the independent public corporation estimated that purchase and conversion of the old Murphy House would cost $80,000 less than construction of a new building of equivalent size. Acquisition and redevelopment of the Greek Revival building, which contains a gross building area of 16,000 square feet, totaled $450,000 and was funded through the Board's capital improvement budget.

52 The Colorado Springs School
Colorado Springs, Colorado

Origin:	Private residence, 1907
Conversion:	Independent school,1967
Developer:	The Colorado Springs School
Architect:	Carlisle B. Guy and Associates, Colorado Springs

Redevelopment: Originally sketched by architect Stanford White, the design of this mansion is a scaled-down copy of the Grand Trianon in Versailles, done in glazed terra-cotta over brick walls. The two-story grand salons were unaltered by the conversion which involved remodeling kitchen and household service areas into classrooms and offices. Acquisition and redevelopment costs were provided by an anonymous donor within the school's management.

53 James B. Colt House (NR)
Hartford, Connecticut

Origin:	Private residence, 1956
Conversion:	Apartments, 1976
Developer:	James B. Colt Partnership, Hartford
Architect:	Susan Willy, New Haven

Redevelopment: All units in the three-story brick and stucco building were rented, without advertising, before completion of the adaptive use project. Each of the eight apartments, which range in size from 425 square feet (two rooms) to 1,180 square feet (five rooms), has an individual plan and different design details. Twelve members of the development partnership raised $51,500 in capital to supplement a $142,000 "participation" mortgage by four local lending institutions. Costs for the project, which also received a $20,000 matching grant from the National Park Service, were $22 per square foot for construction and $27.75 per square foot for the total project.

54 The Cairo
Washington, D.C.

Origin:	Cairo Hotel, 1894
Conversion:	Apartments, 1976
Developer:	Inland Steel Development Company, Washington, D.C.
Architect:	Arthur Cotton Moore/Associates, Washington, D.C.

Redevelopment: The once fashionable Cairo Hotel—the tallest privately owned structure in Washington, built shortly before a restriction on building heights was instituted in 1910—had deteriorated considerably in both status and physical condition before its conversion into apartments. The interior of the steel-frame hotel was gutted and redeveloped to accommodate 170 apartments. An additional eight units, created from the previously unuseable basement, open onto an interior courtyard which was formerly the ballroom and lobby. Permanent financing through FHA 221 (d)(4) program was supplemented by the sale of tax benefits to a syndicate. Purchase costs were about $600,000 and redevelopment totaled $2.9 million.

55 National Trust for Historic Preservation (NR)
Washington, D.C.

Origin:	McCormick (later Mellon) Apartments, 1917
Conversion:	Offices, scheduled for completion in 1979
Developer:	National Trust for Historic Preservation, Washington, D.C.
Architect:	David N. Yerkes and Associates, Washington, D.C.

Redevelopment: The National Trust for Historic Preservation will consolidate its Washington offices, currently scattered in several buildings, by converting a Beaux Arts luxury apartment house into its new headquarters. The five-story limestone building, which has a slate mansard roof, was purchased for $1.3 million and will cost an estimated $1.9 million to rehabilitate. The Trust, which will rent out the upper floors, is seeking foundation grants and private donations to fund the project.

56 Flagler College (NR)
St. Augustine, Florida

Origin:	Hotel Ponce de Leon, 1887
Conversion:	Liberal arts college, 1968
Developer:	Flagler College, Inc., St. Augustine
Architect:	Craig Thorn, St. Augustine

Redevelopment: Once a vacation spot for the rich, the lavish, Spanish-Renaissance-style hotel now serves as a college campus with administrative offices, classrooms, library, dormitory rooms, and dining facilities all centered within one unique complex. Originally designed by the New York architectural firm of Carrere and Hastings, the complex contains five buildings with a gross building area of 270,714 square feet on a 7.2-acre site. Although long-range plans call for expenditures of $7 million for complete renovation and new construction, the hotel buildings were found to be structurally sound and the college opened its doors after only $200,000 of redevelopment work.

57 Glessner House (NHL)
Chicago, Illinois

Origin:	Private residence, 1886
Conversion:	Museum, offices, and meeting spaces; in progress since 1966
Developer:	Chicago School of Architecture Foundation, Chicago
Architect:	Joint efforts from several architects through the years

Redevelopment: The Chicago School of Architecture Foundation, formed in 1966 to save the Glessner House from demolition, has invested manpower, design services, and money in a decade-long redevelopment of this landmark building—an outstanding example of the work of 19th century architect H. H. Richardson. Although several rooms in the Romanesque-style building have been restored as museum space for public tours, most of the house functions in a revenue-producing capacity as offices or meeting spaces for organizations in sympathy with the work of the Foundation. The house was purchased for $35,000, and approximately $400,000 (raised through grants, membership and tour revenues, and rental income) has been spent on the renovation. Under the supervision of various architects over the years, redevelopment of the 20,000-square-foot building has included roof and foundation repairs, installation of new mechanical systems, restoration of woodwork and other interior finishes, and landscaping of the courtyard.

58 Clifton Square
Wichita, Kansas

Origin:	Private residences, 1850s–1930
Conversion:	Shopping complex, 1971
Developer:	Jo S. Zakas, Wichita
Architect:	Kuhnel-Robson-Spangerberg, Wichita

Redevelopment: A dozen houses—some in their original locations and some moved from other parts of the city—comprise this square-block "village" of specialty shops and restaurants. Twenty businesses occupy the houses in the landscaped complex which contains more than 18,000 square feet of retail space. Current valuation of the property is approximately $700,000.

59 Haddie Bishop Speed House (NR)
Louisville, Kentucky

Origin:	Private residence, 1885
Conversion:	Offices, 1975
Developer:	Grossman/Martin/Chapman, Louisville
Architect:	Grossman/Martin/Chapman

Redevelopment: The interior richness of this Victorian mansion—including a music auditorium with organ, seats for 150, and walnut, brass, and crystal interior detailing—was preserved during the conversion of the mansion into offices for a regional planning agency. The architect-developers purchased the house for $75,000 and invested an additional $75,000 in the redevelopment. Loans from a local bank were guaranteed by a local philanthropist with an interest in urban conservation.

60 Oriental Laundry Building (NHL)
New Orleans, Louisiana

Origin:	Two private residences (later a laundry), circa 1860
Conversion:	Restaurant, 1973
Developer:	Edson C. Tung, Metairie, Louisiana
Architect:	Louis Chiodini, St. Louis; and M. Wayne Stoffle, New Orleans

Redevelopment: As the character of Bourbon Street in the Vieux Carré has changed through the years, the uses of these two party-wall structures have also changed. Originally private homes, the brick structures were adapted as a laundry facility in the 1930s when the area became industrialized. Conversion of the street into a pedestrian mall with heavy tourist activity in the early 1970s enabled the owners to renovate the buildings for use as a restaurant. The structures contain a gross building area of 14,880 square feet.

61 Franklin Square House
Boston, Massachusetts

Origin:	St. James Hotel, 1868 (with 1914 addition)
Conversion:	Apartments for the elderly, 1976
Developer:	St. James Company, Boston
Architect:	Boston Architectural Team, Inc., Boston, with Archplan, Inc., Boston

Redevelopment: Originally constructed as a posh hotel in the fashionable French-Second-Empire-style, this six-story building was first converted in 1882 into the New England Conservatory of Music. After the conservatory relocated in 1902, the building served as a nonprofit residence for women until 1970. Adaptation into 193 units of housing for the elderly was done with the assistance of a mortgage loan from the Massachusetts Finance Agency and Section 8 subsidies from the United States Department of Housing and Urban Development. Purchased for $380,000 and redeveloped for $3,778,771, the building totals 89,400 square feet (including 10,000 square feet of community facilities). The conversion to housing for the elderly put this building on the tax rolls for the first time in 94 years.

62 Headland House
Rockport, Massachusetts

Origin:	Private residence, 1797
Conversion:	Condominiums, 1972
Developer:	Thomas S. Grossman, Rockport
Architect:	Boston Architectural Team, Boston

Redevelopment: The interior of this wood-frame, Federal-style residence was gutted and rebuilt to provide five condominiums marketed at an average of $77 per square foot. Although dormers providing a view of Rockport harbor were added to the existing roofline, the remainder of the exterior was restored to its original appearance. A barn on the property has also been converted into a loft-studio. Because local banks were not interested in the project, financing for construction and the permanent mortgage was arranged through a Boston savings bank.

63 The Earle
Ann Arbor, Michigan

Origin:	The Earle Hotel, 1882
Conversion:	Commercial and residential space, 1976-1980
Developer:	Richard Burgess, Ernest Harburg, David Rock & Dennis Webster, Ann Arbor
Architect:	Richard C. Frank, Preservation/Urban Design/Inc., Ann Arbor

Redevelopment: Conversion of the four-story Italianate hotel into commercial and residential uses is phased over a 5-year period in order to make the project more financially feasible. The first phase includes redevelopment of the basement as a nightclub (the largest revenue-producing use planned for the project) and of supporting areas such as kitchen, restroom, and storage facilities. A consortium of five local lending institutions provided a $350,000 permanent mortgage loan.

64 The Boardman Planetarium and Youth Museum (NR)
Ithaca, New York

Origin: Private residence (later the Ithaca Conservatory of Music), 1867

Conversion: Planetarium and museum, 1977-1978

Developer: Center Research Group, Inc., Ithaca

Architect: Tallman and Tallman, Ithaca

Redevelopment: A nonprofit science research cooperative obtained a 20-year lease to convert the county-owned building into a planetarium and museum. Without changing the exterior appearance of the building, a two-story dome will be constructed within the building by removing the third floor of the three-story Italian-style villa. The domed theater, which is to be fully automated, will accommodate 70 in reclining airplane seats donated by an airline company. Museum exhibits will occupy the first floor and the basement will double as space for equipment maintenance and as an after-school youth center involving mechanical and electrical projects. Private foundations and donations are paying for the $50,000 exterior restoration and the $75,000 interior rehabilitation (exclusive of equipment).

65 Clinton House (NR)
Ithaca, New York

Origin: Hotel, 1830 (with additions from 1901)

Conversion: Offices, museum, and commercial space, begun in 1973

Developer: Historic Ithaca, Inc.

Architect: David Taube, (new construction only), Ithaca

Redevelopment: Construction of an addition to accommodate an elevator proved to be the most costly aspect of redevelopment of this 33,000-square-foot, three-story Greek Revival hotel. Funds for the project, including $85,000

for acquisition, $363,000 for rehabilitation, and $136,500 for the elevator construction, were raised through private donations, foundation grants, and state matching grants. Interior spaces were designed according to specifications of tenants, with the first floor and basement providing exhibition, office, workshop, and modern archive storage spaces for a county historical society.

66 Snyder Apartments
Little Falls, New York

Origin: Hotel Snyder, 1905

Conversion: Apartments and commercial space, 1974

Developer: Gaetano Realty Corporation, Utica, New York

Architect: Edmund J. Booth, Utica

Redevelopment: Small shops and a restaurant occupy the basement and first floor of the concrete-frame building, and 39 apartments are housed in the upper five stories. The former hotel was purchased for $55,000 and redeveloped for $300,000. A permanent mortgage from a local bank was secured after the project was completed.

67 Cooper-Hewitt Museum (NHL)
New York, New York

Origin: Andrew Carnegie Mansion, 1901

Conversion: National Museum of Design, 1976

Developer: Smithsonian Institution, Washington, D.C.

Architect: Hardy Holzman Pfeiffer Associates, New York

Redevelopment: The principal rooms in the 64-room, Neo-Georgian mansion were restored, rather than redeveloped, to accommodate gallery and exhibition areas for the federally owned museum collection. Conservation facilities and office, library, archival, and storage spaces have been placed in the basement and on the third and fourth floors. One of the earliest residences in the United States to have a structural steel frame and a central heating and cooling system, the mansion was a gift to the museum from the Carnegie Foundation. Corporate and individual donations provided most of the funding for the $1,750,000 project. A second house on the grounds will be more radically altered to provide additional flexible spaces, and a new museum facility will be constructed later.

68 United States Hotel Building (NHL)
Jacksonville, Oregon

Origin: United States Hotel, 1880
Conversion: Bank, 1965
Developer: City of Jacksonville
Architect: Edson and Pappas, Medford, Oregon

Redevelopment: Built during the gold rush, the United States Hotel was host to President Rutherford B. Hayes almost a century ago. Now owned by the city of Jacksonville, the two-story hotel has been leased to the U.S. National Bank of Oregon as a branch office. The first floor and the ballroom have been restored and furnished with 19th century Oregon memorabilia. The bank project is one of several renovations which are revitalizing Jacksonville's small commercial district while retaining its regional character. It is designated as a National Historic Landmark.

69 Stochman's Building
Ontario, Oregon

Origin: Moore Hotel, 1911
Conversion: Commercial space and offices, 1976
Developer: S.L.S.Q. Corporation, Ontario
Architect: Probart, Gowland, Johanson; Payette, Idaho

Redevelopment: Now recycled as offices with retail and restaurant space, the five-story brick hotel cost $1,030,000 to acquire and develop. A local commercial bank provided a permanent mortgage for the 37,200-square-foot building.

70 Design Research
Philadelphia, Pennsylvania

Origin: Private residence (later the Penn Athletic Club), 1898
Conversion: Commercial use, 1976
Developer: Presbyterian Ministers' Fund
Architect: Colin Smith, Architectural Resources, Inc., Cambridge

Redevelopment: Originally built for the Van Rensselaer family by the Boston architectural firm, Peabody and Stearns, the Renaissance Revival stone mansion on Rittenhouse Square now serves as a retail store for Design Research, Inc. The exterior of the building was restored and certain interior features, such as the fireplaces, a stained glass dome, and an ornamented ceiling, were retained. Most of the interior, however, was gutted and reworked to provide contemporary shopping space. The second floor was raised to allow room for a mezzanine level; other floors were removed to give two-story spaces; and a steel and oak spiral stairway was constructed to provide vertical circulation. Redevelopment costs for the building, which is leased by Design Research, totaled about $1 million.

71 St. Johnsbury House (NR)
St. Johnsbury, Vermont

Origin: Hotel, 1850
Conversion: Apartments for the elderly, 1976
Developer: Northeastern Vermont Development Association, Inc., St. Johnsbury
Architect: Alexander and Truex, Burlington, Vermont

Redevelopment: Once popular with tourists and skiers, this 75-room, wood-frame hotel has been converted into 42 units of housing for the elderly. The lobby and the dining and bar areas (now leased to a private operator) were restored, and the basement was converted to offices for a regional planning commission and an area office on aging. Funding for the $550,000 project included $203,000 from an Economic Development Administration Title X grant; $100,000 from a HUD Community Development Block Grant; and $75,000 from a National Park Service Historic Sites grant. A local bank holds a mortgage for $130,000.

72 309-311 Cameron Street
Alexandria, Virginia

Origin: Norford Inn, 1817
Conversion: Commercial space, offices, and apartments, 1975
Developer: Ellsworth-Howell, Alexandria
Architect: Michael and Michael, Alexandria

Redevelopment: The interior of the four-story Federal-style townshouse was gutted for conversion into retail shops (on the ground floor), offices (second floor), and apartments (top two levels). Permanent mortgages for the $225,000 project, undertaken during a period of tight money, were extremely difficult to obtain. Several commercial banks and savings and loans were involved in the financing.

73 Gadsby's Tavern (NHL)
Alexandria, Virginia

Origin:	Hotel and tavern, 1770 (with major additions in 1792 and 1878)
Conversion:	Museum, restaurant, and meeting hall, 1976
Developer:	City of Alexandria
Architect:	J. Everette Fauber, Jr., Lynchburg, Virginia

Redevelopment: The old hotel and tavern was a gift to the city of Alexandria from the American Legion, now a tenant in the building. A museum occupies a restored portion of the structure; a restaurant with a colonial theme was installed in the original dining and public rooms; and the legion hall was renovated. A $4,000 grant from the National Park Service assisted the $1,644,000 municipal project.

74 The Lloyd House (NR)
Alexandria, Virginia

Origin:	Private residence, 1797
Conversion:	Library annex, 1976
Developer:	The Alexandria Historical Restoration and Preservation Commission and the city of Alexandria
Architect:	Walter M. Macomber and Carrol C. Curtice, Washington, D.C.

Redevelopment: Now used to house the Alexandria Library's extensive collection of rare books, records, and documents on local and state history, the house was purchased in 1969 with funds from a private foundation and from federal, state, and municipal governments. The three-story Georgian brick house, which had been threatened with demolition since 1956, was restored and adapted for $227,000.

75 Swann-Daingerfield Condominiums
Alexandria, Virginia

Origin:	Private residence (Carter Hall), 1802 (with major additions 1835-1905)
Conversion:	Condominiums, 1977
Developer:	OTV, Inc., Alexandria
Architect:	Carroll C. Curtice, Washington, D.C.

Redevelopment: The city of Alexandria organized a competitive bid and proposal process to encourage adaptive use of this large, mansard-roofed residence. The building was sold for $250,000 after acceptance of an $896,000 plan for conversion into 12 residential condominiums. The oldest portion of the structure will be restored as one unit, and the two remaining wings will be gutted for adaptation into two-bedroom units.

76 Richard Johnston House (NR)
Fredericksburg, Virginia

Origin:	Private residence, circa 1799
Conversion:	Commercial and office space, 1975
Developer:	Hunter Greenlaw, Jr., Fredericksburg
Architect:	Grigg, Wood and Browne, Charlottesville

Redevelopment: Probably built as a double townhouse, this 2½-story, Federal-style building was serving as a furniture warehouse before its purchase for conversion into offices and shops. Fireplaces in many of the 16 rooms have been restored, and a landscaped courtyard and parking lot were added behind the building. With renovation costs estimated at $78,000, a 12-month construction loan with permanent financing (20 years at 10 percent) at the end was secured at the outset of the project. Cost overruns of about $40,000 necessitated a second loan (15 years at 10 percent). Developers noted that, as the first project of its kind in downtown Fredericksburg, a good deal of persuasion was necessary in dealing with local financial institutions. The building won fourth place in a nationwide exterior design contest sponsored by the National Association of Realtors.

Project Economics
Hotels, Mansions, and Apartments

Project	Year of Conversion	Gross Building Area (sq. ft.)	Acquisition Cost	Redevelopment Cost	Approx. Cost Per Sq. Ft.	Source of Financing	Rental Rates (annual per sq. ft., unless otherwise noted)
French Flats	1973	6,000	$ 6,500	$ 40,000	$ 7.00	Local bank	$250—500/ mo./unit
Murphy House	1970	16,000	80,000	370,000	(23.13)	Public funds	(not rented)
James B. Colt House	1976	7,800	31,000	171,000	22.00	Local banks, National Park Service grant	—
The Cairo	1976	122,000	600,000	2,900,000	23.77	FHA-Insured perma-nent mortgage 221d4	—
National Trust for Historic Preservation	1979	70,000	1,300,000	1,900,000	27.00	Foundation grants, private donations	—
Flagler College	1968	270,714	1,500,000	200,000	(0.74)		(not rented)
Glessner House	1966	20,000	35,000	400,000	20.00	Grants, rentals, tours, memberships	$0.60
Clifton Square	1971	18,000	—	—	—	Insurance company, local bank	$5.00 plus percentage
Haddie Bishop Speed House	1975	18,000	75,000	75,000	4.16	Local bank	$3.00
Oriental Laundry Building	1973	14,880	Already owned	—	—	S&L	—
Franklin Square House	1976	89,400	380,000	3,778,771	(42.27)	State finance agency, HUD Sec. 8	25 percent of income
Headland House	1972	3,057	—	—	—	Local bank	$77.00 (sale)
The Earle	1976	31,350	116,000	323,000	50.00	5-bank consortium	—
Boardman Planetarium	1978	—	Leased ($300/mo.)	125,000	—	Private foundations, contributions	(leased by developer)
Clinton House	1975	33,000	85,000	Old 363,000 New 136,500	11.00 98.00	Private donations, public grants	$4.25 commer-cial and office
Snyder Apartments	1974	40,670	55,000	300,000	(7.38)	Savings bank (out of town)	$3.00 commer-cial; $170/ mo./apt.
Cooper-Hewitt Museum	1976	—	Gift	1,750,000	—	Foundation, corpo-rate, and indi-vidual donations	(not rented)
United States Hotel Building	1965	—	Leased	76,000	33.00	In-house	(leased by developer)
Stochman's Building	1976	37,200	280,000	750,000	20.00	Local commercial bank	$3.50
Design Research	1976	18,300	Leased	1,000,000	(54.64)		(leased by developer)
St. Johnsbury House	1976	38,940	100,000	450,000	12.00	Local bank, federal funds	$2.60
309–311 Cameron Street	1975	12,000	185,000	225,000	(18.75)	S&Ls, commercial banks	$9.50
Gadsby's Tavern	1976	22,762	Gift	1,644,000	72.00	City funds, National Park Service grant	$6.00
The Lloyd House	1976	2,000	460,000	227,000	(113.50)	City, state, and federal funds; pri-vate foundation	(not rented)
Swann-Daingerfield Condominiums	1977	21,000	250,000	896,000	48.70	S&L	$78.00 (sale)
Richard Johnston House	1975	6,400	27,500	117,500	18.35	Local bank	$5.00

Dashes indicate data not available.
Figures in parentheses were not supplied directly but were derived from other data.

Redevelopment Work
Hotels, Mansions, and Apartments

Project	Exterior Restoration	New Exterior Construction	Structural	Mechanical	Interior Demolition	Interior New Construction	Site Restoration	New Facilities, Parking	Landscaping
French Flats	Extensive	Minor	Minor	Extensive	Extensive	Extensive	—	Minor	Moderate
Murphy House	Extensive	Minor	Minor	Extensive	Extensive	Extensive	—	—	—
The Colorado Springs School	Minor	Moderate	Moderate	Extensive	None	Moderate	—	—	—
James B. Colt House	Extensive	Extensive	Extensive	Extensive	Extensive	Extensive	Extensive	Extensive	Extensive
The Cairo	Minor	Extensive	Moderate	Extensive	Extensive	Extensive	Extensive	Minor	Extensive
National Trust for Historic Preservation	None	None	Minor	Extensive	Moderate	Minor	Minor	None	Minor
Flagler College	Minor	Minor	Minor	Moderate	Minor	Minor	Minor	Minor	Minor
Glessner House	Minor	Minor	Minor	Extensive	Moderate	Moderate	Minor	Moderate	Extensive
Clifton Square	Moderate	Moderate	Moderate	Extensive	Moderate	Moderate	Extensive	Extensive	Extensive
Haddie Bishop Speed House	Minor	Minor	Minor	Extensive	Moderate	Moderate	Minor	Minor	Minor
Oriental Laundry Building	Moderate	Minor	Minor	Extensive	Extensive	Extensive	Minor	Minor	Moderate
Franklin Square House	Minor	Minor	Extensive	Extensive	Extensive	Extensive	Minor	Moderate	Moderate
Headland House	Extensive	Moderate	Moderate	Extensive	Extensive	Extensive	Extensive	Moderate	Extensive
The Earle	Minor	Minor	Moderate	Extensive	Moderate	Moderate	Minor	Minor	Minor
Boardman Planetarium	Extensive	Extensive	Moderate	Extensive	Extensive	Moderate	Minor	Minor	Moderate
Clinton House	Extensive	Moderate	Moderate	Extensive	Extensive	Moderate	Minor	Minor	Minor
Snyder Apartments	Minor	Minor	Minor	Extensive	Extensive	Extensive	Minor	Extensive	Moderate
Cooper-Hewitt Museum	Moderate	Minor	Minor	Extensive	Moderate	Moderate	Minor	None	Minor
United States Hotel Building	Moderate	Minor	Extensive	Extensive	Moderate	Extensive	Minor	Moderate	—
Stochman's Building	Moderate	Extensive	Moderate	Extensive	Extensive	Extensive	Extensive	Minor	Extensive
Design Research	None	None	Extensive	Extensive	Extensive	Extensive	Minor	Minor	Minor
St. Johnsbury House	Moderate	Moderate	Minor	Extensive	Moderate	Moderate	Minor	Minor	Minor
309—311 Cameron Street	Moderate	Minor	Minor	Extensive	Extensive	Extensive	Extensive	—	Extensive
Gadsby's Tavern	Minor	Minor	Minor	Extensive	Minor	Moderate	Extensive	Extensive	Extensive
The Lloyd House	Moderate	None	Extensive	Extensive	Moderate	Extensive	Extensive	—	Extensive
Swann-Daingerfield Condominiums	Extensive	Moderate	Minor	Extensive	Extensive	Extensive	Minor	Moderate	Moderate
Richard Johnston House	Moderate	Moderate	Minor	Extensive	Extensive	Extensive	Moderate	Extensive	Extensive

Dashes indicate data not available.

Carriage Houses, Garages, and Stables

Although a modern parking garage bears little resemblance to a 19th century livery stable, the original function of the two buildings is the same. These structures have changed in design and construction as our principal means of transportation has shifted from the carriage to the car. A few buildings have adapted to the changing times. The Garage in Cambridge, for example, was built as a stable and turnaround shed for horse-drawn trolleys in 1870; in 1916 it was converted to a parking garage, a use which continued until the 1970s. A far greater number of old livery stables and carriage houses, however, have been redeveloped to serve new uses.

Even today the alleyways of many Victorian-era neighborhoods reveal rows of carriage houses. The majority of the buildings were small and utilitarian, originally containing a stable area for the horse, storage for hay and grain, shelter for the carriage and other equipment, and perhaps living quarters above for servants. Often the architectural style of the main house is repeated in miniature in the carriage house. An editor of a leading architectural journal objected to this resemblance in 1902, criticizing carriage buildings for "masquerading as houses."[2]

This small-scale charm, however, has probably been a major factor in saving many carriage houses from demolition. Adaptive use of these buildings became common as quickly as the carriage itself became outmoded, with numerous conversions into apartments, studios, or, of course, automobile garages. On Byron Street on Boston's Beacon Hill, extensive reuse of stables as residences began in the early 1920s.

In more recent times, the character of many older urban neighborhoods has changed from purely residential to mixed uses. Surviving carriage houses such as those in Richmond and Louisville have been recycled as professional offices or commercial space. In many cases, the interior of the building has been gutted during renovation, and contemporary design elements have been introduced to contrast with original features such as exposed brick walls and sturdy structural beams.

Unlike the carriage house, the automobile garage is far from obsolete as a building type. Individual structures, however, sometimes become surplus because of disuse or inadequate space for modern vehicles. They may be attractive for redevelopment because of their location on property suitable for a more intensive use. Designed to accommodate heavy loads of automobiles, garages contructed of concrete or steel are structurally adequate for new uses such as housing or office or commercial space. An enclosed shopping arcade can capitalize on the existing open interiors of a small garage; with large public garages, the space can be subdivided with a minimum of interior demolition. A converted garage, such as Boston's Stoneholm Street Apartments, with some of its parking area preserved, can offer the bonus of parking on the lower levels.

3-3   This concrete parking garage has been converted to apartments. (Photo: Peter Southwick.)

---

[2] *The Architectural Review*, Vol. IX, No. 9 (September 1902), p. 151.

77 The Garage
Birmingham, Alabama

Origin:	Parking garages, 1927
Conversion:	Shopping court, 1974
Developer:	Fritz Woehle, Birmingham
Architect:	Fritz Woehle

Redevelopment: Thirty concrete, single-car garages, originally constructed for residents of an apartment building, now house a series of small shops opening onto a landscaped courtyard. Purchased for $30,000, the garages were refurbished by the architect-developer for $60,000. Antique wooden doors replaced the old garage gates, giving each shop a unique entry. A cedar beam canopy in the courtyard adds to the rustic, open-air atmosphere of the mini-shopping complex.

78 220 East Forsyth Street
Jacksonville, Florida

Origin:	McMurray Livery Stable (later the Court House Garage), 1902
Conversion:	Offices and parking garage, 1973
Developer:	William Morgan, Jacksonville
Architect:	William Morgan Architects, Jacksonville

Redevelopment: Interior walls of exposed brick help to retain the character of this building, which was constructed as a stable but had served as a garage since 1912. The structure was remodeled to accommodate the offices of William Morgan Architects and to provide an additional 7,095 square feet of rental office space. On the ground floor, cars can still pass through the original brick archways into a 19-space garage. Redevelopment costs totaled $210,616 for the structure, which has a gross building area of 17,152 square feet. The conversion received local and national design awards.

79 12 Stoneholm Street
Boston, Massachusetts

Origin:	Parking garage, circa 1920
Conversion:	Apartments, 1970
Developer:	Stoneholm Street Associates, Boston
Architect:	Anderson Notter Associates, Boston

Redevelopment: Studio apartments containing kitchen units and with sleeping lofts over the bathroom occupy three floors of the concrete-frame parking garage. The first two stories of the structure remain in use for parking, and two additional floors have been added to accommodate duplex townhouses. Rooftop terraces and swimming pool serve the 120-unit building, which was redeveloped for $1.4 million.

80 Stella Lass Theatre
Newark, New Jersey

Origin:	Carriage house, circa 1900
Conversion:	Community theater, 1970
Developer:	Newark Community Center of the Arts
Architect:	Hardy Holzman Pfeiffer Associates, New York

Redevelopment: A newly constructed split-level entryway gives access into the former carriage house, now used as an auditorium on the upper floor and a dance rehearsal hall on the lower level. To make optimum use of the building's 2,000 square feet, the auditorium stage is diagonally oriented and moveable seating for 75 is available. Purchase cost of the property, which includes a large residence now used for art classes, was $25,000; redevelopment of the carriage house totaled $46,000.

81 Kent-Valentine Carriage House (NR)
Richmond, Virginia

Origin:	Carriage house and servants quarters, 1840 (with addition, circa 1890)
Conversion:	Offices, 1972
Developer:	Robert Welton Stewart, Richmond
Architect:	Robert Welton Stewart

Redevelopment: Separated from the Kent-Valentine House by a landscaped courtyard, the two-story brick carriage house has been redeveloped as architectural offices. Conversion of the small building (only 1,300 square feet) required removal of interior partitions to yield open drafting areas, replacement of mechanical and electrical systems, and extensive cleaning and painting. Adaptive use of the carriage house resulted from the architect's involvement with the purchase and rehabilitation of the Kent-Valentine House by the Garden Club of Virginia.

Project Economics
Carriage Houses, Garages, and Stables

Project	Year of Conversion	Gross Building Area (sq. ft.)	Acquisition Cost	Redevelopment Cost	Approx. Cost Per Sq. Ft.	Source of Financing	Rental Rates (annual per sq. ft., unless otherwise noted)
The Garage (Birmingham)	1974	6,000	$ 30,000	$ 60,000	$(10.00)	—	$150/mo./unit
220 East Forsyth Street	1973	17,152	102,911	210,616	22.28	Mortgage company	$6.00
12 Stoneholm Street	1970	111,000	—	1,400,000	12.60	—	$7.20
Stella Lass Theatre	1970	2,000	25,000 (includes another bldg.)	46,000	23.00	Local commercial bank	(not rented)
Kent-Valentine Carriage House	1972	1,300	—	12,800	10.00	Personal loans	(not rented)

Dashes indicate data not available.
Figures in parentheses were not supplied directly but were derived from other data.

Redevelopment Work
Carriage Houses, Garages, and Stables

Project	Exterior Restoration	New Exterior Construction	Structural	Mechanical	Interior Demolition	Interior New Construction	Site Restoration	New Facilities, Parking	Landscaping
The Garage (Birmingham)	Moderate	Moderate	Minor	Moderate	Minor	Moderate	Moderate	—	Extensive
220 East Forsyth Street	Minor	—	Minor	Extensive	Moderate	Extensive	Minor	—	Moderate
12 Stoneholm Street	Extensive	Extensive	Minor	Extensive	Minor	Extensive	Minor	Minor	Moderate
Stella Lass Theatre	Moderate	Moderate	Minor	Extensive	Minor	Extensive	Minor	Minor	Minor
Kent-Valentine Carriage House	Minor	Minor	Moderate	Extensive	Extensive	Extensive	Moderate	Extensive	Extensive

Dashes indicate data not available.

Commercial Buildings

Change is a continual part of the life of commercial and office buildings. Businesses are opened, expanded, moved, merged, and closed. Stores relocate to exploit new markets. Offices are remodeled as tenants change. The exteriors of buildings are updated to imitate the newest look. Evolution of economic conditions and growth patterns in a downtown area—traditionally the most dynamic part of a city—cause business activities to shift over a period of time from one block or district to another. Districts which were once important commercial centers can become skid rows with underused or abandoned buildings.

Revitalization of blighted business districts generally is a two-fold process involving reestablishment of the area's credibility for use as well as the actual rehabilitation of individual buildings. Renovation has been preferred over adaptive use in the revitalization of many commercial districts, such as Pioneer Square in Seattle, Larimer Square in Denver, and The Strand in Galveston, or of single structures such as Houston's Old Cotton Exchange. Numerous small towns across the country, from Corning, New York, and Medina, Ohio, to Jacksonville, Oregon, have bolstered their economies by renovating 19th century main streets. In many cases, however, a change of function has provided the most ecnomically feasible use of old banks, stores, or offices.

After the Civil War, the number of commercial buildings in the country increased significantly with the development of new merchandising methods which produced the department store, the chain store, the modern drugstore, and the cafeteria. Inventions such as the telephone and the typewriter made offices more efficient. By the 1880s, tall office buildings had added a new element to the American urban skyline.

America's business buildings have long been shaped by practical concern for economics and building technology. During the second half of the 19th century, the character of commercial and office buildings changed drastically as technology developed more efficient means to meet the demands for maximum exploitation of available space, light, and air. The development of elevators, plate glass, prefabricated cast iron, reinforced concrete, and steel-frame construction all had a major effect on architecture.

The style of commercial buildings, as well as their construction, was of particular importance to the businessman whose building served as a physical advertisement for his company. Banks in particular were anxious to build structures with an appearance of formal dignity and strength, both inside and outside. Projects such as those in Quincy, Illinois and Louisville, Kentucky are examples of former banking rooms which have been converted into public meeting or lobby spaces.

Victorian aspirations toward wealth and prosperity were often expressed in the construction of "cathedrals of commerce" with richly detailed facades of cast iron, stone, or terra-cotta. The original facades of many commercial buildings, covered over through the years in attempts to modernize storefronts, often can be exposed simply by stripping away the new materials. Cleaned and restored, the original exterior decoration can be a valuable commercial asset for a revitalized building such as The Ironfronts in Richmond.

The interior plan of an office and commercial building generally depended on the nature of the business. Department stores had large, open-floor areas; office buildings frequently had numerous small cubicles. Existing interior configurations often influence the choice of a new use for an old building. In many cases, the original finishings within a commercial building have not survived intact, and contemporary planning of space and interior design can be used. Mezzanine levels can often be installed in buildings with high ceilings, with a resulting increase in the gross building area.

A conference sponsored during the summer of 1975 in Seattle by the National Trust for Historic Preservation dealt with the economic benefits of preserving old buildings and focused on the adaptive use of commercial buildings. Now available in book form (Washington, D.C.: Preservation Press, 1976), the conference proceedings included discussions on adaptive office space in old buildings by Boston architect Charles N. Tseckares; on preservation costs of commercial buildings by San Francisco architect Herbert McLaughlin; and on the preservation costs in 19th century commercial buildings and getting the most for your money by Ann Arbor architect Richard C. Frank.

82 Robertson Banking Company Building
Demopolis, Alabama

Origin:	Mayer Brothers Department Store, 1897
Conversion:	Bank and insurance agency, 1975
Developer:	Robertson Banking Company, Demopolis
Architect:	Cobb, Adams, Benton, Birmingham

Redevelopment: Redevelopment of the three-story brick mercantile building, which features Sullivanesque terra-cotta detailing on the facade, earned an award from the Alabama Historical Commission. The conversion, financed by the bank, cost $700,000.

83 FABCO Building
Little Rock, Arkansas

Origin:	Department store (The Blass Building), 1913
Conversion:	Offices and data processing center, 1975
Developer:	Worthen Bank and Trust Company, Little Rock
Architect:	Blass, Riddick, Chilcote, Little Rock

Redevelopment: Redevelopment of the seven-story commercial building, located in central Little Rock, provides more than 80,000 square feet of space for the bank's computer operations and for rental offices.

84 428 Maine Building
Quincy, Illinois

Origin:	State Savings Loan and Trust Company, 1892 (with 1906 addition)
Conversion:	Offices and art facilities, 1966
Developer:	George M. Irwin, Quincy
Architect:	None

Redevelopment: The handsome Romanesque bank building, once threatened with "conversion" into a parking lot, now houses office space and art facilities behind its rusticated granite facade. The main banking room, a two-story area, was adapted to accommodate 160 persons for community concerts, exhibitions, or meetings, and seven walk-in vaults provide 850 square feet of useable space. Redevelopment of the 18,000-square-foot building, purchased for $50,000, cost $350,000.

85 Actors Theatre
Louisville, Kentucky

Origin:	Bank of Louisville, 1834
Conversion:	Repertory theater, 1972
Developer:	Actors Theatre of Louisville, Inc.
Architect:	Harry Weese and Associates, Chicago

Redevelopment: The domed banking area of the Greek Revival bank was restored to serve as the lobby of a new 641-seat theater, constructed behind the old building. The theater box office occupies the bank vault and the former bank's basement contains a restaurant and bar. An adjacent brick warehouse, built circa 1865, was gutted and redeveloped to house a second smaller theater, offices, and scene and property shops.

The theater company acquired the bank by trading another site and building. The bank was subsequently purchased by the city of Louisville for $201,300 and leased back to the theater group for 99 years at a nominal fee. One-half of the purchase and restoration costs for the bank building was paid from a HUD grant, and the remainder was funded by foundation and individual contributions. Project costs for the entire complex, including land acquisition, restoration of the bank, redevelopment of the warehouse, and new construction for the main theater, totaled $1,569,565.

86 Academic Center, University of Baltimore
Baltimore, Maryland

Origin:	Automobile club and dealership, circa 1906
Conversion:	Educational facility, 1971
Developer:	University of Baltimore
Architect:	Fisher, Nes, Campbell and Partners, Baltimore

Redevelopment: Known as "The Garage" when it provided Baltimore's early motoring set with skating, bowling, and billiard facilities, as well as auto repairs and sales, the building was adapted to provide much needed expansion space for the urban university. Classrooms, laboratories, offices, a bookstore, a gymnasium and other recreational facilities occupy a gross building area of 134,464 square feet in the three-story, reinforced concrete building. Federal and state grants totaling $2,225,000 assisted the $4,120,000 project, which received an award from the Baltimore Heritage Foundation, Inc. in 1971.

3-4 Richmond's finest example of cast-iron architecture was converted to commercial and office space in 1976.

87 Chauncy House
Boston, Massachusetts

Origin:	Offices, 1921
Conversion:	Apartments, 1975
Developer:	State Street Development Company, Boston
Architect:	Archplan, Inc., Boston with Boston Architectural Team, Inc. supervising

Redevelopment: Located in Boston's Garment District, the former office building now houses 87 units of low- and moderate-income apartments. The 12-story building, which has a gross building area of 66,911 square feet, also contains 3,300 square feet of street-level commercial space. Rehabilitation costs were financed with a loan from the Massachusetts Housing Finance Agency, and the building has an FHA-insured permanent mortgage for $2,002,400 through the HUD 236 program.

88 One Winthrop Square (NR)
Boston, Massachusetts

Origin:	Mercantile building, 1873
Conversion:	Commercial and office space, 1974
Developer:	Raymond Cattle Company, Boston
Architect:	Childs Bertman Tseckares, Inc., Boston

Redevelopment: Net rentable square footage in the former Boston *Record American* newspaper building was increased by almost 10 percent after conversion into office and commercial space. By using three attic towers, inserting two mezzanines in spaces with 20-foot ceilings, and adding five stories about the ground floor loading dock, the structure gained an additional 10,200 square feet. Project costs totaled $4.7 million ($47 per square foot); construction costs ran to $37.20 per square foot, with $3.6 million invested in building renovation and $120,000 in site improvements. Rents are competitive with nearby Boston skyscrapers.

89 Latta Arcade (NR)
Charlotte, North Carolina

Origin:	Office arcade, 1914
Conversion:	Commercial and office space, 1968
Developer:	F. J. Heath Realty Company, Charlotte
Architect:	Wolf Associates Architects, Charlotte

Redevelopment: A pedestrian link between two blocks in downtown Charlotte, the Latta Arcade gives access to two tiers of small offices and businesses. The redevelopment architects highlighted the original features of the building, including the steel truss arcade system, marble floors, leaded glass windows, and carved woodwork. They received a merit award from the North Carolina chapter of the American Institute of Architects.

90 The Cotton Exchange
Wilmington, North Carolina

Origin:	Nine mercantile buildings, 19th century
Conversion:	Shopping center and offices, begun in 1976
Developer:	Harbor Associates, Inc., Wilmington
Architect:	Reg Narmour, Charlotte; and John Oxenfeld, Wilmington

Redevelopment: The Cotton Exchange represents a major effort by a private corporation to revitalize the waterfront area of Wilmington through development of a specialty shopping complex. Two blocks of buildings, including Wilmington's old Cotton Exchange and a mill structure, are undergoing rehabilitation to provide approximately 89,000 square feet of commercial and office space, unified by a complex of pedestrian malls and arcades. Although a commercial bank has provided construction loans for the $2 million project, arrangements for permanent financing have been hampered by the skepticism of potential lenders concerning the profitability of adaptive use.

91 Galleria
Portland, Oregon

Origin:	Rhodes Department Store, 1906
Conversion:	Shopping mall and offices, 1976
Developer:	Direct Imports, Inc., Portland
Architect:	Colburn Sheldon and Partners, Portland

Redevelopment: An original 75-foot light court, closed in 1949 during a remodeling of the five-story commercial building, was reopened to become the main feature of this multi-use complex. The 240,000-square-foot building, constructed of reinforced concrete, offers commercial space on the first through third floors and office space on the top two levels, with parking for 114 cars in the basement. New elevators, escalators, and mechanical systems service the structure, which was purchased for $565,000 and redeveloped for approximately $3 million. Centrally located in Portland's downtown, the renovated building earned a merit award from the local chapter of the American Institute of Architects in 1976.

92 The Bank Center
Pittsburgh, Pennsylvania

Origin:	Bank buildings, 1890-1927
Conversion:	Specialty shopping center and office tower, 1976
Developer:	The Bank Center Limited (Seach Development Company, General Partner), Pittsburgh
Design Consultant:	Morgan-Stewart, Inc., Pittsburgh

Redevelopment: Five adjacent buildings in Pittsburgh's former financial district have been united in a multiple use complex which covers 190,000 square feet. The three lower levels of each building, including the original banking rooms, have been redeveloped to function as one integrated shopping and entertainment center. This enclosed "bazaar" and the 15-story office tower retain original neoclassical details such as marble columns, stained glass skylights, bronze doors and clocks, and walk-in vaults. Acquisition and redevelopment costs totaled $4.9 million.

93 Burke's Building (NR)
Pittsburgh, Pennsylvania

Origin:	Real estate and tax office, 1836
Conversion:	Commercial space, offices, and apartments, begun in 1974
Developer:	William H. and Carol F. Ferguson, Pittsburgh
Architect:	None

Redevelopment: As Pittsburgh's oldest remaining office building, this landmark of Greek Revival architecture is undergoing gradual adaptation for multiple uses. Plans for restoration of the facade were drawn up by the nonprofit Pittsburgh History and Landmarks Foundation. The stone building has a gross building area of 8,100 square feet.

94 United American Bank
Nashville, Tennessee

Origin:	Noel Hotel, 1930
Conversion:	Bank, 1973
Developer:	United American Bank (formerly Hamilton Bank), Nashville
Architect:	John Cunningham and Associates, Atlanta

Redevelopment: Location and timing were major factors in the decision to purchase and convert the old Noel Hotel into banking headquarters. Adaptation of the former luxury hotel, strategically located near Nashville's major financial institutions, was completed within 9 months. The first floor and mezzanine of the 12-story building were largely restored, and the remaining floors were gutted and remodeled as offices. Acquisition and redevelopment costs totaled approximately $3.5 million.

95 River Square
San Antonio, Texas

Origin:	Commercial building, 1923
Conversion:	Commercial and office space, 1968
Developer:	River Properties, Inc., San Antonio
Architect:	Cyrus Wagner, Austin

Redevelopment: Originally built with its back to the San Antonio River, this one-story building was redeveloped to allow additional commercial access from the riverside at basement level.

Improvements included further digging under the building, pouring of more concrete piers, and replacement of the brick facing on the rear of the structure. An arcade on the riverside and two interior walkways at street level were added. The building, which currently houses three restaurants, two shops, and two galleries within a gross building area of 15,063 square feet, was acquired for $75,000 and redeveloped for $315,000.

96 The Ironfronts (NR)
Richmond, Virginia

Origin:	Stearns Block, 1867
Conversion:	Commercial and office space, 1976
Developer:	Ironfront Associates, Richmond
Architect:	Glave Newman Anderson and Associates, Inc., Richmond

Redevelopment: Richmond's finest remaining example of cast-iron architecture, the old Stearns Block was originally four separate buildings behind a unified Italianate facade. A central entry and circulation space now serve the four-story, 60,000-square-foot office and retail complex. Only the brick walls and wooden floors remained when the interior was gutted during the $1,200,000 redevelopment of the block. The developers, who paid $560,000 to acquire the property, did not attempt to secure a permanent mortgage on the building until 60 percent of the Ironfronts was leased.

97 Prospect Mall
Milwaukee, Wisconsin

Origin:	Automobile dealership, circa 1931
Conversion:	Commercial use, 1976
Developer:	George Bockl, Milwaukee
Architect:	Blake-Wirth, Milwaukee

Redevelopment: Conversion of the automobile dealership into an enclosed shopping mall with 35,000 sqare feet of rentable space was completed within an 11-month period. The interior of the concrete and steel structure was gutted for the redevelopment. About 30 shops and restaurants occupy the three-story building, which rents for $5.50 per square foot.

Project Economics
Commercial Buildings

Project	Year of Conversion	Gross Building Area (sq. ft.)	Acquisition Cost	Redevelopment Cost	Approx. Cost Per Sq. Ft.	Source of Financing	Rental Rates (annual per sq. ft., unless otherwise noted)
Robertson Banking Company Building	1975	36,391	Foreclosure	$ 700,000	$ 25.00	In-house	—
FABCO Building	1975	80,000	Trade	2,950,000	(36.88)	In-house	—
428 Maine Building	1966	18,000	$ 50,000	350,000	(19.44)	Local commercial bank	$2.75
Actors Theatre (bank building only)	1972	5,600	201,300	49,215	8.75	HUD grant, private and foundation grants	
Academic Center	1971	134,464	1,500,000	2,620,000	26.00	Public grants (state and federal), private donations, local bank	(not rented)
One Winthrop Square	1974	100,000	—	3,720,000	37.20	Construction—local bank; permanent—insurance company	—
Latta Arcade	1968	26,819	317,900	—	—	None	$3.50
The Cotton Exchange	1976	89,000	250,000	2,000,000	22.00	Local commercial bank (construction loan only)	
Galleria	1976	240,000	565,000	3,000,000	(12.50)	Undetermined	—
The Bank Center	1976	190,000	1,200,000	3,700,000	40.00	Permanent mortgage with 7 S&Ls, 2 commercial banks	$6.00—24.00
Burke's Building	1974	8,100	290,000	25,000	5.50	S&L	$5.50
River Square	1968	15,063	75,000	315,000	21.00	S&L	$5.40 or 5 percent
The Ironfronts	1976	60,000	560,000	1,200,000	20.00	Insurance co.	$6.75—7.00 office, $7.00—10.00 retail, $2.50 storage
Prospect Mall	1976	40,000	—	—	—	Mortgage broker	$5.50

Dashes indicate data not available.
Figures in parentheses were not supplied directly but were derived from other data.

Redevelopment Work
Commercial Buildings

Project	Exterior Restoration	New Exterior Construction	Structural	Mechanical	Interior Demolition	Interior New Construction	Site Restoration	New Facilities, Parking	Landscaping
Robertson Banking Company Building	Minor	Moderate	Minor	Extensive	Minor	Extensive	—	Extensive	Extensive
FABCO Building	Moderate	Minor	Minor	Extensive	Extensive	Extensive	Minor	Moderate	Minor
428 Maine Building	Moderate	Minor	Moderate	Extensive	Minor	Extensive	Minor	Minor	Minor
Actors Theatre	Minor	None	Moderate	Extensive	Minor	Minor	None	None	None
Academic Center	Moderate	Moderate	Extensive	Extensive	Extensive	Extensive	Minor	Moderate	Moderate
Chauncy House	Moderate	None	Minor	Extensive	Extensive	Extensive	None	None	None
One Winthrop Square	Moderate	Minor	Moderate	Extensive	Extensive	Extensive	Extensive	None	Extensive
Latta Arcade	Minor	Extensive	Minor	None	Minor	Minor	None	None	None
The Cotton Exchange	Moderate	Minor	Moderate	Extensive	Moderate	Extensive	Moderate	Moderate	Moderate
Galleria	Minor	Minor	Moderate	Extensive	Extensive	Extensive	Minor	Extensive	Minor
The Bank Center	Minor	Minor	Moderate	Extensive	Moderate	Moderate	Minor	Minor	Minor
Burke's Building	Moderate	Moderate	Minor	Minor	Minor	Moderate	None	None	None
United American Bank	Minor	Minor	Minor	Extensive	Extensive	Moderate	None	None	Minor
River Square	—	Extensive	Extensive	Extensive	Extensive	Extensive	Moderate	—	Moderate
The Ironfronts	Extensive	Minor	Moderate	Extensive	Extensive	Extensive	Minor	Minor	Minor
Prospect Mall	Minor	Minor	Moderate	Extensive	Moderate	Extensive	Minor	Extensive	Moderate

Dashes indicate data not available.

Railroad Stations

The use and reuse of railroad stations is a complex issue, closely tied to the future of railway transportation in America. A decline in passenger service over the last few decades has made many stations obsolete. Hundreds of small depots are abandoned because trains no longer stop there, and terminals in larger cities house a fraction of the activity which once enlivened their monumental concourses.

Several approaches to the problem of railroad station preservation have been identified. A small station, now bypassed by train service, is often suitable for conversion into a single new use such as a restaurant, retail store, or office. However, if a station is underutilized but not abandoned, a recycling scheme which calls for a complete change of use may be detrimental to railroad transportation. The federally supervised conversion of Union Station in Washington, D.C., into a national visitors' center substantiates this point. With this new facility occupying the entire terminal, another station had to be constructed behind the old building to provide service for 100 daily passenger trains.

This paradox can be avoided by retaining the function of a station but supplementing railroad usage with commercial, office, or cultural facilities. Developers of Union Station in New London, Connecticut, for example, rent space in the terminal to Amtrak as well as to a restaurant, a museum, and professional offices. Other cities have used federal funds to convert stations into intermodal transportation centers for trains, buses, and other mass transit lines.

To Americans, the railroad station symbolizes not only a once popular way to travel but also an important era in the country's history. During the 19th century, the railroads played a vital role in the growth and industrialization of the nation. When the final spike for the transcontinental railroad was driven in 1869, the railroad companies became a determining force in urban development of the Midwest and the West. Towns with railroad stations thrived and grew into cities; towns which were not on train routes declined.

During the heyday of train transportation, the railroad station was a pivotal building in both cities and towns. Union Station served as a gateway into a city, a mark of the pride and prosperity not only of the railroad companies but also of the community. Many of the larger terminals were designed by the country's finest architects, and some (such as Grand Central in New York City) rank among the greatest structures in America.

Exteriors of the city terminals were massive and monumental, and interiors were grand and richly detailed with great vaulted spaces built to imitate the ancient Roman baths. Even the larger train sheds form an important chapter in engineering technology, showing progressive advancements in iron and steel construction.

The smaller depots provide a catalog of American architectural styles. Simplicity, exuberance, dignity, whimsy, and severity have all been expressed in the architecture of different stations across the country. Living quarters were occasionally provided on the second floor, and for a short span of years stations combined with hotels were popular. In Holly Springs, Mississippi, one of the few remaining depot-hotels has been recycled as a private residence.

Unfortunately many stations, large and small, are now in blighted areas, perhaps isolated by a wasteland of abandoned tracks, surplus railway equipment, or industrial buildings. The central city location of most stations, however, may mean that active commercial or office districts are still close by. Renewal of stations in cities such as Chattanooga has proved to be a catalyst for revitalization of surrounding areas. The multi million dollar conversion of Station Square in Pittsburgh into a multiple use facility is expected to have a similar impact on the neighborhood.

Acquisition of stations can be an early stumbling block for some adaptive use projects. Larger terminals are usually jointly owned by several railroad companies, and legal negotiations for purchase may be complicated. Amtrak, which leases its facilities from the railroads, frequently finds that it is economically unsound to maintain a building many times larger than its needs warrant.

The vast interiors of the larger stations can sometimes be used as "found space" in adaptive use projects. Sensitive designs such as that of Mount Royal Station in Baltimore can capture extra floor space through the addition of mezzanines without damaging the integrity of the building. Original interior finishings such as marble tiles and columns, woodwork, and art glass are often among the finest features of a station and should be restored if possible.

Adaptive use schemes often can capitalize on America's nostalgic fondness for railroads. The Chattanooga Choo-Choo (probably the best known of all recycled stations), the Gandy Dancer Restaurant in Ann Arbor, and The Depot in Pittsford, New York, are among many projects which depend on a railroad theme as their special calling card. Depots in Batavia, Illinois, and Lawton, Oklahoma, and numerous other towns have been converted into railroad museums to record the flavor of train travel through artifacts and exhibitions.

Several technical reports which can assist local communities or developers have been generated by federal and private investigations of adaptive use of stations. In cooperation with the National Endowment for the Arts, the Educational Facilities Laboratories has published two studies and in 1974 co-hosted a national conference in Indianapolis on the subject. The reports (*Reusing Railroad Stations*, New York: 1974, and *Reusing Railroad Stations Book Two*, New York: 1975) examine reuse strategies and economic aspects of recycling and include several case studies. A paper prepared for the Indianapolis conference by the Advisory Council on Historic Preservation analyzes federal involvement with railroad station preservation and describes 28 federal programs which might aid reuse ("Federal Programs for Reusing Railroad Stations," Washington, D.C.: 1974). A film entitled "Stations" (available from Roger Hagan Associates, 1019 Belmont Place East, Seattle 98102) also explores recycling projects.

The Railroad Revitalization and Regulatory Reform Act, passed in 1976, includes provisions which promote the reuse of railroad stations for commercial, cultural, educational, or recreational activities. The National Endowment for the Arts plans to distribute $2.5 million in planning grants to local public or nonprofit organizations for preparation of reuse studies for historically or architecturally significant stations. Federal funds are also available through the Urban Mass Transportation Administration of the Department of Transportation for conversion of stations into intermodal transportation centers.

98 Yuma Art Center (NR)
Yuma, Arizona

Origin:	Southern Pacific Railroad Depot, 1926
Conversion:	Art center, 1976
Developer:	Yuma Fine Arts Association, Yuma
Architect:	Liberty-Pogue and Associates, Yuma

Redevelopment: A Spanish Colonial building, the depot was acquired by the Yuma Arts Association through a trade rather than a purchase. Conversion of the 7,000-square-foot stucco depot required replacement of the mechanical systems and the addition of a temperature control system for the exhibitions. Redevelopment costs totaled $80,000 and were financed by private donations amounting to 80 percent, and by state and federal grants.

99 Santa Fe Depot (NR)
San Diego, California

Origin:	Santa Fe Depot, 1914
Conversion:	Multi-modal transportation center and commercial complex, 1978
Developer:	City of San Diego
Architect:	Innis-Tennebaum, San Diego

Redevelopment: Using a $2.8 million grant from the Urban Mass Transportation Administration (U.S. Department of Transportation), the city of San Diego is joining with a private developer to adapt the depot into a mixed-use transportation and commercial complex. The depot, a Spanish Colonial Revival building with twin entrance towers, will serve as an Amtrak and bus station and will contain shopping, restaurant, and entertainment facilities within its grandly arched interior spaces. The private developer will contribute $5.6 million to the project.

100 Union Railroad Station (NR)
New London, Connecticut

Origin:	Union Railroad Station, 1885
Conversion:	Amtrak passenger station, commercial and office space, 1976
Developer:	Union Station Associates of New London
Architect:	Anderson Notter Associates, Boston

Redevelopment: One of the last buildings designed by 19th century architect H. H. Richardson, the Romanesque station was threatened with demolition by urban renewal for many years. Two consultant service grants from the National Trust for Historic Preservation helped to mobilize efforts to save the building, which was purchased in 1975 by the architect-developer. The station continues to serve as a regional rail transportation center, with Amtrak occupying about 30 percent of the building. A mezzanine, added in the former waiting room, now accommodates a two-level restaurant, and an opening through the first floor gives access to new basement-level passenger facilities. A 20-year lease commitment from Amtrak encouraged a Hartford bank to provide financing for the project, which also received preservation grants from HUD ($90,000) and the National Park Service ($36,100), and a loan from the National Trust revolving fund ($30,000).

101 Louisiana Arts and Science Center Riverside
Baton Rouge, Louisiana

Origin:	Illinois Central Railroad Passenger Station, circa 1890s (remodeled in 1925)
Conversion:	Museum, 1976
Developer:	City of Baton Rouge
Architect:	Desmond-Miremont Architects, Baton Rouge

Redevelopment: Situated on the banks of the Mississippi River, the passenger station was doubled in size by new construction during conversion to use as a museum. Containing a gross building area of 50,300 square feet, the museum features a two-story gallery area; a 200-seat auditorium adapted from the old railway express office; exhibition, office and storage spaces; and an outdoor sculpture garden. The $2.5 million redevelopment of the station, which is leased to the city of Baton Rouge by Illinois Central for $1 a year, was financed by an urban renewal grant.

102 Mount Royal Station
Baltimore, Maryland

Origin:	Mount Royal Station, 1896
Conversion:	Art school, 1967
Developer:	Maryland Institute, College of Art, Baltimore
Architect:	Cochran, Stephenson and Donkervoet, Baltimore

Redevelopment: Built of granite and trimmed with limestone, Mount Royal stood as a monumental example of Renaissance Revival architecture even after trains ceased to run in 1961. The first art students moved into the station that same year, when the Maryland Institute rented the building for $1 a year to accommodate overflow classes. In 1964, the school purchased the building for $250,000 and undertook a major fund drive to raise the $600,000 needed for redevelopment. Useable space was increased from 22,500 to 47,000 square feet, primarily by extending the original balconies over the cavernous waiting room area. The baggage platform was adapted as a glass-walled school for sculpture, and other parts of the station now function as lecture halls, studios, galleries, library, and cafeteria.

103 Gandy Dancer Restaurant (NR)
Ann Arbor, Michigan

Origin:	Michigan Central Railroad Depot, 1886
Conversion:	Restaurant, 1970
Developer:	C. A. Muer Corporation, Detroit
Architect:	Jack Green Associates, Southfield, Michigan

Redevelopment: Although financing was initially unavailable, because of the "track record" of the Chuck Muer Corporation—owner of several restaurants in Michigan and elsewhere—a $250,000 term loan was finally acquired for this conversion. Refinanced twice (first with a $35,000 permanent mortgage and subsequently for $650,000), the cost of the Romanesque-style stone station totaled $850,000. The baggage building, renovated in 1976, has been connected by a glass enclosure to the main depot, which retains many of the original interior fixtures. With the encouragement of the developer, the city of Ann Arbor passed an ordinance to protect the historical and architectural integrity of the building by extending a local historic district to include the depot complex.

104 Union Center (NHL)
St. Louis, Missouri

Origin:	St. Louis Union Station, 1894
Conversion:	Multi-use complex, in progress since 1976
Developer:	Union Center Venture, St. Louis
Architect:	Robert Moore, St. Louis

Redevelopment: Adaptive use of the 56-acre Union Station complex in St. Louis—planned to enclose over 33 million cubic feet of space under one roof—would make this project the largest conversion in the world. The megastructure (1,500,000 square feet) is within the St. Louis central business district and forms the western anchor for a landscaped mall which originates at the Gateway Arch. Proposed re-uses of existing buildings include conversion of the train station into a hotel and of the railroad mail building into an athletic club. The 11½-acre train shed will shelter a variety of activities, including theaters, restaurants, shops, markets, an amusement park, and an underground aqua center. The long-forgotten cellars of a brewery which occupied the site before the station will accommodate a ratskeller. Project developers, who received a $4 million acquisition loan for the complex from a Denver savings and loan, anticipate an investment of $51 million over a period of 5 to 7 years. The complex has been designated as a redevelopment area by the city of St. Louis to allow the developers some local tax relief.

105 Citibank Depot Drive-Up (NR)
Lincoln, Nebraska

Origin:	Chicago Rock Island and Pacific Railroad Passenger Depot, 1893
Conversion:	Drive-up banking facility, 1969
Developer:	Citibank and Trust Company, Lincoln
Architect:	Clark & Enersen, Hamersky, Schlaebitz, Burroughs and Thomsen, Lincoln

Redevelopment: Cars, not trains, now pull up to Lincoln's old passenger station, a fanciful chateauesque building. To accommodate drive-up banking, the 45,000-square-foot site was landscaped and redeveloped with parking, driveways, and brick walks. Rehabilitation of

3-5   One of the last buildings designed by 19th century architect H. H. Richardson, this railroad station in New London, Connecticut, still serves as an AMTRAK station, but the remaining space has been programmed for commercial and office use.   (Photo: Randolph Langenbach.)

the small depot and baggage room required sandblasting, replacement of the roof, and restoration of the interior with railroad and banking furnishings from the 19th century.

106   The Depot
Pittsford, New York

Origin:	New York Central Railroad Station, 1865
Conversion:	Restaurant, 1962
Developer:	Edward B. Plenge and Peter B. Heinrich, Rochester
Architect:	Harvey L. Sibley, Jr., Warren, Vermont

Redevelopment: One of the earliest restaurants in the country with a railroad theme, The Depot was an immediate financial success and has spawned adjacent development of a motel and a nightclub. A one-story brick passenger station was connected to a wood-frame freight house with new construction, creating additional multilevel dining space on the former track area. The complex was acquired for $25,000 and redeveloped for $75,000.

107   Saratoga Springs Drink Hall (NR)
Saratoga Springs, New York

Origin:	Trolley Station, 1915
Conversion:	Offices, 1975 and 1977
Developer:	City of Saratoga Springs
Architect:	The Saratoga Associates, Saratoga Springs

Redevelopment: First converted many years ago from a trolley station to a mineral water "drink hall," the city-owned building now serves as headquarters for the chamber of commerce and the Saratoga Springs Historic Foundation. Two fires in early 1976 destroyed much of the interior of the Beaux Arts stucco building, which is being redeveloped for $120,000 through the Community Development Block Grant program.

108 Station Square (NR)
Pittsburgh, Pennsylvania

Origin: Pittsburgh and Lake Erie
               Railroad Station, 1901
Conversion: Commercial, office, and
               hotel space; in progress
Developer: Pittsburgh History and
               Landmarks Foundation
Architect: Urban Design Associates;
               Williams/Trebilcock/
               Whitehead; James A.
               Morgan & Associates; and
               Pittsburgh History and
               Landmarks Foundation,
               Pittsburgh

Redevelopment: A $5 million grant from a private foundation in Pittsburgh supplied seed money for redevelopment of a 40-acre railroad and industrial complex along the Monongahela River as a commercial, office, residential, and entertainment center. The first phase of the project—a $30-million redevelopment scheme scheduled for completion in 1979—will include conversions of the Terminal Building into luxury office space, and of the freight house into a specialty shopping center, as well as construction of a 250-room hotel. Although the railroad company will continue to have its headquarters in the Terminal, the station's lavishly ornamented Grand Concourse is being restored and converted into a 550-seat restaurant by the developer of the Gandy Dancer Restaurant in Ann Arbor (project #103 in the catalog). The redevelopment will provide 120,000 square feet of commercial space, 360,000 square feet of office space, and 2,000 parking spaces. Profits from the complex, leased from the railroad company for 50 years, will be used for conversion of a freight house into a specialty shopping center and of a seven-story warehouse into luxury office space, as well as for construction of a 250-room hotel.

109 Chattanooga Choo-Choo (NR)
Chattanooga, Tennessee

Origin: Terminal Station, 1909
Conversion: Restaurant and hotel, 1973
Developer: Chattanooga Choo Choo
               Corporation
Architect: Klaus Nentwig & Associates,
               Chattanooga

Redevelopment: An investment of more than $2.4 million by two dozen local businessmen initiated the conversion of Chattanooga's Terminal Station into a major restaurant and hotel complex with a railroad theme. An additional $1.6 million was provided through bank financing. The property was purchased for $350,000 from the Southern Railway System through a subordinated bond which makes the railroad company a major stockholder in the development corporation. More than 1,300 visitors can be seated in numerous dining rooms, which include the old baggage area and the former waiting room, a vast space with a dome rising 85 feet above floor level. Adjoining the landscaped track and platform area behind the terminal are several shops, a newly constructed 103-room hotel, and 24 railroad cars converted into motel rooms. An old railroad warehouse on the edge of the 24-acre site provides convention facilities for as many as 1,000 persons, and an old trolley shuttles visitors to and from the 800-car parking area.

110 North Bennington Railroad Station (NR)
North Bennington, Vermont

Origin: North Bennington Railroad
               Station, 1879
Conversion: Village and private offices,
               1972
Developer: Village of North Bennington
Architect: Timothy D. Smith and
               Associates, North
               Bennington

Redevelopment: Transferred from state to village ownership for $1, the station was converted to offices with a $55,000 private donation. Redevelopment included restoration of the polychromatic Victorian interior wood detailing; construction of a new entrance and stairs; replacement of mechanical systems; and reconstruction of the original mansard-roofed clock tower. The French-Second-Empire-style station contains 3,900 square feet, with village offices and meeting spaces on the first floor and rental office space on the second.

Project Economics
Railroad Stations

Project	Year of Conversion	Gross Building Area (sq. ft.)	Acquisition Cost	Redevelopment Cost	Approx. Cost Per Sq. Ft.	Source of Financing	Rental Rates (annual per sq. ft., unless otherwise noted)
Yuma Art Center	1976	7,000	Trade	$ 80,000	$ (11.43)	Private donations (80%), Public grants (state and federal: 20%)	(not rented)
Santa Fe Depot	1978	55,000	$ 2,849,000	8,000,000	30.00	Federal grant, private developer	$10.00— 12.00
Union Railroad Station (New London)	1976	20,000	11,400	615,000	30.00	Out of town commercial bank, federal grants, National Trust revolving fund loan	$7.25
Louisiana Arts and Science Center (Riverside)	1976	55,000	$1/year Leased	2,500,000	50.00	Public grant (urban renewal)	(not rented)
Mount Royal Station	1967	47,000	250,000	600,000	18.00	Fund drive	(not rented)
Gandy Dancer Restaurant	1970	13,000	180,000	850,000	100.00	Bank (local)	(not rented)
Union Center (St. Louis)	Planned	1,500,000	4,000,000	51,000,000	(34.00)	S&L (acquisition loan)	$5.00— 10.00
Citibank Depot Drive-Up	1969	3,560	100,000	100,000	(28.01)	In-house	(not rented)
The Depot (Pittsford)	1962	7,000	25,000	75,000	(10.71)	Local bank; investments from ltd. corp.	—
Saratoga Springs Drink Hall	1977	—	City-owned	120,000	—	Community Development Block Grant	—
Station Square	In-process	(47 acres)	Lease	30,000,000	—	Private foundations	—
Chattanooga Choo-Choo	1973	24 acres	350,000	4,000,000	—	Private investors, 2 local banks, insurance company	—
North Bennington Railroad Station	1972	3,900	$1	55,000	14	Private donation	—

Dashes indicate data not available.
Figures in parentheses were not supplied directly but were derived from other data.

Redevelopment Work
Railroad Stations

Project	Exterior Restoration	New Exterior Construction	Structural	Mechanical	Interior Demolition	Interior New Construction	Site Restoration	New Facilities, Parking	Landscaping
Yuma Art Center	Moderate	Minor	Minor	Extensive	Moderate	Moderate	Minor	Minor	Extensive
Santa Fe Depot	Minor	Minor	Extensive	—	Minor	Minor	Minor	Minor	Minor
Union Railroad Station (New London)	Extensive	Minor	Moderate	Extensive	Moderate	Moderate	Minor	Minor	Minor
Louisiana Arts and Science Center (Riverside)	Moderate	Extensive	—	Extensive	Extensive	Extensive	—	Moderate	Moderate
Mount Royal Station	Minor	Minor	Extensive	—	Minor	Extensive	Minor	Minor	Minor
Gandy Dancer Restaurant	Moderate	Moderate	Minor	Extensive	Moderate	Moderate	Extensive	Extensive	Extensive
Union Center	Minor	Minor	Minor	Extensive	Extensive	Extensive	Extensive	Extensive	Extensive
Citibank Depot Drive-Up	Moderate	Minor	Minor	Moderate	Minor	Moderate	Extensive	Extensive	Extensive
The Depot (Pittsford)	Moderate	Moderate	Minor	Extensive	Minor	Minor	Minor	Extensive	Moderate
Saratoga Springs Drink Hall	Moderate	Minor	Minor	Extensive	Moderate	Moderate	Minor	None	Minor
Station Square	Moderate	Moderate	Minor	Extensive	Minor	Extensive	Minor	Extensive	Extensive
Chattanooga Choo-Choo	Minor	Minor	Minor	Extensive	Minor	Moderate	Extensive	Extensive	Extensive
North Bennington Railroad Station	Extensive	—	Moderate	Extensive	Minor	Minor	Moderate	Moderate	Moderate

Dashes indicate data not available.

Mills

The evolution of industry in America has left the country with a great legacy of mills, ranging from small flour-grinding gristmills or village-scaled New England textile companies, to vast midwestern grain milling operations. Although the diversity in age, size, and function makes generalizations difficult, many of the mill buildings still standing today are characterized by structural strength and by large open interiors which make them highly adaptable for new uses. This potential for reuse is fortunately joined by a growing awareness of the mill's value as a physical record of America's historical, technological, and social development.

The early gristmills and sawmills, which had become a familiar part of the American landscape by the early 18th century, represent a tradition distinct from the 19th century textile mills. The former were typically barn-shaped structures, situated beside running waterways and constructed of stone or clapboard with heavy timber frames. The exteriors were without ornament, and the interiors were functionally arranged to accommodate grinding or sawing machinery, hoists, and other equipment.

As technological advancements transformed weaving from a cottage industry to a mechanized process, the textile mill became one of the earliest forms of the factory in America. The mills of the industrial revolution were large, multistoried structures of stone or brick, pierced with multiple windows, dormers, or clerestories to capture as much natural light as possible. Built to support heavy machinery, they had vast open floors broken only by timber posts or cast-iron columns. They sometimes so dominated the local economy that entire towns were established around a complex of mills, with the industrialist supplying housing, stores, churches, and schools for the laborers.

In most parts of the country the original function of the mill, unlike the functions of buildings such as schools, theaters, or courthouses, is no longer part of our experience. As a means for preserving our knowledge of the milling process, a great number of grist and sawmills have been restored and operate as historic sites or tourist attractions. Working mills like Byrd Mill in Louisa County, Virginia, can be found all over the country.

Other larger complexes, such as Slater Mill in Pawtucket, Rhode Island, and the Eluetherian Mills in Wilmington, Delaware, serve appropriately as museums of industrial technology. The Brandywine River Museum in Chadds Ford, Pennsylvania, represents a particularly sensitive adaptation of a mill structure for use as an art gallery.

Recognized as having historical value by the local community, many mills have been cleaned up to serve as recreation, art, or craft centers. A citizens' group in North Adams, Massachusetts, for instance, has formed a nonprofit corporation to rehabilitate the Windsor Mill as a regional arts center. The project has been awarded federal, state, and county funds in addition to private grants.

Perhaps because of their picturesque locations on waterways, countless small mills have been converted into single-family houses or into restaurants. Small professional firms have also found suitable space in modest-sized mills. For example, Zion and Breen Associates, an architectural firm in Imlaystown, New Jersey, gained a new office through the conversion of an early wooden gristmill.

The larger mills, on the other hand, present more challenging problems for economically feasible reuse. Fortunately, they have qualities which facilitate conversion into multiple housing units or into commercial and office space. Heavy structural systems provide ample support for intensive usage; high ceilings allow adequate space for installation of mechanical equipment; open floor areas minimize the need for interior demolition and allow convenient subdivision with modern materials.

In many situations, a developer or community has to consider the future of mill buildings within the broader context of an entire town, rather than as isolated structures. Viable reuse of a mill complex may affect an entire community psychologically as well as economically, and may spark additional revitalization. The experience of Harrisville, New Hampshire, provides a notable example of this kind of success. A local citizens' group secured new uses for more than 25 mill-related structures.

The Society for Industrial Archaeology and the Society for the Preservation of Old Mills (Box 435, Wiscasset, Maine 14578) are particularly concerned with the restoration and reuse of this building type.

111 Montchanin Mills Building
Montchanin, Delaware

Origin:	Dupont Company mill, circa 1870
Conversion:	Commercial, office, and warehouse use, 1970
Developer:	H. W. Booker Construction Company, Montchanin
Architect:	The Architects Studio, Inc., Montchanin

Redevelopment: The Howe trusses in the roof structure of the old mill became an integral part of the design for the architectural offices which now occupy the upper level of the building. Offices comprise 6,600 square feet of the 15,300-square-foot building; retail space occupies 4,850 square feet; and 1,500 square feet are used for warehousing. With the exception of four skylights, the exterior of the mill has not been altered.

112 Cotton Mill Apartments
Northbridge, Massachusetts

Origin:	Whitinsville Cotton Mill (later the Spiras Building), 1847 (with 1870 addition)
Conversion:	Apartments for the elderly, 1977
Developer:	E. Denis Walsh, Schochet-Whitinsville, Associates, Boston
Architect:	Glaser, DeCastro and Vitols, Boston

Redevelopment: Conversion of the five-story granite mill into 55 apartment units will yield a gross building area of 75,000 square feet on a 2.37-acre site. Originally planned as conventional apartments and later as condominiums, the mill project encountered financial difficulties until funding was secured from the Massachusetts Housing Finance Agency for housing units for the elderly. HUD Section 8 subsidies have also been used.

3-6 Aerial view of the Quaker Square complex in Akron, Ohio.

113 The Tannery
Peabody, Massachusetts

Origin:	A. C. Lawrence Leather Corporation, 1814 (mansion), 1890s (tannery buildings)
Conversion:	Apartments, 1972
Developer:	Crowninshield Apartments Associates, Inc., Peabody
Architect:	Anderson Notter Associates, Boston

Redevelopment: The unique character of the recycled leather mill is further enhanced by the wide variety in the sizes and plans of the 284 apartment units contained in two timber frame mill buildings. An early Federal-style mansion on the grounds serves as a community center and as offices for Crowninshield Corporation. An old smoke tower remains as a landmark, leftover machinery provides planters and sculptural elements, and bridges for transporting industrial goods from building to building now act as skyways among the residential units. The Massachusetts Housing Finance Agency funded the $4.4 million redevelopment, which accommodates low-income residents in 25 percent of the units.

114 Glen Arbor Roller Mills
Glen Arbor, Michigan

Origin:	Flour mill, 1879
Conversion:	Recording studio, 1974
Developer:	Frederick C. Ball, Glen Arbor
Architect:	Frederick C. Ball

Redevelopment: Multi-track recording equipment now sits beside restored flour sifters and grinding stones in the former gristmill. A control room and two studios with facilities for 45 performers occupy the four-story, wood-frame building. Redevelopment, totaling $100,000 included extensive electrical and acoustical work.

115 E. E. Cooley Building (NR)
Starkville, Mississippi

Origin:	John M. Stone Cotton Mill, 1902
Conversion:	University offices and maintenance shops, 1968
Developer:	Mississippi State University
Architect:	Mississippi State University Physical Plant Department

Redevelopment: The two-story mill structure, with masonry exterior walls and wooden interior framing, was purchased by the state of Mississippi in 1966 for $125,687. The university disposed of the old mill equipment, repaired deteriorated structural parts, replaced the mechanical systems and added interior finishes to convert the 107,558-square-foot building into offices and maintenance shops for its physical plant. Redevelopment costs for the building totaled $276,813.

116 Contoocook Mills Industrial District (NR)
Hillsboro, New Hampshire

Origin:	Hillsboro Hosiery Mill complex, 1846–1888
Conversion:	Apartments, offices, and commercial space, 1972
Developer:	Bean Mountain Corporation, Hillsboro
Architect:	Paul and Leslie Belliveau, Hillsboro

Redevelopment: Two brick structures in this six-building mill complex now contain 10 apartment units, and two attached wood-frame buildings are undergoing conversion to commercial and office use. Redevelopment of the ¾-acre complex, located in downtown Hillsboro, has received general support from the community but encountered resistance from local politicians and lending institutions. The developers, who paid $2,500 for the mill buildings, secured a mortgage loan from a savings bank out of town.

117 One Mill Plaza (NR)
Laconia, New Hampshire

Origin:	Busiel-Seeburg Mill, 1857
Conversion:	Offices, 1973
Developer:	One Mill Plaza, Inc., Laconia
Architect:	Brian F. Larson, Eau Claire, Wisconsin

Redevelopment: A campaign by local citizens to prevent demolition by the city of two important mill complexes in downtown Laconia received a boost when the Busiel Mill was privately purchased and converted into professional office space. The $375,000 redevelopment of the building, purchased for $8,000, was assisted by a first mortgage from local banks and a second mortgage from the Small Business Administration. A bell tower with an interior spiral staircase, now restored, distinguishes the 3½-story brick building, which was originally a hosiery mill.

118 Zion and Breen Associates, Inc.
Imlaystown, New Jersey

Origin:	Salter's Mill, circa 1695 (burned and reconstructed in 1897)
Conversion:	Offices, 1972
Developer:	Robert Zion, Imlaystown
Architect:	Zion and Breen Associates, Inc.

Redevelopment: A landscape architectural firm rescued and recycled the wood-frame gristmill, preserving much of the mill equipment as features of the contemporary design. An interior bridge over the open mill brace leads to offices and drafting rooms which are arranged on three levels. The deteriorated structure was purchased for $5,000 and redeveloped for $110,000.

119 Old City Hall Restaurant (NR)
Lockport, New York

Origin:	Flour mill (later Lockport City Hall), 1860
Conversion:	Restaurant and museum, 1976
Developer:	SWACC Enterprises, Inc., Lockport
Architect:	None

Redevelopment: Plans by urban renewal to demolish the Old City Hall—built as a mill but used for many years as municipal offices—were abandoned in recognition of the structure's historic importance and its redevelopment potential. One side of the 2½-story building, constructed of local limestone, forms a retaining wall for the Erie Canal. Leased by the city of Lockport to a private corporation for $7,800 annually, the building has been converted into a restaurant with a canal museum on the lower floor. Replacement of window sashes, structural repairs, and electrical work were paid for with $38,000 from Community Development funds and an additional $140,000 was invested privately.

120 Carr Mill (NR)
Carrboro, North Carolina

Origin:	Alberta Cotton Mill, 1899
Conversion:	Shopping mall, 1977
Developer:	Carr Mill, Charlotte, North Carolina
Architect:	Miller Steever Finch, Charlotte

Redevelopment: An interior shopping mall with about 20 retail outlets occupies the main floor of the two-story brick mill, a 62,000-square-foot structure which was purchased for $400,000. Two new buildings will be added to the 8.3-acre site, which includes parking for 350 cars.

121 Quaker Square
Akron, Ohio

Origin:	Grain storage and packing plant, 1875 to 1930
Conversion:	Commercial and office space, 1975
Developer:	Quaker Square Associates, Inc., Akron
Architect:	Curtis and Rasmussen, Akron

Redevelopment: The "birthplace of the breakfast cereal industry," this complex of brick, timber-frame mill buildings is centrally located in downtown Akron. Purchased for $825,000, the property now functions as a multi-use commercial and office center containing a gross building area of 150,000 square feet. An enclosed gallery unites several structures, which have been renovated to retain the general character of the old mill and many of its original materials. Future plans call for conversion of a block of silos into a hotel.

122 Cedar Creek Settlement
Cedarburg, Wisconsin

Origin:	Wittenburg Woolen Mills, 1864
Conversion:	Commercial space, 1974
Developer:	James B. Pape, Grafton, Wisconsin
Architect:	W. R. Prokopowicz, Milwaukee

Redevelopment: Acquired in 1972 for $55,000, this complex of three limestone buildings has been restored as a historical village featuring specialty shops. Because of initial difficulties in obtaining financing for the $495,000 project, redevelopment had to be phased over a 2-year period. A small office and stable building were converted to shops in 1972 and retail spaces were available in the main mill building by 1974. The complex, which covers 45,000 square feet, is designated as a state and local landmark.

Project Economics
Mills

Project	Year of Conversion	Gross Building Area (sq. ft.)	Acquisition Cost	Redevelopment Cost	Approx. Cost Per Sq. Ft.	Source of Financing	Rental Rates (annual per sq. ft., unless otherwise noted)
Montchanin Mills Building	1970	15,300	Already owned	—	—	—	—
Cotton Mill Apartments	1977	75,000	$ 330,000	$ 1,757,000	$ 23.43	Public (state)	$23.43
The Tannery	1972	251,000	—	4,400,000	17.50	MHFA (state)	$4.50
Glen Arbor Roller Mills	1974	9,000	40,000	100,000	17.00	Personal funds	—
E. E. Cooley Building	1968	107,558	125,687	276,813	3.74	Public (state)	(not rented)
Contoocook Mills Industrial District	1972	12,000	2,500	125,000	(apts.) 7.00, (storage) 2.50	Savings bank (out of town)	$100/mo./ studio; $160/mo./ duplex; $0.75/ storage
One Mill Plaza	1973	13,500	8,000	375,000	27.78	Local banks and SBA; stockholder loans	$5.11
Zion and Breen Associates, Inc.	1972	6,200	5,000	110,000	(17.74)	—	(not rented)
Old City Hall Restaurant	1976	—	Leased per year: 7,800	178,000	—	Public (CDA); private investment	(leased by developer)
Carr Mill	1977	62,000	400,000	800,000	(12.90)	S&L (out of town)	$5.25
Quaker Square	1975	150,000	825,000	2,200,000	15.00	Local S&L	$12.00 re- tail; $8.00 office
Cedar Creek Settlement	1974	—	55,000	495,000	11.00	Commercial bank (local)	$3.00

Dashes indicate data not available.
Figures in parentheses were not supplied directly but were derived from other data.

Redevelopment Work
Mills

Project	Exterior Restoration	New Exterior Construction	Structural	Mechanical	Interior Demolition	Interior New Construction	Site Restoration	New Facilities, Parking	Landscaping
Montchanin Mills Building	Minor	Minor	Minor	Moderate	Extensive	Extensive	—	Extensive	—
Cotton Mill Apartments	Minor	Minor	Minor	Extensive	Minor	Extensive	Minor	Moderate	Extensive
The Tannery	Minor	Minor	Minor	Extensive	Minor	Extensive	—	Moderate	Extensive
Glen Arbor Roller Mills	Extensive	Moderate	Moderate	Extensive	Minor	Extensive	Extensive	Moderate	Moderate
E. E. Cooley Building	Moderate	Minor	Extensive	Extensive	Extensive	Extensive	Extensive	Extensive	Minor
Contoocook Mills Industrial District	Extensive	Moderate	Extensive	Extensive	Moderate	Moderate	Extensive	Extensive	Extensive
One Mill Plaza	Extensive	Moderate	Moderate	Extensive	Extensive	Extensive	Minor	Minor	Minor
Zion and Breen Associates, Inc.	Minor	—	—	Moderate	Extensive	Extensive	Minor	Minor	Minor
Old City Hall Restaurant	Minor	—	Moderate	Extensive	Minor	Extensive	—	—	Moderate
Carr Mill	Extensive	Extensive	Extensive	Extensive	None	Extensive	Extensive	Extensive	Extensive
Quaker Square	Moderate	Minor	Minor	Extensive	Moderate	Moderate	Moderate	Extensive	Extensive
Cedar Creek Settlement	Minor	Minor	Minor	Extensive	Moderate	Moderate	Moderate	Moderate	Moderate

Dashes indicate data not available.

FACTORIES, WAREHOUSES, AND INDUSTRIAL BUILDINGS

Reuse projects involving industrial buildings—warehouses, factories, bakeries, breweries, powerhouses, and many others—were probably the first adaptive use efforts to capture widespread public attention. Loft living became a familiar practice in light industrial districts such as SoHo in New York City. Ghirardelli Square in San Francisco and Trolley Square in Salt Lake City demonstrated that recycling could be both popular and profitable, and similar commercial complexes have opened all over the country.

But the proliferation of these adaptive use projects has depended on more than economics. A new appreciation of industrial buildings, aesthetically as well as historically, has reinforced their value as important resources within the urban environment. These buildings provide visual documentation of America's industrial development, reflecting both changes in manufacturing methods and advancements in building technology. Their brick, stone, or concrete facades are often designed to reflect the functions of the buildings. A sense of strength, simplicity, and dignity can be expressed in these utilitarian structures. Windows are usually arranged in rhythmic patterns, and decorative elements such as arches, brick corbeling, or corner quoins break the severity of exterior walls. Interiors are characterized by exposed structural elements of heavy timber or cast iron and by great volumes of unobstructed space.

Because of changes in manufacturing patterns, in transport systems, and in the location of the labor force, many industries have left the center city for the suburbs or other regions. This migration has left abandoned or underutilized many industrial buildings, often on the fringe of a city's central business district. Empty and lifeless, large-scale industrial buildings can have a negative visual and social impact on an area and can cost a city a great deal in lost tax revenues. These buildings, however, frequently can contribute to the vitality and interest of an urban area by being recycled.

In areas like SoHo, artists and other renters of loft studios live in harmony with preexisting light industry structures. Attracted and supported by the new resident population, small businesses such as galleries, art supply stores, bookstores, and restaurants add to the mixture of uses in the old buildings. As a result of these adaptations, such districts are alive around-the-clock, rather than only during working hours.

The original impetus for loft living was more pragmatic than romantic; artists sought out inexpensive studio space suitable for dancing, painting, sculpting, or other work. The interior spaces of old warehouses—large, open, and flexible—answered their needs and have since proved attractive as living quarters for other city dwellers as well. In many buildings, all improvements are left up to the tenants. Assistance is available in the form of construction manuals, most notably *Loft Living, Recycling Warehouse Space for Residential Use* by Kingsley C. Fairbridge and Harvey-Jane Kowal (Saturday Review Press, 1976).

Industrial buildings which have been rehabilitated by private developers as multiple rental units for artists have been designed to provide special amenities such as moveable partitions, extra-wide doorways and corridors, and ceiling-height electrical outlets. The Piano Craft Guild in Boston and Westbeth Artists Housing in New York City are both popular redevelopments oriented toward artists.

Far greater numbers of industrial buildings, however, have been adapted for commercial or office use. San Francisco became an early leader in this movement, with several large-scale, well-publicized conversions. Ghirardelli Square, opened in 1964 and completed in 1968, stands out as the pioneer. The Cannery, The Showplace!, The Ice House, Jackson Place, and the China Basin Building are other examples. In other parts of the country, projects include Canal Square, Washington, D.C.; The Powerhouse, Cleveland; Hansen's Bakery, Seattle; the Ybor Cigar Factory, Tampa; St. Paul Court, St. Paul; and Bakery Square, Louisville. Like those of San Francisco, many of these developments have played significant roles in the revitalization of surrounding districts.

In general, recycled industrial buildings can show a high degree of imagination and creativity on the part of the developer. Unlike many other types of buildings in which the existing fabric of the building can be a determining factor in the adaptive use de-

sign, industrial buildings are often no more than shells with interior framing. This lack of constraint in the interior allows great flexibility in introducing contemporary design elements. The original characteristics of the building—wide spaces and rough materials—can be appropriately highlighted through open-space planning or through exposed mechanical or electrical systems. Tall ceilings also offer the bonus of "found" space, which can be used for the addition of lofts or mezzanines.

123 China Basin Building
San Francisco, California

Origin:	Produce warehouse, 1920
Conversion:	Offices, 1973
Developer:	Fourth Berry Street Corporation, New York City
Architect:	Robinson and Mills, San Francisco

Redevelopment: A huge six-story structure—825 feet long and 100 feet deep—the China Basin Building is within San Francisco's former shipping district, an area which is currently experiencing revitalization because of its convenient location to commuter transportation and the waterfront. The first phase of redevelopment involved 120,000 of the total 500,000 square feet, with renovations focusing on new mechanical and service systems. New entrances and exterior graphics were designed to soften the building's massive scale; a first floor restaurant was added; and the wharf at the rear of the building was redeveloped for public access.

124 The Feather Factory
San Francisco, California

Origin:	Feather processing plant, 1919
Conversion:	Offices and showrooms, 1973
Developer:	950 Battery Street Associates, San Francisco
Architect:	Don Knorr and Associates, San Francisco

Redevelopment: An unusual steel framework of supports for vats, catwalks, blowers, and pipes—the necessary equipment for washing, drying, fluffing, and stuffing feathers—presented a unique design challenge for conversion of the three-story loft building into professional office space. The architect and developers designed a free-flowing space, patterned by exposed steel ties and braces (added to bring the building up to earthquake code standards) and lighted by the original factory windows and

3-7   This 1919 vintage feather processing plant in the Embarcadero district of San Francisco now serves as offices. (Photo: Robert Brandeis.)

skylights. By expanding catwalks into decks, a gross building area of 30,000 square feet was achieved in the structure, which is located in the revitalized Embarcadero district of San Francisco. Purchased for $190,000 and redeveloped for $350,000, the project has earned awards from the American Institute of Steel Construction (1973) and other groups.

125 Ghirardelli Square
San Francisco, California

Origin:	Ghirardelli Chocolate Company, 1893
Conversion:	Commercial space, 1964
Developer:	William M. Roth and Mrs. William P. Roth, San Francisco
Architect:	Wurster, Bernardi and Emmons; Lawrence Halprin & Associates (landscaping); John Matthias; San Francisco

Redevelopment: Perhaps the best known of all large-scale adaptive use projects, Ghirardelli Square initiated the revitalization of an industrial district on San Francisco's north waterfront. More than a half dozen brick buildings were converted to specialty commercial uses and linked with landscaped, multiple level terraces and walkways. Seventy shops, 14 restaurants, and two theaters occupy the buildings, which are identified according to their original manufacturing uses (The Cocoa Building, The Mustard Building, the Power House, etc.). The two-phase redevelopment, completed in 1964 and 1968, included construction of a 300-car underground garage and replacement of the deteriorated wood-frame Box Factory with a new structure. The chocolate complex was purchased for $2,500,000 with redevelopment costs in excess of $10,000,000. Financing by a major life insurance company was provided according to a special formula related to the project's performance. The owners report that although the cost of redevelopment was high, the investment is now fully seasoned and profitable and promises an increasingly fine return in future years.

126 Musto Plaza
San Francisco, California

Origin:	Marble cutting factory, 1906
Conversion:	Offices, 1970
Developer:	Musto Estate Company, San Francisco
Architect:	Bull, Field, Volkmann, Stockwell, San Francisco

Redevelopment: Earthquake upgrading necessary for conversion of the three-story brick building was accomplished by connecting new plywood diaphragms to walls and interior timber frames. A public gallery on the ground floor of the 41,728-square-foot building leads to a landscaped rear courtyard, developed out of a former parking lot.

127 450 Pacific Avenue Building
San Francisco, California

Origin:	Warehouse, 1907
Conversion:	Offices, 1973
Developer:	Barbary Coast Development Company, San Francisco
Architect:	Bull, Field, Volkmann, Stockwell, San Francisco

Redevelopment: Large sawtooth skylights were added to bring daylight to the lower levels of the four-story brick warehouse, now used as offices. A new lighting system was integrated within the existing system of wooden beams and joists, which were left exposed. Redevelopment costs for the 28,000-square-foot structure, formerly the Saturday Review Building, totaled $950,000.

128 Blake Street Bath and Racquet Club
Denver, Colorado

Origin:	Light industry and boarding rooms, circa 1890
Conversion:	Condominiums and offices, 1976
Developer:	Wazee Design and Development, Ltd., Denver
Architect:	David Decker, Denver

Redevelopment: A row of 10 attached, two-story buildings in Denver's lower downtown has been recycled as condominium units with a common tennis court and swimming pool in a rear courtyard. First floors can be rented for office or commercial uses or combined with living spaces on the second floor, at the discretion of each condominium owner. A one-story rear addition (1940) to the complex now houses a conference room and recreation facility with showers and saunas. Financing for the $125,000 purchase was provided by the previous owner but the developer went to 40 institutions over an 18-month period before securing renovation financing from a Denver subsidiary of First Pennsylvania Corporation. The age of the buildings and their location outside the city's downtown urban renewal area were seen as drawbacks by potential lenders. Financing for the condominiums, costing about $75,000 each, is available from three local commercial banks.

129 The Cable Building
Denver, Colorado

Origin:	Powerhouse, offices and shops for cable cars, 1889
Conversion:	Commercial space and offices, 1973
Developer:	E. J. Judd, Denver
Architect:	James Sudler, Denver

Redevelopment: The wrecker had been scheduled to begin demolition of the derelict powerhouse only days before its purchase by a developer who saw the reuse potential of this downtown Denver landmark. Reinforced at the time of purchase by rental agreements covering more than half of the 53,750-square-foot structure, the developer converted the first floor to restaurant and retail space and the second floor to offices, adding parking facilities in the basement. Redevelopment of the building, which has elaborate brick detailing and features a two-story arched entry, earned an award from the Downtown Denver Association as the best improvement to the central city in 1973.

130 Tivoli (NR)
Denver, Colorado

Origin:	Tivoli Brewery Company complex, late 19th century
Conversion:	Commercial center, 1977
Developer:	Associates for the Redevelopment of Tivoli, Denver
Architect:	Hellmuth, Obata, Kassabam, St. Louis

Redevelopment: The oldest brewery in Colorado, the Tivoli complex is scheduled for major redevelopment into a shopping, entertainment, and recreation center. The brewery is leased to private developers by the Auraria Higher Education Center, a commuter college of 30,000 which includes the Tivoli buildings within its urban campus. Of the seven Tivoli structures, the prominent 1890 tower building (where hops were fed by gravity into processing machines) will feature an interior arcade and the Turnhalle Opera House will be restored for concerts and dramatic productions. The project will cost $6.8 million, of which $4.8 million will be provided by local lending institutions and the remainder will be raised through a limited partnership.

131 Canal Square
Washington, D.C.

Origin:	IBM Warehouse, circa 1880–1890
Conversion:	Commercial and office uses, 1971
Developer:	Richard Bernstein, Washington, D.C.
Architect:	Arthur Cotton Moore/Associates, Washington, D.C.

Redevelopment: A blend of adaptive use and new construction, this pedestrian-oriented complex features an interior brick-paved courtyard bordered by shops and a restaurant. A late 19th century warehouse with exposed stone foundation walls forms one side of the courtyard, and a new, six-story building wraps around two other sides. A narrow shopping arcade links the complex, which has underground parking, to a busy Georgetown commercial street. The $2.4 million redevelopment project, which received construction financing from a local security and trust company, has been refinanced since completion. Canal Square has earned several awards, including an American Institute of Architects National Honor Award in 1977.

132 CFC Square (South)
Washington, D.C.

Origin:	Warehouse, 1927
Conversion:	Commercial, offices, and restaurant, 1977
Developer:	National Rural Utilities Cooperative Finance Corporation, Washington, D.C.
Architect:	Arthur Cotton Moore/Associates, Washington, D.C.

Redevelopment: As one phase of a three-part redevelopment scheme for property along the C & O Canal in Georgetown, this concrete-frame warehouse was stripped to its structural basics and outfitted with a new brick and tile exterior. The width of the building was reduced to eliminate hard-to-rent deep spaces, and two additional floors were added. Other elements in the scheme include a four-story, 1956 office building, dramatically renovated by the addition of a triangular glass-covered atrium and a new elevator tower, a proposed apartment building, and a public plaza with underground parking.

133 Bakery Square (NR)
Louisville, Kentucky

Origin:	Hellmueller Bakery, 1870
Conversion:	Commercial use, 1973
Developer:	J. Clifford Todd, Louisville
Architect:	J. Clifford Todd and Donald J. Allen, Louisville

Redevelopment: Redevelopment costs, originally estimated at $220,000, reached $550,000 for total conversion of the three-story brick bakery into a shopping complex with 36 stores. Several shops open onto a brick-paved courtyard, which separates the main building from a restaurant housed in the bakery's old stable. The Louisville Chamber of Commerce lists Bakery Square as the second most popular tourist attraction in the city. The developer estimates that 40 percent of business in Bakery Square comes from tourists.

134 Piazza d'Italia
New Orleans, Louisiana

Origin:	Warehouses and mercantile buildings, 1860
Conversion:	Commercial and office space, in progress since 1977
Developer:	City of New Orleans/Piazza d'Italia Corporation
Architect:	August Perez and Associates, New Orleans

Redevelopment: The city of New Orleans traded land parcels to assemble a complex of six 19th century structures, valued at $3 million, for redevelopment as commercial and office space. A private developer has been chosen to undertake the $6.3 million project, which will involve a combination of facade restoration, renovation, and new construction. An Italian-American community center will be an integral part of the complex. Matching grants, totaling $1.7 million, from the Economic Development Administration and the state of Louisiana have been used to develop a major public plaza within the interior of the city block. The keyhole-shaped plaza, recipient of a design citation from Progressive Architecture in 1976, replaced the rear portions of the warehouses, which were lost in a fire.

135 111 Rue Iberville Building (NHL)
New Orleans, Louisiana

Origin:	Louisiana Sugar Refinery Warehouse, 1888
Conversion:	Offices and restaurant, 1971
Developer:	Joseph C. Canizaro, New Orleans
Architect:	Curtis and Davis, New Orleans

Redevelopment: Overcoming the strong odor of molasses, developers converted this seven-story brick warehouse into an office building with a restaurant on the first floor. Existing structural elements were left exposed wherever possible, providing a visual potpourri of cast-iron columns and braces, wooden joists, and steel trusses. The project, which cost a total of $1,071,058, received the Vieux Carré Commission Honor Award in 1971.

136 Mercantile Wharf Building (NR)
Boston, Massachusetts

Origin:	Storage and distribution house for ship chandlers and sail makers, 1857
Conversion:	Apartments and commercial space, 1976
Developer:	Mercantile Associates, Boston
Architect:	John Sharratt Associates, Boston

Redevelopment: The granite-faced wharf building, within Boston's historic waterfront district, has been converted to 122 mixed-income apartment units with 13,400 square feet of commercial space on the ground floor. Interior balconies surrounding a central skylighted atrium give access to individual apartments, which feature exposed brick walls, heavy timbered ceilings, and modern appliances. Financing for the $5.1 million redevelopment of the building was obtained through the Massachusetts Housing Finance Agency.

137 Piano Craft Guild
Boston, Massachusetts

Origin:	Chickering piano factory, 1853
Conversion:	Artists' housing and studios, 1974
Developer:	Gelardin/Bruner/Cott, Inc., Cambridge
Architect:	Gelardin/Bruner/Cott, Inc., with Anderson Notter Associates, Boston, as architects of record

Redevelopment: Redesigned to provide working-living spaces for artists in the Boston area, the converted piano factory contains 174 apartments and 30,000 square feet of commercial space. The 220,000-square-foot structure (the second largest building in the country when it was constructed in 1853) takes the shape of a square doughnut, with a landscaped interior courtyard. The apartments, arranged around central corridors, contain moveable partition walls and other design features of special value to artists. The architect-developers adhered to a tight budget, finishing the project for $10.50 per square foot. Construction costs of $2.3 million were covered by the Massachusetts Housing Finance Agency, which provided a $3.5 million permanent mortgage.

138 The Prince Building (NR)
Boston, Massachusetts

Origin:	Prince Spaghetti Factory, 1917
Conversion:	Apartments and offices, 1966
Developer:	Trident Realty Trust, Boston
Architect:	Anderson Notter Associates, Boston

Redevelopment: Three new penthouse stories were constructed, and existing floors were raised to accommodate horizontal utility lines during redevelopment of the nine-story, concrete-frame pasta factory. Balconies for most of the 42 residential units overlook the Boston waterfront. The first two floors of the structure serve as parking areas, and the third story contains office space. Financing for the project was difficult to obtain because revitalization of the industrial waterfront area for commercial and residential uses had not yet taken hold.

139 1455 Centre Street
Detroit, Michigan

Origin:	Warehouse, 1911
Conversion:	Commercial and office space, 1974
Developer:	Harmonie Park Development Company, Detroit
Architect:	John Hilberry and Associates, Inc., Detroit

Redevelopment: Conversion of the three-story, steel-frame warehouse, purchased for $50,000, provided a total of 9,000 square feet for retail space and law and architectural offices. Although a local commercial bank did provide a permanent mortgage, the lenders required a large portion of cash investment before agreeing to participate in financing for the $120,000 project.

140 Detroit Cornice and Slate (NR)
Detroit, Michigan

Origin:	Sheet metal and stone factory, 1897
Conversion:	Offices and restaurant, 1975
Developer:	J. A. Citrin Sons Company, Southfield, Michigan
Architect:	William Kessler and Associates, Inc., Detroit

Redevelopment: Redevelopment included careful restoration of the pressed metal facade, designed to give the appearance of cut stone, of this three-story landmark building in downtown Detroit. The Victorian exterior contrasts with the contemporary interior spaces of the 13,500-square-foot building, which now accommodates an architect's office, artist's studio, and restaurant.

141 Butler Square (NR)
Minneapolis, Minnesota

Origin:	Warehouse, 1906
Conversion:	Retail/office complex, 1974
Developer:	Development Associates, Inc., Minneapolis
Architect:	Miller Hanson Westerbeck Bell Architects, Inc., Minneapolis

Redevelopment: Butler Square occupies the former Butler Brothers Warehouse, a massive nine-story building located on a 1.4-acre site on the edge of downtown Minneapolis. The Butler Brothers Warehouse was first acclaimed for its impressive facade, but it has been the imaginative and striking reuse of the interior space which has generated so much interest. The most important interior modification was the creation of an expansive atrium extending from the first floor to a skylight on the roof. The atrium was built in part to reduce the floor area to less than 20,000 square feet per floor, so that the floors would be compatible with luxury office space. This reduced the square footage in the eastern half of the building by 18 percent. More importantly, however, the atrium created a dramatic interior space which introduced light into the building and gave Butler Square an inward orientation. The building now consists of 29,441 square feet of commercial space and 139,005 square feet of office space.

142 Ideal Laundry Building
Fremont, Nebraska

Origin:	Warehouse for wholesale produce (later a laundry building), 1884
Conversion:	Offices, 1975
Developer:	Ray C. Simmons, Fremont
Architect:	Andrew Morrow, Lincoln

Redevelopment: Although use as a laundry for 78 years had led to deterioration of its ceilings and walls, the two-story brick building was structurally sound enough to warrant conversion of the first floor into law offices. Original tin ceilings and beadboard were reused in the interior renovation and a 20th century rear addition in bad repair was removed to expand a parking lot. Situated on the main highway between Lincoln and Sioux City, the building forms the southern anchor of a short historic district on Fremont's Broad Street. The property was purchased for $16,250 and redeveloped for $60,136.

143 Bently Nevada Corporation
Minden, Nevada

Origin:	Minden Creamery, 1908
Conversion:	Electronics plant, 1970 (with additions in 1973 and 1977)
Developer:	Donald E. Bently, Minden
Architect:	None

Redevelopment: Although a metal bas-relief sign over the door still reads "Eggs and Poultry," the entrance of this building now leads into a modern industrial plant for the manufacture of electronic equipment. The interior of the former creamery was gutted, a new floor plan established, and major additions made during extensive redevelopment of the brick structure. The 2.5-acre site was purchased for $70,000 and redeveloped for $650,000.

223

144 Stephens Square
Binghamton, New York

Origin: Warehouse, 1888
Conversion: Commercial and office
                 space, 1972-1976
Developer: James Mowry, Binghamton
Architect: James Mowry, Binghamton
Redevelopment: A shopping arcade with 25 businesses arranged on three levels now revitalizes the interior of Stephens Square, a brick industrial building originally constructed by a Binghamton cigar maker. Building acquisition and redevelopment of three floors (termed a "vertical marketplace") totaled $395,000; renovation of three remaining floors will be undertaken in a second phase of the project. Redevelopment efforts, initiated in 1972, were snagged for 2 years by the possibility of condemnation and demolition of the building by the city for another urban revitalization project.

145 Warehouse Apartments
Binghamton, New York

Origin: Warehouse, 1898
Conversion: Apartments and offices, 1971
Developer: James Mowry, Binghamton
Architect: James Mowry
Redevelopment: A narrow four-story building, the converted warehouse contains seven apartment units and one office. Costs for the project were kept low ($100,000) by highlighting existing brick walls, wooden joists, and open spaces. Two of the units in the 8,000-square-foot building are duplexes which occupy the basement and first floor.

146 Bedford-Stuyvesant Commercial Center
Brooklyn, New York

Origin: Industrial buildings,
                 turn of the century
Conversion: Commercial, office, and
                 recreational uses, 1975
Developer: Bedford Stuyvesant
                 Restoration Corporation,
                 Brooklyn
Architect: Arthur Cotton
                 Moore/Associates,
                 Washington, D.C.
Redevelopment: An entire city block in Bedford Stuyvesant has been recycled into neighborhood shops, offices, and public spaces, through the reuse of older buildings and the construction of new. A converted milk bottling plant, now housing retail stores and restaurants, is a major feature in the project, which also includes a skating rink and underground parking garage. The facades of three demolished tenements were retained and braced to serve as a gateway to the complex and to preserve the visual continuity of the street. A permanent mortgage for the project, partially financed with federal funds from the Office of Economic Opportunity, is still being sought.

147 The Hallie Flanagan Davis Powerhouse Theater
Poughkeepsie, New York

Origin: Electrical powerhouse, 1912
Conversion: Drama workshop, 1972
Developer: Vassar College,
                 Poughkeepsie
Architect: Robertson Ward, Jr.,
                 Chicago
Redevelopment: Flexibility was the key for the design of a small theater within the shell of an old brick power plant on the Vassar College campus. A modular scaffolding and platform system together with a modular seating unit allow frequent rearrangement of the performance and audience spaces within the 3,600-square-foot building. Old machinery pits for electrical equipment were converted to central trap areas and the original machinery crane rail now serves as a track for the new lighting system. Lobby and support facilities are contained in a new addition to the building, which was redeveloped for $935,000.

148 GP Warehouse and Emporium
Bismarck, North Dakota

Origin: Grocery warehouse, 1922
Conversion: Restaurant and shops, 1976
Developer: Vernon F. Peterson,
                 Bismarck
Architect: Vernon F. Peterson
Redevelopment: The governor of North Dakota played the fiddle at the grand opening of the GP Warehouse and Emporium, a restaurant and bar with a nostalgic 1880s decor. Above the restaurant, the second floor of the four-story brick and concrete warehouse has been developed as "Village Square," a series of 10 small shops offering handcrafted goods. The developer received a 20-year $195,000 mortgage through the Small Business Administration and a $40,000 loan through a local bank. Financing arrangements were complicated by SBA's

3-8 Musto Plaza in San Francisco was transformed from a marble cutting factory to office use in 1970.

"after-acquired clause," which specifies that all capital improvements are considered part of the original mortgage.

149 The Marketplace (Mid-Atlantic Design Center) Philadelphia, Pennsylvania

Origin:	Automobile assembly plant (later Gimbel's Warehouse), 1920s
Conversion:	Merchandise market, 1975
Developer:	Herbert S. Goldstein, Managing Partner, Philadelphia
Architect:	Levinson Lebowitz Zaprauskis, Philadelphia

Redevelopment: One hundred modern showrooms occupy a formerly undistinguished warehouse, providing a merchandising market where design professionals and their clients can examine the latest line of residential and contract furnishings, fabrics, and accessories. Each floor of the five-story concrete-frame structure, which retains its central circulation core with automobile ramps and elevators, features a central mall punctuated with freestanding concrete support columns and opening onto individual showrooms. For the brick exterior, a unique painting scheme was designed to integrate conflicting building materials, improve the structure's proportions, and emphasize the original terra-cotta decoration.

150 Gassner Nathan and Partners Memphis, Tennessee

Origin:	Memphis Elevator Company, 1910
Conversion:	Offices, 1968
Developer:	Gassner Nathan and Partners, Memphis
Architect:	Gassner Nathan and Partners, Memphis

Redevelopment: The long narrow shell of the former elevator factory was redeveloped for $65,000 as offices and design studios for an architectural and planning firm. The firm, which first leased the two-story masonry building in 1968, exercised an option to purchase the building in 1976 for $60,000 with financing provided by the seller.

151 Olla Podrida Dallas, Texas

Origin:	Car warehouse
Conversion:	Shopping mall, 1972
Developer:	Park Central, Dallas
Architect:	Pratt, Box and Henderson, Dallas; and Architects Partnerships, Dallas

Redevelopment: Loosely translated from Latin, Olla Podrida means "a pot of stew," a light reference to the mixture of artists, craftsmen, and collectors who maintain studios and shops in the old warehouse. Although all interior construction within the steel-frame building is new, old salvaged materials were extensively used for both structural and decorative elements in the complex. A Plexiglas skylight stretches the length of the building, lighting a central mall with access to three levels of shops and to a dinner theater and indoor tennis facility. Redeveloped in three phases from 1972 to 1976, the structure has a gross building area of 72,000 square feet.

152 Blum Building (NHL)
Galveston, Texas

Origin: Wholesale house, 1870
Conversion: Commercial space and
               offices, 1977
Developer: George P. Mitchell, Houston
Architect: Ford, Carson & Powell, San
               Antonio

Redevelopment: The cast-iron storefronts of this three-story masonry warehouse are being restored during the first phase of work, which also includes development of a restaurant and retail shops on the first floor. The structure, which formerly served as a clothing house for cotton factors, as a wholesale grocer, and as a hardware store, contains 26,000 square feet. A permanent mortgage will be provided by a six-bank consortium in accordance with special arrangements between the lending institutions and the Galveston Historical Foundation for financing of rehabilitation projects within The Strand Historic District.

153 Whiteside Townflats (NHL)
Galveston, Texas

Origin: Paint factory (later Knapp
               Printing Company), 1870
Conversion: Apartments, 1974
Developer: Emily M. Whiteside,
               Galveston
Architect: Ford, Carson & Powell, San
               Antonio

Redevelopment: By dropping a three-story atrium into the center of the narrow 20-foot-long building, the apartments in the former printing company were given access to light and air. A full loan of $110,000 (30 years at 8½ percent) was provided by the trust fund of a local foundation interested in preservation of historic Galveston. The adaptive use project encouraged rehabilitation of other buildings on The Strand, Galveston's 19th century cast-iron commercial district. Revitalization on The Strand has in turn motivated the recycling of projects in other parts of the central business district.

154 River Square
San Antonio, Texas

Origin: Warehouse, circa 1875
Conversion: Commercial, office, and
               residential spaces, 1976
Developer: William W. Atwell, San
               Antonio
Architect: Martin and Artega, San
               Antonio

Redevelopment: Winner of a San Antonio Conservation Award for this project, the developer nevertheless encountered resistance from local lending institutions at the time of purchase of the $225,000 property. Although acquisition and improvement costs were personally financed through a local bank, the developer is now seeking a permanent mortgage from institutions outside of the city. The limestone structure, with a gross building area of 29,400 square feet, was redeveloped for $300,000.

155 The Ice House
Burlington, Vermont

Origin: Ice house (later a mattress
               company), 1868
Conversion: Restaurant and office, 1976
Developer: Numerous Enterprises, Ltd.,
               Burlington
Architect: Colin Lindberg, Burlington

Redevelopment: A $75,000 grant from the Economic Development Administration helped to make this $220,000 project possible, despite the developer's initial difficulty in convincing bankers to provide financing for adaptive use of the former ice storage plant. Conversion involved removal of an 8,000-square-foot warehouse addition built in the early 20th century and new construction of a 1,000-square-foot contemporary kitchen, yielding a gross building area of 8,000 square feet. All dimensional lumber contained in the demolished section was salvaged for reuse at a substantial saving.

156 Crilley Warehouse (NHL)
Alexandria, Virginia

Origin:	Hill Steam Cracker Manufactory, 1895
Conversion:	Commercial space and offices, 1976
Developer:	Marilyn Hansen and Michael M. Reddan, Alexandria
Architect:	Michael M. Reddan

Redevelopment: A three-story skylighted atrium in the center of the square warehouse (100 feet square) provides a common lobby for the shops, restaurants, and offices which now occupy the brick building in Old Town Alexandria. Interiors feature heavy timber posts and beams and exposed brick walls. The third floor is leased to an office management company which sublets executive suites and provides secretarial, telephone, copying, and other office services to tenants. Acquisition and redevelopment, financed by a local savings and loan, totaled $1,230,535.

157 Green's Steam Furniture Works
Alexandria, Virginia

Origin:	Steam furniture factory, circa 1830s
Conversion:	Condominiums, 1977
Developer:	Ellsworth-Howell, Alexandria
Architect:	Michael and Michael, Alexandria

Redevelopment: Sixteen residential condominiums, ranging in size from 595 to 1,500 square feet, occupy the former industrial building, which now features a central atrium. The ground floor is used for parking, and a fourth floor was added within the existing exterior walls to provide three levels for residential use. The original heavy timber frame of the brick structure was previously replaced with a steel skeleton and concrete floors. A $1-million construction loan for the project was given with the condition of a percentage of pre-sales of condominium units.

158 Torpedo Factory Art Center (NHL)
Alexandria, Virginia

Origin:	Torpedo factory, 1917-1918
Conversion:	Art center, 1974
Developer:	City of Alexandria
Architect:	None

Redevelopment: Purchased from the federal government by the city of Alexandria, the Torpedo Factory became the focus of a unique bicentennial experiment to serve community artists and to attract tourists. Twenty percent of the structure—a two-story industrial building with 20-foot ceilings and large open spaces—has been adapted as rental studio and gallery space for artists, craftsmen, and art organizations. Redevelopment work was kept to a minimum, with 8-foot partitions used to separate studio spaces; the public (averaging 7,000 visitors a week) can view the artists at work and buy their wares. Although the center is financially self supporting (annual rents of $3 per square foot cover utilities and pay back the city's $140,000 renovation loan), it is reaching the end of its 3-year trial period and faces an uncertain future.

159 The Warehouse (NR)
Richland Center, Wisconsin

Origin:	A. D. German Warehouse (grocery storage), 1915-1920
Conversion:	Museum and cultural center, 1976
Developer:	Richland Museum Ltd., Richland Center
Architect:	Robert Blust/Center Architects, Richland Center

Redevelopment: The only structure designed by Frank Lloyd Wright in the town of his birth, this four-story brick and concrete warehouse is topped by an elaborate, geometrically patterned concrete frieze which recalls the architect's interest in Mayan architecture. Conversion of the 14,000-square-foot building includes development of a rooftop garden restaurant, a shop, a theater, studios, and exhibition spaces; the site and rooftop will be extensively landscaped with native plants in accordance with Wright's traditions. The building is being purchased for $70,000 via a land contract at 8 percent over a 20-year period. The conversion is being financed by donations from individuals, businesses, and industries; grants from public and private foundations; and revenues from membership, admissions, and special events.

Project Economics

Factories, Warehouses, and Industrial Buildings

Project	Year of Conversion	Gross Building Area (sq. ft.)	Acquisition Cost	Redevelopment Cost	Approx. Cost Per Sq. Ft.	Source of Financing	Rental Rates (annual per sq. ft., unless otherwise noted)
China Basin Building	1973	500,000 Phase I: 120,000	(Already owned by developer)	($ 1,656,000) Phase I	($13.80) Phase I	Insurance company	$7.20
The Feather Factory	1973	30,000	$ 190,000	350,000	11.66	Securities company	$45.00
Ghirardelli Square	1964	180,000	2,500,000	10,000,000	(55.56)	Insurance company	$12.00
Musto Plaza	1970	41,728	—	(459,843)	11.02	—	—
450 Pacific Avenue Building	1973	28,000	—	950,000	34.00	Local commercial bank	—
Blake Street Bath and Racquet Club	1976	22,000	125,000	500,000	22.73	Purchase financing from previous owner; local banks	$37.50 (sale)
The Cable Building	1973	53,750	—	—	—	Construction—local commercial bank; permanent mortgage—NY S&L	$5.50—8.00
Tivoli	1977	160,000	Leased	6,800,000	42.50	Local banks; funds from ltd. partnership	$8.46
Canal Square	1971	150,000	—	2,400,000	Old 17.00 New 15.00	Construction—local security and trust company; permanent—NY Life; refinanced by Bank of America	$9.00—office; $13.00—retail
CFC Square (South)	1971	107,000	—	4,700,000	28.60	Construction—self-financed; permanent—not yet obtained	—
Bakery Square	1973	(50,000)	70,000	550,000	19.00	Local commercial bank	$5.00
Piazza d'Italia	1977	150,000	Trade (3,000,000 value)	6,300,000 (buildings); 1,700,000 (public space)	40.00	Federal and state funds for public space; remainder undetermined	
111 Rue Iberville Building	1971	42,000	135,000	836,058	22.00	Mortgage company	$7.00
Mercantile Wharf Building	1976	294,000	100,000	5,100,000	26.00	MHFA (state)	$410—490/mo./1 br/market; $235/mo./1 br/moderate; $550—595/mo./2 br/market; $285/mo./2 br/moderate; 25% income/low
Piano Craft Guild	1974	220,000	500,000	2,300,000	10.50	MHFA (state)	$91—140/mo./low-income; $151—198/mo./moderate; $205—401/mo./market

Project	Year of Conversion	Gross Building Area (sq. ft.)	Acquisition Cost	Redevelopment Cost	Approx. Cost Per Sq. Ft.	Source of Financing	Rental Rates (annual per sq. ft., unless otherwise noted)
The Prince Building	1966	87,000	120,000	1,218,000	14.00	Savings bank	—
1455 Centre Street	1974	9,000	50,000	120,000	13.30	Local commercial bank	$4.80
Detroit Cornice & Slate	1975	13,500	—	—	—	—	
Butler Square	1974	248,774 (after atrium construction)	500,000	3,900,000 Phase I	19.05	Construction— local commercial bank	$10.00–15.00 commercial; $8.50–9.25 retail; length generally 5 years.
Ideal Laundry Building	1975	7,216	16,250	60,136	(8.33)	—	(not rented)
Bentley Nevada Corporation	—	39,000	70,000	650,000	(16.67)	—	(not rented)
Stephens Square	1976	60,000	125,000	270,000 Phase I	13.00	6-bank consortium	$4.00—10.00
Warehouse Apartments	1971	8,000	15,000	100,000	12.00	Local bank	$3.00
Bedford-Stuyvesant Commercial Center	1975	146,500	—	—	—	Federal funds (CEO); construction— 2 NYC commercial banks; permanent— not yet obtained	$7.50 office; $8.00—11.00 retail
The Hallie Flanagan Davis Powerhouse Theater	1972	3,600	(Already owned)	953,000	135.00	College funding	(not rented)
GP Warehouse and Emporium	1976	37,500	82,500	225,000	6.00	SBA and local bank	3.00
The Marketplace	1975	351,126	—	—	—	—	—
Gassner Nathan and Partners	1968	10,360	60,000	65,000	9.85	Financed by seller	$3.50
Olla Podrida	1972	72,000	—	—	—	—	$6.25 or percentage
Blum Building	1977	26,000	69,000	400,000 Phase I	(15.38)	6-bank consortium	—
Whiteside Townflats	1974	6,000	—	110,000	25.00	Local foundation (loan)	$3.60
River Square	1976	29,400	225,000	300,000	(10.20)	(In process)	$4.08 office; $6.00 + percentage retail
The Ice House	1976	8,000	90,000	220,000	26.25	EDA grant (75,000); bank loan	$6.50—7.00
Crilley Warehouse	1976	28,797	315,000	915,535	31.79	Local S&L	$12.50
Green's Steam Furniture Works	1977	27,600	100,000	1,100,000	(39.86)	S&L (metro area)	$90.00— 115.00 (sales)
Torpedo Factory Art Center	1974	85,000	1,500,000	140,000	(1.65)	City capital bond issue	$3.00
The Warehouse	1977	14,000	70,000	67,712 (first two floors)	7.34	Public and private grants; donations; membership and special events admittance revenue	(not rented)

Dashes indicate data not available.
Figures in parentheses were not supplied directly but were derived from other data.

Redevelopment Work
Factories, Warehouses, and Industrial Buildings

Project	Exterior Restoration	New Exterior Construction	Structural	Mechanical	Interior Demolition	Interior New Construction	Site Restoration	New Facilities, Parking	Landscaping
China Basin Building	Moderate	Moderate	Minor	Extensive	Moderate	Extensive	Moderate	Moderate	Moderate
The Feather Factory	Minor	Minor	Extensive	Moderate	Moderate	Minor	None	None	None
Ghirardelli Square	Minor	—	Moderate	Moderate	Minor	Extensive	—	Extensive	Extensive
Musto Plaza	Minor	Moderate	Moderate	Extensive	Minor	Extensive	Extensive	—	Moderate
450 Pacific Avenue Building	Moderate	Minor	Extensive	Extensive	Moderate	Extensive	Minor	None	Minor
Blake Street Bath and Racquet Club	Extensive	Moderate	Moderate	Extensive	Extensive	Extensive	Extensive	Extensive	Moderate
The Cable Building	Moderate	Minor	Minor	Extensive	Extensive	Extensive	—	Extensive	Moderate
Tivoli	Minor	Moderate	Moderate	Extensive	Extensive	Extensive	Moderate	Minor	Moderate
Canal Square	Moderate	Extensive	Moderate	Extensive	Minor	Moderate	Minor	Extensive	Moderate
CFC Square (South)	Extensive	Extensive	Moderate	Extensive	Extensive	Extensive	Extensive	Extensive	Extensive
Bakery Square	Minor	Minor	Minor	Extensive	Extensive	Extensive	Minor	Extensive	Extensive
Piazza d'Italia	Extensive	Extensive	Extensive	Extensive	Extensive	Extensive	Extensive	None	Extensive
111 Rue Iberville Building	Minor	Minor	Moderate	Extensive	Moderate	Moderate	Minor	Minor	Minor
Mercantile Wharf Building	Moderate	Moderate	Extensive	Extensive	Extensive	Extensive	Moderate	Moderate	Extensive
Piano Craft Guild	Moderate	Moderate	Moderate	Extensive	Moderate	Extensive	Moderate	Extensive	Extensive
The Prince Building	Extensive	Moderate	Minor	Extensive	Minor	Extensive	Minor	Extensive	Minor
1455 Centre Street	Minor	Minor	Minor	Extensive	Moderate	Moderate	Moderate	Minor	Minor
Detroit Cornice & Slate	Extensive	Minor	Extensive	Extensive	Extensive	Extensive	Minor	Moderate	Moderate
Butler Square	Minor	Minor	Minor	Extensive	Moderate	Moderate	Moderate	Moderate	Moderate
Ideal Laundry Building	Minor	—	—	—	—	Extensive	Moderate	Moderate	—
Bentley Nevada Corporation	Moderate	Moderate	Moderate	Extensive	Extensive	Extensive	Moderate	Minor	Minor
Stephens Square	Moderate	Minor	Minor	Extensive	—	Extensive	Minor	Minor	Minor
Warehouse Apartments	Minor	Minor	Minor	Extensive	Extensive	Extensive	Minor	Minor	Minor
Bedford-Stuyvesant Commercial Center	Moderate	Extensive	Extensive	Extensive	Moderate	Extensive	Moderate	Extensive	Moderate
The Hallie Flanagan Davis Powerhouse Theater	Minor	Moderate	Moderate	Extensive	Minor	Extensive	Extensive	Extensive	Extensive
GP Warehouse and Emporium	Minor	Minor	Minor	Moderate	Moderate	Moderate	Minor	Minor	Minor
The Marketplace	Minor	Moderate	Minor	Extensive	Minor	Extensive	Minor	—	—
Gassner Nathan and Partners	Minor	Minor	Minor	Extensive	Extensive	Extensive	None	None	Minor
Olla Podrida	Minor	Minor	Minor	Extensive	Minor	Extensive	Moderate	Moderate	Moderate
Blum Building	Extensive	Minor	Moderate	Extensive	Minor	Extensive	Minor	Moderate	Minor
Whiteside Townflats	Extensive	None	Moderate	Extensive	Moderate	Extensive	Moderate	Minor	Moderate
River Square	Minor	Minor	Minor	Moderate	Moderate	Minor	Minor	Minor	Minor
The Ice House	Extensive	Moderate	Extensive	Extensive	Extensive	Extensive	Extensive	Extensive	Moderate
Crilley Warehouse	Moderate	Moderate	Moderate	Extensive	Extensive	Extensive	Minor	Extensive	Minor
Green's Steam Furniture Works	Moderate	Moderate	Moderate	Extensive	Extensive	Extensive	—	Extensive	—
Torpedo Factory Art Center	Minor	None	None	Moderate	None	Moderate	None	None	None
The Warehouse	Moderate	Minor	Minor	Extensive	Minor	Moderate	Minor	Moderate	Moderate

Dashes indicate data not available.

Miscellaneous

Many types of buildings have escaped classification within the previous nine categories. Of these, many are associated with community welfare, be it spiritual (churches and synagogues), physical (hospitals and sanitariums), or cultural (libraries and museums). Other buildings are identified with public amusement (social halls, bowling alleys, and roller rinks).

Churches and synagogues probably face the most serious situation as surplus buildings. High maintenance costs of the buildings themselves coupled with a change in housing patterns among members have led many congregations to sell central city churches and build in the suburbs. Other churches have been concerned that shrinking congregations have greatly reduced the use of the religious buildings during the week. In 1975, a multidenominational conference in Cambridge, Massachusetts, dealt specifically with the challenge of underutilized church property and the search for alternatives. The conference proceedings stressed the need for community-oriented supplemental uses of church buildings, such as child care facilities, centers for youth or the elderly, or adult education programs.

Once transferred to private ownership, many smaller churches have been converted into single-family homes. Larger buildings have been adapted as multi-family housing, educational centers, or restaurants. In general, these adaptations have attempted to retain the aesthetic elements of the original design, such as stained glass windows, fine woodwork, and lofty interior spaces.

The large number of unused country barns have also made these utilitarian structures attractive for recycling schemes. Essentially structural shells enclosing highly adaptable spaces, barns have frequently been converted into private residences, theaters, or commercial complexes. The special relationship of a barn to its surrounding landscape and the use of local construction materials and regional building forms most likely contribute to the popularity of barn redevelopments.

Even the ubiquitous gas station has become a candidate for reuse. During the 1974 gasoline crisis, hundreds of small stations closed, only to reopen later as pizza parlors, record stores, beauty shops—the list could be endless. Once the pumps are gone, the vacant station offers a small structure suitable for a single enterprise on a lot with the advantages of on-site parking and good access. Fifty proposals for adaptation are presented by A. L. Kerth in *A New Life for the Abandoned Service Station* (New York, 1974).

Several uncommon building types have been the subjects of reuse schemes as well. Windmills and lighthouses, for example, have been converted to private homes or small shops. In North Carolina, a water tower in Raleigh serves as office space and a water tank in Rocky Mount as an arts center. Lucy, a six-story structure shaped Ike an elephant in Margate, New Jersey, built as an ocean resort attraction in 1881, has been restored and adapted as a children's library. An elevator in one leg carries visitors into the library. Railroad boxcars serve as a discotheque in Ithaca, New York; and in Hoboken, New Jersey, an ocean liner has been docked and adapted as a dormitory for students of the Stevens Institute of Technology.

Concrete grain elevators, such as those at Old Mill Plaza in Newton, Kansas, (see Case Studies) or at Quaker Square in Akron, offer a still unmet challenge for adaptive use.

**160   Golden Mall Playhouse
Burbank, California**

Origin: Bowling alley, circa 1923
Conversion: Live theater, 1973
Developer: Walter L. Gilmore, Burbank
Architect: None
Redevelopment: On-site parking, proximity to a commercial area, and accessibility to freeway exits contributed to the choice of a dilapidated cement-block bowling alley for conversion into a 230-seat, air-conditioned theater. Redevelopment costs for the 6,000-square-foot building, which is used by a nonprofit theater organization as a showcase for new talent, were kept to $33,000 through the use of volunteer labor and salvaged materials.

3-9 The interior colonnade of Quincy Market, part of Faneuil Hall Marketplace. (Photo: Edward C. Benner.)

161 The Stanford Barn
Palo Alto, California

Origin:	Winery (later a dairy barn), 1888
Conversion:	Commercial and office space, 1961 and 1977
Developer:	Stanford Barn Enterprises, Palo Alto
Architect:	Herand der Sarkissian, Palo Alto

Redevelopment: First converted to a specialty shopping facility in 1961, the three-story brick barn has recently undergone a major renovation, doubling the amount of commercial space. The structure, which features interior patios and open hallways, is within the Stanford Shopping Center area which serves the university as well as residents of adjacent communities. The developers purchased a leasehold on the property (until 2006) for $1 million through a savings and loan association, and used personal funds to cover rehabilitation costs. The project will be refinanced upon completion.

162 Mammoth Gardens
Denver, Colorado

Origin:	Roller skating rink, 1907
Conversion:	Marketplace, 1976
Developer:	Warren Bailey, Denver
Architect:	Warren Bailey, Denver

Redevelopment: Once a grand roller skating rink, this block-long building housed wrestling matches, basketball games, bicycle races, a gambling casino, jitterbug marathons, revival meetings, political conventions, and rock and roll concerts before its purchase for redevelopment as an inner-city marketplace. The building's 35,000 square feet are occupied by more than 50 food markets, restaurants, craft studios, and specialty shops; on the weekends an additional 50 temporary booths offer homemade, handcrafted, and homegrown goods.

163 Educational Center for the Arts
New Haven, Connecticut

Origin:	Temple Mishkin Israel, late 19th century
Conversion:	Regional public high school for the arts, 1972
Developer:	Board of Education, city of New Haven
Architect:	Charles Brewer, New Haven

Redevelopment: Financed by a grant from the Connecticut State Department of Education, the conversion of the Spanish-Renaissance-style temple resulted in new theater, studio, classroom, office, and storage spaces for the public school system of New Haven. The main temple area, comprising one-third of the 15,000-square-foot building, was gutted to form a performance area with modern sound and lighting systems.

164 Light Designs, Inc. (NR)
Pensacola, Florida

Origin:	St. Michael's Creole Benevolent Association Hall, circa 1895
Conversion:	Commercial showroom, 1972
Developer:	Roy M. Stark and Robert N. Quigley, Pensacola
Architect:	None

Redevelopment: Used by the Creole Association as a meeting hall from 1895 until 1972, the one-story wooden building required only minor remodeling for its conversion into a showroom for lamps and lighting fixtures. The new owners felt that the contrast between the old building and the products of Light Designs would prove their contention that contemporary lighting compliments good period architecture. The structure, which features a steeply pitched roof and turned wooden porch details, was repainted according to research on the original colors.

165 Rafford Hall (NR)
Pensacola, Florida

Origin:	Pensacola Athletic Club, 1890
Conversion:	Offices and community center, 1976
Developer:	North Hill Preservation Association, Pensacola; and Pensacola JayCees, Inc.
Architect:	Look and Morrison, Pensacola

Redevelopment: Acquired without cost from a nonprofit organization, the former athletic club has been restored as a meeting hall and headquarters for community groups. The three-story frame building contains a gross building area of 7,912 square feet. The $100,000 redevelopment was funded through private donations, and grants from the state bicentennial organization, the U.S. Department of the Interior, and Bird and Sons, Inc.

166 The Abbey Restaurant
Atlanta, Georgia

Origin:	Congregational Church, 1915
Conversion:	Restaurant, 1968
Developer:	W. F. Swearingen, Atlanta
Architect:	W. F. Swearingen

Redevelopment: No major changes in the interior spaces were required for the conversion of the brick Gothic Revival church into a restaurant. The nave serves as the main dining area. Redevelopment yielded a gross building area of 9,000 square feet.

167 Faneuil Hall Marketplace (NR)
Boston, Massachusetts

Origin:	Wholesale food market, 1826
Conversion:	Specialty retail/restaurant and office complex, 1978
Developer:	The Rouse Company, Columbia, Maryland
Architect:	Benjamin Thompson and Associates, Inc., Cambridge

Redevelopment: Strategically located between downtown and the waterfront in Boston, Faneuil Hall Marketplace is being redeveloped as a retail and office complex. In 1826, Quincy Market was built as an annex to Faneuil Hall, the first public market in Boston. Shortly thereafter North and South Market Buildings were added. These two buildings together with Quincy Market comprise Faneuil Hall Marketplace and are under the control of the Boston Redevelopment Authority (BRA). The BRA signed a 99-year lease with The Rouse Company, which has the responsibility to continue restoration, find tenants, arrange financing, and manage the project on an ongoing basis. The Rouse Company is spending nearly $30 million to rehabilitate the three buildings into 225,000 square feet of specialty retail/restaurant use and 150,000 square feet of office space. Permanent financing is from Teachers Insurance and Annuity Association. Half of the construction financing is from Chase Manhattan Bank of New York, and half from a consortium of Boston financial institutions.

168 Coolidge Bank and Trust Company
Cambridge, Massachusetts

Origin:	Gas station, circa 1930
Conversion:	Bank, 1971
Developer:	Stonemill Trust, Watertown, Massachusetts
Architect:	Mintz Associates, Architects & Planners, Inc. (formerly Pard Team, Inc.), Boston

Redevelopment: Bright contemporary graphics call attention to the former gas station, now a branch bank located just off Harvard Square. A brick-paved courtyard replaces the old pump area, and one arm of the building serves as a drive-up banking facility. Redevelopment costs for the project, which includes underground parking for 20 cars, totaled $247,065.

169 Academy Knoll
Marlborough, Massachusetts

Origin:	St. Anne's Academy, 1888–1925
Conversion:	Apartments for the elderly, 1976
Developer:	Academy Knoll Associates, Boston
Architect:	Anderson Notter Associates, Boston

Redevelopment: Serving as a convent and boarding school until 1972, the rambling brick structure now contains 109 apartments for the elderly. The exterior of the building and the former academy's landscaped grounds have been preserved, as have many interior architectural details. Units in the subdivided chapel and auditorium feature stained glass windows and gold-leaf vaulted ceilings, and other apartments contain wainscoted walls and built-in wooden cabinets from former classrooms and dormitories. Funded by the Massachusetts Housing Finance Agency, the $2 million project receives HUD Section 8 rent subsidies.

170 Exeter Assembly Hall
Exeter, New Hampshire

Origin:	Chapel, 1914
Conversion:	School assembly hall, 1969
Developer:	Phillips Exeter Academy, Exeter
Architect:	Hardy Holzman Pfeiffer Associates, New York

Redevelopment: The seating capacity of the former chapel was increased from 600 to 1,100 during redevelopment, which also improved the sight lines and acoustics of the hall. Exposed steel and chromium piping were introduced to support a new curvilinear balcony, and original plasterwork was repainted with antique glazes to accentuate the 1914 details. Construction costs totaled $500,000.

171 Santuario de Guadalupe (NR)
Santa Fe, New Mexico

Origin:	Guadalupe Church, pre-1795
Conversion:	Museum and cultural institute, 1976
Developer:	Guadalupe Historical Foundation, Santa Fe
Architect:	Johnson-Nestor/Architects-Planners, Santa Fe; Nathaniel Owings (consulting architect), Big Sur, California

Redevelopment: Vacated by its parish in 1961, this adobe mission church has been rehabilitated by a private foundation to serve as a performing arts and exhibition facility. Redevelopment work included partial restoration of the much-remodeled building to its 18th century appearance, installation of new heating and museum lighting systems, and extensive landscaping of the surrounding gardens and riverfront parkway. Largely financed by public grants, the project received funds from the American Revolution Bicentennial Administration ($168,544), the New Mexico Arts Commission ($3,000), and the U.S. Department of Housing and Urban Development through the city of Santa Fe ($130,000).

172 Ithaca Hair Stylists
Ithaca, New York

Origin:	Gas station, 1936
Conversion:	Beauty salon, 1976
Developer:	Joseph E. and Mary H. Burun, Ithaca
Architect:	None

Redevelopment: Acquired in October for $27,000, the Colonial-Revival-style gas station was reopened as a beauty salon by the following December. Garage doors were remodeled as bay windows, a new concrete floor was laid, and interior spaces were plastered during the $10,000 conversion. The slate-roofed building, which contains 1,000 square feet, still sports a wrought-iron weather vane in the shape of an old-fashioned car.

173 Bridgemarket
New York, New York

Origin:	Farmers' market, 1908
Conversion:	Commercial use, 1977
Developer:	Harley Baldwin, New York
Architect:	Hardy Holzman Pfeiffer Associates, New York

Redevelopment: A complex of indoor and outdoor markets, located under and around the vaults at the Manhattan end of the 59th Street Bridge, has been reused as markets, boutiques, restaurants, and public spaces. The city-owned markets are leased to the developer, who invested $1.5 million in rehabilitation.

174 New York Shakespeare Festival Public Theater (NR)
New York, New York

Origin:	Astor Library (later the Hebrew Immigrant Aid Society), 1853–1881
Conversion:	Theater facility, in progress since 1966
Developer:	New York Shakespeare Festival, New York
Architect:	Giorgio Cavaglieri, New York

Redevelopment: Three separate buildings behind a unified Renaissance Revival facade now provide performance spaces and support facilities for the New York Shakespeare Festival. Redevelopment work on the buildings, which were purchased in 1965 for $575,000, was initially financed by private donations; the complex has since been sold to the city of New York. Although interior spaces have been used by the theater company for a decade, work continues on the 84,000-square-foot complex, with costs to date estimated at $3 million.

175 Old Saratoga Square
Saratoga Springs, New York

Origin:	Young Men's Christian Association, 1870 (with addition circa 1900)
Conversion:	Commercial and office use, 1976
Developer:	Old Saratoga Square Partnership, Saratoga Springs
Architect:	The Saratoga Associates, Saratoga Springs

Redevelopment: Subjected to several remodelings which had destroyed many of the original features of the building, the old YMCA had been empty for several years prior to its purchase for reuse. Rather than attempt to recapture the original cast-iron storefronts, the architects redesigned the ground level in brick to harmonize with the masonry construction of the other three floors. Four retail outlets, occupying 3,000 square feet, were developed in the first phase of work, at $17 per square foot. Costs for the second phase, involving rehabilitation of the third and fourth floors into offices for the project architects, were kept to $2.35 per square foot through in-house professional services and construction labor. The third phase, estimated at $60,000, will consist of adding 13 more retail spaces, and the fourth phase of retrofitting the 18,300-square-foot building for energy conservation.

176 CAG Building and Highland Apartments
Utica, New York

Origin:	St. Luke's Home and Hospital, 1905
Conversion:	Apartments and offices, 1968
Developer:	Gaetano Realty Corporation, Utica
Architect:	Jonza & Montay, Utica; also Charles A. Tomaselli, Louis Carl DiOrio, Andrew Alesia, Lawrence Fliorentino, Utica

Redevelopment: A U-shaped brick building with limestone detailing, the former hospital now contains offices on the ground floor and apartments on the three upper floors. Conversion of the Jacobean Revival building totaled $500,000 for acquisition and renovation.

177 The AIA Tower (NR)
Raleigh, North Carolina

Origin:	Raleigh Water Tower, 1887
Conversion:	Offices, 1963
Developer:	North Carolina Chapter of the American Institute of Architects, Raleigh
Architect:	Committee of AIA members

Redevelopment: A four-story tower of granite and brick no longer stores water for the Raleigh community but provides, 1,800 square feet of unique office spaces. The tower and an attached two-story building were first converted to office use in 1931 by an architect who deeded the building to the state chapter of the AIA in 1963. Renovation was financed through contributions from AIA members.

178 Rocky Mount Arts and Crafts Center
Rocky Mount, North Carolina

Origin: Water storage tank, early
                    1930s
Conversion: Arts and crafts center, 1960
Developer: City of Rocky Mount
Architect: Edwards, Dove and Knight,
                    Rocky Mount

Redevelopment: A round, metal storage tank, 40 feet high and 57 feet in diameter, now houses three floors of community arts facilities—including offices, a circular art gallery, an arena-auditorium with seating for 110, and five classrooms. A brick and glass facade was added to the front of the tank, and exterior redevelopment of the property included extensive landscaping and construction of parking facilities. The tank was a donation from the Atlantic Coastline Railroad, and financing was provided by the city through tax revenues.

179 Spring House Village Center
Spring House, Pennsylvania

Origin: Dairy farm complex, circa
                    1850
Conversion: Shopping center, 1972
Developer: Penn Eastern Development
                    Company, Spring House
Architect: Lynn Taylor Associates,
                    Spring House

Redevelopment: Several buildings from the former Martin Century Dairy Farms form the core of this enclosed shopping mall, which mixes old construction with contemporary architecture. A timber barn (circa 1850), carriage house, and ice cream manufacturing plant comprise 40,000 of the 130,000-square-foot complex. Serving an upper-middle-class suburb of Philadelphia, the center composed of 45 stores was developed for $3,700,000. The project received a Land Development Award from the Montgomery County (Pennsylvania) Planning Commission, and design awards from the Pennsylvania Society of Architects and the Philadelphia Chapter of the American Institute of Architects.

180 George Washington Bicentennial Center (NR)
Alexandria, Virginia

Origin: The Lyceum, 1839
Conversion: Museum and community
                    hall, 1974
Developer: City of Alexandria
Architect: Carroll C. Curtice,
                    Washington, D.C.

Redevelopment: Originally used as a hall for weekly lectures and debates, the old Lyceum now serves as a travel information center, museum, and community meeting space. Both the interior and exterior of the two-story Greek Revival building were restored to original appearances with funds from HUD, the state of Virginia, the city of Alexandria, and the Historic Alexandria Foundation. Acquisition and redevelopment costs totaled $1,100,532.

Project Economics
Miscellaneous

Project	Year of Conversion	Gross Building Area (sq. ft.)	Acquisition Cost	Redevelopment Cost	Approx. Cost Per Sq. Ft.	Source of Financing	Rental Rates (annual per sq. ft., unless otherwise noted)
Golden Mall Playhouse	1969–73	6,000	$ 34,000	$ 33,000	$ 6.50	Private investment	$1.20
The Stanford Barn	1977	40,000	1,000,000 for leasehold	500,000	20.00	S&L	$12.00
Mammoth Gardens	1976	35,000	250,000	150,000	(4.29)	SBA (502-C)	$12.00—18.00
Educational Center for the Arts	1972	15,000	44,000	774,345	(51.62)	Public grant (state)	(not rented)
Light Designs, Inc.	1972	2,020	—	10,000	5.00	Personal funds	(not rented)
Rafford Hall	1976	7,912	Gift	100,000	12.64	Fund-raising, private and public grants	—
The Abbey Restaurant	1968	9,000	—	—	—	Insurance company	—
Faneuil Hall Marketplace	1973–78	—	City owned; 99-year lease to developer	30,000,000	(80.00)	Construction—New York commercial bank and 12 Boston financial institutions; Permanent—Teachers Insurance	$8.00–12.00 average retail; $10.00–11.00 office; length 5—15 yrs.; percentage clauses; old tenants $3 for 3 years
Coolidge Bank and Trust	1971	5,000	—	247,065	50.00	—	—
Academy Knoll	1976	128,000	—	2,016,500	15.75	MHFA (state)	$305/mo./1 br; $360/mo./2 br
Exeter Assembly Hall	1969	—	Already owned	500,000	—	—	(not rented)
Santuario de Guadalupe	1976	4,000	Gift	250,000	(62.50)	Public grants (state and federal)	(not rented)
Ithaca Hair Stylists	1976	1,000	27,000	10,000	(10.00)	Local bank	(not rented)
Bridgemarket	1977	—	Leased from city	1,500,000	—	—	—
New York Shakespeare Festival Public Theater	1966+	84,000	575,000	(3,008,710)	(35.82)	Private donations; city funds	(not rented)
Old Saratoga Square	1976	18,300	97,500	135,000	9.00	—	—
CAG Building and Highland Apartments	1968	60,000	70,000	430,000	(7.17)	Local savings bank	$3.50—4.50 office; $145—225/mo./apt.
The AIA Tower	1963	1,800	Gift	40,000	(22.22)	Private donations	—
Rocky Mount Arts and Crafts Center	1960+	10,475	Donation	200,000	—	City tax revenues	(not rented)
Spring House Village Center	1972	130,000 (old and new)	370,000	3,700,000	28.50	Insurance company (out of state)	8.00
George Washington Bicentennial Center	1974	11,237	209,000	891,532	79.33	City, state, and federal grants; private foundation	(not rented)

Dashes indicate data not available.
Figures in parentheses were not supplied directly but were derived from other data.

Redevelopment Work
Miscellaneous

Project	Exterior Restoration	New Exterior Construction	Structural	Mechanical	Interior Demolition	Interior New Construction	Site Restoration	New Facilities, Parking	Landscaping
Golden Mall Playhouse	Minor	Minor	Minor	Extensive	Extensive	Extensive	Extensive	Extensive	Minor
The Stanford Barn	Minor	—	Moderate	Moderate	Moderate	Extensive	Minor	Minor	Moderate
Mammoth Gardens	Minor	Minor	Minor	Extensive	Moderate	Extensive	Minor	Moderate	Minor
Educational Center for the Arts	Minor	Moderate	Moderate	Extensive	Moderate	Extensive	Minor	Minor	Minor
Light Designs, Inc.	Minor	None	None	Extensive	None	Minor	Minor	Extensive	Minor
Rafford Hall	Extensive	Minor	Minor	Extensive	Minor	Moderate	Minor	None	Minor
The Abbey Restaurant	Minor	Moderate	Minor	Extensive	Minor	Minor	Minor	Moderate	Moderate
Faneuil Hall Marketplace	Moderate	Moderate	Moderate	Extensive	Extensive	Extensive	Extensive	Minor	Extensive
Coolidge Bank and Trust	Minor	Moderate	Minor	Extensive	Moderate	Extensive	Minor	Minor	Minor
Academy Knoll	Minor	Minor	Moderate	Extensive	Minor	Moderate	Minor	Moderate	Minor
Exeter Assembly Hall	—	—	Minor	Minor	Moderate	Extensive	—	—	—
Santuario de Guadalupe	Moderate	Moderate	Minor	Extensive	Minor	Moderate	Extensive	Extensive	Extensive
Ithaca Hair Stylists	Moderate	Extensive	Minor	Extensive	Moderate	Extensive	Moderate	Moderate	Moderate
Bridgemarket	Minor	Minor	Minor	Extensive	Minor	Extensive	Minor	None	Minor
New York Shakespeare Festival Public Theater	Minor	Moderate	—	—	—	Moderate	Minor	None	None
Old Saratoga Square	Minor	Minor	Minor	Extensive	Moderate	Moderate	None	None	None
CAG Building and Highland Apartments	Minor	Minor	Minor	Extensive	Moderate	Extensive	Minor	Extensive	Minor
The AIA Tower	Minor	None	None	Extensive	Moderate	Moderate	Extensive	—	Extensive
Rocky Mount Arts and Crafts Center	Extensive	Minor	Extensive	Extensive	Moderate	Extensive	Extensive	Extensive	Extensive
Spring House Village Center	Extensive	Extensive	Extensive	Extensive	Extensive	Extensive	Extensive	Extensive	Extensive
George Washington Bicentennial Center	Extensive	Moderate	Extensive	Extensive	Extensive	Extensive	Moderate	Extensive	Extensive

Dashes indicate data not available.

Cross Reference to Catalog Projects: By New Use

Banks, 34, 68, 82, 94, 105, 168

Commercial (retail, restaurants, services), 2, 3, 14, 16, 17, 21, 22, 33, 35, 41, 42, 58, 70, 77, 97, 99, 108, 120, 122, 125, 130, 133, 140, 141, 148, 149, 151, 162, 164, 167, 172, 173, 179

And offices, 18, 19, 69, 72, 76, 88, 89, 90, 91, 92, 93, 95, 96, 100, 104, 111, 116, 121, 129, 131, 132, 139, 144, 146, 152, 154, 156, 161, 175

And residential, 63, 72, 93, 136, 154

Educational Facilities, 1, 24, 31, 52, 56, 86, 102, 115, 163, 170

Factory, 143

Hotels, 104, 109

Library, 28, 29, 74

Museums, Art Galleries, and Craft Centers, 11, 16, 20, 21, 26, 27, 57, 64, 65, 67, 73, 84, 98, 101, 119, 158, 159, 171, 178, 180

Offices, 4, 9, 10, 12, 15, 25, 32, 51, 55, 59, 81, 83, 107, 110, 117, 118, 123, 124, 126, 127, 128, 135, 140, 141, 142, 150, 175, 177

And other uses, 50, 57, 65, 78, 84, 134, 138, 145, 155, 165, 167

Parking, 78

Performing Arts Centers and Theaters, 2, 5, 21, 38, 39, 40, 44, 45, 46, 47, 48, 49, 80, 85, 147, 160, 174

Planetarium, 64

Public Buildings, 4, 13, 23, 28, 29, 37, 74, 99, 110, 180

Recording Studios, 114

Recreational Facilities, 16, 29, 43, 104, 146

Restaurants, 30, 60, 73, 103, 106, 109, 119, 148, 155, 166

Residential,
And other uses, 50, 66, 116, 136, 137, 138, 145, 176
Condominium ownership, 62, 75, 128, 157
For the elderly, 7, 61, 71, 112, 169
Multifamily, 6, 7, 8, 36, 53, 54, 79, 87, 113, 153

Transportation Centers, 99, 100

Cross Reference to Catalog Projects: By Geographical Location

Alabama:	Birmingham, 77
	Demopolis, 82
	Fort Payne, 50
	Mobile, 1, 13
	Montgomery, 51
Arizona:	Yuma, 98
Arkansas:	Little Rock, 83
California:	Burbank, 160
	Claremont, 2
	Los Gatos, 3
	Oakland, 38
	Palo Alto, 161
	San Diego, 99
	San Francisco, 123, 124, 125, 126, 127
	Santa Cruz, 14
Colorado:	Colorado Springs, 52
	Denver, 128, 129, 130, 162
Connecticut:	Hartford, 53
	New Haven, 163
	New London, 100
Delaware:	Montchanin, 111
	Wilmington, 15

District of Columbia:	54, 55, 131, 132
Florida:	Jacksonville, 78
	Pensacola, 164, 165
	St. Augustine, 56
Georgia:	Atlanta, 39, 166
Idaho:	Boise, 16
Illinois:	Aurora, 40
	Chicago, 41, 57
	Quincy, 84
	Woodstock, 4
Kansas:	Wichita, 58
Kentucky:	Louisville, 17, 18, 59, 85, 133
Louisiana:	Baton Rouge, 101
	New Orleans, 60, 134, 135
Maryland:	Baltimore, 5, 86, 102
Massachusetts:	Boston, 6, 19, 20, 61, 79, 87, 88, 136, 137, 138, 167
	Cambridge, 168
	Gloucester, 7
	Marlborough, 169
	Northbridge, 112
	Peabody, 113
	Rockport, 62

BIBLIOGRAPHY

General

"A Boom in Recycled Buildings." *Business Week.* (July 11, 1977), pp. 100-101.

"And Now Recycled Buildings." Time, 106: (July 7, 1975), pp. 52-53.

" Architects' Office Interiors: the 'Bare Brick School.' " *Architectural Record,* 158:4 (April 1975), p. 95.

Boston Redevelopment Authority. *Recycled Boston.* Boston: author, 1976.

"Building Types Study 478: Rehabilitation and Re-Use." *Architectural Record,* 158:8 (August 1975), pp. 67-82.

Bunnell, Gene. *Built to Last, A Handbook on Recycling Old Buildings.* Washington, D. C.: Preservation Press, 1977.

Cantacuzino, Sherban. *New uses for Old Buildings.* London: The Architectural Press, 1975.

Cavaglieri, Giorgio. "Design in Adaptive Reuse." *Historic Preservation,* 26:1 (January-March 1974), pp. 12-17.

————. "Old Buildings Need Lots of New Love." *AIA Journal,* 54:1 (July 1970), pp. 25-26.

"Conservation in the Context of Change." *Architectural Record,* 158:8 (December 1974), issue.

Dean, Andrea O. "Adaptive Use: Economic and Other Advantages." *AIA Journal,* 65:6 (June 1976), pp. 26-40.

————. "A Boston Firm that has made a Specialty of Adaptive Use." *AIA Journal,* 66:4 (April 1977), pp. 64-67.

Department of the Environment, Scottish Development Department, Welsh Office. *Aspects of Conservation One: New Life for Old Buildings.*

Dunlop, Beth. "Six Architects' Offices in Recycled Buildings." *AIA Journal,* 63:1 (January 1975), pp. 35-38.

Educational Facilities Laboratories and the National Endowment for the Arts. *The Arts in Found Places.* New York: EFL, 1976.

Fracchia, Charles A. *Converted into Houses.* New York: The Viking Press, 1976.

"The Future of the Past." *Progressive Architecture,* 53:11 (November 1972), issue.

Harney, Andy Leon. "Adaptive Use: Saving Energy (and Money) as well as Buildings." *AIA Journal,* 62:2 (August 1974), pp. 49-54.

"The Home Towns Come Back." *Architectural Record,* 160:12 (December 1976), issue.

Interiors, 135:9 (April 1976), issue.

Ketchum, Morris, Jr. "Recycling and Restoring Landmarks: An Architectural Challenge and Opportunity." *AIA Journal,* 64:3 (September 1975), pp. 31-39.

Knight, Carleton, III. "Adaptive Use, Cont., Apartments from a Factory and a Store." *AIA Journal,* 62:5 (November 1974), pp. 38-41.

McLaughlin, Herbert P., Jr. "Commercial Renovation Proves Its Worth." *Historic Preservation,* 27:4 (October-December 1975.)

————. "A 'Preservation Addict' looks at the Practical Side of Rehabilitating for Profit." *Architectural Record,* 159:3 (March 1976), pp. 65-67.

McQuade, Walter. "Buildings Can Be Recycled Too." *Fortune,* XCI:5 (May 1975), pp. 192-199.

Marlin, William. "Uses of the Past." *Architectural Forum,* 137:2 (September 1972), pp. 24-33.

Martin, Thomas J. and Gamzon, Melvin A. "Adaptive Reuse Gives Life to Old Buildings." *Real Estate Review,* 6:3 (Fall 1976).

"New Life for Old Buildings: The Architect's Renewed Commitment to Preservation." *Architectural Record.* 150:6 (December 1971), issue.

"New Places in Old Spaces." *Progressive Architecture,* LI:12 (December 1970), pp. 62-64.

Preservation News Supplements. "Business and Preservation" (April 1976); "Living Places" (April 1975); "New Life for Old Buildings" (April 1973).

"Preserving the Recent Past." *Progressive Architecture*, LV:7 (July 1974), issue.

"Recycled City Buildings Provide New and Beautiful Living Spaces." *House and Home Remodeling Guide* (Winter 1974).

"Recycling." *Architecture Plus*, 2:2 (March/April 1974), issue.

"Recycling for New Uses." *Buildings*, 70:6 (June 1976), issue.

"Rehabilitation and Re-use." *Architectural Record*, 158:8 (August 1975), pp. 67-82.

"The Renovation Market." *Building Design and Construction*, 16:1 (January 1975), pp. 24-44.

"Restoration and Remodeling." *Progressive Architecture*, LVII:11 (November 1976), issue.

Robinson, Michael J. "Urban Rehab $10.50 A Square Foot." *House and Home.* 47:2 (February 1975), pp. 68-73.

Rothenberg, Alan E. "A New Look at Building Recycling: It Pays to Preserve." *Cry California*, 10:1 (Winter 1974/1975), pp. 6-12.

"Same Place, New Face." *Real Estate Today*, 8:5 (May/June 1975), pp. 23-41.

Shopsin, William C. *Adapting Old Buildings to New Uses.* New York: New York State Council on Architecture, 1974.

Smith, Baird. "Adaptive Use: A Survey of Construction Costs." Advisory Council on Historic Preservation *Special Report*, IV:4 (June 1976).

Stanforth, Deirdre. *Restored America.* New York: Praeger, 1975.

Tseckares, Charles. "One Winthrop Square, Boston." *Urban Land*, 35:7 (July/August 1976), pp. 14-17.

Ware, Merrill. *Federal Architecture: Adaptive-Use Facilities.* Washington, D.C.: The Federal Architecture Project, National Endowment for the Arts, 1975.

Woodbridge, Sally. "The Great Northwest Revival." *Progressive Architecture*, LV:8 (August 1974), pp. 46-53.

Economic and Legal Aspects

Costonis, John J. *Space Adrift, Saving Urban Landmarks through the Chicago Plan.* Urbana: University of Illinois Press, 1974.

Crawford, Dana. "The Economics of Rehabilitated Downtown Areas." *Historic Preservation*, 21:1 (January-March 1969), pp. 29-31.

The Foundation Library Center. *The Foundation Directory.* New York: Russell Sage Foundations, 1967.

Gammage, Grady, Jr.; Jones, Philip N.; and Jones, Stephen L. *Historic Preservation in California, A Legal Handbook.* Stanford: Stanford Environmental Law Society, 1975.

Gerber, Edward F. "Historic Georgetown, Inc.: The Economics Involved in Preservation." *Urban Land*, 34:7 (July/August 1975), pp. 14-22.

Hillman, Howard and Ararbanel, Karin. *The Art of Winning Foundation Grants.* New York: Vanguard Press, 1975.

Knight, Carleton, III. "State Agency Finances Rehab, Reuse." *Preservation News*, XV:8 (August 1975).

Latus, Mark. "Preservation and the Energy Crisis." *Historic Preservation*, 25:2 (April-June 1973), pp. 10-13.

Nannen, Howard. *A Guide to the Financing and Development of Small Restoration Projects.* Hartford, Connecticut: Hartford Architecture Conservancy, 1976.

National Endowment for the Arts. *Grant Program Guidelines, Architecture + Environmental Arts.* Washington, D.C.: author, 1976.

National Trust for Historic Preservation. *Economic Benefits of Preserving Old Buildings.* Washington, D.C.: Preservation Press, 1976.

———. *A Guide to Federal Programs and Activities Related to Historic Preservation.* Washington, D.C.: author, 1974.

———. *A Guide to Federal Programs for Historic Preservation, 1976 Supplement.* Washington, D.C.: Preservation Press, 1976.

———. *A Guide to State Historic Preservation Programs.* Washington, D.C.: Preservation Press, 1976.

———. *Historic Preservation Law: An Annotated Bibliography.* Washington, D.C.: Preservation Press, 1976.

———. "Information, Factors Affecting Valuation of Historic Property." Washington, D.C.: Preservation Press, 1976.

Nicholson, Sy. "Developers Find Profit in Adaptive Reuse Projects, But Lack of Financing Could Stymie Further Growth." *National Real Estate Investor.* July 1977, pp. 22-31.

"Preservation and Taxation." *Preservation News* Supplement, May 1976.

Reynolds, Judith and Anthony. "Factors Affecting Valuation of Historic Property." *Information* series. Washington, D.C.: National Trust for Historic Preservation, 1976.

Schmertz, Mildred F. "The Effect of Current Methods of Financing Downtown Renewal." *Architectural Record,* 160:12 (December 1976), pp. 124-127.

United States Department of the Interior, National Park Service, Office of Archeology and Historic Preservation, National Register of Historic Places. *Historic Preservation Grants-in-Aid: Policies and Procedures.* Washington, D.C.: author, 1973.

———. Office of Archeology and Historic Preservation. *11593* (periodical).

———. *The National Register of Historic Places.* Washington, D.C.: U.S. Government Printing Office, 1976.

Ziegler, Arthur P., Jr.; Adler, Leopold, III; and Kidney, Walter C. *Revolving Funds for Historic Preservation: A Manual of Practice.* Pittsburgh: Ober Park Associates, Inc., 1975.

Conservation Technology

American Institute of Architects. *Architect's Handbook of Professional Practice.* Washington, D.C.: author, 1973. "The Architect as a Preservationist."

Association for Preservation Technology. *Bulletin* (periodical).

"Building Codes for Preservation." *Preservation News* Supplement, November 1976.

Bullock, Orin M., Jr. *The Restoration Manual.* Norwalk, Connecticut: Silvermine Publishers, Inc., 1966.

Chambers, J. Henry. *Cyclical Maintenance for Historic Buildings.* Washington, D.C.: United States Government Printing Office, 1976.

Fairbridge, Kingsley C. and Kowal, Harvey-Jane. *Loft Living, Recycling Warehouse Space for Residential Use.* New York: Saturday Review Press, 1976.

Harvey, John H. *Conservation of Buildings.* London: John Baker, Ltd., 1972.

Insall, Donald W. *The Care of Old Buildings Today, A Practical Guide.* London: The Architectural Press, 1972.

National Trust for Historic Preservation. *Preservation and Building Codes.* Washington, D.C.: Preservation Press, 1975.

Neal, Wallace. "Preserving Historic Buildings." *The Construction Specifier,* 29:5 (May 1976), pp. 36-43.

O'Bannon, Robert E. "Historic Buildings and the Uniform Building Code." *Building Standards,* 43:5 (September/October 1974), pp. 26-27.

The Technology Organization, Inc. *Technology and Conservation* (periodical).

Timmons, Sharon, editor. *Preservation and Conservation: Principles and Practices.* Washington, D.C.: Preservation Press, 1976.

United States Department of the Interior, National Park Service, Office of Archeology and Historic Preservation, Interagency Historic Architectural Services Program. *Preservation Briefs* (intermittent publications). Washington, D.C.: United States Government Printing Office.

Project Categories

Schools

Allen, Bob. "Public Schools for Public Uses." *Current Municipal Problems,* XV:4 (September 1974), pp. 406-412.

American Association of School Administrators. *To Recreate a School Building, "Surplus" Space, Energy and Other Challenges.* Arlington, Virginia: author, 1976.

Dean, Andrea O. "Surplus School Buildings: New Opportunities for Adaptive Use." *AIA Journal,* 66:4 (April 1977), pp. 58-63.

Educational Facilities Laboratories, *Schoolhouse* (periodical).

————. *Surplus School Space: Options and Opportunities.* New York: author, 1976.

Getzels, Judith N. "Don't Scrap that School." *Planning,* 42:10 (November 1976), pp. 22-24.

Holmes, Hendrik S. *Surplus Schools/A Study of Adaptive Reuse.* Brookline, Massachusetts (privately printed, undated).

Marline, William. "Some Old School Solutions." *Historic Preservation,* 26:3 (July-September 1974), pp. 10-15.

Meir, James. "Found Space into Schools." *Architecture Plus,* 2:2 (March/April 1974), pp. 74-75.

Stephens, Suzanne. "Up from Institutionalism." *Progressive Architecture,* 52:2 (February 1971), pp. 82-91.

Color Film: "Back to School to Live" (Conversion of Central Grammar School in Gloucester, Massachusetts, into housing for the elderly). Eighteen minutes, 16 mm. Contact Albert Viator, 3 Calder Street, Gloucester 01930.

Public Buildings

Getzels, Judith N. *Recycling Public Buildings.* Planning Advisory Service Report No. 319. Chicago: American Society of Planning Officials, 1976.

Historic Preservation, 14:2 (1962), issue.

Knight, Carleton, III. "Ringing in the Old." *Architectural Forum,* 138:3 (April 1973), pp. 50-54.

Legner, Linda. "How To Save our County Courthouses." *Inland Architect,* 19:5 (May 1975), pp. 20-21.

National Trust for Historic Preservation. *A Courthouse Conservation Handbook.* Washington, D.C.: Preservation Press, 1976.

————. Department of Field Services. "Fact Sheet: Preservation of County Courthouses." Washington, D.C.: author, 1973.

Osman, Mary. "A St. Paul Landmark Saved by a Bill." *AIA Journal,* 61:3 (March 1974), pp. 32-35.

Ware, Merrill. *Federal Architecture: Adaptive Use Facilities.* Washington, D.C.: The Federal Architecture Project, National Endowment for the Arts, 1975.

Weese, Ben. "The County Courthouse, Rediscovering a National Asset." *Architectural Record,* 157:6 (June 1975), pp. 114-116.

Theaters

Chesley, Gene A. "Encore for Nineteenth Century American Theaters." *Historic Preservation,* 25:4 (October-December 1973), pp. 20-25.

Frausto, Robert. "The Decline of the Great Movie Palaces." *Planning,* 40:2 (February 1974), pp. 15-19.

Huxtable, Ada Louise. "Theaters, Recycled." *New York Times Magazine* (April 17, 1975), pp. 74-75.

Sharp, Dennis. *The Picture Palace and Other Buildings for the Movies.* New York: F. A. Praeger, 1969.

Stoddard, Robert. "Preservation of Opera Houses, Movie Theaters and Concert Halls." *Information* series. Washington, D.C.: National Trust for Historic Preservation, 1976.

Theatre Historical Society. *Marquee* (periodical).

Hotels, Mansions, and Apartments

Blackall, C. H. "The American Hotel." *The Brickbuilder,* 12:2,3,4 (February, March, April 1903), pp. 24-30, 47-53, 68-72.

Bowman, LaBarbara. "Office Use Sought for Mansions," *The Washington Post.* December 26, 1973.

"Famous American Hotels," *Interiors,* 103 (May 1944), pp. 38-40, 66-78.

Hepburn, Andrew. *Great Resorts of North America.* New York, 1965.

"The Hotel: Its History, Development and Its Present Design Problems," *Interiors,* 106 (October 1946), pp. 79-80, 172-174.

National Trust for Historic Preservation. "Adaptive Use of Mansions," unpublished, no date.

"The Redesign of Existing Hotels," *Architectural Record,* 159:2 (February 1976), p. 118.

Seindenberg, Roderick. "Apartment House Architecture," *The American Architect,* 135:2562 (February 5, 1929), pp. 141-177.

Sexton, R. W. *American Apartment Houses, Hotels and Apartment Hotels of Today.* New York, 1929.

———. *American Apartment Houses of Today.* New York, 1926.

Williamson, Jefferson. *The American Hotel.* New York, 1930.

Carriage Houses, Garages, and Stables

Boston Redevelopment Authority. *Recycled Boston.* Boston: author, 1976.

Commercial and Office Buildings

Brink, Peter H. "Commercial Area Revolving Funds for Preservation." *Information* series. Washington, D.C.: National Trust for Historic Preservation, 1976.

"Business and Preservation." *Preservation News Supplement.* April 1976.

National Trust for Historic Preservation. *Economic Benefits of Preserving Old Buildings.* Washington, D.C.: Preservation Press, 1976, pp. 75-94.

Uhlman, Wes. "Preserving Pioneer Square in Seattle." *HUD Challenge,* 4:6 (June 1973), pp. 10-12.

Railroad Stations

Advisory Council on Historic Preservation. "Federal Programs for Reusing Railroad Stations." Washington, D.C.: author, 1974.

Educational Facilities Laboratories. *Reusing Railroad Stations.* New York: author, 1974.

———. *Reusing Railroad Stations Book Two.* New York: author, 1975.

Hale, Jonathan. "Railroad Stations: An Endangered Species." *Architectural Record,* 150:12 (December 1971), pp. 120-124.

———. "Sic Transit." *Architectural Forum,* 140:4 (November 1973), pp. 74-81.

Houstoun, Lawrence O. "Let's Concentrate on Saving Rail Service Instead of Stations." *AIA Journal,* 62:3 (September 1974), pp. 50-52.

Kidney, Walter C. *Working Places, the Adaptive Use of Industrial Buildings.* Pittsburgh, Pennsylvania: Ober Park Press, 1976, pp. 48-77.

National Register of Historic Places. *Historic Railroad Stations: A Selected Inventory.* Washington, D.C.: author, 1974.

National Trust for Historic Preservation, Department of Field Services. "Fact Sheet: Preservation of Railroad Stations." Washington, D.C.: author, 1974.

"New Life for Old Railroad Stations—Thousands and Thousands of Them." *Building Design and Construction,* 15:11 (November 1974), pp. 58-66.

Pfeiffer, Norman. "Right Side of the Tracks." *Architectural Forum,* 140:4 (November 1973), pp. 66-73.

"Railroading, Saving America's Stations." *Preservation News Supplement.* April 1974.

Color Film: "Stations" (adaptive use of railroad stations). Two versions of 27 and 63 minutes in length. Contact Roger Hagan Associates, 1019 Belmont Place East, Seattle, Washington 98102.

Mills

Candee, Richard M. "New Hampshire: Preservation Redefined." *Historic Preservation*, 27:3 (July-September 1975), pp. 20-25.

Kidney, Walter C. *Working Places, the Adaptive Use of Industrial Buildings*. Pittsburgh: Ober Park Press, 1976, pp. 20-24, 30-38.

Society for Industrial Archeology. *Newsletter* (periodical).

Society for the Preservation of Old Mills. *Old Mill News* (periodical).

Weymouth, George A. "From Mill to Museum." *Historic Preservation*, 24:1 (January-March 1972), p. 13.

Zimiles, Martha and Murray. *Early American Mills*. New York: Bramhall House, 1973.

Factories, Warehouses, and Industrial Buildings

Beckman, Ronald. "Experiments in Energy Conservation." *Historic Preservation*, 27:1 (January-March 1975), pp. 28-33.

Fairbridge, Kingsley C. and Kowal, Harvey-Jane. *Loft Living, Recycling Warehouse Space for Residential Use*. New York: Saturday Review Press, 1976.

Kidney, Walter C. *Working Places, the Adaptive Use of Industrial Buildings*. Pittsburgh: Ober Park Press, 1976.

Newell, Diane. "With Respect to Breweries." *Historic Preservation*, 27:1 (January-March 1975), pp. 24-27.

Ryder, Sharon Lee. "From Piano to Forte." *Progressive Architecture*, LVI:2 (February 1975), pp. 60-67.

————. "A Very Lofty Realm." *Progressive Architecture*, LV:10 (October 1974), pp. 92-97.

Sande, Theodore A. *Industrial Archeology*. Brattleboro, Vermont: The Stephen Greene Press, 1976.

Society for Industrial Archeology. *Newsletter* (periodical).

Color Slidefilm: "Working Places" (adaptive use of industrial buildings). Contact Society for Industrial Archeology, Room 5020, National Museum of History and Technology, Smithsonian Institution, Washington, D.C. 20560.

Miscellaneous

The Cheswick Center. *The Challenge of Underused Church Property and the Search for Alternatives*. Cambridge, Massachusetts: author, 1975.

————. "Preservation of Churches." *Information* series. Washington, D.C.: National Trust for Historic Preservation, 1977.

Farley, John H. "Costs in Recycled Gas Stations." *Architectural Record*, 156:8 (August 1974), p. 71.

Kerth, A. L. *A New Life for the Abandoned Service Station*. Massapequa, New York: author, 1974.

Schmertz, Mildred F. "Upgrading Barns to be Inhabited by People." *Architectural Record*, 115:6 (June 1974), pp. 117-122.